Parmigianino

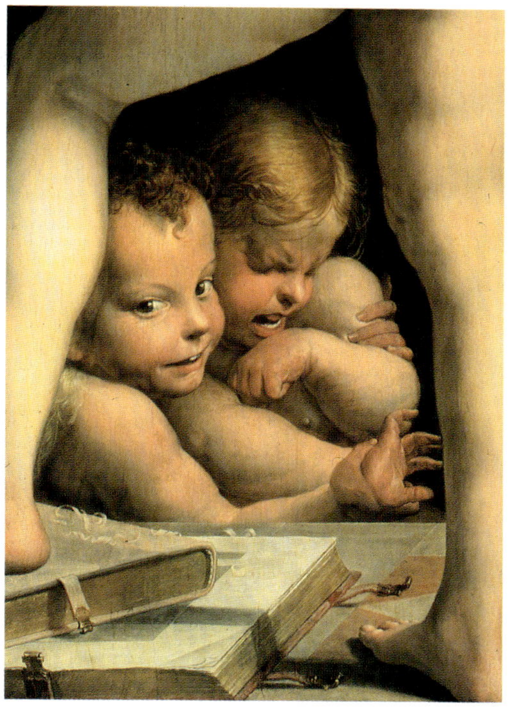

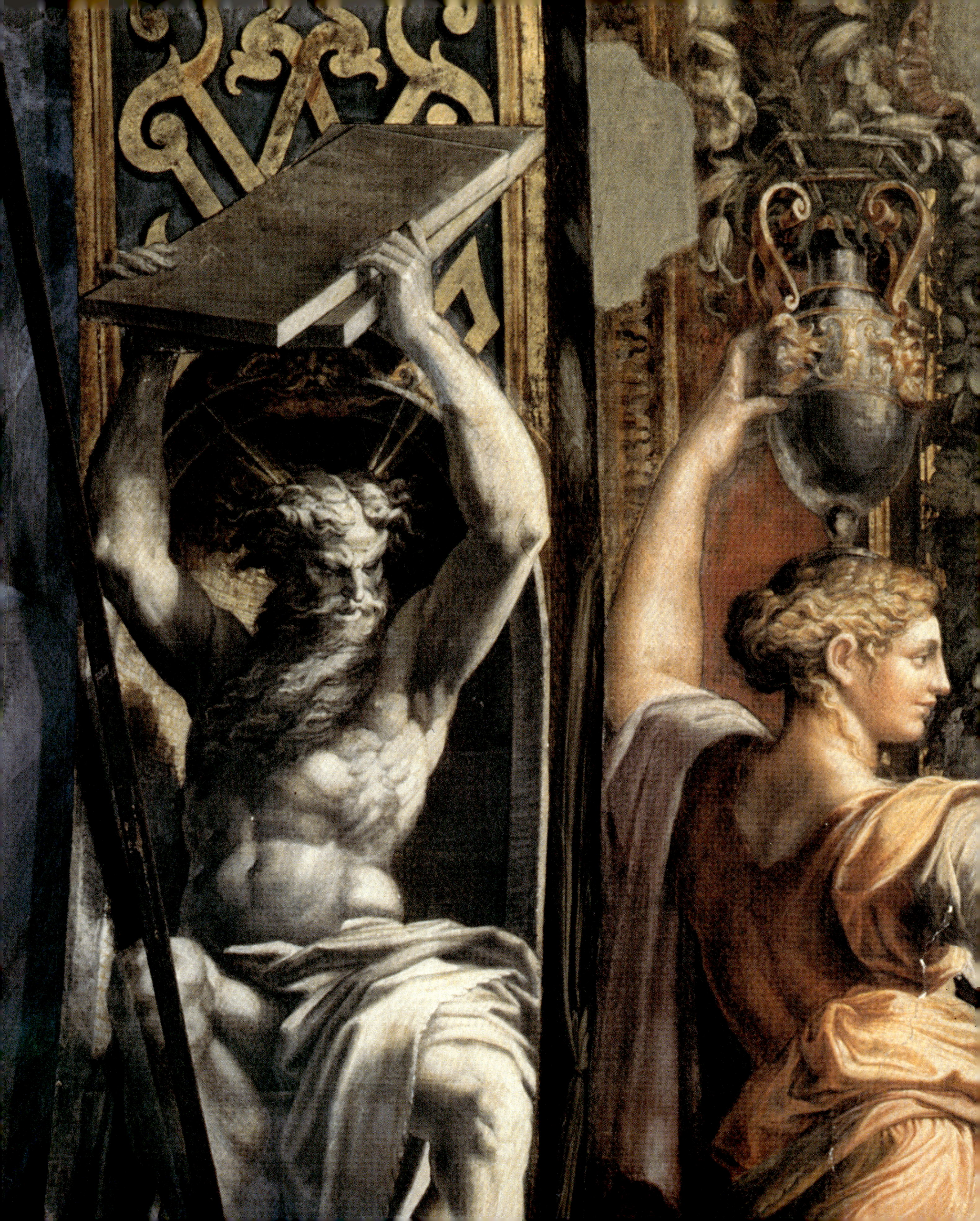

CECIL GOULD

Parmigianino

ABBEVILLE PRESS PUBLISHERS
New York London Paris

FRONT COVER: Detail of *Madonna dal Collo Lungo.* See page 143.

BACK COVER: *Cupid Cutting His Bow.* See page 121.

PAGE 1: Detail of *Cupid Cutting His Bow.* See page 121.

FRONTISPIECE: Detail of vault of Santa Maria della Steccata. See page 132.

PAGE 9: Detail of *David.* See page 31.

PAGE 175: Studies for the Fontanellato fresco. See page 39.

PAGE 181: Detail of study of trees. See page 162.

PAGE 201: Detail of *Diana and Nymphs.* See page 154.

For the English-language edition:
EDITOR: Abigail Asher
TYPOGRAPHIC DESIGN: Barbara Sturman
JACKET DESIGN: Sandy Burne

First edition

10 9 8 7 6 5 4 3 2 1

LIBRARY OF CONGRESS CATALOGING-IN-PUBLICATION DATA
Gould, Cecil Hilton Monk, 1918–1994
Parmigianino / Cecil Gould.
p. cm.
Includes bibliographical references and index.
ISBN 1-55859-892-8
1. Il Parmigianino, 1503–1540—Criticism and interpretation.
2. Mannerism (Art)—Italy. 3. Il Parmigianino, 1503–1540—Catalogs.
I. Title.
ND623.P255G68 1995
760′.092—dc20 94-39742

CONTENTS

PREFACE 7

I *Parma, the Beginnings* 11

II *Rome* 55

III *Bologna* 83

IV *Parma and the End* 125

APPENDIXES 176

NOTES 177

WORKS CITED 179

CATALOG 182

INDEX 202

PHOTOGRAPHY CREDITS 216

NOTES TO THE READER

The reader will find the following abbreviations in the text of *Parmigianino:*

> **Fig. (followed by a number)** refers to illustrations in this volume.
>
> **P (followed by a number)** refers to drawings by Parmigianino, numbered according to A. E. Popham's *Catalogue of the Drawings of Parmigianino* (1971).
>
> **P.O.C. (followed by a number)** stands for "Popham as Old Copy," and refers to works judged by Popham to be old copies of works by Parmigianino.
>
> **P.O.R. (followed by a number)** stands for "Popham as Old Reproduction," and refers to works judged by Popham to be old reproductions of works by Parmigianino.

At the end of each caption describing works by Parmigianino is the number of the corresponding entry in the catalog that begins on page 182. The captions for drawings also recall the Popham catalog number for each work.

The majority of Parmigianino's drawings are mentioned in the catalog, under the heading "Corresponding drawings" in the entries regarding paintings or engravings.

PREFACE

It is surprising that despite the revival of interest in mannerist painting very little has been published outside Italy on Parmigianino, one of its greatest precursors. The only major general book in English—by S. J. Freedberg—appeared in the United States more than forty years ago. In many respects this remains the standard work of reference, but since then the study of the subject has been enriched by A. E. Popham's masterly edition of the drawings, and some more paintings and some more facts have come to light.

In planning the present book I finally abandoned the current practice of allotting most of the space to the catalog, thereby restricting the consecutive writing to a short introduction. I believe that a catalog should be primarily for purposes of reference; for this reason it is counterproductive for it to consist of long, essaylike entries. It is more useful if restricted to presenting the established facts as clearly and succinctly as possible. Discussion of controversial matter is then relegated to the text. While it would be possible to split the latter, in this case, into sections on the religious panels, the portraits, the frescoes, the drawings, and the etchings, such an arrangement obscures both the artist's development and the interrelation of the genres. Since, in addition, Parmigianino's career happened to fall into four phases—his successive residences at Parma, Rome, Bologna, and finally Parma again—there seemed sufficient justification for planning the text on a chronological basis. Depending on the mood of the reader, the result can be seen either as a survival of an old-established form or as a revival. I hope that such an approach may also help to smooth the largely artificial distinction between specialist and general appeal.

In the space of nearly a decade that this book has been underway, I have had help from more colleagues and friends than I can now name, but I would record particular gratitude to Sir Michael Levey and Dr. Paul Joannides and the staff of the National Gallery library and the National Art Library.

C.G.

Cecil Gould died as this volume was going to press; it is a great loss. Despite his illness, Mr. Gould worked closely with the publisher on every phase of the editing and layout of Parmigianino, *though sadly he did not live to see the published book. As his publisher, we mourn his passing and remember him with affection and gratitude.*

ALSO BY CECIL GOULD

An Introduction to Italian Renaissance Painting

Trophy of Conquest: The Musée Napoleon and the Creation of the Louvre

Leonardo da Vinci: The Artist and the Non-Artist

The Paintings of Correggio

Bernini in France: An Episode in Seventeenth-Century History

The Sixteenth-Century Italian Schools: National Gallery Catalogue

I *Parma, the Beginnings*

II *Rome*

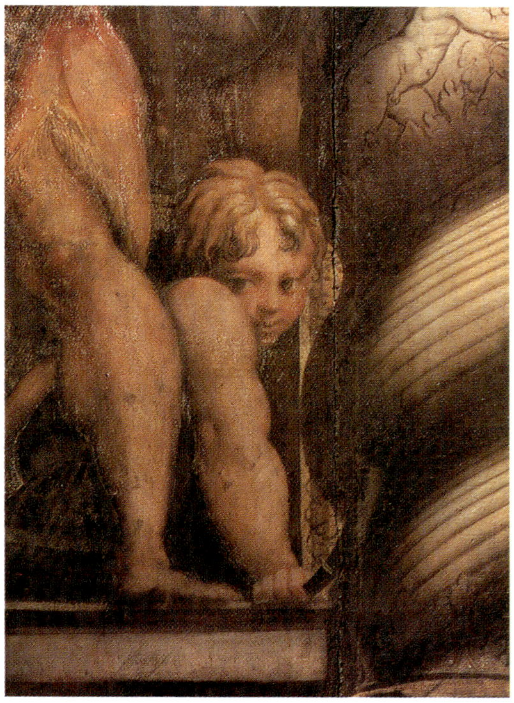

III *Bologna*

IV *Parma and the End*

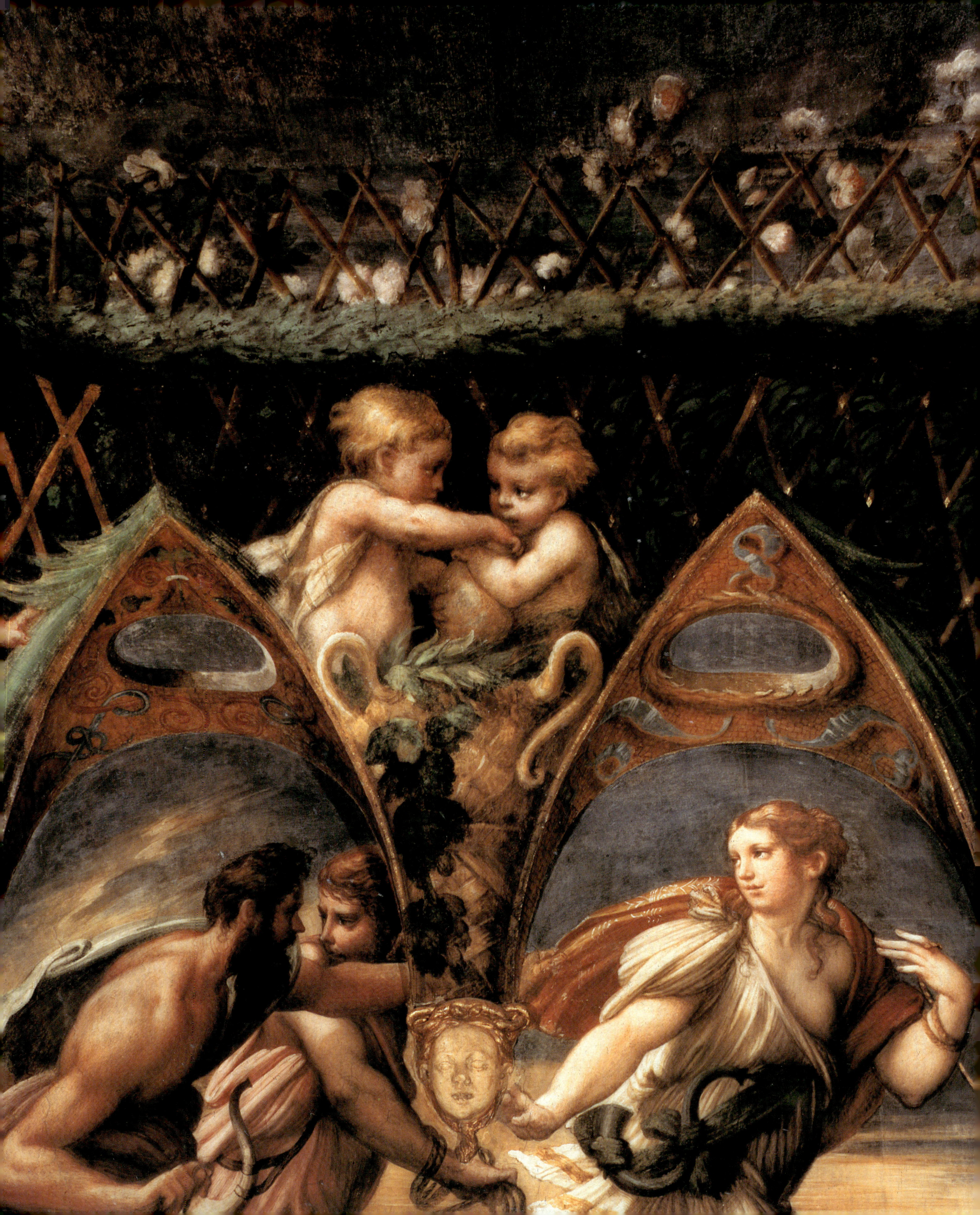

I

Parma, the Beginnings

The first modern monograph on Parmigianino, published by the Austrian scholar L. Fröhlich-Bum in 1921, was entitled *Parmigianino und der Manierismus.* The label *mannerism* was at that time still a novelty, and for many years afterward it continued to be associated with Parmigianino. It is true that his art and that of other highly gifted painters, such as the Florentines Pontormo and Rosso, who came to maturity around the 1520s was essentially mannered. But though Parmigianino is likely to have come in contact with both of these, and though there were significant exchanges of ideas, there was no real homogeneity in their art. And while Parmigianino exercised considerable influence on painting in North Italy, as well as influencing aspects of art in France and northern Europe, neither he nor his contemporaries were crucial to the formation of artists of the next wave in Florence and Rome. It is true that the most gifted of these, Francesco Salviati, had been at Bologna and had absorbed something of Parmigianino's elegance; but in general it was the legacy of the earlier Michelangelo, both as regards the extreme of *contrapposto* and the use of vivid coloring with minimal shadows, that dominated painting in Rome and Florence in the middle years of the century.

If Salviati and the other mid-century painters in Rome and Florence are currently labeled, rightly or wrongly, as marking the central core of mannerism, some other label should be found for the generation that succeeded that of Raphael and the first half of Michelangelo's long career. Pontormo, Rosso, Parmigianino, and others might therefore be termed proto-mannerists. But since the word *mannerism* is still applied variously it may be less misleading to invent a new label for these late-Renaissance painters, namely the post-peak generation. Such a term reflects the central issue that confronted them, and it has the additional advantage of conforming with the sense of an observation made by Vasari in his biography of one of them, namely Rosso. Writing in his *Vite de' più eccellenti pittori (Lives of the Artists)* of what he considered the inferiority of the fresco in Santa Maria della Pace, which was the first work that Rosso executed after his arrival in Rome in the 1520s, Vasari said that a change of scene sometimes affected artists adversely and went on to say, "This could well have been the case with Rosso in the atmosphere of Rome on account of the stupendous works of architecture and sculpture [of antiquity] which confronted him, and of the paintings and statues of Michelangelo which alone may have been enough to throw

Detail of fig. 17
PARMIGIANINO
Diana and Actaeon
(Nymph pursued by huntsmen)

him off balance. It was indeed those which had already caused Fra Bartolommeo and Andrea del Sarto to flee the city without leaving any testimony of their stay there." In modern times the point was expressed more trenchantly by Kenneth Clark: "Looking at the masterpieces of Leonardo, Michelangelo and Raphael, they [Pontormo, Rosso, Giulio, Perino, and Polidoro] may well have felt that every possible line of advance had been blocked by an apparently final solution."[1]

Vasari adduces a different factor to account for what he saw as Parmigianino's failure to realize his enormous talent, namely his obsession with alchemy in an attempt to become richer. This view in its turn was countered by another near-contemporary, Lodovico Dolce, on the ground that Parmigianino was indifferent to money.[2] This may have been the case, but it need not entirely discredit what Vasari says. There can be no doubt that Parmigianino was indeed fascinated by alchemy, but primarily for its own sake. It was bound up with his preoccupation with the idea of magic. But while the time that he spent in this way would necessarily have been lost to his art, the shortcomings attributed to him by Vasari cannot be explained by this alone.

Detail of fig. 67
PARMIGIANINO
Madonna and Child with Saints Margaret and Jerome, a Mitered Saint, and an Angel

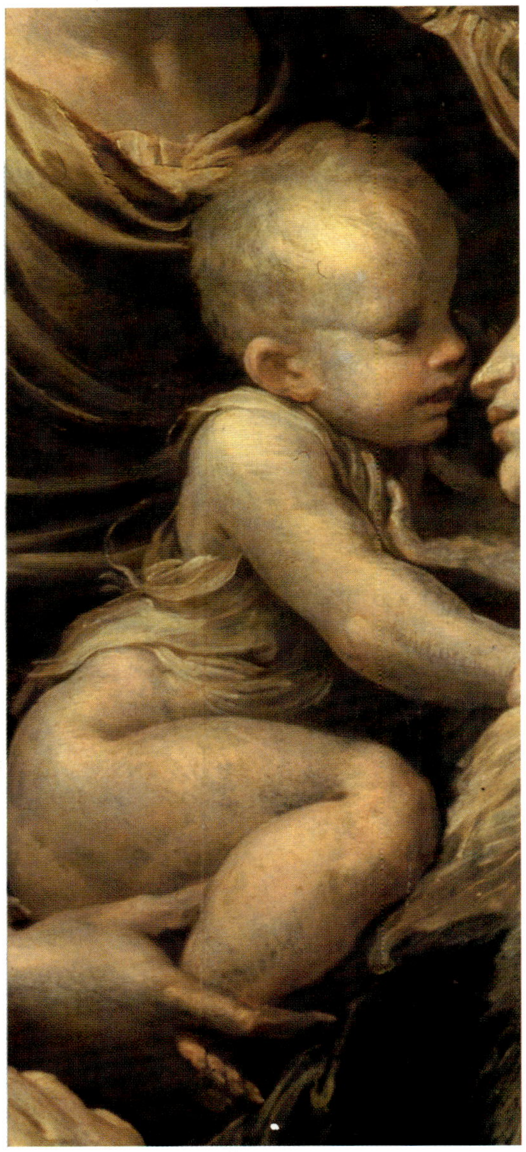

Coming to maturity in the post-peak period, Parmigianino's contemporaries were forced to set themselves new aims. The weapons that the generation of Raphael had perfected in the struggle to emulate nature now proved double-edged. Raphael himself had been aware of the incidental imperfections of nature, but he had held the balance between reproducing them and improving on them. Now, when reproduction had become less difficult, the balance was no longer held. Other post-peak painters—Pontormo and Rosso among the Florentines, Beccafumi at Siena, and Giulio Romano, Polidoro, and Perino among Raphael's assistants in Rome—though differing from each other and from Parmigianino, were at one with him to the extent that they tended no longer to use the fundamental discoveries of Renaissance painting, that is, perspective, anatomy, and light and shade, merely to imitate natural appearances. Any or all of them were now of interest in their own right. Limbs could be lengthened, tricks could be played with pictorial space, and light used not only to simulate volume but also to suggest magic and the supernatural. In the process, art diverged from nature.

A problem endemic to Christian art that surfaced with increased urgency at this stage and affected Parmigianino with particular acuteness was how to introduce novelty into age-old, hackneyed religious themes. The demand for Madonnas would have seemed endless, and Nativities, Adorations, and the rest only slightly less. The challenge could be met in different ways. The artist could try to reinterpret orthodox designs in his own way; or he could try to break loose. Of Parmigianino's four altarpieces of the Madonna and Child with Saints, two adopt the first solution and the other two the second. *The Madonna with Saint Margaret* (Bologna) is a brilliant variation on Correggio's *Madonna with Saint Jerome,* and the *Madonna with Saint Stephen and the Baptist* (Dresden) an inspired variant on Raphael's Sistine *Madonna.* In both cases an amazingly new and effective use of light was the chief element in creating effects that are entirely different from the prototypes.

In the other two altars—the *Madonna with Saint Jerome and the Baptist* (London) and the *Madonna dal Collo Lungo* (Uffizi)—the derivative features are less basic, and it seems that in both cases Parmigianino was determined to overcome tradition and create something quite new. But though both pictures contain ravishing individual elements, neither could count as a totally successful altarpiece.

The graceful elegance that has always been considered the hallmark of Parmigianino's art did not come all at once. It could hardly do so, since it depends on technical mastery. However much it had been codified by this time, the young artist must still learn it; and we shall see that Parmigianino's training seems to have left something to be desired. In his early painting, and even in some of the early drawings, the will to elegance is already there, but the hand is still not fully obedient. One of the most usual concomitants of unnatural elegance, namely attenuation of the limbs, though popularly associated with him, is really obtrusive only in a single painting, the *Madonna dal Collo Lungo.* But there were other sacrifices on the altar of elegance. When he paints hair, for example, the result is marvelously beautiful, the strands falling in infinitely inventive patterns. But, looking on occasion like fine gold wire, it does not suggest softness. And his flesh still less. The comparison already made between his *Saint Margaret* altar (fig. 67) and its prototype, Correggio's *Madonna with Saint Jerome* (Parma; fig. 68), illustrated this. Correggio's Christ Child has cheeks into which a spectator might want to sink his fingers. But the magic light that produces a dreamlike effect in Parmigianino's altarpiece turns the color and texture of the skin into something almost reptilian.

Girolamo Francesco Maria Mazzola was born on January 11, 1503. His near-contemporary Lodovico Dolce refers to him as Francesco Parmigiano. The diminutive form, Parmigianino, has been usual since the end of the sixteenth century. His native city of Parma had a turbulent political history. During much of the fifteenth century it had been controlled by the great Lombard dynasties of Visconti and Sforza. From 1500 to 1512, and again between 1515 and 1521, it was occupied by the French, and then fell to the papacy, which had already controlled it for three years following the battle of Ravenna in 1512. Soon after Parmigianino's death the reigning pope, Paul III, annexed it on behalf of his family, the Farnese, who ruled it until the eighteenth century and left a lasting mark on its architecture. But the lack throughout Parmigianino's career of a princely ruling house—always the principal source of demand for art of antique subject matter (see appendix 1)—greatly reduced opportunities for work of this type.

In Parmigianino's youth, and for very many years previously, there was a conspicuous lack of local artistic talent in Parma. The city had produced great architecture and sculpture during the Romanesque period, but it could boast no preeminent native painter until Parmigianino himself matured. It thus offered opportunities for artists from outside. There were several altarpieces by the Bolognese Francia in churches in Parma, and others by the Venetian Cima. Most of these would have been set up during Parmigianino's youth and would for that reason have been calculated to leave an impression on his

Detail of fig. 68
CORREGGIO
Madonna and Child with Saint Jerome and Others

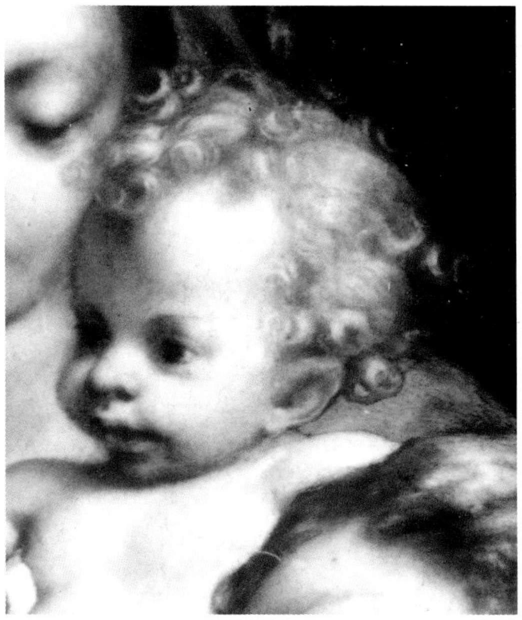

adolescent susceptibility. In fact this seems to have been rather stronger in the case of Francia's work than of Cima's, though neither was essential to his formation. Neither of these painters settled in Parma, and both of them died before 1520. But others came and stayed. Anselmi settled there from Siena some years before 1520. As a painter of talent and one with experience of the current trends in Central Italy, he would doubtless have exercised a stronger influence on the young Parmigianino than he did had it not been for the arrival at Parma, soon afterward, of another painter. In Parmigianino's eyes Anselmi would now have appeared as one of the "meaner beauties of the night. . . . What are you when the moon shall rise?" The moon in question, the new arrival, was Antonio Allegri from the neighboring city of Correggio, from which he took his name. He and Anselmi and the young Parmigianino worked alongside each other in the early 1520s at the monastery church of San Giovanni Evangelista. As a result of his work there Correggio was overwhelmed with commissions by the end of the year 1522, while Parmigianino, for his part, was awarded a contract for painting an apse and a vault in Parma cathedral.[3]

During this time it is certain that he learned an incalculable amount from Correggio. A small but tangible indication of this is one of his drawings at Oxford (P330; fig. 1), which is a copy of part of Correggio's cupola at San Giovanni Evangelista and was more probably made from Correggio's preparatory drawings than from the fresco itself. And a perceptive recent observation—the attribution by Lucia Fornari-Schianchi of part of the pendentives of Correggio's cupola to Parmigianino—indicates that at this time he was actually working as Correggio's assistant (fig. 14).[4] At the same time it must be borne in mind that although Correggio had evidently already been in Rome by the time of his arrival in Parma and had profited by the experience of Michelangelo and Raphael, his own style was still incompletely formed. It was precisely now, in the early 1520s at San Giovanni, that he was taking a giant stride into his astonishing maturity. By working alongside him, Parmigianino was witnessing the crucial stage in Correggio's development. There is every reason to believe that he realized the magnitude of the result, perhaps sooner than anyone else. And indeed, when first unveiled, Correggio's cupola at San Giovanni Evangelista must have seemed an astonishing, an unbelievable miracle, nothing like it having been done before. The heroic figures of the apostles, majestically enthroned on realistic clouds high above the congregation, would have inspired awe and incredulity in anyone who saw them and desperation in a young aspiring painter. Henceforth, and for the rest of his life, an indefinable mixture of admiration, envy, and resentment of Correggio's greatness was to be perhaps the chief emotion of Parmigianino's life. This was reflected in its pattern. We know that from then on he was never to be in the same place as Correggio for any length of time. While Correggio remained at Parma—Parmigianino's native city, not his—Parmigianino absented himself from it for three periods in quick succession. Some time before the summer of 1524 he had been working in the medieval castle of Fontanellato, twelve miles from Parma. Then he left for Rome, where he remained until he was driven out by the sack of 1527. But instead of returning home, he

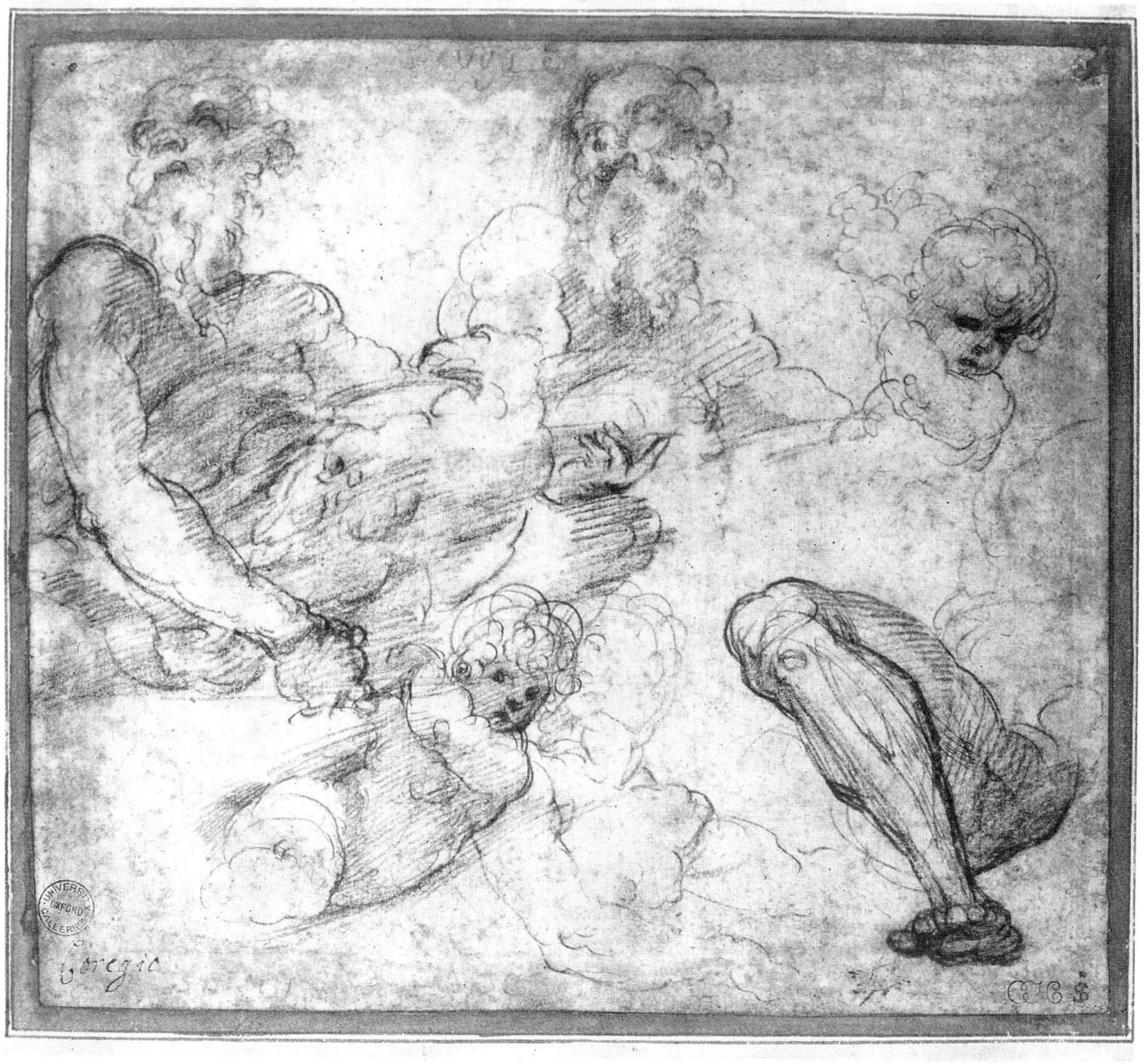

1. PARMIGIANINO
Studies after Correggio, n.d. P330
Black chalk on paper, 2⅞ × 4⅛ in.
(7.2 × 10.5 cm)
Ashmolean Museum, Oxford, England

remained for another three or four years at Bologna—until Correggio finally departed from Parma.

In the decade between 1510 and 1520, when a talented youth living at Parma would gradually take stock of the situation of the arts in the region, the scene was many-faceted and complex. Leonardo had left Milan in 1513. The great years of the Brescian school were still ahead, as was Giulio Romano's highly productive residence at Mantua. Torbido, Caroto, and others were active at Verona, Francia at Bologna, Dosso Dossi and Garofalo at Ferrara, and Costa at Mantua. But the most enterprising pictorial undertaking within reach during this decade was a major program of redecoration in the ancient cathedral of Cremona (there was a tenuous connection between the city and Parmigianino's family in the person of Francesco Tacconi).[5] Between 1515 and 1520 Altobello Melone, Romanino, and Pordenone continued the series of frescoes that Boccaccio Boccaccino had started a decade previously, and which eventually almost encircled the interior of Cremona cathedral. The influence on the young Parmigianino of Pordenone's dramatic contributions to the series has been acknowledged. Less obvious, but equally fundamental, is the influence of Melone's and Romanino's Cremona frescoes. These are essentially picturesque rather than monumental; and the accumulation in them of details such as palm trees, painted

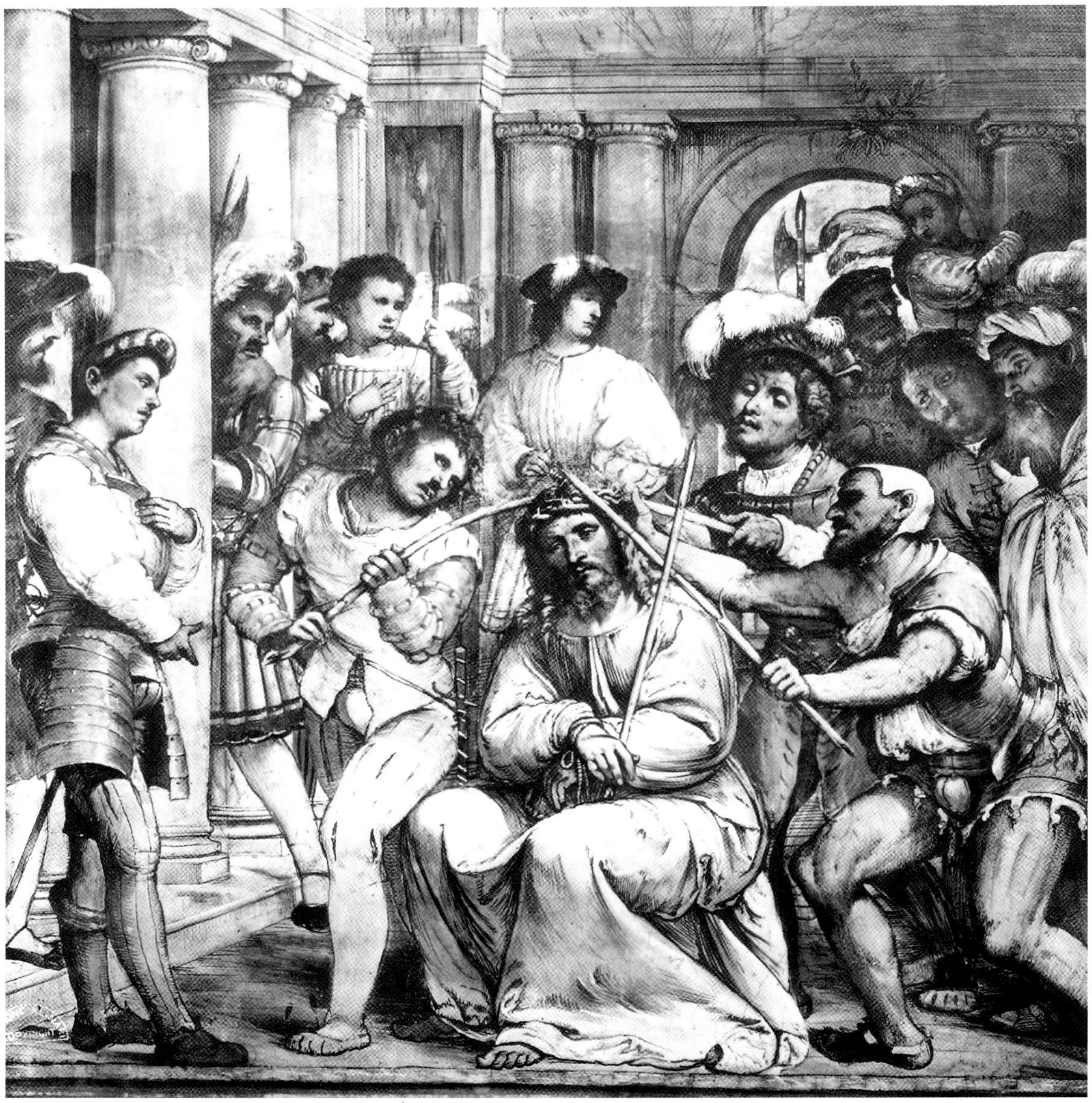

2. ROMANINO
Christ before Caiaphas, c. 1519–20
Fresco
Duomo, Cremona, Italy

marble reliefs, and soldiers in elaborate costumes with slashed sleeves and plumed hats, depicted in a fluid, almost freehand technique, is echoed by the young Parmigianino (fig. 2). To judge by the result, the sight of the Cremona frescoes would have been the most traumatic experience in his life before the impact of Correggio burst on him. Even then, Cremonese influence is perceptible for a time alongside that of Correggio.

Another source of influence—from Ferrara—on the young Parmigianino is more difficult to pin down. But Dosso Dossi's altarpiece *Saint Sebastian with the Baptist and Saint Jerome* is dated 1522 (fig. 3). It is still in Modena cathedral, and Modena is near Parma. Dosso's altarpiece has a background of undulating hills with plentiful foliage, the whole painted with strong contrasts of lurid light, as usual with him. Though I assume that Parmigianino would have known at least this example of Dosso's art, and that Dosso's treatment of light was indeed a formative influence, Dosso's approach to landscape was evidently less so. It is nearer and less impetuous than that of Parmigianino himself or of his Cremonese prototypes.

Documents recently discovered (Dall'Acqua 1984) show that Parmigianino had two elder brothers and a sister. Like Raphael, he lost his father at an early age, and as in Raphael's case again, the father, Filippo Mazzola, had been a known but essentially provincial painter. Two uncles, Pier Ilario and Michele, who brought up the boy, were also painters but even more obscure. Vasari stated in his first edition that the young Parmigianino had been apprenticed to Correggio. By the time he came to revise his history he

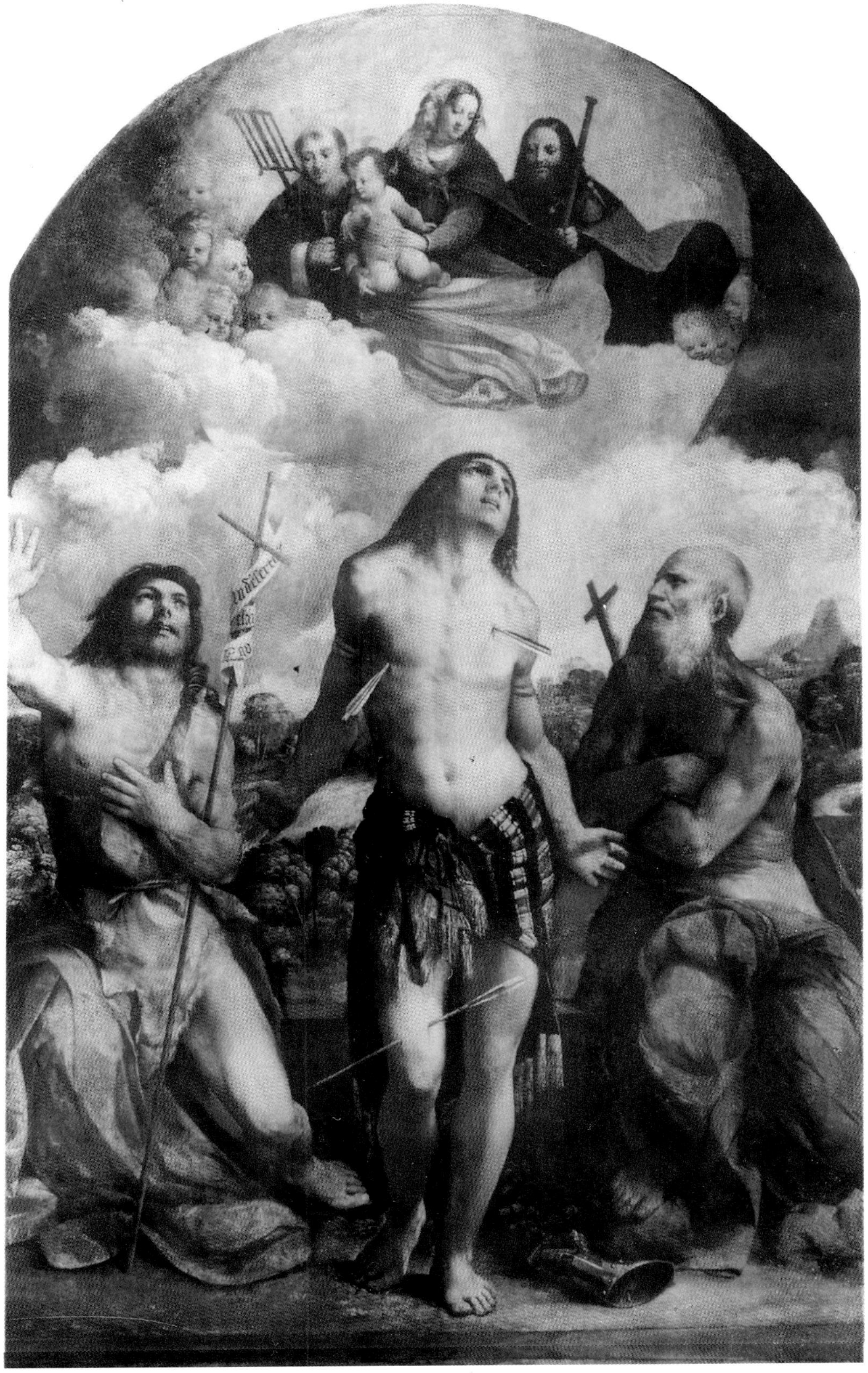

3. DOSSO DOSSI
Saint Sebastian with the Baptist and Saint Jerome, c. 1522
Oil on panel, 144½ × 74⅜ in. (367 × 190 cm)
Duomo, Modena, Italy

had met Girolamo Mazzola Bedoli, who had been connected with Parmigianino and who would have convinced him of his mistake (Vasari may or may not have met Parmigianino in Bologna in 1530; see appendix 2). In his second edition he merely states that the boy was apprenticed to "excellent masters." The best painters in Parma at the time would have been Araldi and Rondani. Both, in the present state of knowledge, are shadowy figures, Rondani the more advanced painter of the two. Vasari does not mention either, and his silence, together with the appearance of Parmigianino's earliest work, particularly the Bardi altarpiece, leads one to think that apart from what he would have learned from his uncles he was probably largely self-taught.

4. PARMIGIANINO
The Baptism of Christ, c. 1519
Tempera on panel, 76 × 50 in.
(193 × 127 cm)
Staatliche Museen, Berlin (cat. A2)

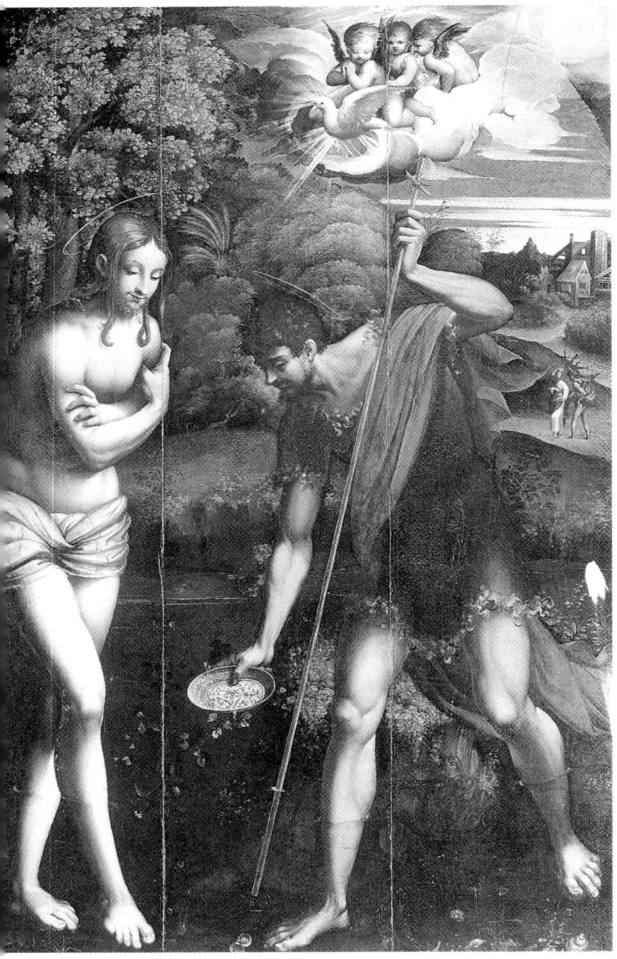

Vasari does tell us, however, that at the age of sixteen Parmigianino painted a *Baptism of Christ.* Despite a gap in its pedigree there can be little doubt that this is the picture that entered the Bode Museum in Berlin as early as 1821 (fig. 4). It is much tighter in handling than the earliest of the universally accepted paintings, the Bardi altar, and bears only minimal relation, at the most, to any of the acknowledged works. For this reason the statement on an inscription formerly annexed to the picture, to the effect that Parmigianino was no more than fourteen when he painted it, may be more plausible than Vasari's. When attention was redrawn to the picture in the present century by Voss and Freedberg there was widespread skepticism, but there is no valid reason to doubt the attribution. As with other work attributed to infant prodigies, some of the alien appearance of the Berlin picture may be due to the "help" of older painters, presumably his uncles. As might be expected, it is hardly possible to speak of style in a work produced in these circumstances. The general idiom seems to approximate that of Francia, but the greater interest already shown in effects of light distinguishes it from his work.[6]

As with the Berlin *Baptism* the pedigree of the Bardi altarpiece—the *Marriage of Saint Catherine*—is not complete (fig. 5). But as a recognizably early work of Parmigianino it is reasonable to identify it with an altarpiece specified by Vasari as of that subject and as painted by Parmigianino at Viadana. He had been taken there by his uncles to escape the hostilities between the papal forces and the French in the Parma area in 1521. Preliminary drawings for the painting show, insofar as it is possible to chart their sequence, an increasing tendency toward austerity. An early design in the Louvre (P381) shows a picturesque composition of the Cremonese type, with luxuriant foliage breaking into the figure group both above and below. In a drawing in the Uffizi (P76r) this is relegated to a window at the back, while another sketch, in Cambridge, Massachusetts (P51), replaces the foliage with a double colonnade. It also includes an elaborate frame, with bizarre curved column shafts, the entablature surmounted by a vase—a feature that was to be obsessive with Parmigianino throughout his career and which has been seen as a symptom of his interest in alchemy[7] (fig. 6). This and other studies for the painting illustrate a peculiarity that will be encountered in the later work. The subject matter varies during the evolution of the design. In this case various saints appear in the drawings who do not figure in the painting. Though it is possible that such developments were made with the agreement of

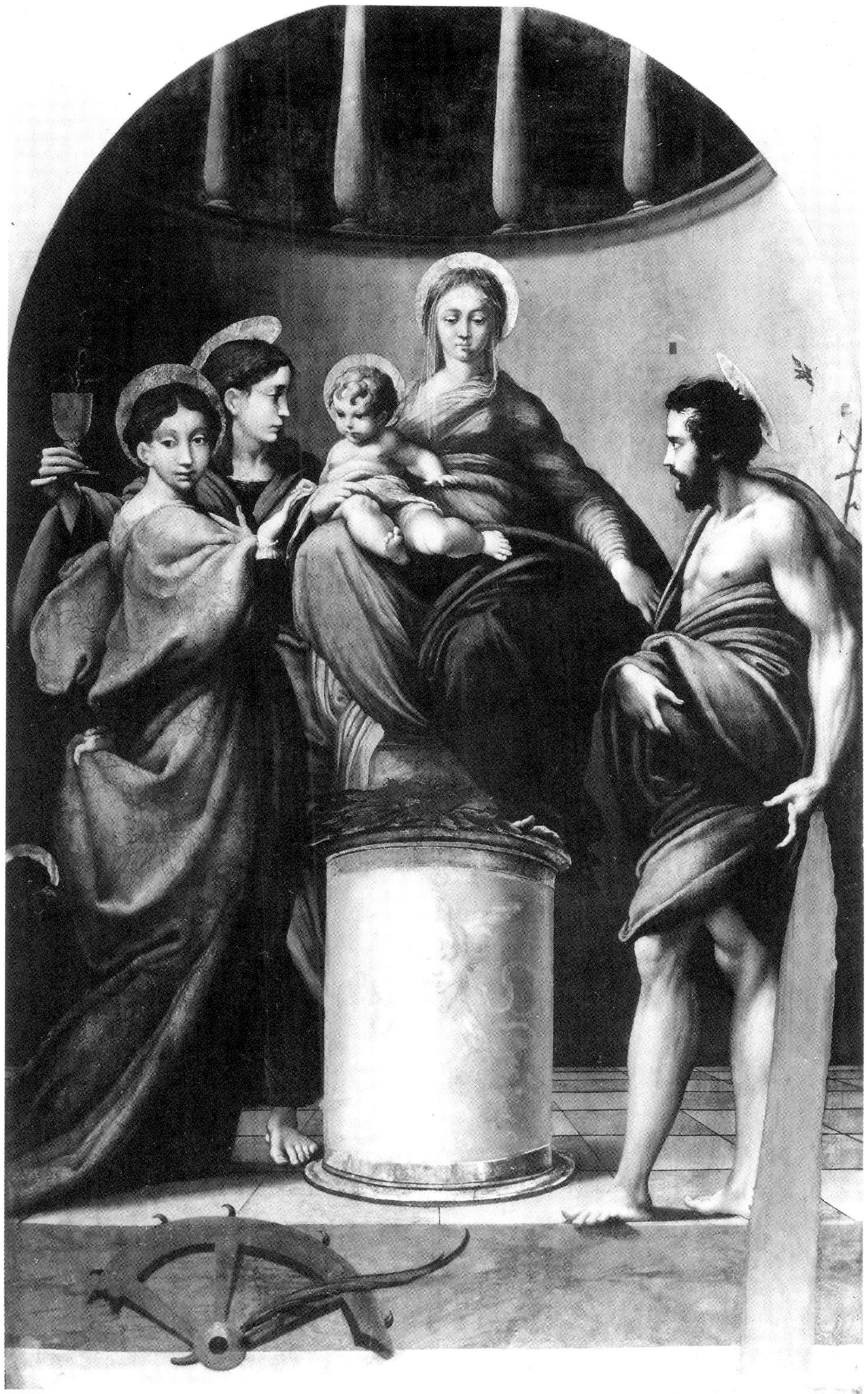

5. PARMIGIANINO
The Mystic Marriage of Saint Catherine, c. 1522
Tempera on panel, 80 × 51⅛ in. (203 × 130 cm)
Santa Maria, Bardi (Parma), Italy
(cat. A1)

the patron, the fact that Parmigianino did it so often and in such different contexts argues that he habitually permitted himself, as of right, considerable iconographic flexibility and that he got away with it. This practice also favors the assumption (which has been questioned) that the drawings associated with the Bardi altar really do connect with it.

In the painting as executed the pillars in the background have been reduced in number, and the rest of the surround left blank. The inspiration for this was probably Francia's altarpiece *Madonna Enthroned with Saints* (Galleria Nazionale, Parma), which is dated 1515 and has a semicircular colonnade or stone arbor behind the figures. But the pose

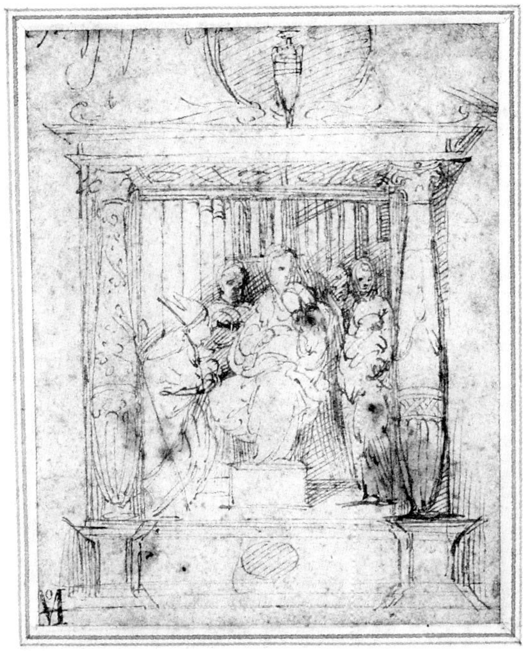

6. PARMIGIANINO

Study for the Bardi altarpiece, n.d. P51

Pen and ink on paper, $4\frac{7}{8} \times 3\frac{3}{4}$ in.

(12.5×9.5 cm)

Fogg Museum, Cambridge,

Massachusetts

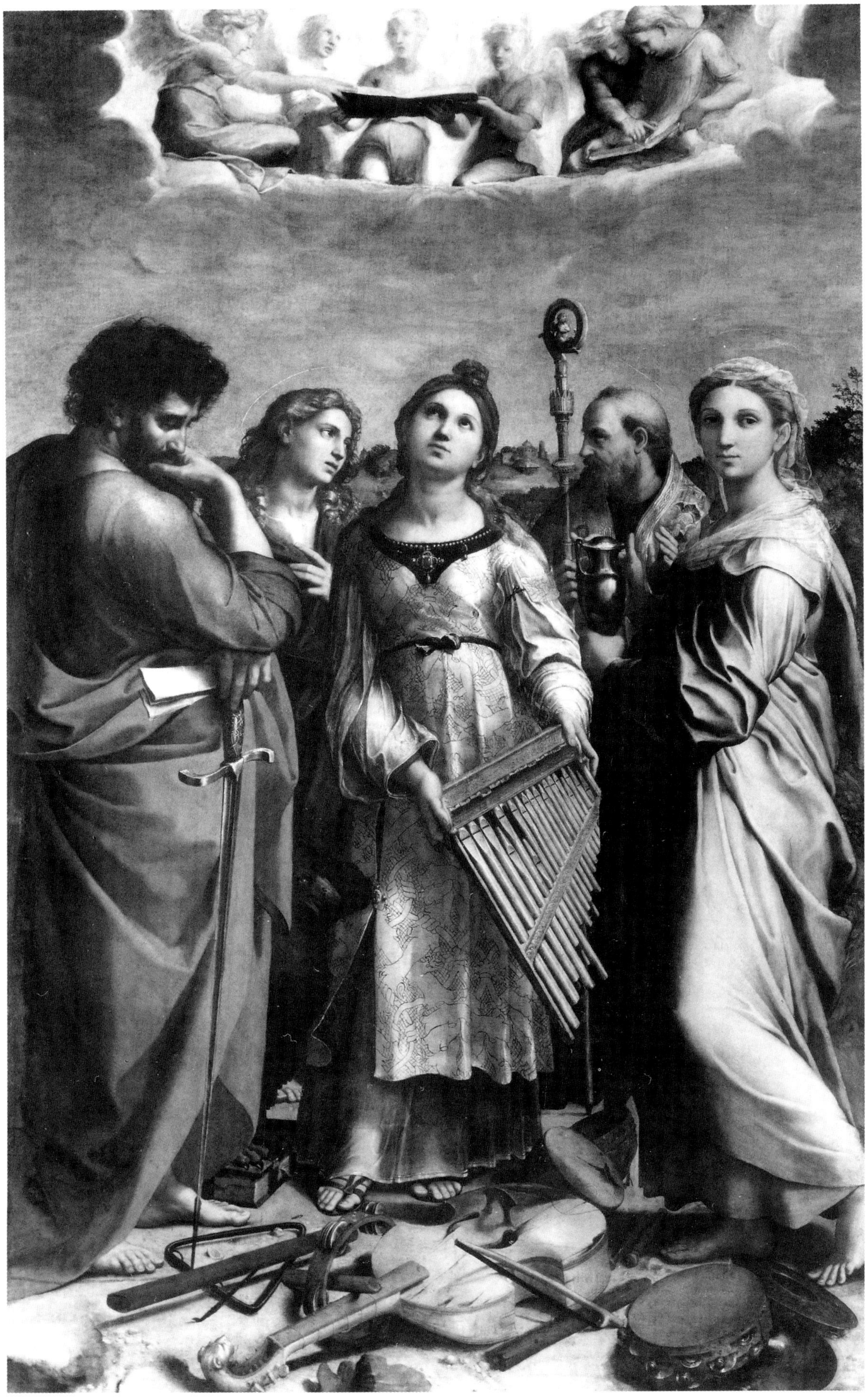

7. RAPHAEL

Saint Cecilia, c. 1515

Oil on canvas, removed from panel,

$93\frac{3}{4} \times 59$ in. (238×150 cm)

Pinacoteca Nazionale, Bologna, Italy

of Saint Catherine in Parmigianino's painting, on the left and seen from the back, has been thought to echo that of the saint—Saint Paul—in the corresponding position in the altarpiece which was currently the most sensational in North Italy—Raphael's *Saint Cecilia* in San Giovanni al Monte in Bologna (fig. 7).[8] The cylindrical pedestal of the Madonna's throne in the Bardi altar was a device that had been used, apparently, by Cima in his altarpiece of c. 1507 for Parma cathedral (now in the Galleria Nazionale, Parma).

Although the drawings show that prolonged experiment and thought had gone into the making of the Bardi picture, it gives the impression, more than any other of Parmigianino's early works, that he was wanting to run before he could walk—that he was taking shortcuts before he had fully mastered the long way round. For instance, the hair is painted with calligraphic finesse, but the bodies are not fully modeled. Sir Joshua Reynolds expressed this well when he said of Parmigianino, "He endeavors at grace and grandeur of manner before he has learnt correctness of drawing."[9] In a word, the technique appears amateurish. The same could be said of the earliest work of both Rosso and Tintoretto, both of whom are also likely to have been partly self-taught. Unlike the Berlin *Baptism,* however, the Bardi altarpiece shows, particularly in the facial types, unmistakable pointers toward the mature Parmigianino.

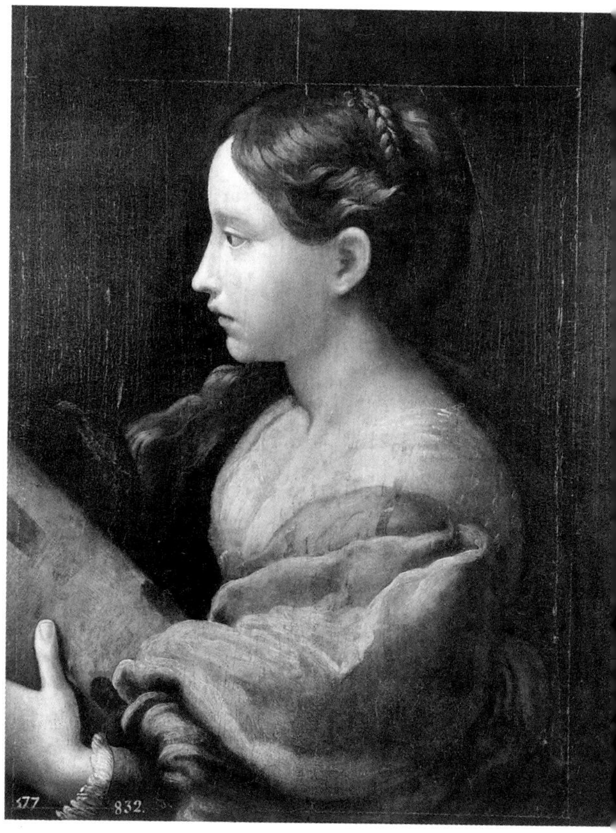

8. PARMIGIANINO
Saint Barbara, c. 1523
Oil on panel, 18⅞ × 15⅜ in.
(48 × 39 cm)
Museo del Prado, Madrid (cat. A22)

Very close to the Bardi altarpiece in its combination of freedom of brushwork and insecure draftsmanship is the small picture of Saint Barbara (Prado; fig. 8). An early profile sketch in Bayonne (P6) has been claimed as a study for it. The fact that the drawing seems to be of a young man need not preclude this; but the degree of resemblance is not enough to be conclusive.

Though none of the surviving paintings executed before the Rome visit are precisely datable from documents, a rough chronology can be established. The number of commissions that were involved, and their relative importance, shows that by the age of twenty the young Parmigianino was already established in the Parma area as a force in the world of art. Vasari implies that Parmigianino started the frescoes in the San Giovanni Evangelista chapels (figs. 9–11) before fleeing to Viadana, but it is assumed that what is now visible dates from after his return, that is, from 1522. The frescoes in the Rocca in Fontanellato are evidently more mature, and therefore later, and their style can be used as a yardstick for dating panel pictures such as the portrait in Naples of Galeazzo Sanvitale, the owner of Fontanellato, and the male portrait in the National Gallery, London. Finally, Vasari states that Parmigianino took three of his pictures with him to Rome (to show what he could do) and two of these are identifiable with the *Self-Portrait in a Convex Mirror* (Kunsthistorisches Museum, Vienna; fig. 36) and a *Holy Family* in the Prado. The third was almost certainly the *Circumcision* now in Detroit. A few others can be grouped stylistically around these few landmarks.

If pictures such as the Sanvitale and London portraits are compared with the Bardi altarpiece, the technical progress made within the space of no more than about three years is almost incredible—from amateurish fumbling to mastery of technique and style alike.

Granted that between the ages of about eighteen and twenty-one a talented artist may be expected to make giant strides, in this case the improvement is such as to leave very little doubt that even without having been apprenticed to Correggio (or any other major painter) he had at this period spent much time watching Correggio paint and studying his drawings and his technical methods.

As for the San Giovanni frescoes, the ancient Benedictine monastery had recently been rebuilt, and by the early 1520s Anselmi, Correggio, and the young Parmigianino were working in different parts of the handsome new church. Vasari makes the surprising (and improbable) claim that Parmigianino painted seven of the side chapels. Authentic drawings survive for frescoes in two of them—the first and second in the north aisle of the nave, coming from the west—and those two, which at that time were still unallocated to private patrons, are the only ones whose existing decoration is attributable to him with confidence. It has nevertheless been suggested in modern times that he was also active in a third chapel—the fourth from the west. The frescoes in question consist of full-

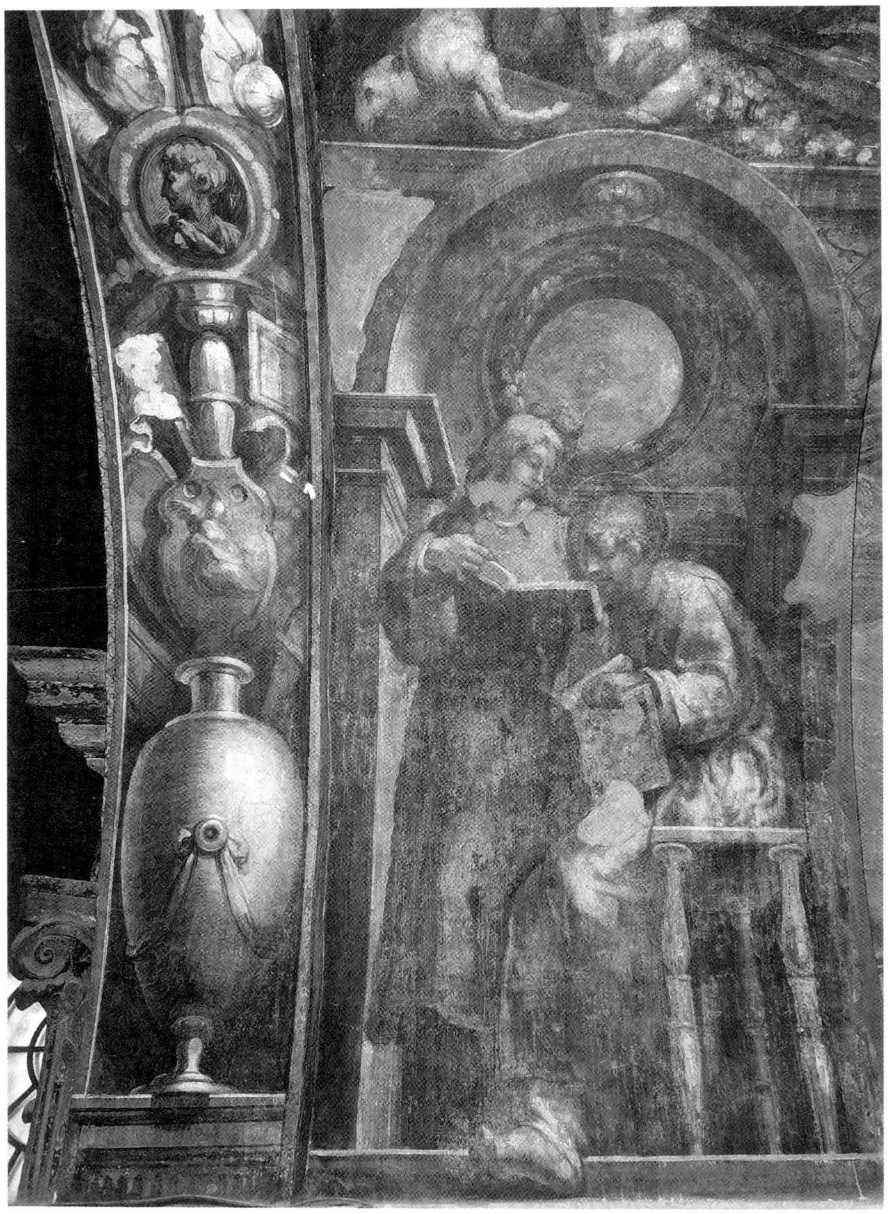

9. PARMIGIANINO
Two Deacons, c. 1522
Fresco
San Giovanni Evangelista, Parma, Italy
(cat. A34)

length seated figures of the saints Hilary of Poitiers and Nicholas of Bari. As regards style, the grinning Saint Hilary strongly recalls Saint Augustine in Rondani's signed altarpiece in the Parma gallery. Nevertheless it would be very difficult to reconcile an attribution of the frescoes to Rondani with the documentation. A document of 1515 records past payment to Parmigianino's uncles, Pier Ilario and Michele.[10] But the technique, which is relatively free and painterly, and the style are incompatible with the uncles' retarded quattrocento idiom, as represented by the altarpiece from Scurano that they signed jointly.[11] On the other hand, the employment of an independent master would run counter to the contract. In default of a second contract reallocating the work to another painter, it might be assumed that Parmigianino's uncles had taken it on themselves to subcontract it unofficially; and since the sale of the chapel to the patron was not finalized until 1522, by which time Parmigianino was already nineteen, it has been suggested that it was to him that they did so. The argument might also be applied to Girolamo Mazzola Bedoli, since he was apparently resident in the house of Parmigianino's uncles and

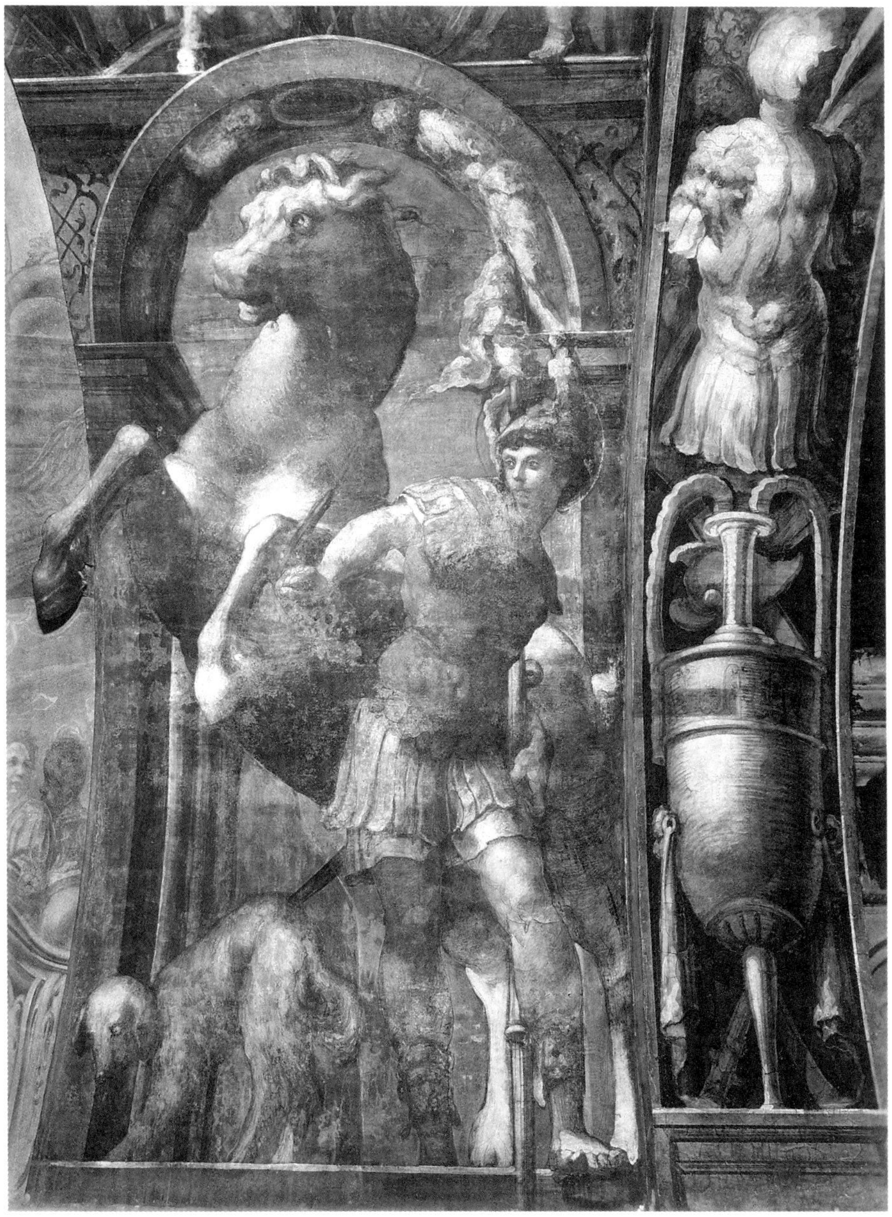

10. PARMIGIANINO
Saint Vitalis, c. 1522
Fresco
San Giovanni Evangelista, Parma, Italy
(cat. A34)

married Pier Ilario's daughter some time before 1530. He eventually painted the altarpiece that is still in position in this very chapel, but his style as a fresco painter is not known before 1538. In view of the conflicting evidence, the verdict on the authorship of the frescoes should remain open.[12]

The space available for frescoes in these chapels consists of the soffits of two arches, a broad inner one and a narrower one nearest the nave aisle. It would be almost impossible to treat such spaces in a unified manner, and even Correggio, at the height of his powers, was unable to do much with a corresponding site on the opposite side of the nave.[13] In the event Parmigianino, in the first two chapels, split the surface on the broader inner soffit into three separate fields in each case, the painting on the central one facing the altar and the flanking scenes facing the side walls in opposite directions, thus forcing the spectator to take up three positions in order to see them. In both cases the principal figures are martyrs, and in both the scenes depicted are planned on a basis of contrast: in both cases one of the flanking frescoes is of a placid subject and the other of a violent one. In one chapel the participants are female saints, in the other, male. Thus in the first chapel, where the frescoes seem more accomplished, and therefore probably later than those in the second, Saint Lucy (in profile, like the Prado *Saint Barbara*) and Saint Apollonia are shown seated while Saint Agatha (fig. 11) is seen in the throes of martyrdom. This chapel was originally dedicated to saints Lucy, Cecilia, Agatha, and Agnes. In the second chapel two young men, without attributes but one of them perhaps Saint Laurence and the other perhaps Saint Stephen, occupy one field, one of them seated, the other standing. The foil to them, on the other side, is a young soldier, identified as Saint Vitalis, who tries to restrain a violently rearing horse. The center painting in the first chapel is *God the Father* (now much damaged), and in the corresponding position in the second chapel is a complex design in which four putti are accompanied by a tambourine, a helmet and shield, a lamb, and a bear, apparently standing for the sanguine, choleric, melancholic, and phlegmatic temperaments respectively. This, and the prominent inclusion of vases on the outer arch of the same chapel, has been seen as evidence of an interest in alchemy, though whether reflecting the interests of the patron as well as those of the artist would be open to discussion.[14]

From a stylistic point of view the most interesting aspect of these frescoes is their eclecticism. The decoration of the outer arch of the first chapel includes putti for which there are admirable drawings in the Louvre (P396 and P405). These drawings and the resulting paintings bear an obvious relationship to the putti that Correggio had painted in the Camera di San Paolo and to those which he was to include in the decoration of the cupola at San Giovanni. It has been suggested (by Popham) that Correggio drew them from wax models, and that Parmigianino had access to these.

The group of Saint Vitalis and his charger has been thought to derive from part of Pordenone's fresco *Christ on the Road to Calvary* at Cremona, but in some respects it is closer to what was probably Pordenone's own ultimate inspiration—the antique *Horse Tamers* in

11. PARMIGIANINO
Saint Agatha and Executioner, c. 1522
Fresco
San Giovanni Evangelista, Parma, Italy
(cat. A33)

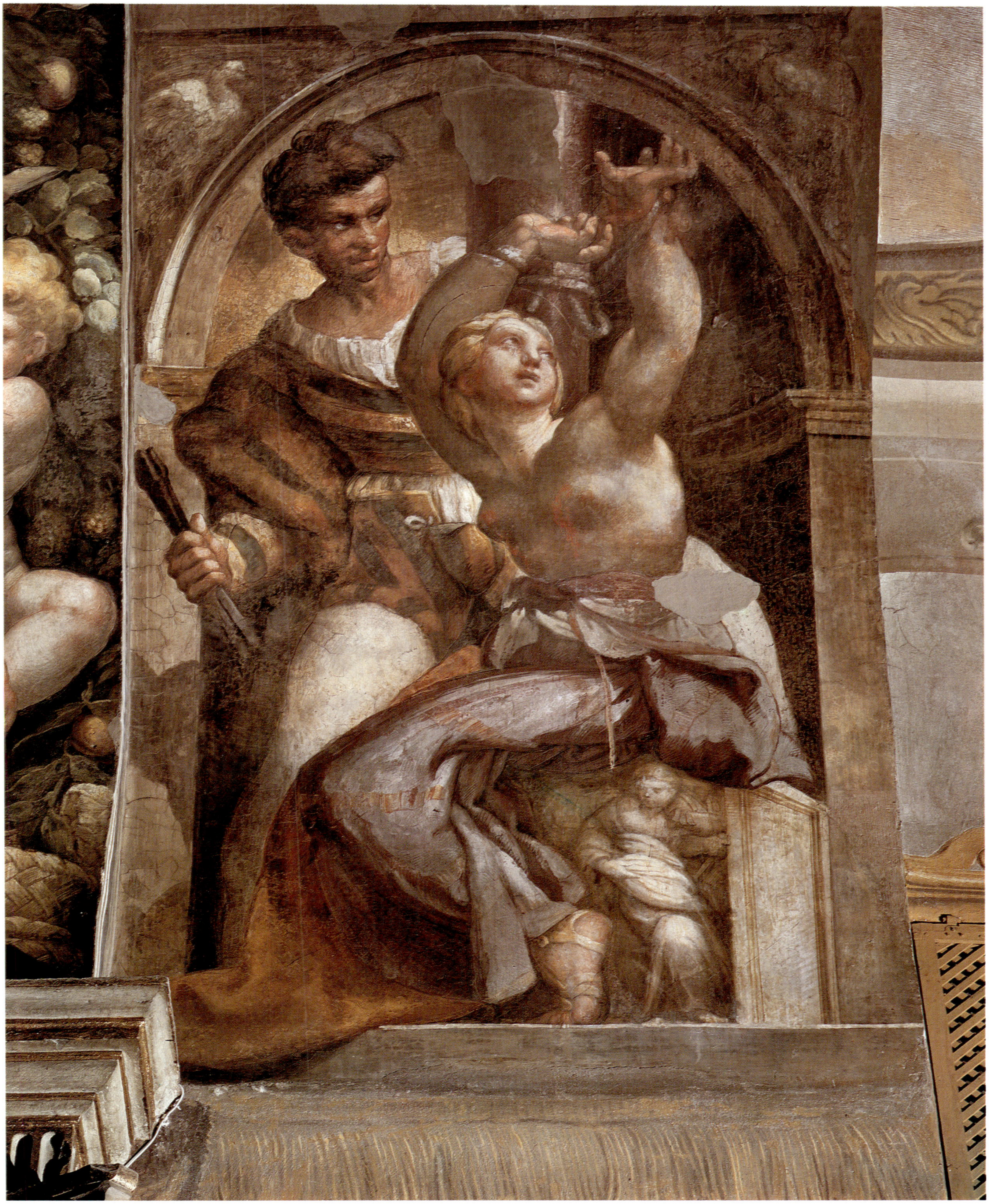

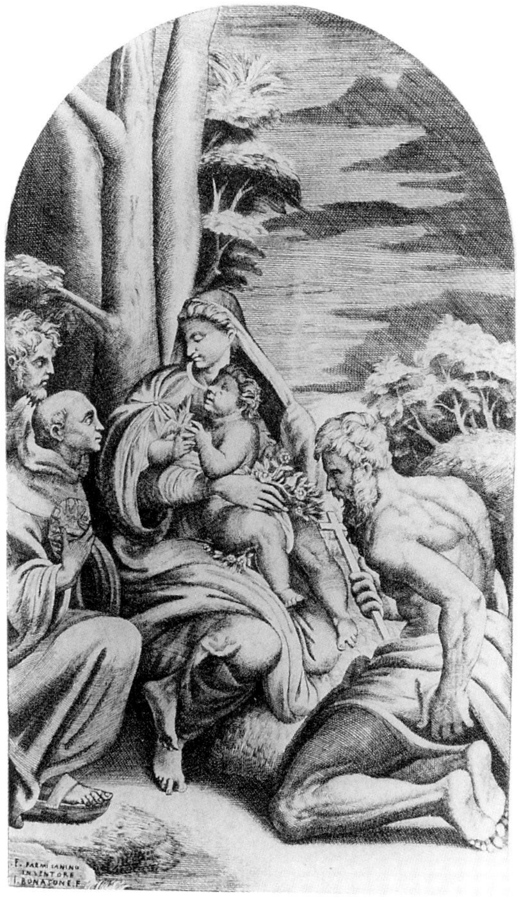

12. GIULIO BONASONE (AFTER PARMIGIANINO)
Madonna and Child with Saint Jerome and the Blessed Bernardino da Feltre, c. 1525–50
Engraving (cat. B2 and G11)

the Quirinal. And one of the gimmicks that Pordenone permitted himself in the Cremona frescoes is echoed in Parmigianino's device in allowing the feet of one of the young male saints to project over the parapet in the foreground. A further derivation from the Cremona frescoes in general is the inclusion of painted marble reliefs under the seats in both the *Saint Lucy* and the *Saint Agatha* scenes. More remarkable is the debt to Michelangelo's Sistine ceiling, since there are signs of it both in the frescoes and in some of Parmigianino's early drawings; and he had not yet been to Rome. The *Saint Agatha,* for example, is a pastiche of Michelangelo's Eve in the *Temptation* (itself an evident derivative from an antique bacchante or maenad), while the *God the Father* in the central reserve of the first chapel closely echoes Michelangelo's *Eternal.* In addition, two drawings of this period (P328 and P410v) are clearly after two of the Sistine *Ignudi;* and a sketch after Michelangelo's *Prophet Isaiah* (P712v) may also date from this time. A further sketch by Parmigianino (P168v) after part of Raphael's fresco *Poetry* on the ceiling of the Stanza della Segnatura poses no problem, as this had already been engraved by Marcantonio Raimondi. But Michelangelo's figures had not by this time. The least improbable explanation of Parmigianino's knowledge of them, and of antique monuments such as the *Horse Tamers,* would be that he had seen sketches of them by Correggio and perhaps others.[15]

Correggio's influence was evidently strong in an altarpiece that Vasari mentions as painted by Parmigianino after his return from Viadana. The subject was the Madonna and Child with Saint Jerome and the Blessed Bernardino da Feltre. The original has disappeared, but the composition is known from an engraving (in reverse) by Bonasone (fig. 12) and a painted copy. There is also a study for it (P275). The design is totally different from that of the Bardi altarpiece, and evidently looks to works of Correggio such as the *Madonna of Albinea* of c. 1517 (itself known only from copies) or the Uffizi *Holy Family with Saint Francis.* In both of Correggio's compositions, as in Parmigianino's, the setting is in the open air, with the Madonna seated against a tree trunk.

The extreme of Correggio's dominance over Parmigianino at this stage of his career may be traced in a different composition, once again known only from copies. This is the oblong *Marriage of Saint Catherine,* of which there is a copy in the Parma gallery (fig. 13). There is no documentation of the intended destination of this composition. Though the facial types, insofar as it is possible to recognize them in a copy, are in line with early works such as the Bardi altar or the Madrid *Saint Barbara,* the design as a whole is virtually a pastiche of elements in Correggio's half-dome for San Giovanni Evangelista as known from copies and fragments. And this, together with the painting's inherent characteristics—a low eye level, a background of clouds, and a design that curves in depth—may give a hint as to the purpose of Parmigianino's composition. I suggest that this copy may record part of his project for one of the half-domes at the Duomo. His contract, dated November 21, 1522, assigns to him both the painting of the northern wall and half-dome of the north transept (there are also apses on the east side of the transepts) and of the large quadripartite vault of the same transept, which has only a single bay, without side aisles.

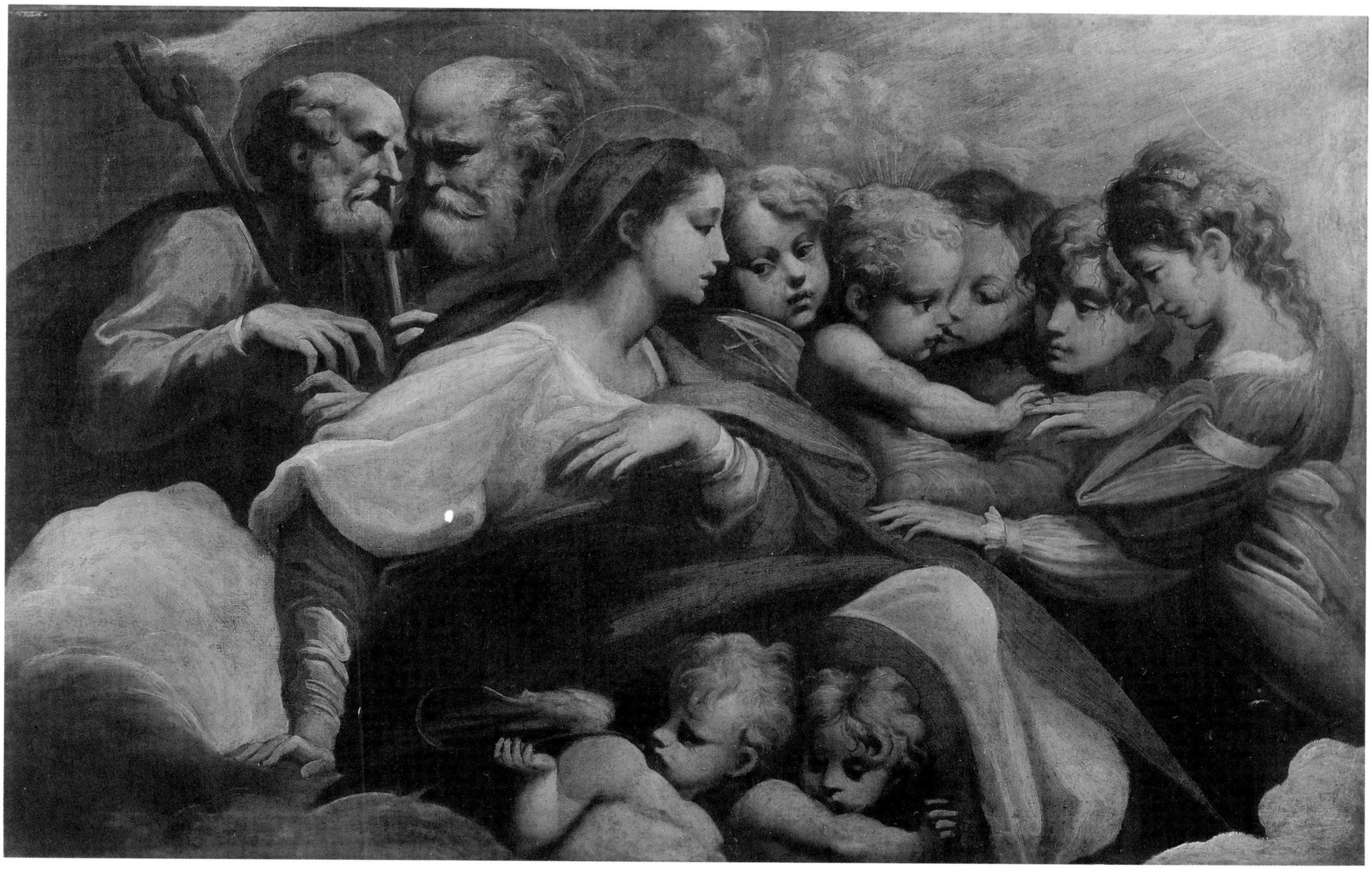

The contract gives the artist permission to erase existing paintings in those areas. Popham suggested reasonably that drawings of heroic figures in the Louvre and British Museum (P401 and P166), and perhaps two others (P14 and P165), are Evangelists and that they were intended for the four compartments of this vault. The style of the drawings is a patent essay in the epic manner of Correggio and San Giovanni Evangelista. One of them (P166) is also comparable in design with Parmigianino's organ shutters for the Steccata.

A feature of Parmigianino's contract at the Duomo is that his uncles, Pier Ilario and Michele, are named in it as guarantors that the work be done—this evidently because Parmigianino himself was still only nineteen. For this reason alone we cannot help speculating why the work was not in fact done. A decade later Parmigianino's failure to fulfill his obligations in frescoing the half-dome of the Steccata may have been due to diverse factors—his being out of practice in mural work at that time and his fear that he might not be an effective rival to Correggio, despite his wish to be so. But at the Duomo the first of these explanations is unlikely, since he had recently been engaged on fresco work at San Giovanni. As to the second, I doubt if at this stage he was as much obsessed with Correggio as he became later. I would suggest instead that the cause was a practical one

13. AFTER PARMIGIANINO
Mystic Marriage of Saint Catherine,
c. 1522
Oil on canvas, 29⅛ × 46 in.
(74 × 117 cm)
Galleria Nazionale, Parma, Italy
(see cat. B10)

beyond the artist's control. And this leads to a review of the situation in general at the Duomo at this moment.

The spectacular enterprise of the adjoining monastery church of San Giovanni Evangelista had evidently fired the Duomo authorities to emulate and, if possible, surpass it. They decided to engage the services of the painters who were working at the monastery, the aim being to modernize the interior of the huge and austere Romanesque cathedral. They evidently acted—on paper—with a degree of alacrity rare in the chapter of a cathedral. Correggio, the great new star, was first commissioned, on November 3, 1522, to undertake the vast program consisting of the decoration of the cupola, half-dome, and choir. This was followed by three more contracts drawn up on the same day, less than three weeks later—November 21. These are Parmigianino's, Rondani's (for work in the Cappella del Ferro), and Anselmi's (for the south transept, corresponding with Parmigianino's commitment for the northern one). Finally, on December 20, Araldi was assigned two bays of the nave.[16]

What happened in the event was disappointing. Correggio seems not to have started work for another four years, and what he eventually painted—the cupola—though it was soon recognized as epoch-making, was no more than half of what he had agreed to do. Parmigianino, Rondani, and Araldi did nothing. Anselmi did nothing at the time. Many years later, in 1548, he did paint the vault of the south transept, but only as a result of a fresh contract. What precisely had happened is not documented. Presumably the Duomo funds had failed, or enthusiasm for the project, or both. Conceivably the cathedral authorities were primarily interested in Correggio's contribution (his contract, after all, had preceded all the others), and his delay brought about a general cooling off. In any case I deduce that to Parmigianino the situation would have seemed sufficiently fluid for him to take the risk of working for some months in Fontanellato and then, by the year 1524, to visit Rome. Neither the duration of the Rome visit nor the succeeding years at Bologna would have been foreseen at the time; and when at last he did return to Parma, in 1530 or 1531, it must have been clear that the Duomo contract was null and void. In the event, the apses in the north transept were painted, in the second half of the sixteenth century, by Orazio Sammichini.

The recent attributions to Parmigianino, already mentioned, of one or more of the putti on Correggio's pendentives of the cupola of San Giovanni Evangelista can be dated with some confidence to the year 1523, on the ground that this part of Correggio's work was among the last, and that the end payment to him is dated January 1524. Following the recent restoration of these frescoes, it was stated that cartoons were not used for these figures. Whether Parmigianino had sketches for them by Correggio, or whether he was designing them himself on the model of Correggio's, there would have been little scope for his own idiosyncrasies except in the treatment. And in fact the features of the putto on the left of the north arch (fig. 14) are closer to those in Fontanellato than to the standard Correggesque type, and the shadows are rather less strong. The putto on the right of the south arch seems also of this kind. Since Parmigianino was already an independent master and not a pupil of Correggio or of anyone else the relationship was evidently of an informal as well as a temporary nature; and since Parmigianino had been at work on two of the side chapels in the same church there is nothing implausible in his assisting Correggio.[17]

Similar in style to Parmigianino's frescoes in the San Giovanni chapels, and therefore probably of similar date, are the organ shutters—representing Saint Cecilia and David—of the Steccata (figs. 15 and 16). They are not mentioned by Vasari, but are semi-documented. The attribution is confirmed by drawings.[18] The shutters are now in an unsatisfactory condition as a result both of damage and of the additions that were made subsequently to accommodate them to a large instrument. As at San Giovanni, the influence of both Pordenone and Correggio is clear—of Pordenone in the exaggerated *contrapposto* and of Correggio most obviously in the enchanting child who peeps out from behind David's left leg, and who is virtually repeated in one of the putti in the Fontanellato fresco.

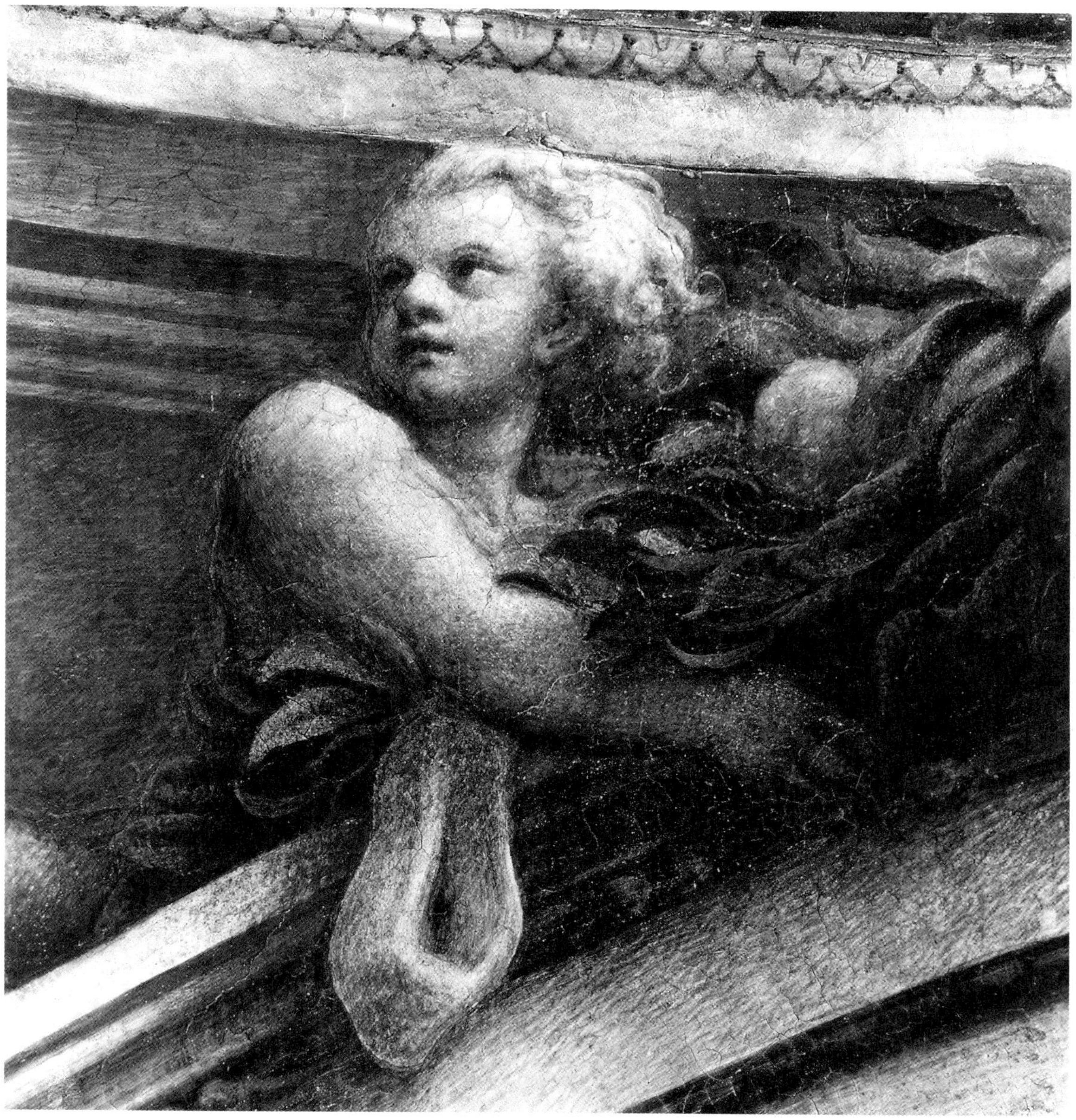

14. PARMIGIANINO
Detail of the north arch of San Giovanni Evangelista, c. 1523
(Putto)
Fresco
San Giovanni Evangelista, Parma, Italy
(cat. A34)

Much more rewarding is Parmigianino's next fresco—the decoration with scenes from the story of Diana and Actaeon on the vault of a small room, thought to have been a bathroom or *stufa,* in the medieval castle of Fontanellato (figs. 17–21). The patron in question, Count Galeazzo Sanvitale, was the current head of one of the surviving feudal dynasties in the country around Parma. Being in a remote region, the Fontanellato fresco is not mentioned by Vasari; but though not documented, its authenticity is assured by a number of preparatory drawings. It was formerly thought to be a late work, but there is no doubt, from these drawings, and when one looks back from them at the fresco itself, that it dates from shortly before the Rome journey.

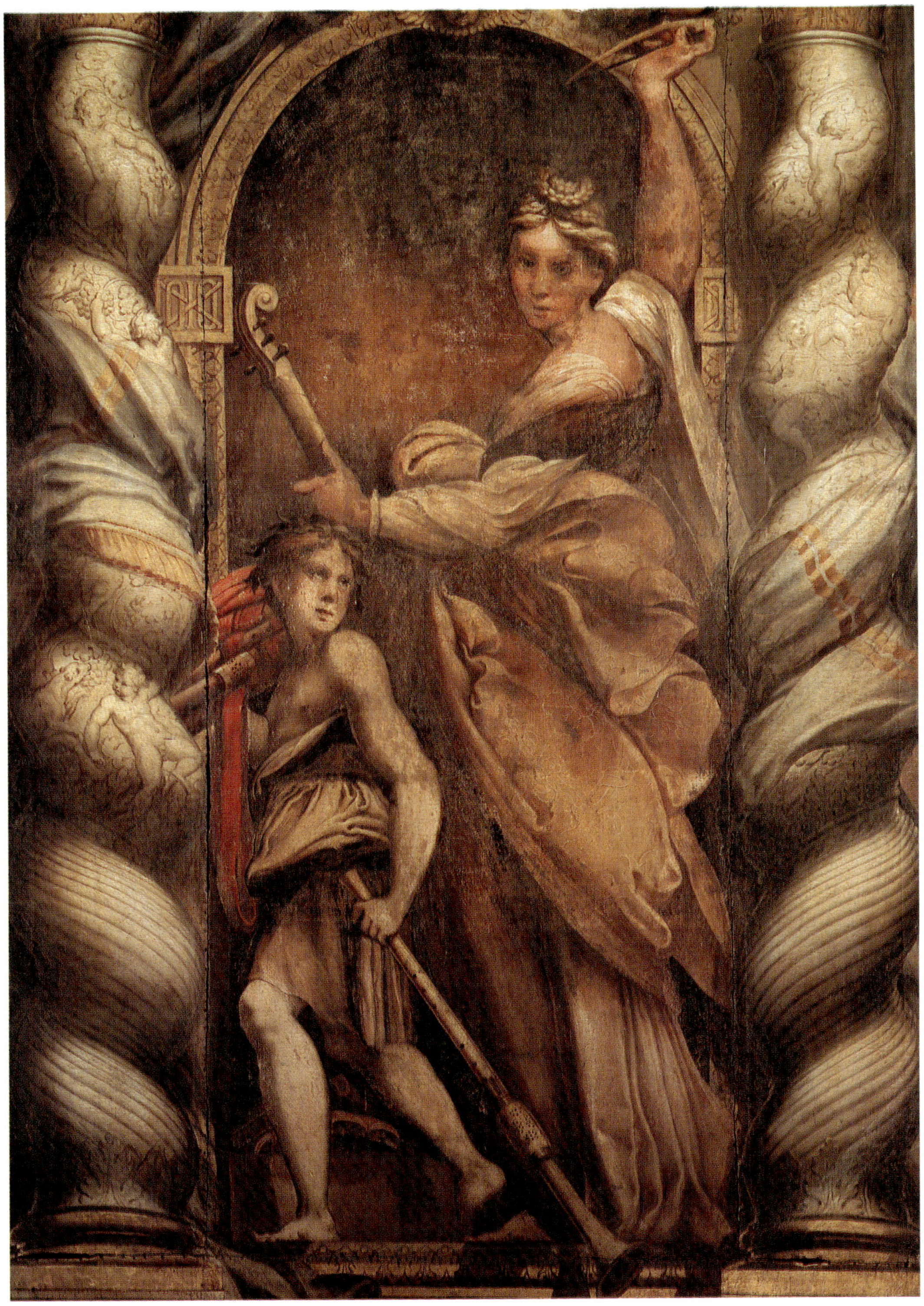

15. PARMIGIANINO
Saint Cecilia, c. 1523
Oil on canvas, 211¾ × 109⅜ in.
(538 × 278 cm)
Santa Maria della Steccata, Parma, Italy
(cat. A36)

The room is constructed on similar principles to the Camera di San Paolo at Parma, which Correggio had painted several years previously (fig. 22). In both cases the structure of the vault included a series of vertical lunette shapes on all four walls. In Fontanellato there are pendentives between the lunettes (the Camera di San Paolo is different in this respect). These pendentives—four on each of the long walls and three on each short one—are supported by small, Medusa-like heads in stucco or terra-cotta, certainly designed and perhaps also executed by Parmigianino himself. A drawing in Berlin (P12; fig. 23) shows a frieze of putti and a scene from the story of Diana and Actaeon, apparently below a head of similar type. This may have been intended for a different room,

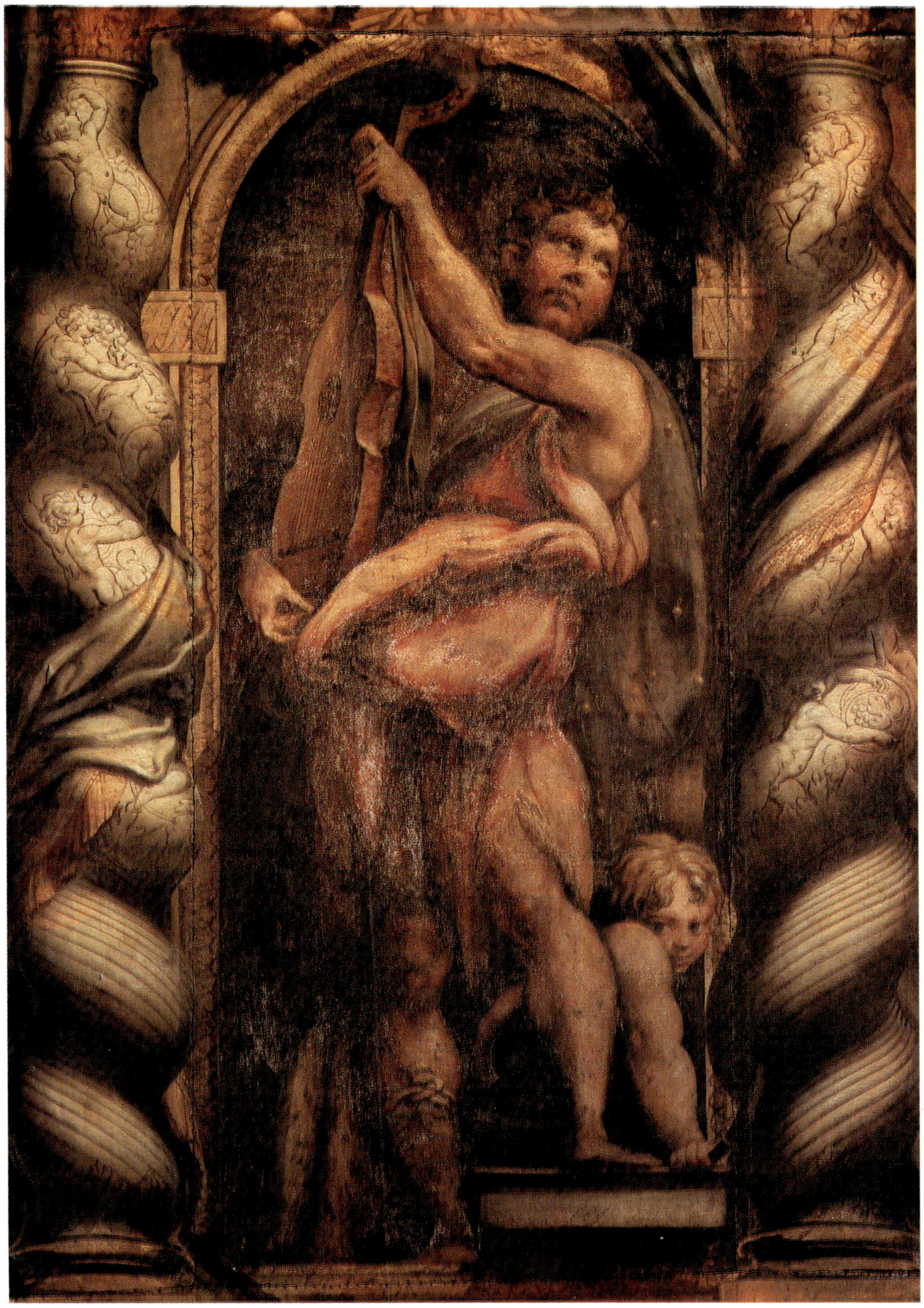

16. PARMIGIANINO
David, c. 1523
Oil on canvas, 211¾ × 109⅜ in.
(538 × 278 cm)
Santa Maria della Steccata, Parma, Italy
(cat. A37)

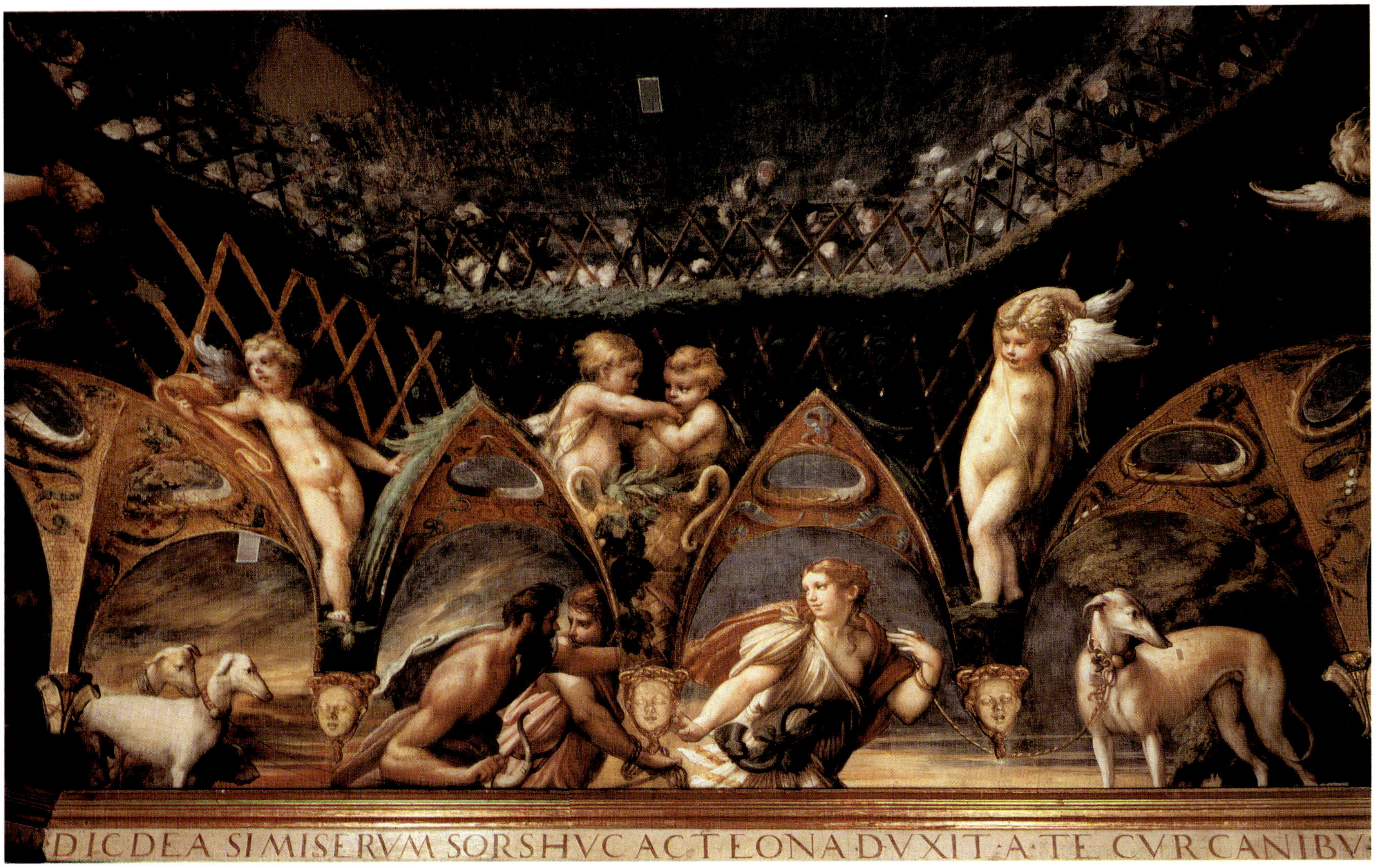

17. PARMIGIANINO
Detail of *Diana and Actaeon*, c. 1523
(Nymph pursued by huntsmen)
Fresco
Rocca Sanvitale, Fontanellato (Parma), Italy (cat. A12)

but might equally indicate an intention to paint the walls of this one as well as the ceiling. On the verso of the same sheet is a study for a *Rape of Europa.*

Though the Fontanellato room is considerably smaller even than the Camera di San Paolo and is oblong, while Correggio's is square, it is clear that Parmigianino made Correggio's scheme his starting point by treating the curved vault as a trellised arbor, pierced by a central "opening," apparently revealing the sky. There are smaller "openings" in the tiny triangular vaults above each of the lunettes. In addition Parmigianino may have drawn on one of Correggio's own sources, the trellised ceiling fresco of Andrea Mantegna's funerary chapel in Sant'Andrea of Mantua. We shall see later that he seems to have displayed knowledge of this work in another context. But despite the more restricted space, Parmigianino's design is actually more elaborate than Correggio's; and perhaps for that reason, as well as owing to his relatively younger age, the result is less perfect. Correggio's Camera gives the impression that nothing could be added or subtracted without loss. But Parmigianino's room, though extremely beautiful and his finest work to date of this kind, does not quite convey this impression. For one thing, he uses different scales in juxtaposition. The full-length putti seem too big for the pendentives, which truncate them in

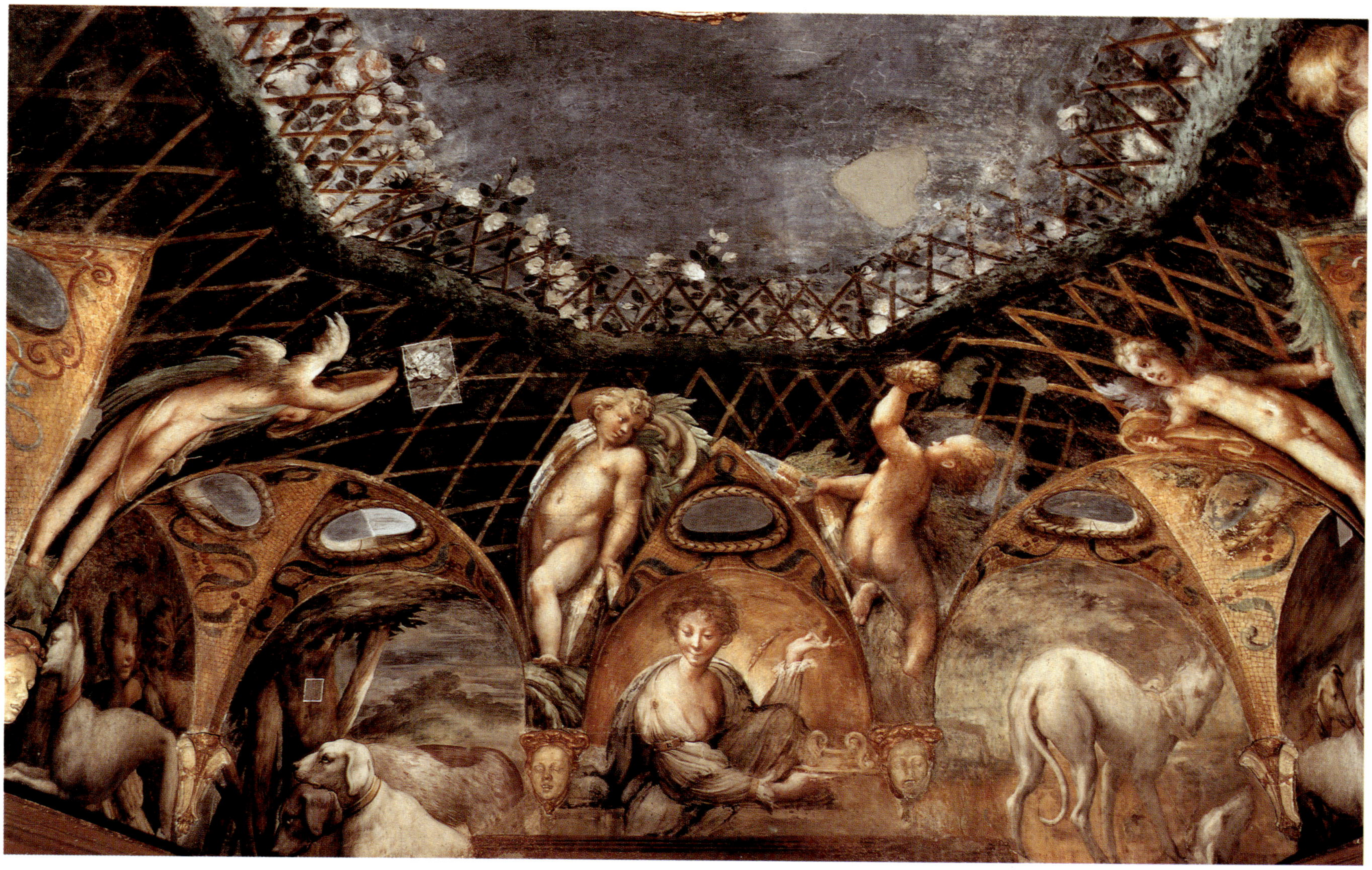

18. PARMIGIANINO
Detail of *Diana and Actaeon,* c. 1523
(Cupbearer and dogs)
Fresco
Rocca Sanvitale, Fontanellato (Parma), Italy (cat. A12)

some cases, and also too big for the half-length figures in the lunettes. An essential difference is that whereas Correggio's room is purely decorative in effect, Parmigianino's is narrative. The action shown in the lunettes—the most conspicuous area—continues from one to another, though not always consecutively: several lunettes separate Diana's transformation of Actaeon into a stag from its sequel—his death. A sketch in the Morgan Library (P313V) shows that changes were made, since on this sketch Diana and Actaeon appear in the same scene (and apparently in a pendentive rather than a lunette), whereas in the fresco the episode is distributed across two lunettes. The cursive nature of the painting is emphasized by the inscription that runs around all four walls and consists of a paraphrase of Ovid's complaint that Actaeon was unjustly punished. Despite the grim ending of the story the general effect of the fresco, accentuated by the playful behavior of the putti, is one of beauty.

In recent years various allegorical "interpretations" of the fresco have been postulated (summarized in the catalog). In default of contemporary documentary support, these theories, which are mutually incompatible, can neither be proved nor disproved. Nevertheless, certain elements remain mysterious. Neither Ceres (on the window wall)

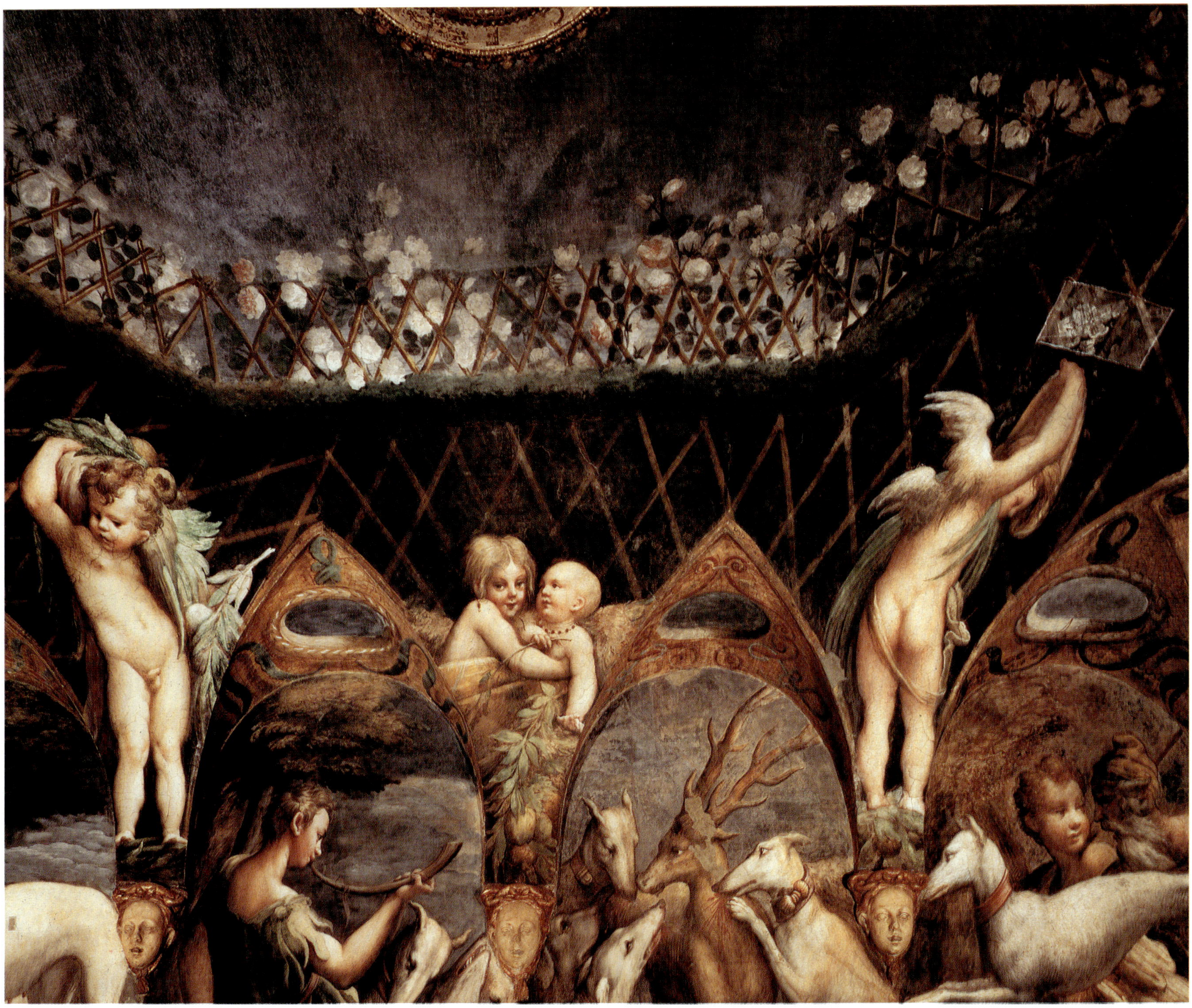

19. PARMIGIANINO
Detail of *Diana and Actaeon,* c. 1523
(Actaeon attacked by hounds)
Fresco
Rocca Sanvitale, Fontanellato (Parma),
Italy (cat. A12)

Opposite:
20. PARMIGIANINO
Diana and Actaeon, c. 1523
Fresco
Rocca Sanvitale, Fontanellato (Parma),
Italy (cat. A12)

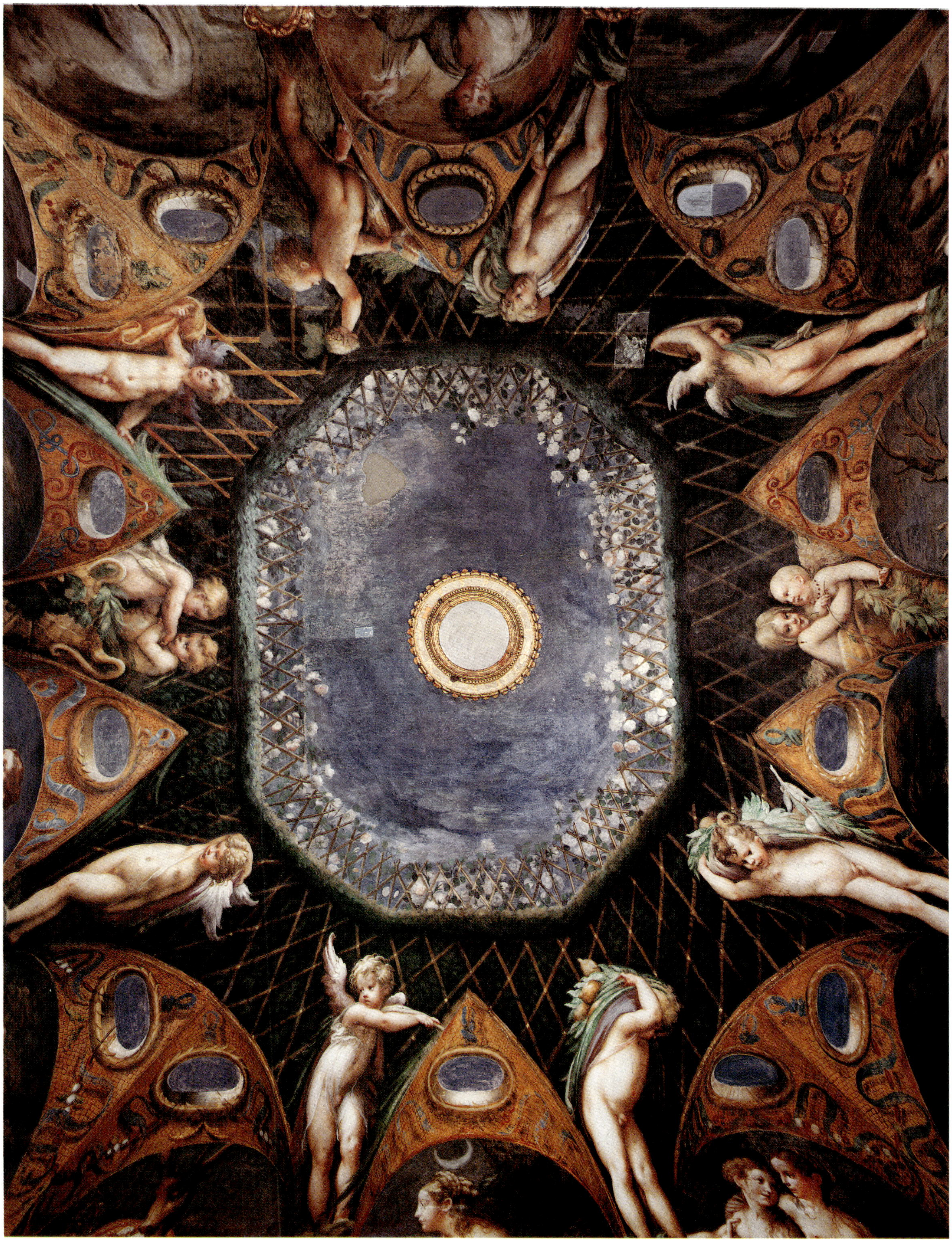

21. PARMIGIANINO

Detail of *Diana and Actaeon*, c. 1523

(Actaeon transformed into a stag)

Fresco

Rocca Sanvitale, Fontanellato (Parma), Italy (cat. A12)

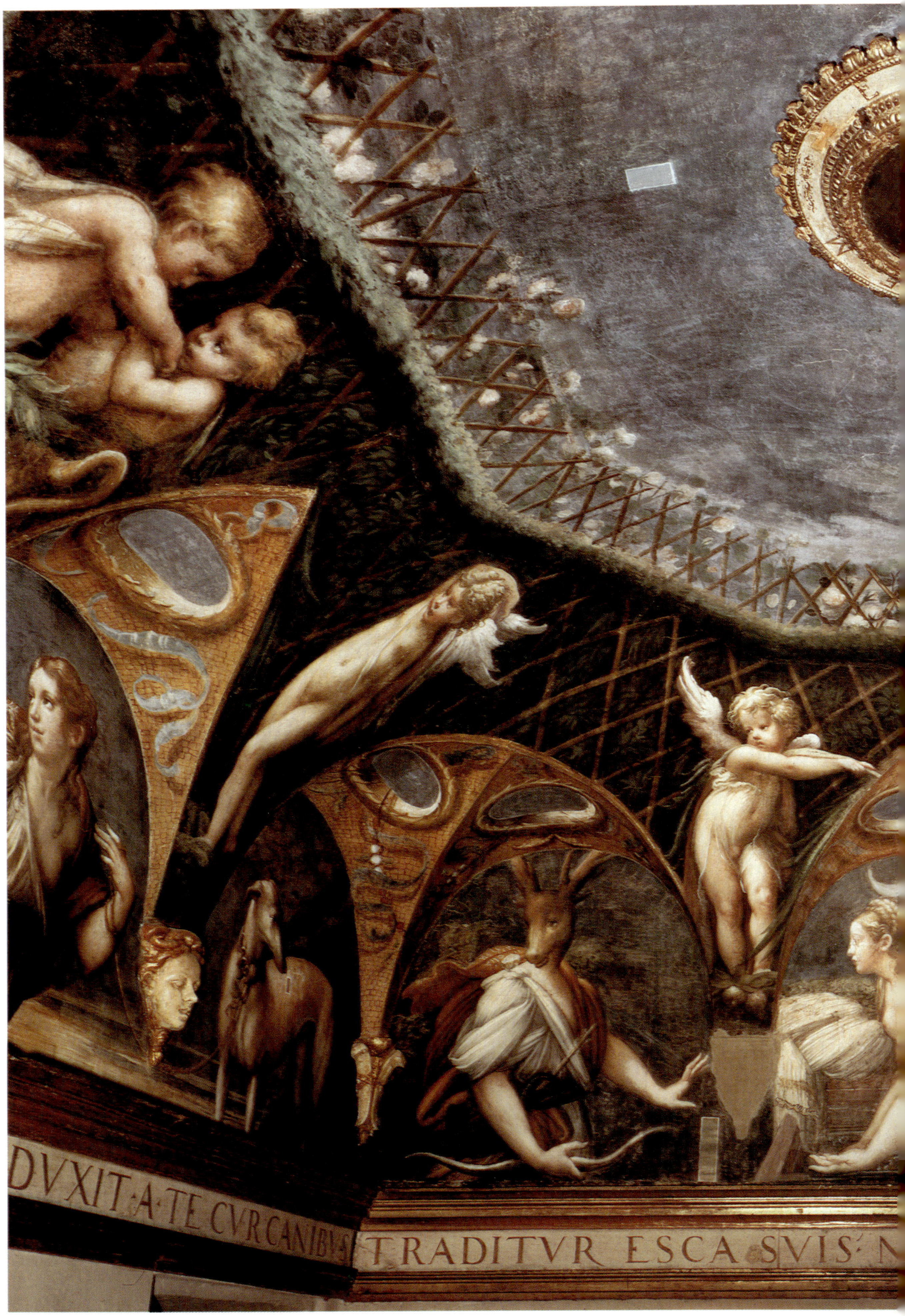

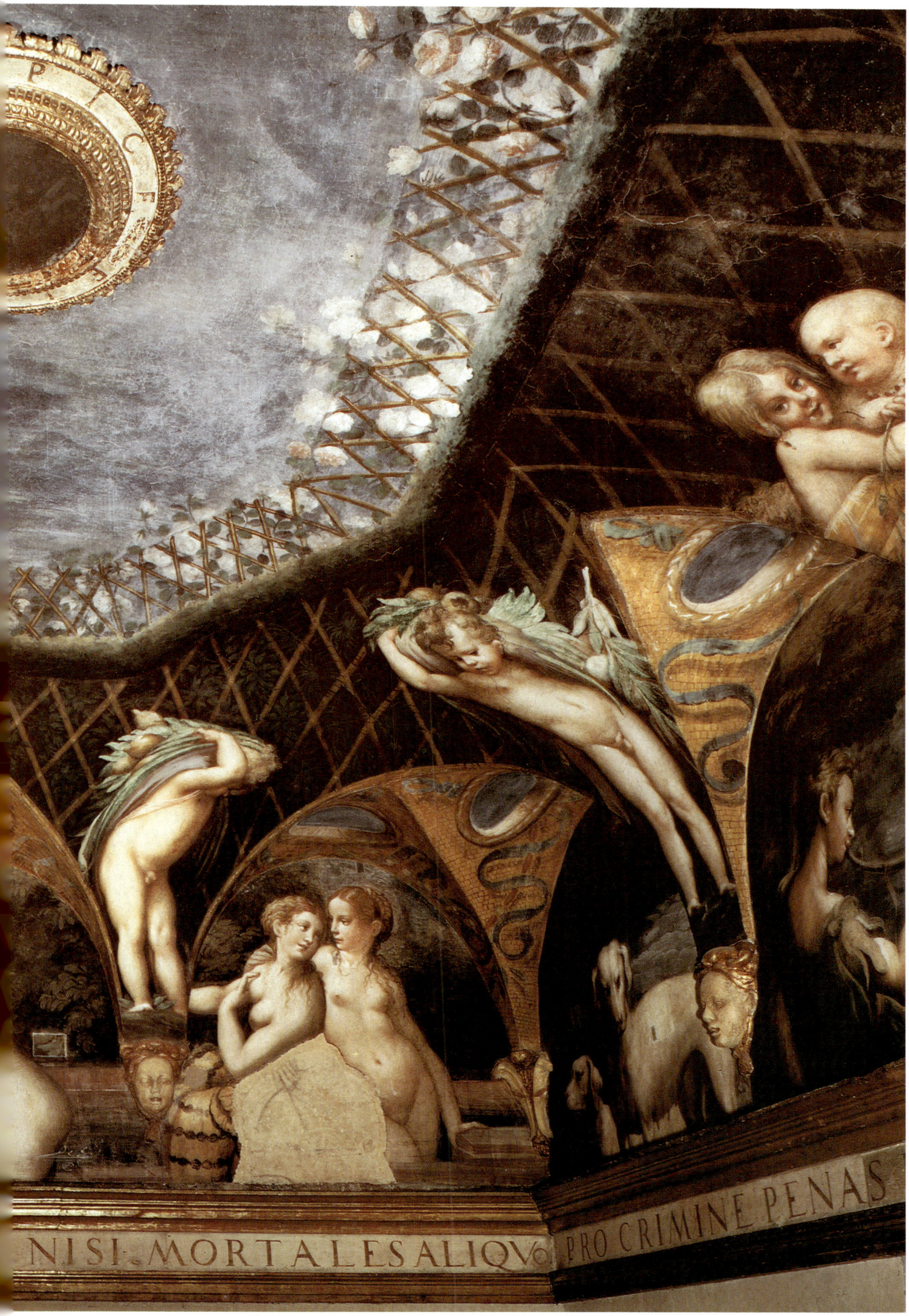

NISI MORTALES ALIQVO
PRO CRIMINE PENAS

22. CORREGGIO
Cupola of the Camera di San Paolo, c. 1519
Fresco
Camera di San Paolo, Monastery of San Paolo, Parma, Italy

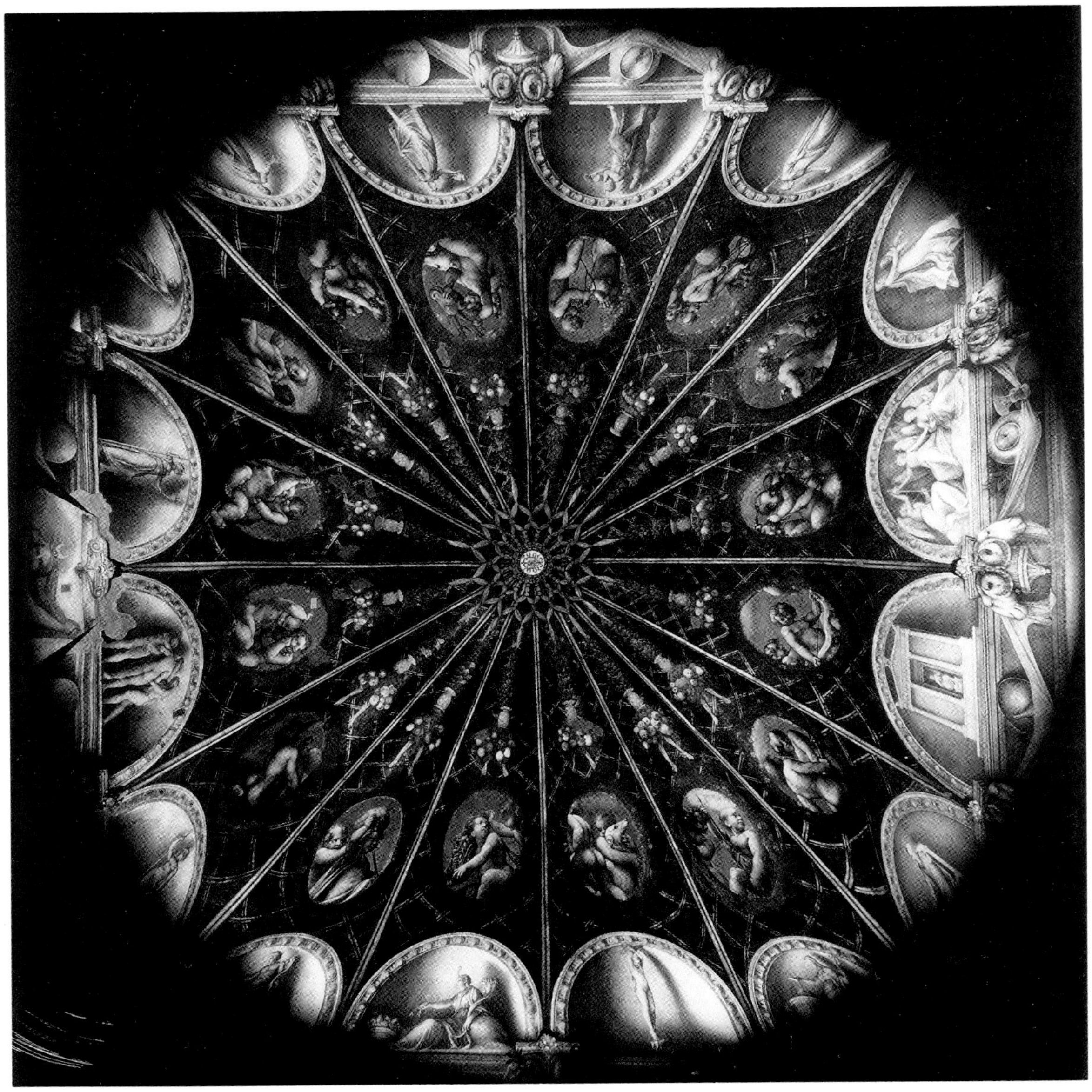

nor the huntsmen who pursue a nymph (on the wall to the right of the window) figure in Ovid's account of the story of Diana and Actaeon. The fact that the nymph is dressed in the same clothes as Actaeon is a particularly puzzling feature. Despite the lack of an authentic key to a hidden meaning in the fresco, Parmigianino's portrait of Galeazzo Sanvitale (Naples; fig. 34), the patron, discussed later, does suggest his arcane interests and supports the idea of a collaboration between him and the painter in the program of the fresco.

One other fresco, now reduced to a mere fragment but known from a print, may perhaps have been commissioned at this time by Sanvitale. This was the lunette in grisaille in the Palazzetto Eucherio Sanvitale in the ducal park at Parma. A document refers to the building as belonging in 1527 to Galeazzo and adds that he had bought it from Scipione della Rosa. As the composition and Parmigianino's drawings for it are in his pre-Roman style, and therefore not later than 1524, and since we do not know how long before 1527 the building changed hands, the patron could have been either of these two. The decision to paint a Madonna and Child within a lunette evidently dictated the separation of the two figures in order to fill the space, and this brought with it the difficulty of devising a pose for a detached infant. In the event Parmigianino showed the Christ Child impulsively shooting one leg forward—an idea that he had foreshadowed at San Giovanni Evangelista, where God the Father is supported by an angel's projecting leg, and which he was to develop in studies for the *Madonna della Rosa* (fig. 90) and then discard. Despite the imposed separation of mother and child the fresco was evidently a very delicate work, and its virtual destruction a disaster.

The pictorial language of the Fontanellato fresco seems to derive from the picturesque design and fluid handling of the Cremona frescoes, greatly refined by experience of Correggio. The Sanvitale portrait is closely related, as is shown in the drawings. Also related is the London portrait (fig. 31) and two small panels of the Nativity or Adoration (figs. 24 and 25). The Madonna in the Courtauld picture (fig. 24) echoes the Bardi *Madonna,* but the Christ Child seems to show awareness, in the spiral pose, of Raphael's *Bridgewater Madonna* (Edinburgh), a work that, to our knowledge, had not been engraved at this time, and whose original location is unknown. As in the San Giovanni Evangelista frescoes, the slab under Saint Joseph in the Courtauld picture is adorned with a marble relief, and reliefs are also prominent as bases for the columns in the other Nativity, which has only recently come to light (fig. 25). Unlike the Courtauld picture the latter includes the shepherds and also shows an early interest in supernatural light—which in this case attracts the gaze of Saint Joseph away from the Christ Child. The angels and the almost comically anthropomorphic livestock are similar in both paintings, which are among the most original of Parmigianino's early work. Both of these little panels portray the Nativity with a degree of domesticity probably unprecedented in Italian painting. It is this informality that encourages the view that they may be the earliest surviving examples of those pictures that, as we shall see, Parmigianino seems to have been in the habit of painting without a commission. If that was the case, he is likely to have disposed of these two before leaving for Rome, as they are not among those that Vasari says he took with him.

The even smaller *Saint Catherine* (Frankfurt; fig. 26) is rather more stylish and perhaps therefore rather later. The type of the saint's head is virtually a repetition of that of Saint Cecilia in the Steccata organ shutter, and also similar to the Ceres figure at Fontanellato and to the Madonna in the Prado *Holy Family.* The Frankfurt picture has two very Correggesque putti on the right, and also uses a motive of Correggio's of a different kind—the act of pulling down palm branches. Incidentally, this provides an illustration of the interaction of visual and functional factors with Parmigianino. For in the picture that was probably his source of inspiration in this respect—Correggio's *Holy Family with Saint Francis* (Uffizi)—Saint Joseph pulls down the palm branch to provide food for the Christ Child (the motive also occurs, though in a form less close to Parmigianino's, in a fresco, *The Flight into Egypt,* by Altobello Melone at Cremona). The action evidently pleased Parmigianino from a visual point of view, but he changed its meaning. Now the palm is the attribute of the saint's future martyrdom.

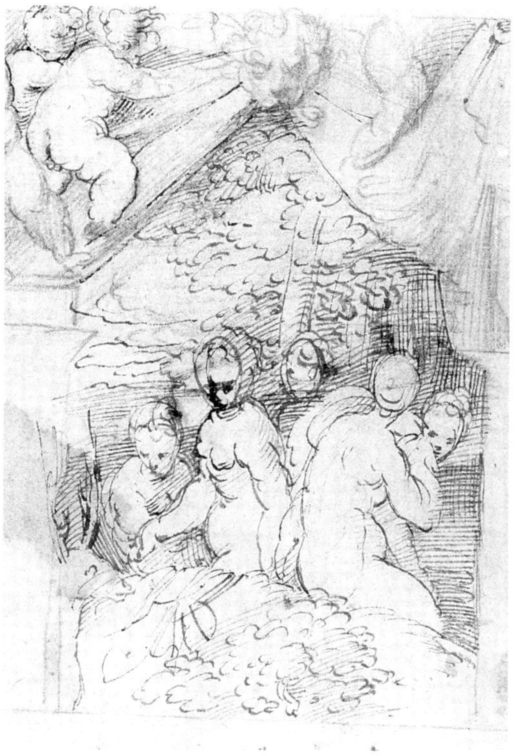

23. PARMIGIANINO
Detail of studies for the Fontanellato fresco, n.d. P12
Red chalk and pen and ink on paper, $9\frac{1}{4} \times 6\frac{3}{4}$ in. (23.6 × 17.1 cm)
Kupferstichkabinett, Berlin

24. PARMIGIANINO
Holy Family with an Angel ("Nativity"), c. 1522–24
Oil on panel, 17 × 18⅝ in. (43.1 × 47.3 cm)
Courtauld Institute, Seilern collection, London (cat. A20)

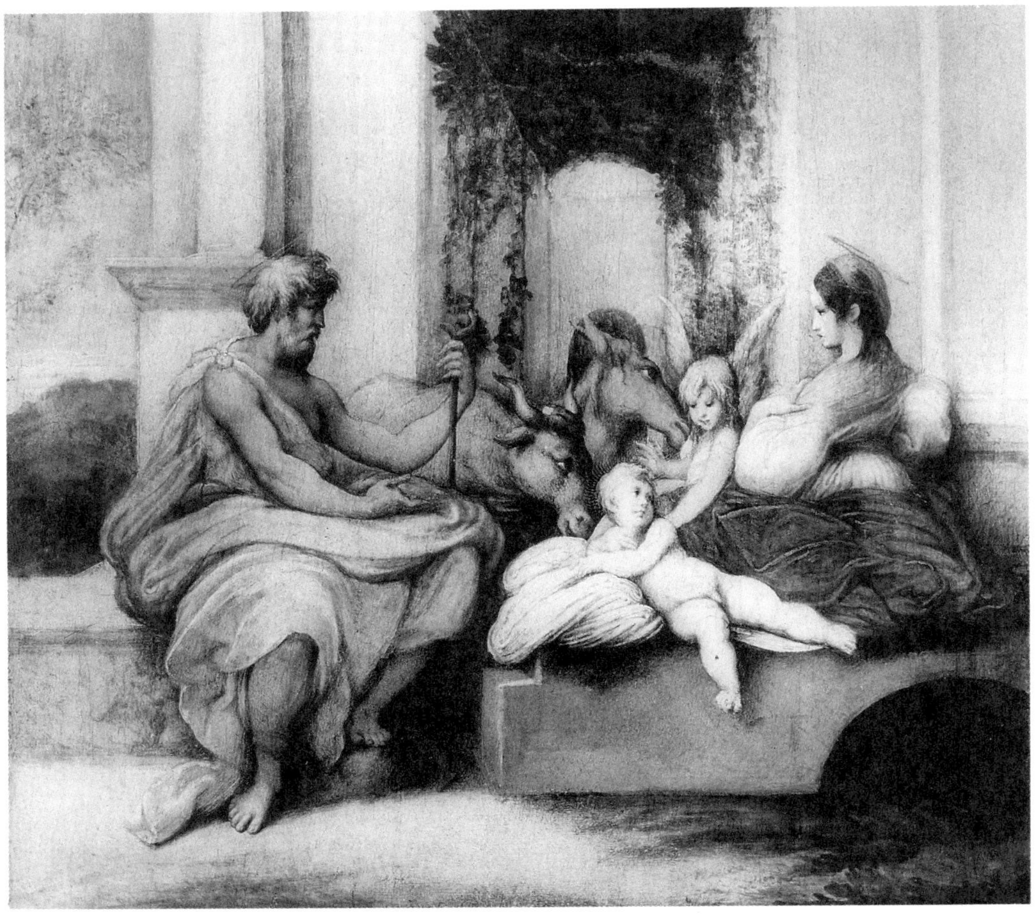

25. PARMIGIANINO
Adoration of the Shepherds ("Nativity"), c. 1522–24
Oil on panel, 16½ × 16⅝ in. (41.9 × 42.3 cm)
Location unknown (cat. A54)

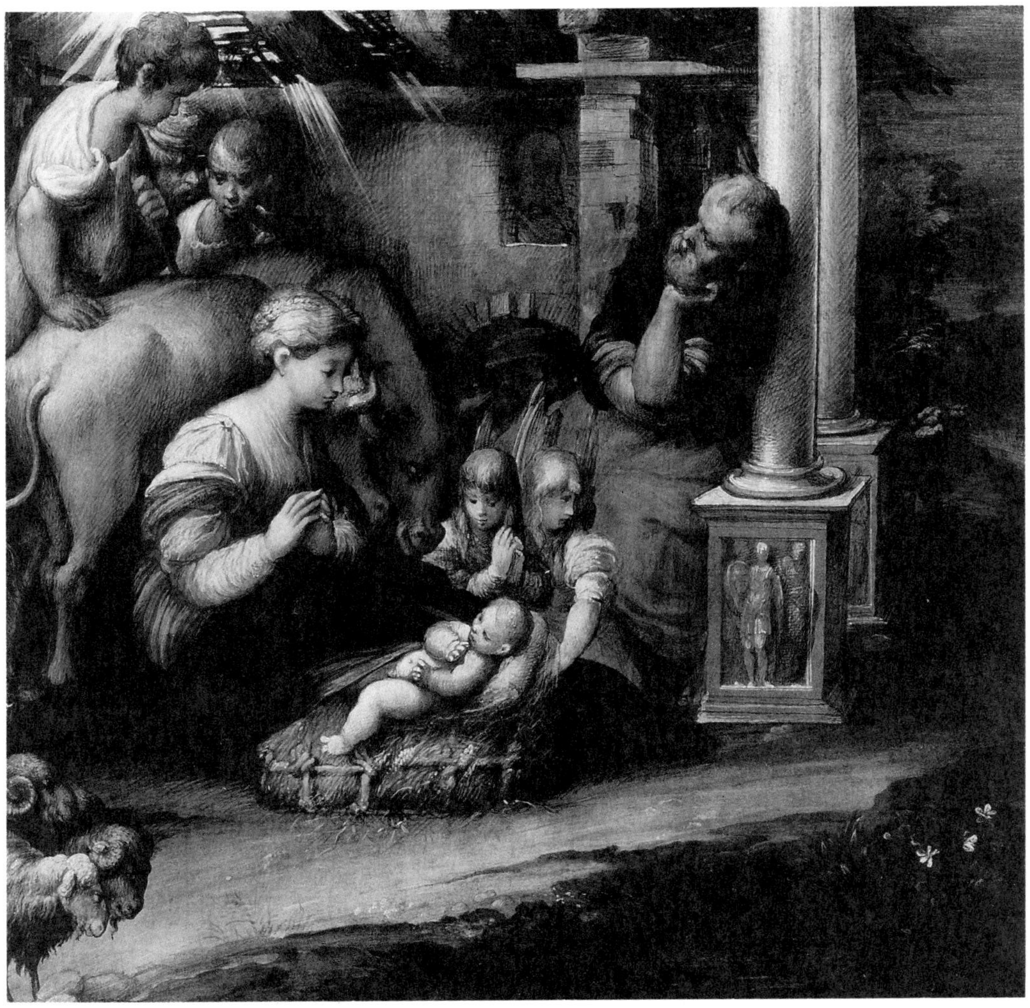

Opposite:
26. PARMIGIANINO
Saint Catherine of Alexandria, c. 1523–24
Oil on panel, 10¼ × 7½ in. (26 × 19 cm)
Städelsches Kunstinstitut, Frankfurt (cat. A13)

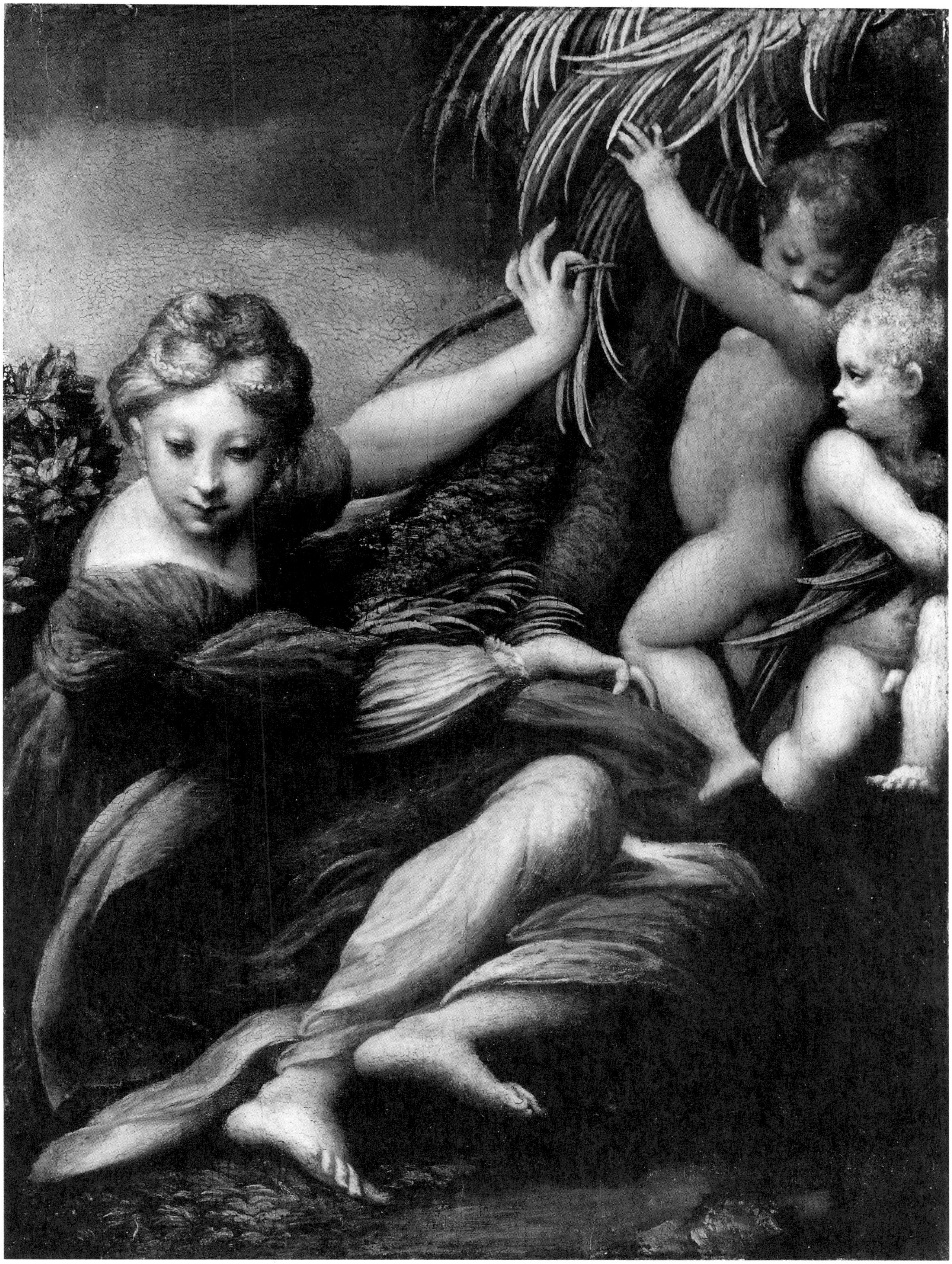

On the face of it the evidence for the date of the Rome journey is conflicting or ambiguous. Parmigianino's portrait of Galeazzo Sanvitale (Naples) has the date 1524 on the back. Galeazzo was a native of the Parma area, which suggests that Parmigianino did not leave home before that year. On the other hand, the portrait of Lorenzo Cybo (Copenhagen; fig. 38) bears the date 1523; and Cybo, a native of Massa, was currently employed (as captain of the papal guard) in Rome. Nevertheless the sum of the evidence favors the later date. Vasari tells us that it was soon after he reached Rome that Parmigianino was presented to the Pope, Clement VII, who was not elected until November 1523, and he adds, in his biography of Lappoli, that the artist did not reach Rome until after the plague had ceased, which was not until July 1524. I conclude that the date inscribed on the Cybo portrait, which is repeated in a replica now at Columbia, was an error.

It has usually been assumed that the pictures which Parmigianino took with him to Rome were painted ad hoc, or at least that they dated from just before the time of the journey; and in these circumstances a young artist, conscious of his own rapid development and concerned with making an impression, might indeed be expected to choose examples of his latest work. However, as already mentioned, we shall see that there are indications that Parmigianino was in the habit of painting small pictures for his own amusement and without commission and retaining them for considerable periods. In the present case Freedberg suggested on stylistic grounds that the Detroit *Circumcision* was likely to have preceded the Rome journey by several years; and for my part I think it very possible that the same, in principle, may have been the case with the other two pictures that Vasari specifies that Parmigianino took with him. One of them, the Prado *Holy Family* (fig. 27), has encroaching foliage of the Cremonese type in the background, and a preliminary study in the Louvre (P396) has, on the verso, sketches for the putti in the first of the San Giovanni chapels, which are therefore datable to the early 1520s. The study for the *Holy Family* illustrates Parmigianino's consistent tendency to crowd heads together so densely as to leave insufficient room for their bodies. In the painting this was modified to some extent, but in the Detroit *Circumcision* (fig. 28) it reappears in an extreme form. Six or seven heads are shown in the background in space that would hardly accommodate more than three of them—very much as in the oblong *Marriage of Saint Catherine* copies (fig. 13), where the effect of overcrowding of the heads is partly justifiable on account of the low eye level. Vasari says that what was probably this little picture (the *Circumcision*) was painted immediately after Parmigianino reached Rome as a present for the Pope; but it is almost certain that, with the *Holy Family* and the self-portrait (fig. 36), it was the third of the trio that he took with him. Here there is likely to be northern influence—Dürer's print of this subject from his *Marienleben* (1511). This shows a general similarity and an even greater crowding of figures. A further northern affinity may be recognized in the magical lighting that is apparent even in the preliminary drawing in the Louvre (P369; fig. 29). In it, merely by means of ink, brown wash, and a little white paint, the artist has suggested the illumination coming from the head

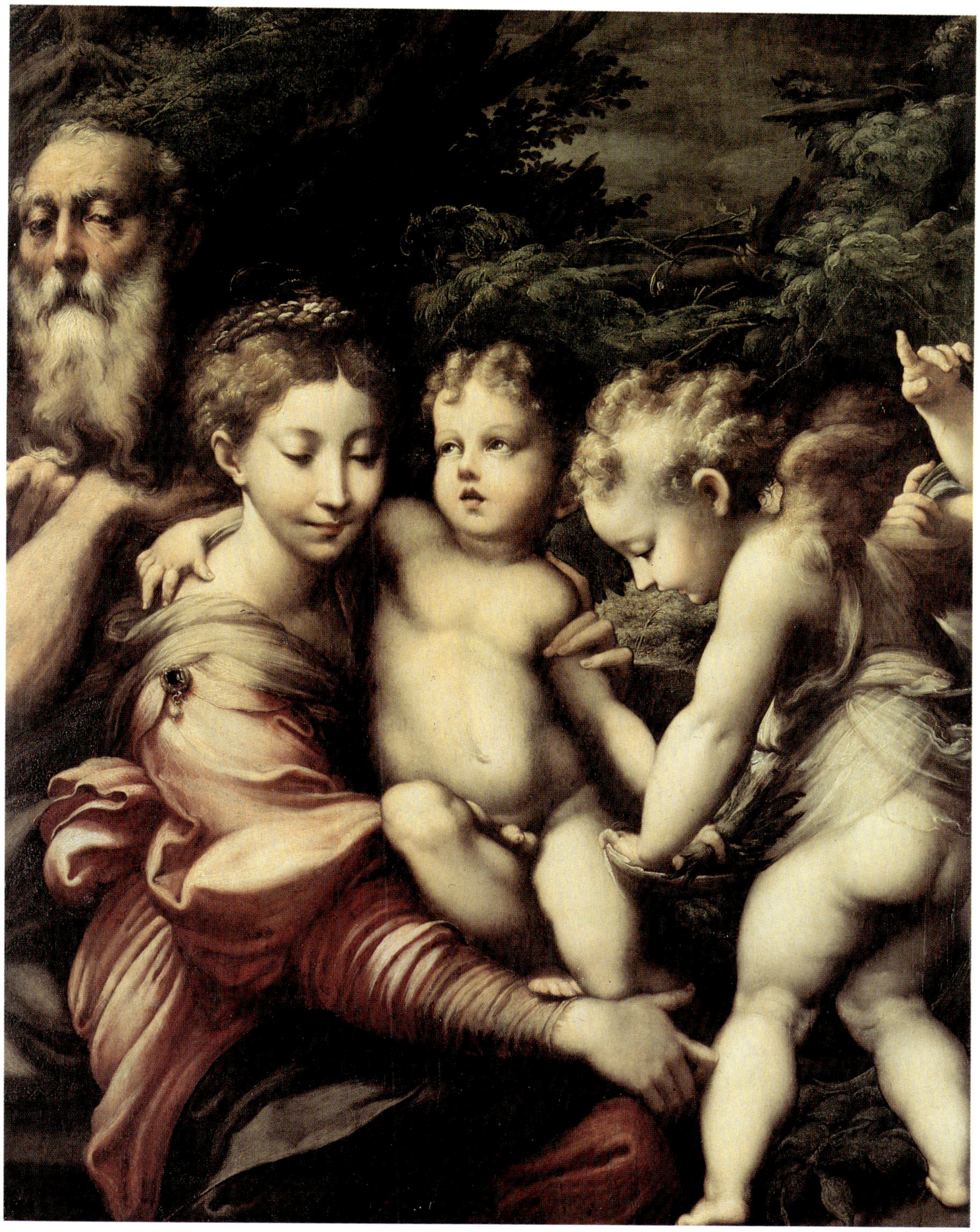

27. PARMIGIANINO
Holy Family with Angels, c. 1524
Oil on panel, 43¼ × 35 in. (110 × 89 cm)
Museo del Prado, Madrid (cat. A23)

of the Christ Child. In the painting itself additional mysterious lighting comes from the sky in the background. Vasari, commenting on the illumination, adds a third source—from torches. Perhaps his memory was at fault.

The early self-portrait, already mentioned, introduces the subject of portraiture in general. It was a highly critical moment, since it was now, in the first half of the sixteenth century, that the modern portrait evolved. In the preceding century, both in Italy and the north, the form of the portrait—in which male sitters greatly outnumbered females—had normally been restricted to the head-and-shoulders type. And though the greatest exponents—Jan van Eyck, Rogier van der Weyden, or Hans Memling in Flanders, or

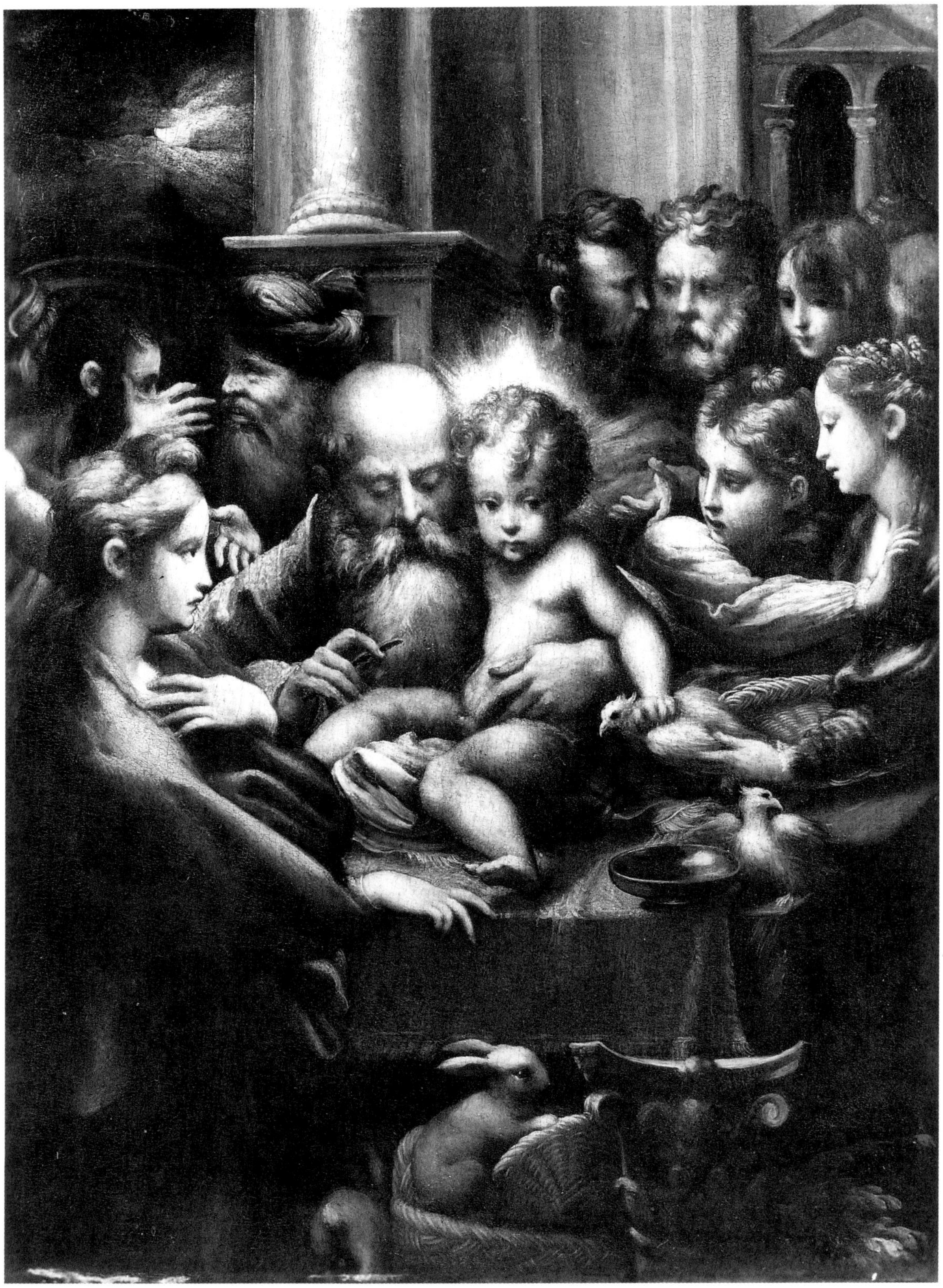

28. PARMIGIANINO
The Circumcision, c. 1522
Oil on panel, 16½ × 12¼ in.
(42 × 31 cm)
Detroit Institute of Arts, Michigan
(cat. A6)

Sandro Botticelli, Domenico Ghirlandaio, Antonello da Messina, or Giovanni Bellini in Italy—had evoked vivid characteristics, the form did not permit of much elaboration. Now, with the expansion of the field to half-length, three-quarter, or even full-length, a vast potentiality was revealed. Poses could be varied, the sitter's face looking in one direction and his body turning toward another. There was almost infinite scope for varying the design through the attitude of the sitter's arms, his hands fingering a book, his gloves, or the hilt of his sword, while the details of his costume could be arranged to provide telling contrasts of both form and color. Finally, it was now possible to include adjuncts—a servant, a child, a dog, or a horse, or on occasion the sitter's wife or mistress—and this not only as an element in the design but also to throw light on his character and interests.

Unlike an altarpiece, a portrait is normally not accessible to the public, and in theory this would seem a fatal obstacle to the development of portraiture as an art-historical trend. If it was so much more difficult for a painter to see what his seniors had accomplished in portraiture than it was in religious painting, it would be reasonable to deduce that progress in this genre would be that much slower. In the event it was not. The great and exciting possibilities that now opened seem to have been explored in different parts of Italy and the north more or less simultaneously. Just as bad news or scandal is frequently disseminated so rapidly as to defeat analysis, so it seems to be with important advances in the arts. The new portraiture blossomed and spread rapidly through channels

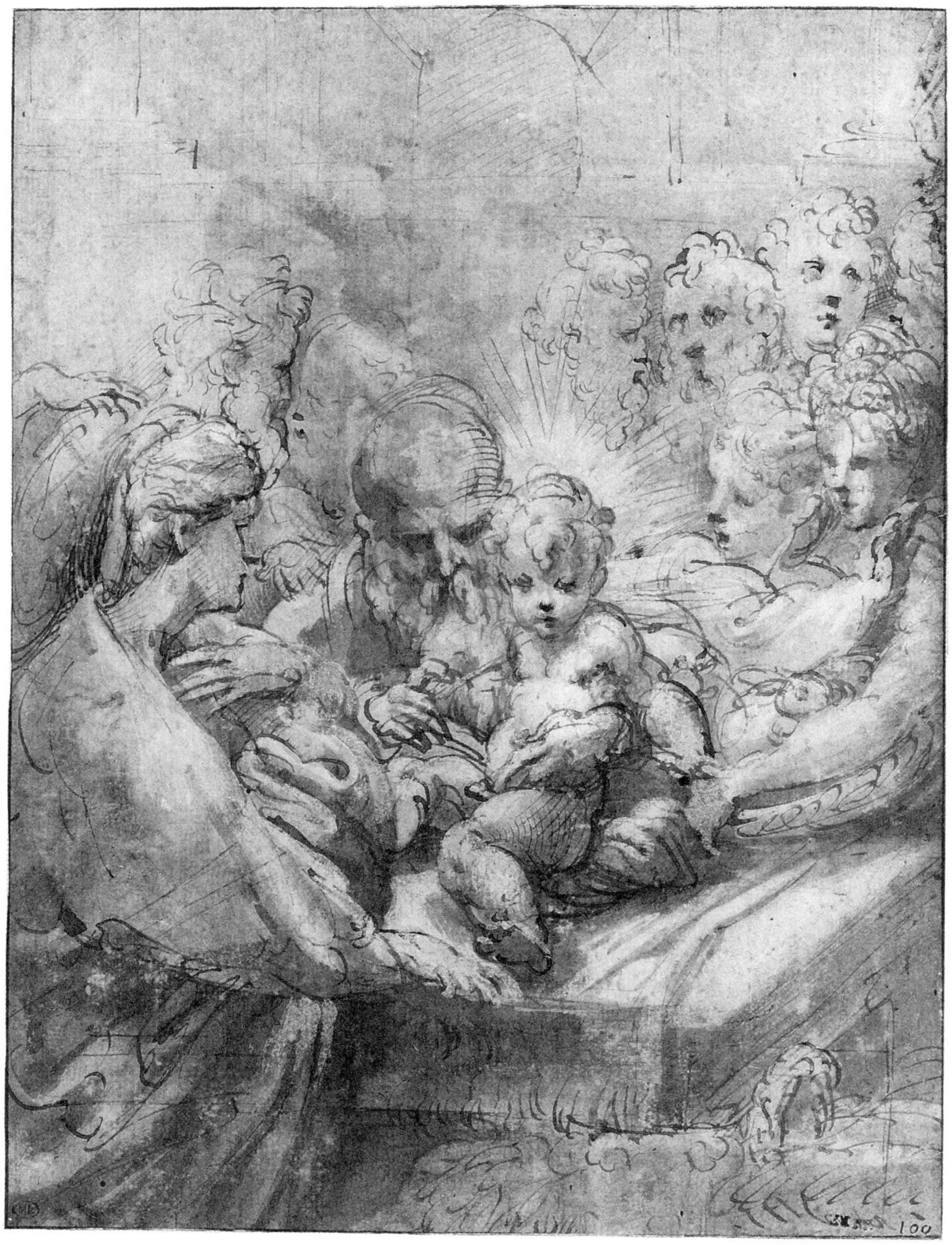

29. PARMIGIANINO
Study for *The Circumcision*, n.d. P369
Pen and wash on paper, 7¾ × 5⅝ in. (19.6 × 14.2 cm)
Musée du Louvre, Paris

so tenuous as to defy precise charting, though the fact that portraits would normally be painted in the artist's studio and not in the sitter's house offered a limited possibility of dissemination of influence. In fact the extent of this was extraordinary. In Florence alone Leonardo da Vinci, Franciabigio, Andrea del Sarto, Jacopo da Pontormo, and Bronzino traversed the development of a century or more in half of that time. Fundamental advances were also made in Rome by Raphael and Sebastiano del Piombo, while in Venice all the leading painters of the first half of the sixteenth century contributed—Giorgione da Castelfranco, Titian, Lorenzo Lotto, Palma Vecchio, and Bordone. The Brescians followed. In the north Albrecht Dürer, Lucas Cranach, Quentin Massys, Mabuse, and Hans Holbein brought about a parallel revolution during the same period.

In this field Parmigianino's contribution was preeminent. Here it was a question of riding the crest of the wave rather than of trying, in a mood of post-peak depression, to find new solutions to old problems of religious imagery. A crucial factor was that the element of emulation in this case was less. Michelangelo scorned portraiture, and Correggio practiced it only rarely, and then with less than his usual distinction. In the event it may be claimed that it was here that Parmigianino achieved his greatest feat as painter. For a combination of originality of design, brilliance of execution, and immediacy and vitality of the result these are among the greatest of Renaissance likenesses.

To what extent Parmigianino may have been affected by the sight of the work of older portraitists is very difficult to estimate. The odd examples by Romanino might be a possibility, and just possibly one or more by Dosso Dossi. But on the whole the most likely forebear would be the strange and itinerant figure of Lorenzo Lotto. He, like Parmigianino, united a vein of pictorial exuberance with an interest in original lighting effects, and in the course of his restless career in different parts of Italy he had exerted some degree of influence on aspects of Correggio's art at about the same time.[19]

One of Parmigianino's earliest portraits is probably the little canvas of a man in black in the Castello Sforzesco at Milan (fig. 30). This had been implausibly attributed to Correggio. But the billowing Cremonese foliage points to the young Parmigianino at a time before his style as portraitist was fully developed. Much more remarkable is the London portrait of a collector (fig. 31). It may or may not represent the Cavaliere Baiardi, the collector and patron of Parmigianino. It is, in any case, an astonishing performance both visually and as a character study. The image is memorably vivid and memorably unpleasant. With a small, elaborately embossed metal box in his left hand, a bronze statuette and coins in front, and a fragment of marble relief in the background behind him, he scrutinizes the spectator suspiciously. The status of the foliage behind him is ambiguous, perhaps deliberately. It might be either the reality or a painting: if a window, no glazing bars; if a picture, no molding on the frame. Most remarkable is the lighting—an intense, rather lurid illumination coming from high on the right.

The sitter of the York portrait (fig. 32), which probably dates from the same period, is less unsympathetic but the image is astonishingly, almost alarmingly frank—a man in

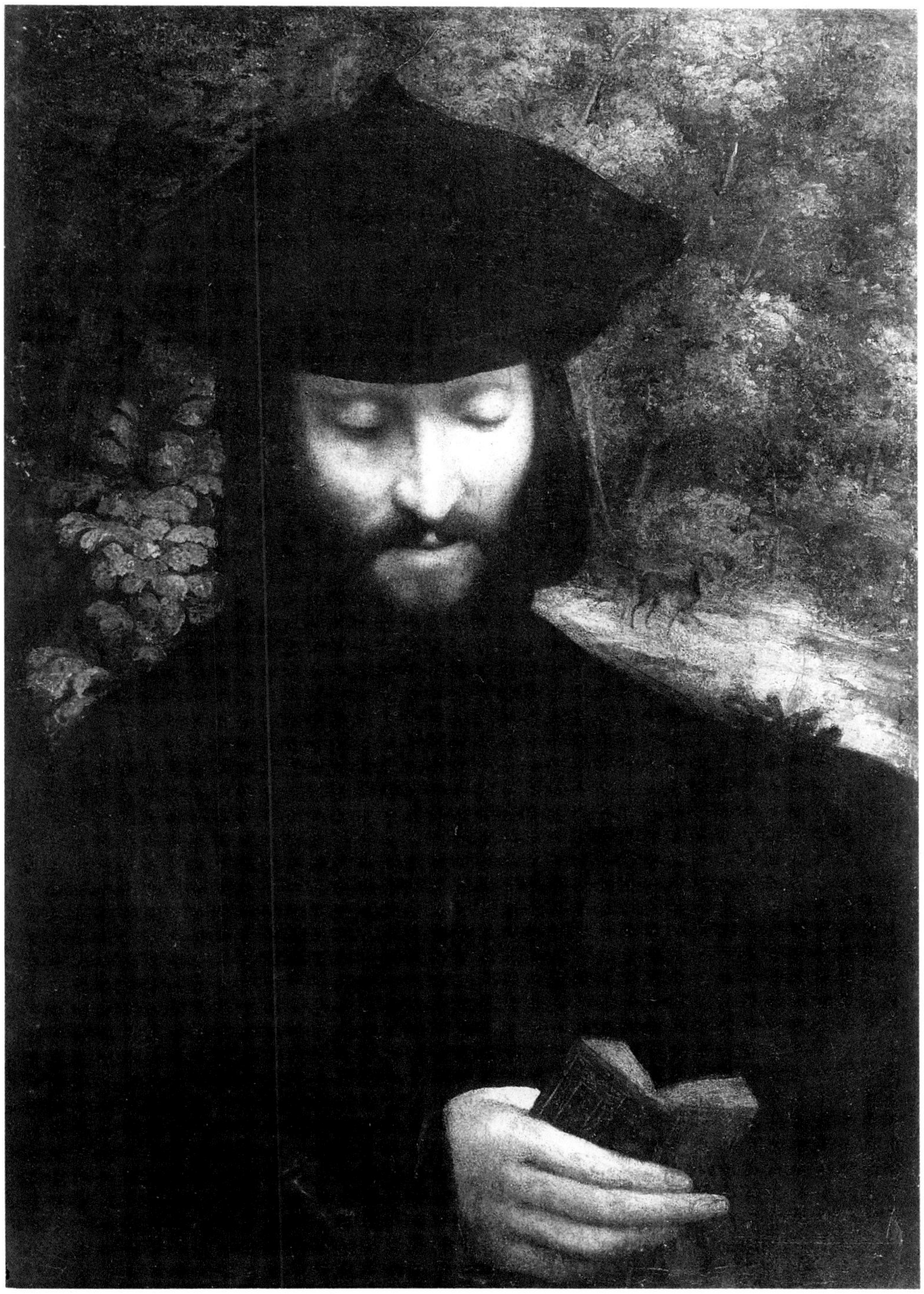

30. PARMIGIANINO
A Man in Black, c. 1520
Oil on canvas, removed from panel, $23\frac{5}{8} \times 16\frac{7}{8}$ in. (60 × 43 cm)
Castello Sforzesco, Milan (cat. A26)

early middle age, fierce, unkempt, perhaps even in his cups. He is likely to have been a prominent figure in Parma in the 1520s, as his features recur in two paintings by Correggio dating from the middle years of that decade—the executioner on the right of the *Martyrdom of Four Saints* (Parma) and the apostle to the spectator's right of Saint Peter on the cupola of San Giovanni Evangelista (fig. 33).

In the case of the Galeazzo Sanvitale portrait (Naples; fig. 34), which has a date, 1524, on the back, there are, exceptionally, no less than four preliminary drawings (P458r and v, also P748v and P.O.R. III). It may be that the original idea was to include the portrait in the fresco. The recto of P748 may also have studies for the sculpted heads in the Diana and Actaeon room. The verso shows the sitter in the same chair as in the painting, but

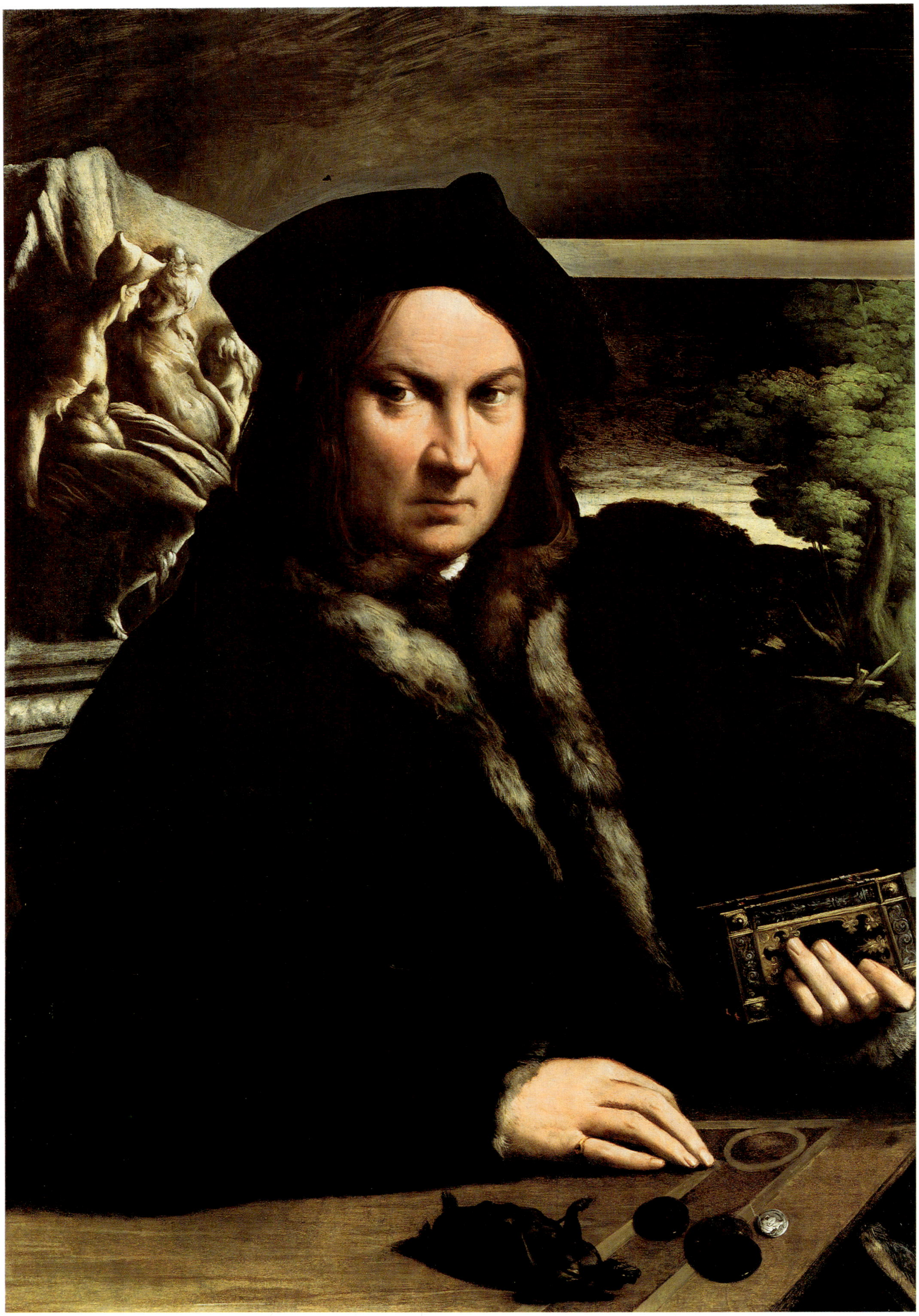

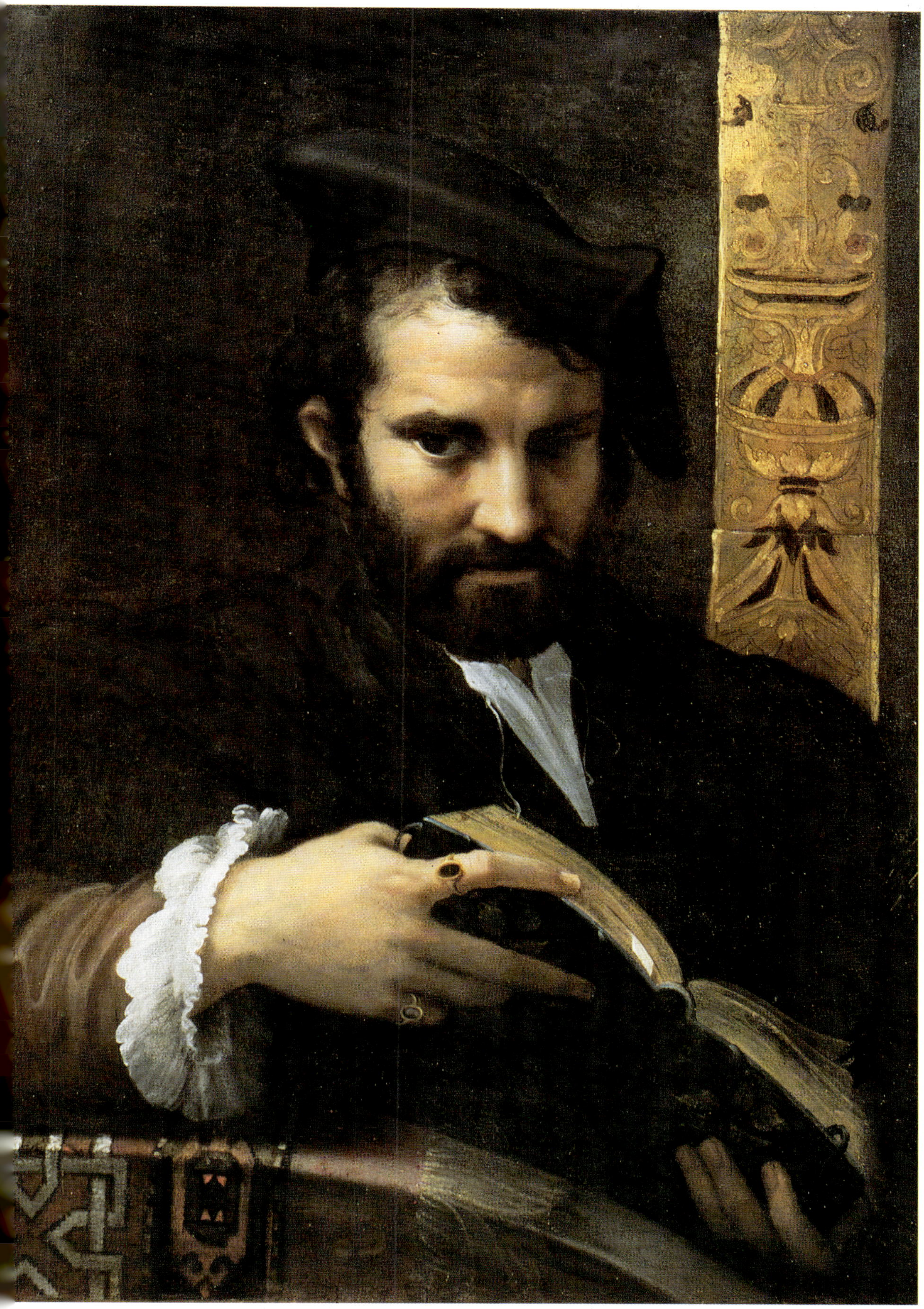

Opposite:
31. PARMIGIANINO
A Priest or Collector, c. 1523
Oil on panel, 35 × 25¼ in. (89 × 64 cm)
National Gallery, London (cat. A19)

32. PARMIGIANINO
A Man with a Book, c. 1523–24
Oil on canvas, lined, 27½ × 20½ in. (70 × 52 cm)
City Art Gallery, York, England (cat. A53)

33. CORREGGIO
Detail of the cupola of San Giovanni Evangelista, c. 1520–24
(Apostles to the right of Saint Peter)
Fresco
San Giovanni Evangelista, Parma, Italy

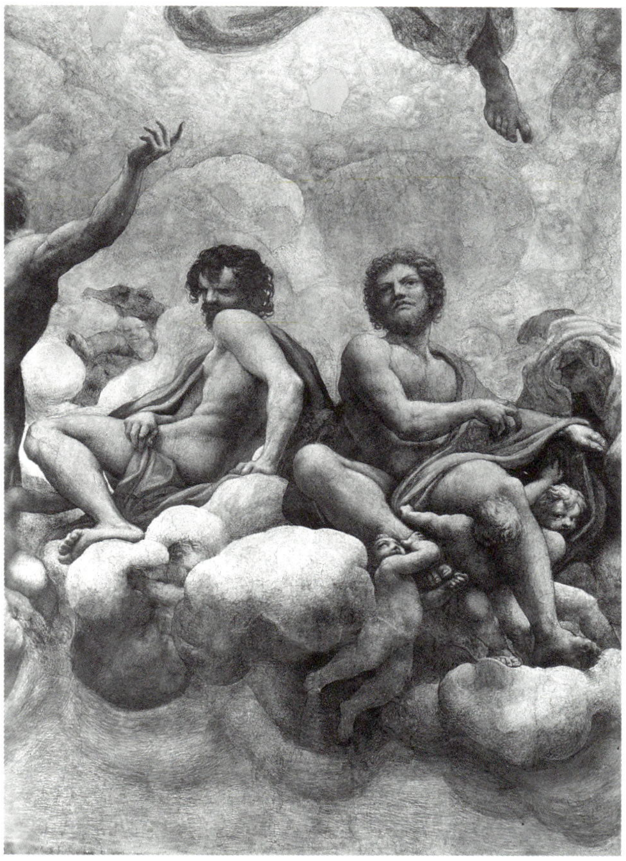

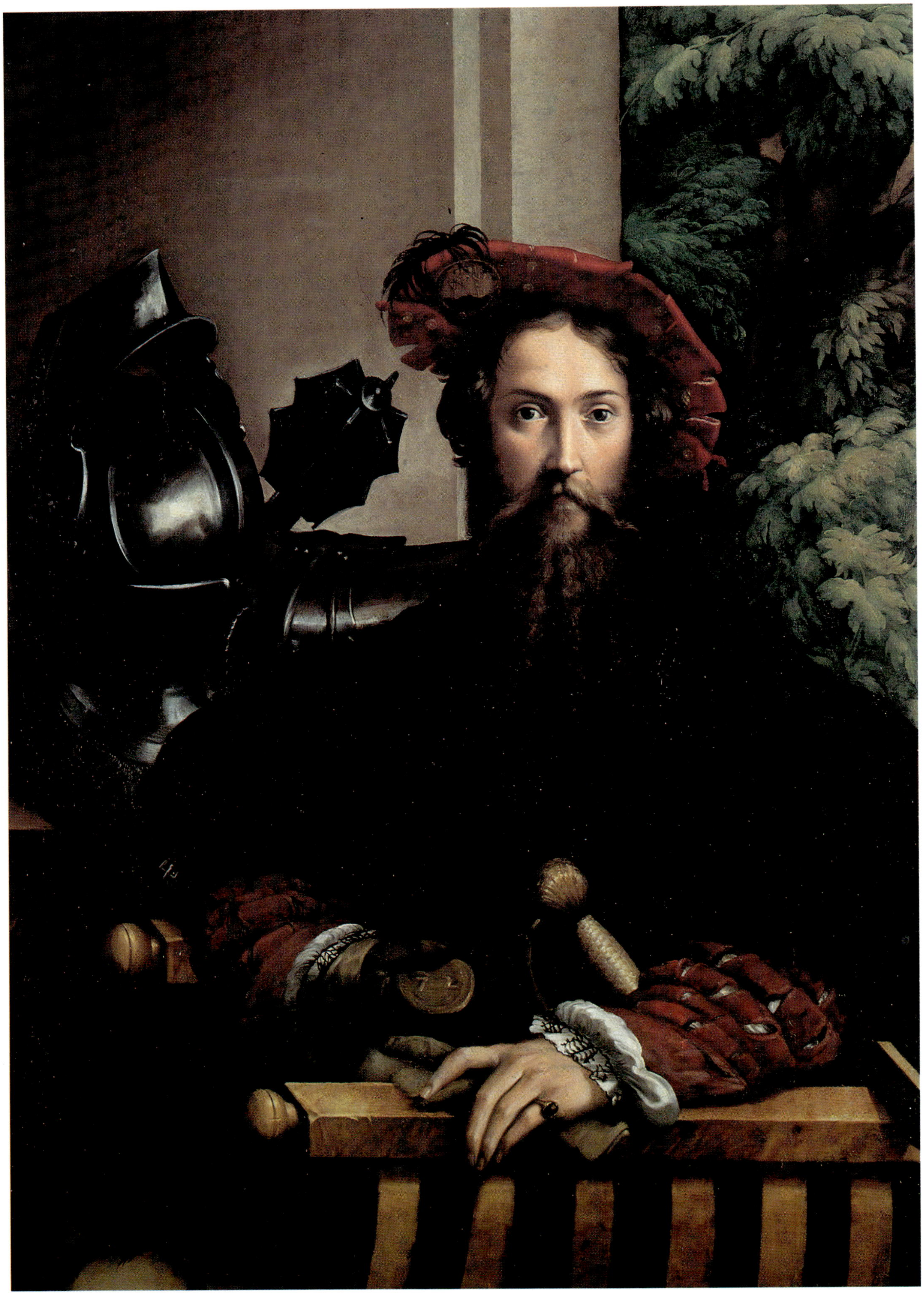

looking back to speak to a woman (fig. 35). The foliage behind them seems to encroach more than ever and was restrained in the finished painting. In two of the other sketches only the male sitter is included, but he is still looking over his shoulder as in the first drawing. The omission of the woman in the painting suppressed this idea, and the man's face was given, so far as one can judge, a different and less sympathetic expression. Now, in the finished portrait, without the woman to condition his reaction, he seems intolerably smug. Dressed up to the nines in marvelously elaborate clothes, the count peers at us self-consciously, holding out ostentatiously a medal with characters that have been claimed as alchemical—therefore constituting a bond with the painter. The equally ostentatious but highly decorative inclusion of military allusions—the huge helmet, mace, and a piece of body armor on the ledge behind the sitter—seems incongruous with the foppish image.[20]

How amazing and original these three portraits are! Unlike Titian and the portraitists of the next generation, Parmigianino makes no attempt to show his sitters in a

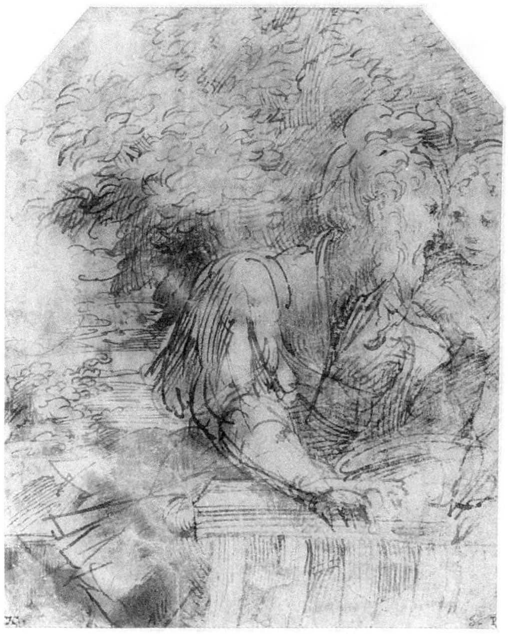

35. PARMIGIANINO
Study for the Sanvitale portrait, n.d. P748v
Pen and brown ink on paper, 7¼ × 1¾ in. (18.5 × 4.5 cm)
Donnington Priory, England (formerly)

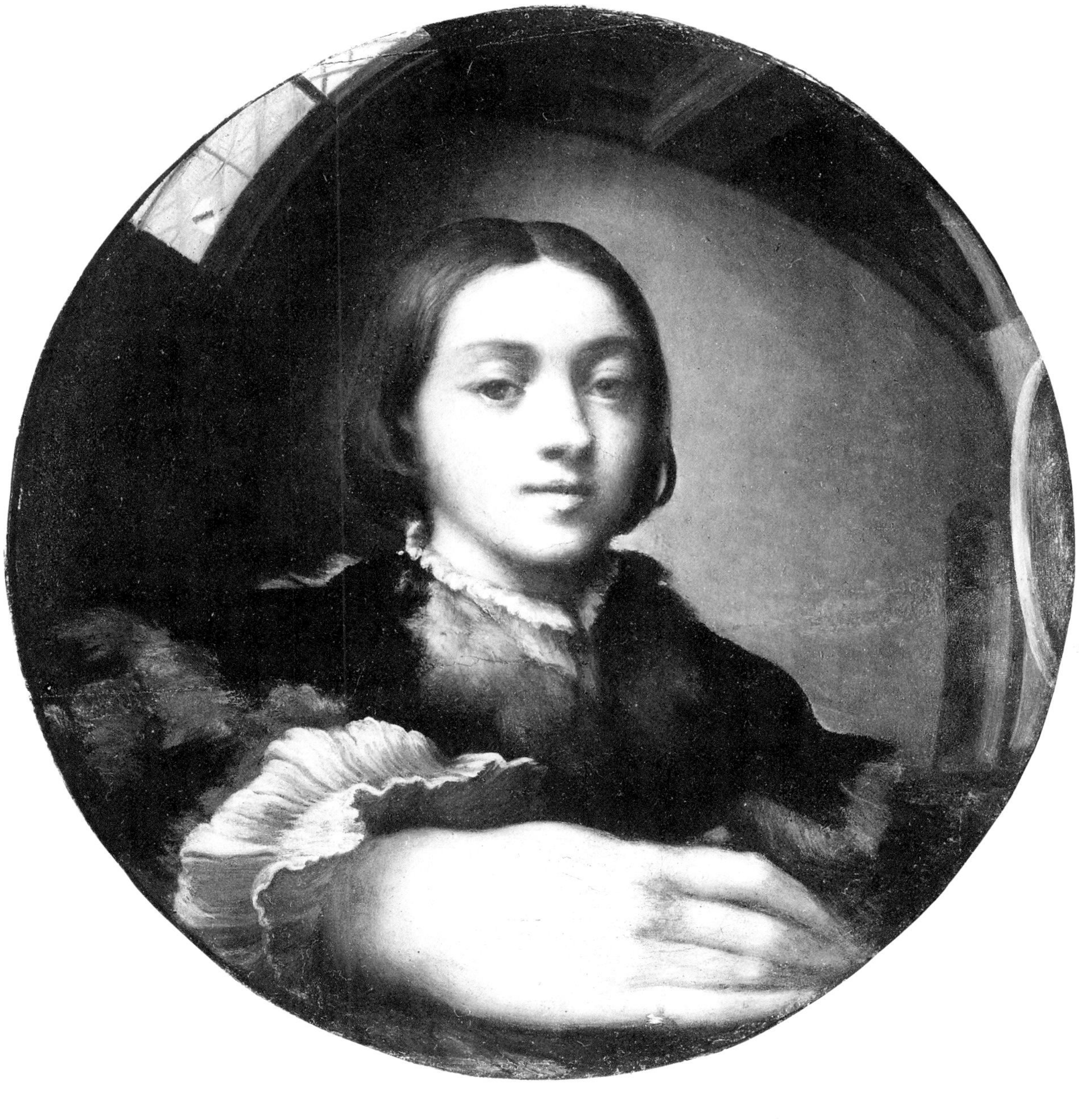

36. PARMIGIANINO
Self-Portrait in a Convex Mirror, 1524
Oil on (convex) panel, diameter: 9⅝ in. (24.4 cm)
Kunsthistorisches Museum, Vienna (cat. A48)

Opposite:
34. PARMIGIANINO
Galeazzo Sanvitale, Count of Fontanellato, 1524
Oil on panel, 42⅞ × 31⅞ in. (109 × 81 cm)
Galleria Nazionale di Capodimonte, Naples (cat. A29)

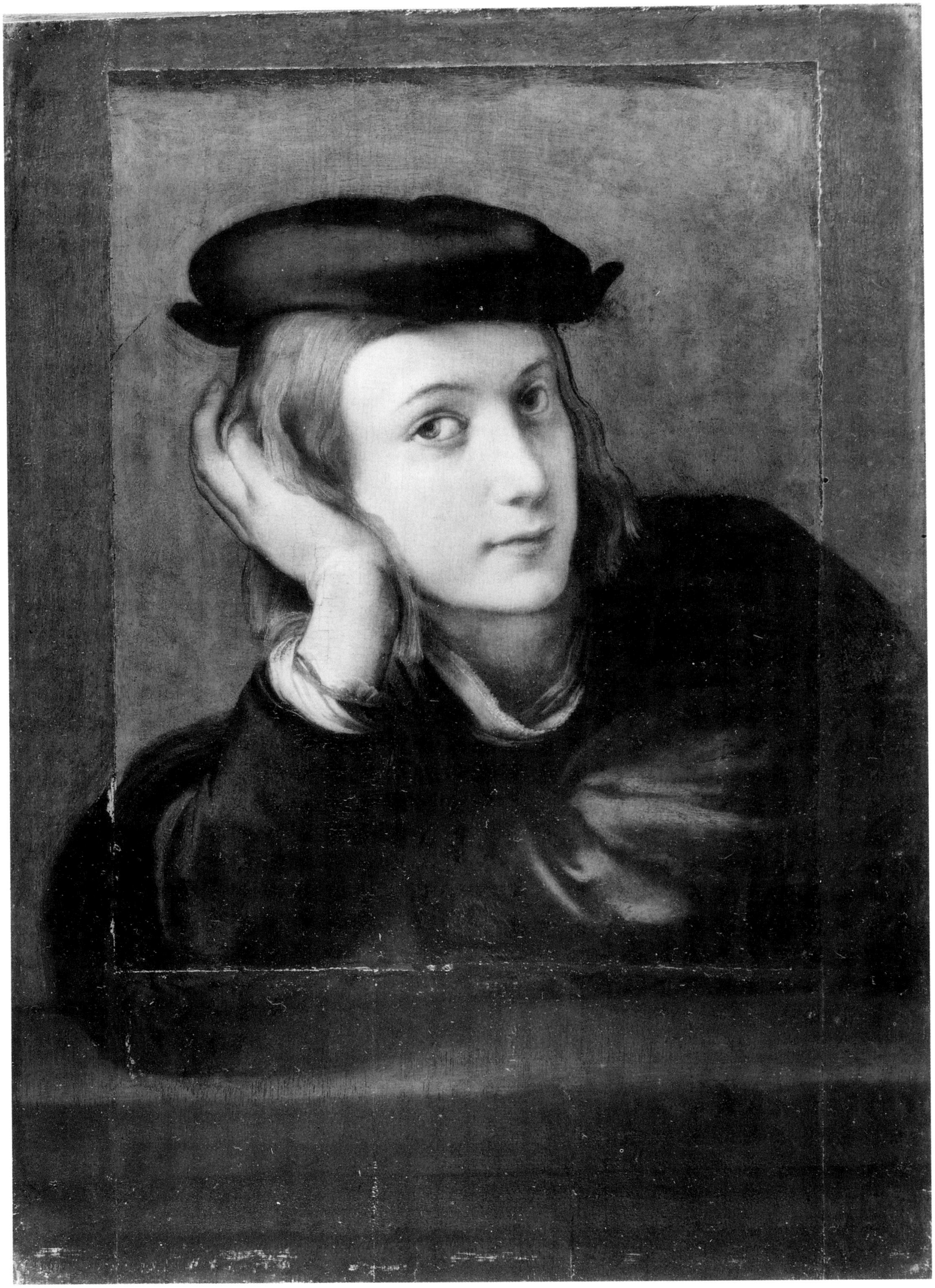

favorable light. No effort has been made to soften the expression of the London collector, or to smooth the hair and adjust the hat of the pugnacious reader of York; and in the case of Galeazzo Sanvitale one might even suspect some positive cynicism on the painter's part. It is hard to equate such maturity of outlook with the image presented by the Vienna self-portrait (fig. 36)—a self-confident youth admiring his own beauty in a convex mirror and copying its effects on a small piece of convex wood. It is what it was meant to be—a witty visual conceit, typical of its century. (We may compare it with the famous portrait in the Louvre of a youth with his hand to his face [fig. 37], long attributed to Parmigianino, among many others, but now thought to be *by* Correggio and *of* the young Parmigianino.[21]) Such was the brilliant and beautiful boy who now set out, bringing with him this very picture, to see and conquer Rome.

37. CORREGGIO
Portrait of Parmigianino (?), n.d.
Oil on canvas, 27⅛ × 17⅜ in.
(59 × 44 cm)
Musée du Louvre, Paris

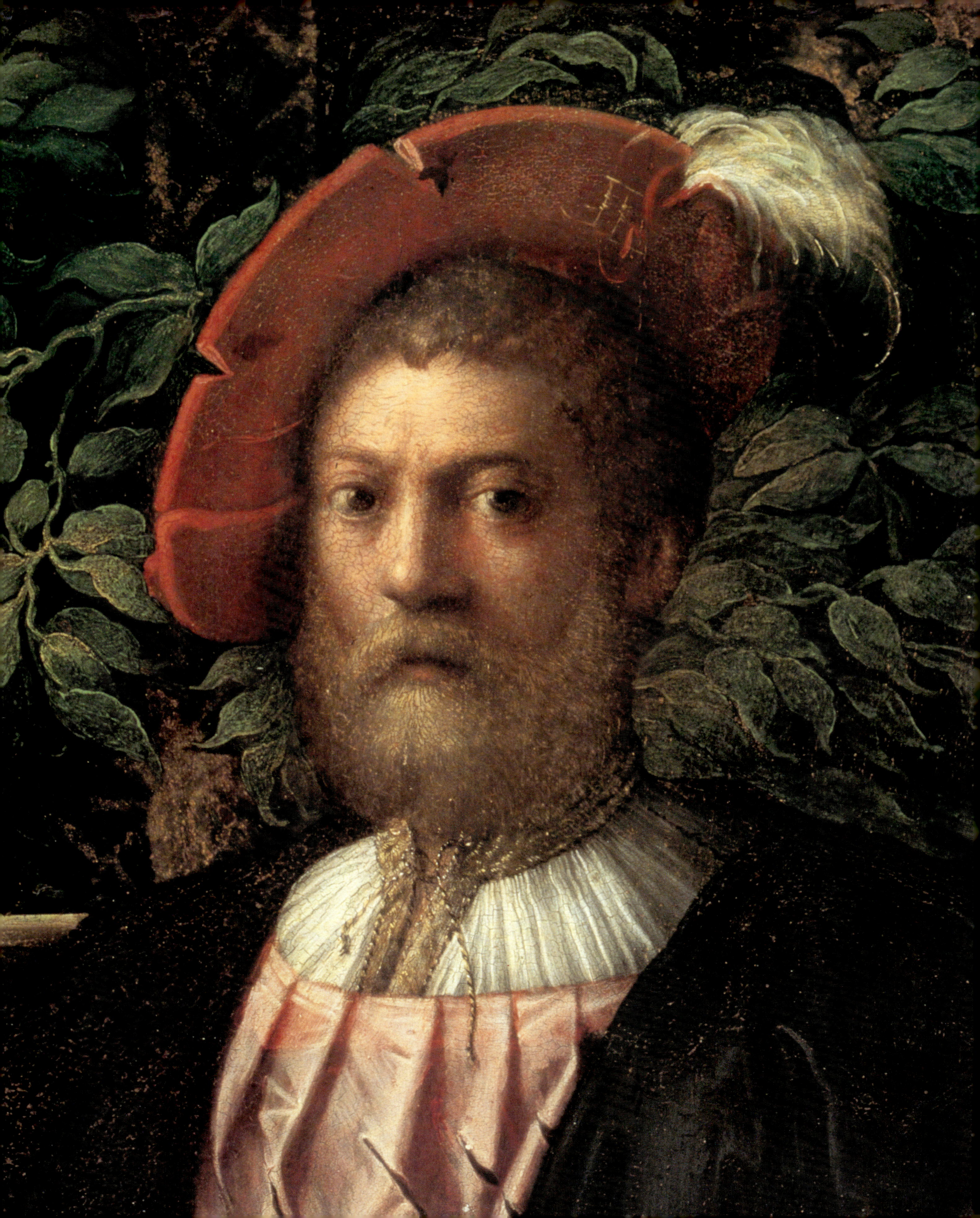

II

Rome

Vasari gives a vivid account of Parmigianino's arrival in Rome. A Vatican official, he says, was so much taken with the pictures he had brought with him that he presented him to the Pope—Clement VII—who was equally impressed and said he would like him to paint in the Sala dei Pontefici. The reference was evidently to the walls of that room, since Vasari tells us that the ceiling, which was to exert a significant effect on Parmigianino later in his career, was already finished at the time.

What followed was an anticlimax. Parmigianino never did paint in the Sala dei Pontefici, nor was he given any other public work in Rome. Compared with the series of commissions that had already come his way in Parma, and with what he was to obtain when he stopped at Bologna on his way home, his pickings in Rome were very meager. In the course of the three years that he spent there he only obtained, as far as we know, a single contract—for the altarpiece now in London—and that was financed by a private patron. As to the pictures that he had brought with him, Vasari notes that the Pope retained only one—the *Circumcision*—for himself. He gave Parmigianino's self-portrait to the young adventurer Pietro Aretino, and the *Holy Family* to his young kinsman Ippolito de' Medici, who was thirteen years old at the time. The latter was soon to be created cardinal against his will, and his features are familiar from Titian's extraordinary portrait now in the Pitti. He was to prove an enthusiastic admirer of Parmigianino's art.

If we pay careful attention to Vasari's wording we may find the key to the riddle: "Clement, having seen the pictures, and Francesco so young, was amazed." The implication is that the Pope's goodwill was due not so much to appreciation of Parmigianino's pictures as to amazement that so small and young-looking a painter could have done them at all. Though already twenty-one he was still treated as a child to the extent that he had not been allowed to come to Rome alone but had been escorted by one of his uncles, who seems to have remained there to look after him. Vasari describes him at this time as looking more like an angel than a human and reports that the people of Rome looked upon him as the reincarnation of Raphael, the divinely gifted, short-lived genius.

In pondering Parmigianino's failure to consolidate his initial advantage in Rome this may be the time to consider Vasari's sobering observation on the adverse effect of the Eternal City on visiting artists. To what extent Parmigianino may have been overwhelmed

Detail of fig. 38
PARMIGIANINO
Lorenzo Cybo and His Page
(Lorenzo Cybo)

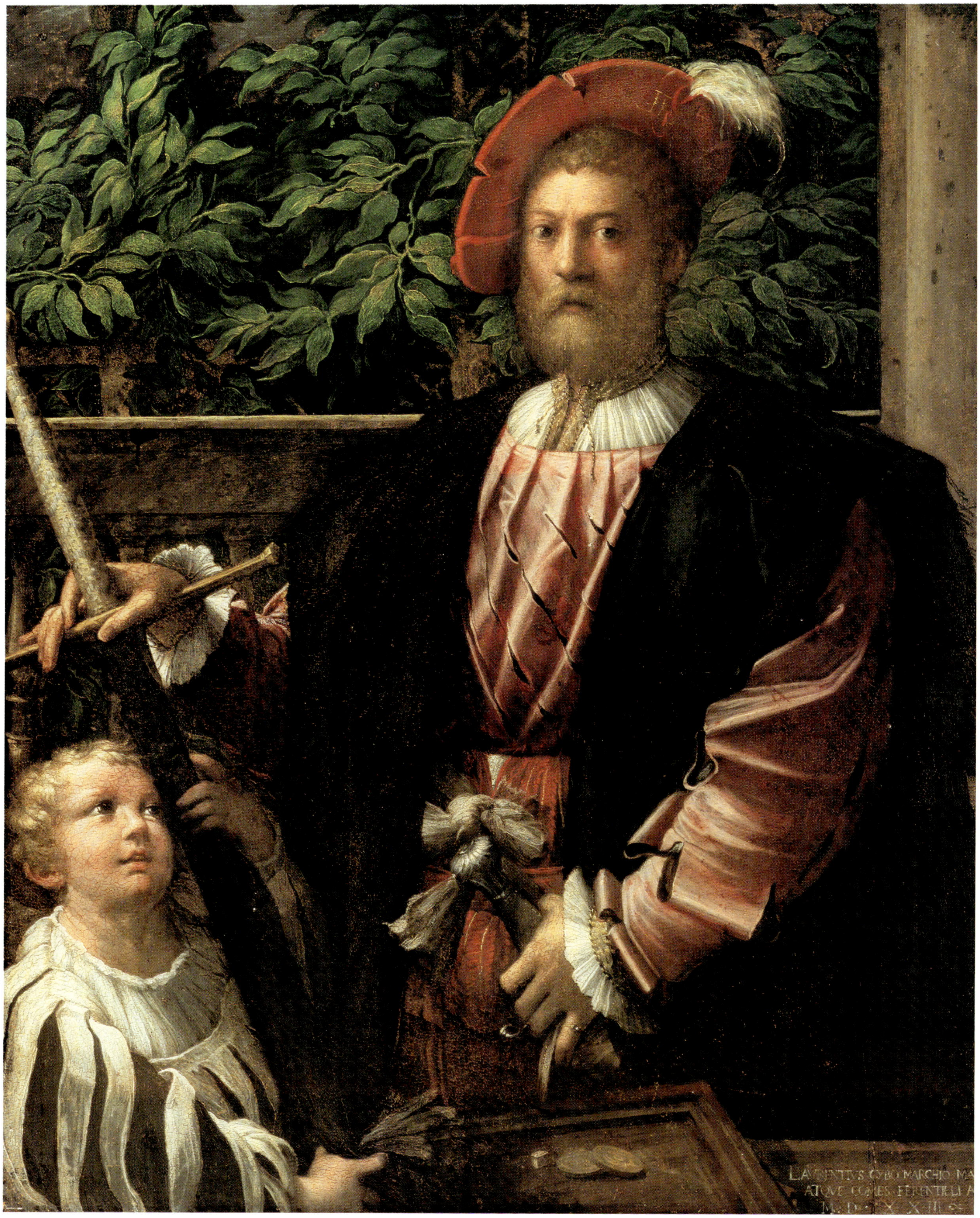
LAVRENTIVS CYBO MARCHIO MA
ATQVE COMES FERENTILLI A
M D X X III

by it would be difficult to estimate. As regards antiquity, it seems he was less moved by its grandeur than by the delicacy and refinement of the best relief sculpture. This is clear from many of his finest drawings, such as those he was to do for the *canephorae* of the Steccata, which come as close to the spirit of antiquity as those of a neoclassical artist of the eighteenth century.

The moment of his arrival in Rome was a lull between storms. The city was recovering from the brief but disastrous reign of the Dutch pope, Adrian VI. But there was an unrest in the air in the aftermath of reform in the north; a sinister, almost apocalyptic mood prevailed, as though anticipating the catastrophe of 1527, when the emperor's troops sacked the city.[1] Raphael had died four years previously, and Michelangelo had left Rome as early as 1516. He was based at this time in Florence. Parmigianino had evidently stopped there on his way to Rome, and there is, as we shall see, a suggestive indication that he may have met Michelangelo there. Finally, Giulio Romano left Rome sometime in the year that Parmigianino arrived. Painters who remained included Perino del Vaga and the team of Polidoro da Caravaggio and his partner, Maturino. The chief activity of this duo was the painting of the external walls of Roman palaces, almost all of which has perished. There is some indication that Parmigianino may have been planning at one time to break into this field.[2] These artists had been part of Raphael's team, which had worked on the great composite decorative schemes in the loggia of the Vatican and in the Sala di Costantino, in which a highly sophisticated system had been evolved by Raphael and transmitted by him to his assistants. Of the three painters Perino was the one whose natural bent—to the graceful—was closest to Parmigianino's, and in one or two of his rare panel pictures he approximates to some extent Parmigianino's manner. In modern times the attribution of one of them, the Taggia *Adoration,* has actually oscillated between the two of them, though there can be no doubt, as we shall see, that it is the work of Parmigianino. But as Perino was only two years Parmigianino's senior, it might be nearest the truth to suggest that the two developed on roughly parallel lines.

Very much apart from this group artistically, and probably still smarting after his failure to participate in the work of the Sala di Costantino, was Michelangelo's protégé, Sebastiano del Piombo. We shall see that Parmigianino is likely to have been in personal contact with him on at least one occasion. A further painter, Rosso Fiorentino, had, like Sebastiano, never been a member of Raphael's team and may in fact have arrived in Rome at about the same time as Parmigianino. Relations between them were probably fairly close (in his biography of Lappoli Vasari mentions them, and also Perino del Vaga, Giulio Romano, and Sebastiano, as though mutually acquainted). Parmigianino had evidently been impressed by Rosso's altarpiece *Marriage of the Virgin* of 1523. This was for the Ginori chapel in San Lorenzo in Florence, and Parmigianino would have seen it there on his way to Rome. He later adapted the composition for his own engraved design of the same subject (GI).[3] Like himself, Rosso seems to have been partly self-taught as painter, and like him again was a fine draftsman. And the most striking characteristic of his art—a strong

38. PARMIGIANINO
Lorenzo Cybo and His Page, c. 1524–26
Oil on panel, 49¾ × 41⅛ in.
(126.5 × 104.5 cm)
Statens Museum fur Kunst,
Copenhagen (cat. A5)

impulse toward the diabolical—might be thought to chime with Parmigianino's interest in alchemy and magic.

The existing drawings by Parmigianino after the work of other artists illustrated his interests at this time—that is, the antique, Michelangelo, and Raphael. There are exquisite studies after the head of Läocöon and his sons (P71, P404, P694). He sketched a version of the Spinario—from the back (P710): he had also sketched Michelangelo's *David* from the back (P175) and an *Apollo* from the front (P518). There is also a free sketch, perhaps from memory, after Michelangelo's *Pietà* in Saint Peter's (P311), as well as a separate sketch of the outstretched left arm of the Adam on the Sistine ceiling (P131). There are several copies after Marcantonio's prints after Raphael, but these may well date from before the Rome visit. They include a careful drawing of the whole of the cartoon of *Paul Preaching at Athens* (P144). This may have been used for an etching, as Vasari says that Parmigianino did one after one of Raphael's tapestries, though an etching after another of Raphael's series—the *Healing of the Lame Man*—is attributed to him. There is a free sketch after Marcantonio's print of the *Feast in the House of Simon* (P746) and a figure from the *Massacre of the Innocents* (P756). A sketch copy after Raphael's *School of Athens* (P666r) was evidently not made from the fresco itself, as it omits the figure of the seated philosopher, left center, which is also omitted from Raphael's own cartoon, now in the Ambrosiana in Milan. By compressing some of the figures, particularly on the left, Parmigianino shows no respect for Raphael's marvelously subtle intervals. Oddly enough, since this type of formal composition was what he did least well, Parmigianino designed, but apparently never painted, a variation of this composition in the form of a *Presentation of Christ in the Temple*, recorded in drawings, which will be discussed later, in the Victoria and Albert Museum (P273) and British Museum (P218).

Vasari tells us that Parmigianino painted many small pictures while he was in Rome. He adds that most of them were acquired later by Cardinal Ippolito de' Medici, and this throwaway statement may shed some light on Parmigianino's working procedure. Vasari was in a position to have reliable information on this subject, as he tells us that he lived for a time under Cardinal Ippolito's protection. The future Cardinal was, as we have seen, only thirteen when Parmigianino arrived in Rome, and was being educated in Florence.[4] His taste for Parmigianino's art doubtless sprang from the gift of his kinsman, the pope, of the *Holy Family* that Parmigianino had brought with him to Rome. But Ippolito's youth at this time, together with his absence from Rome and Vasari's implication that the transaction took place at a later date ("poi"), suggests a different occasion. The most likely time and place for Ippolito and Parmigianino to conclude the sale would have been during the Pope's visit to Bologna in 1529–30. Though it would be possible, in theory, that Ippolito obtained Parmigianino's pictures from an intermediary who could have bought them from the artist in Rome, Vasari's words suggest a bulk purchase. This would be more likely to be made from the artist himself, and some support for the theory that the transaction took place at Bologna

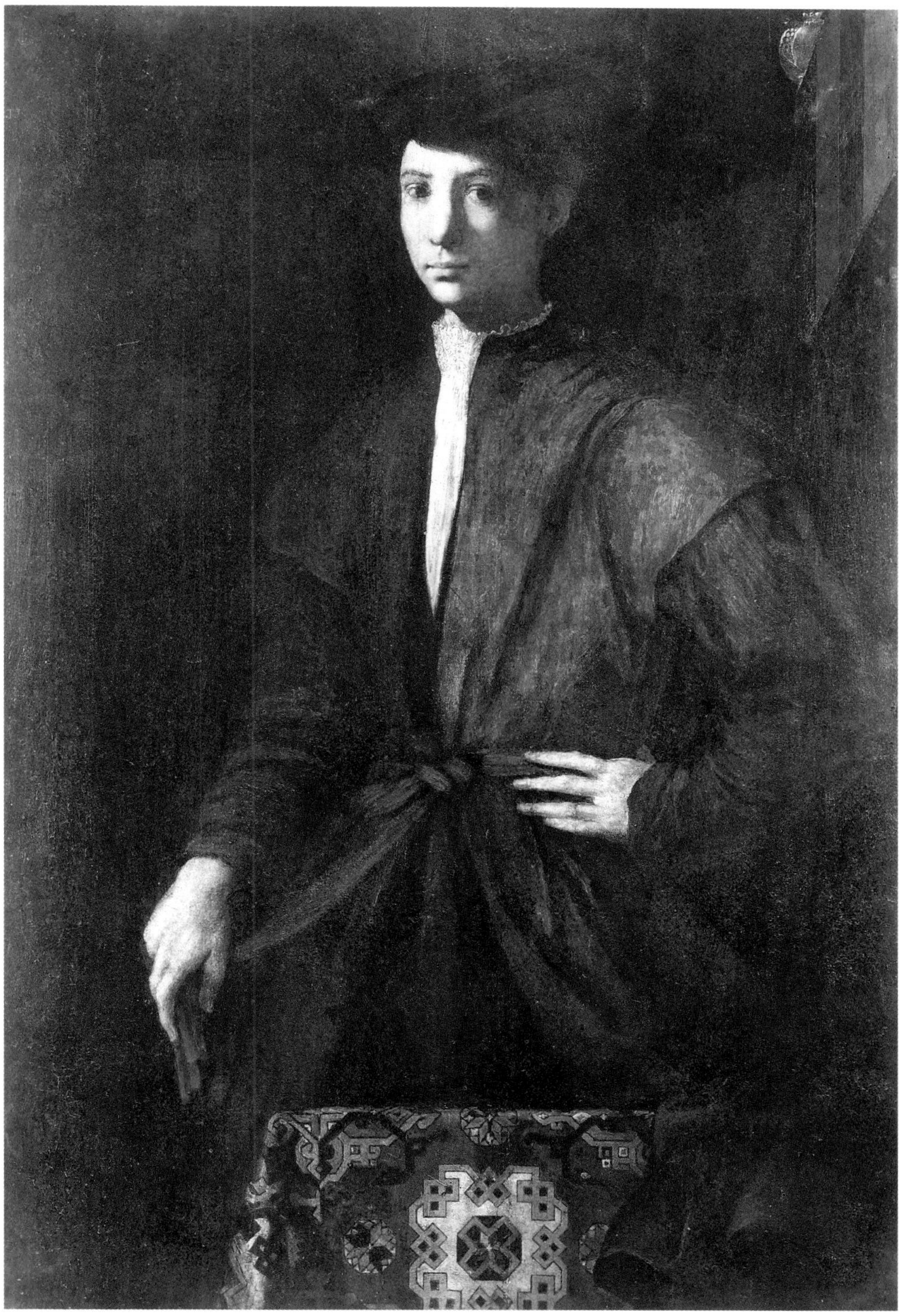

39. ROSSO FIORENTINO
Young Man, c. 1523–24
Oil on panel, 47¼ × 33⅞ in.
(120 × 86 cm)
Galleria Nazionale di Capodimonte, Naples

may be found in Vasari's statement that Cardinal Ippolito also acquired Parmigianino's portrait of Charles v, as this was actually painted at Bologna. It would follow that the possibility suggested in connection with the pictures that Parmigianino brought with him to Rome may be confirmed—namely that he was in the habit of painting small pictures of his own volition and without commission, of keeping them by him, and of taking the unsold ones with him when he changed his place of residence. A further deduction—of some importance to our picture of his life at this time—would be that if the Cardinal bought most of Parmigianino's Roman pictures at Bologna, the young artist's circumstances while in Rome would have been straitened.

Some of the pictures painted in Rome were probably portraits, but only one of those that survive can be dated to this time. That is the portrait of Lorenzo Cybo, now at Copenhagen and already mentioned (fig. 38). The design adheres fairly closely to the type evoked in the Sanvitale portrait. The sitter's eyes appear anxious, almost neurotic, but he looks a more serious soldier than Sanvitale. Once again the foliage is prominent, but the design is perhaps even more subtle. The diagonals of the sword and the tray in the foreground are contrasted with the horizontals of the balustrade behind and the ledge in front. The novelty is in the inclusion of the page, who holds one of his knight's gloves in his right hand and rests his left on the scabbard of the sword. The inclusion of a child as adjunct in a portrait had been adopted in a tentative form before the end of the fifteenth century by Domenico Ghirlandaio. Early in the sixteenth the idea of introducing a subsidiary figure had caught on at Venice in the circle of Giorgione,[5] and a rather later Venetian example, Titian's portrait of Laura Dianti and a Negro page (Kisters collection), offers a fairly close parallel with Parmigianino's portrait, as being at three-quarter length and in a more developed idiom. In this case there could be no question of a connection, but in another, comparable portrait, also datable to the 1520s, some degree of it is more probable than not. This concerns Parmigianino's relations, already mentioned, with Rosso Fiorentino. The probability of the connection in this case is indicated by the fact that the portrait in question, now at Capodimonte (fig. 39), of a young man was actually attributed to Parmigianino when in the Farnese collection in the seventeenth century, and that it was only in recent times that it was convincingly reattributed to Rosso. It has, admittedly, no subsidiary figure, but its brilliant use of adjuncts—the Turkish rug, the curtain, and the door frame, with their contrasts of contour, color, and pattern alike as elements in the design—does suggest an exchange of ideas between the two painters in Rome in the mid-1520s. There is greater tension in Rosso's portrait, but Parmigianino dwells with greater authority on the elaborately varied textures of the garments and accessories.

A further link with Rosso is indicated by Parmigianino's composition, of which the original is lost, representing Saturn disguised as a horse courting Philyra. It is recorded in a print by Lepicié (fig. 40) and in Parmigianino's own studies (P245, 387, 510, 654, 718v, P.O.C. 20). This, which was a late work, was evidently inspired by Giovanni Jacopo Caraglio's print (fig. 41) after Rosso's design of the same rare subject.

Of the small paintings that may date from the Roman period none is precisely dated, and therefore none can be assigned with certainty to this stage of Parmigianino's career. The two most favored candidates are the *Holy Family* and *Madonna* now in the Galleria Doria in Rome (figs. 42, 43). A modern critic, suggesting an alternative dating within the early period of Parma, has remarked wittily that the reason for the usual assumption that they date from Parmigianino's Roman years may be merely the fact that for at least two centuries they have been in a collection in Rome. It is true that the gesture of the figure on the left in the *Holy Family* who raises both arms can be paralleled in two of Anselmi's frescoes at San Giovanni Evangelista at Parma—*Saint Catherine* and *Saint*

Agnes—which are datable to the period not long before Parmigianino left Parma for Rome.[6] Nevertheless the Doria pair are obviously more mature than pre-Roman pictures such as the Prado *Holy Family.*

The Doria *Holy Family* is usually entitled the *Adoration of the Shepherds,* but the two bearded figures whose heads are seen in the center are not visibly on their knees in adoration—an arrangement that results logically in an oblong format. It may not have been pointed out that a drawing—P778—corresponds closely with the foremost of these bearded heads and may also originally have included the other one. In both Doria pictures the upright shape of the panel seems too lofty for the composition, as though the artist had been required to paint on panels that already existed and that could not be cut down because of their function, while the brilliant handling suggests that they were painted in haste. Most interestingly, the *Holy Family* seems to show knowledge, presumably derived from copies, of both of Leonardo's compositions of the *Madonna with Saint Anne*—of the Louvre version in the impulsive, swooping gesture of the Madonna, and of the London cartoon in the upward-pointing hand of one of the shepherds.

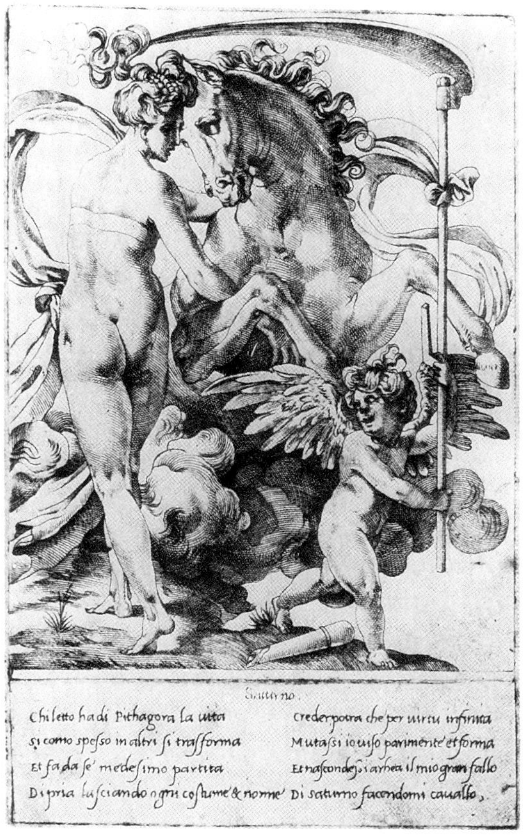

41. GIOVANNI JACOPO CARAGLIO (AFTER ROSSO)
Saturn and Philyra, 16th century
Engraving

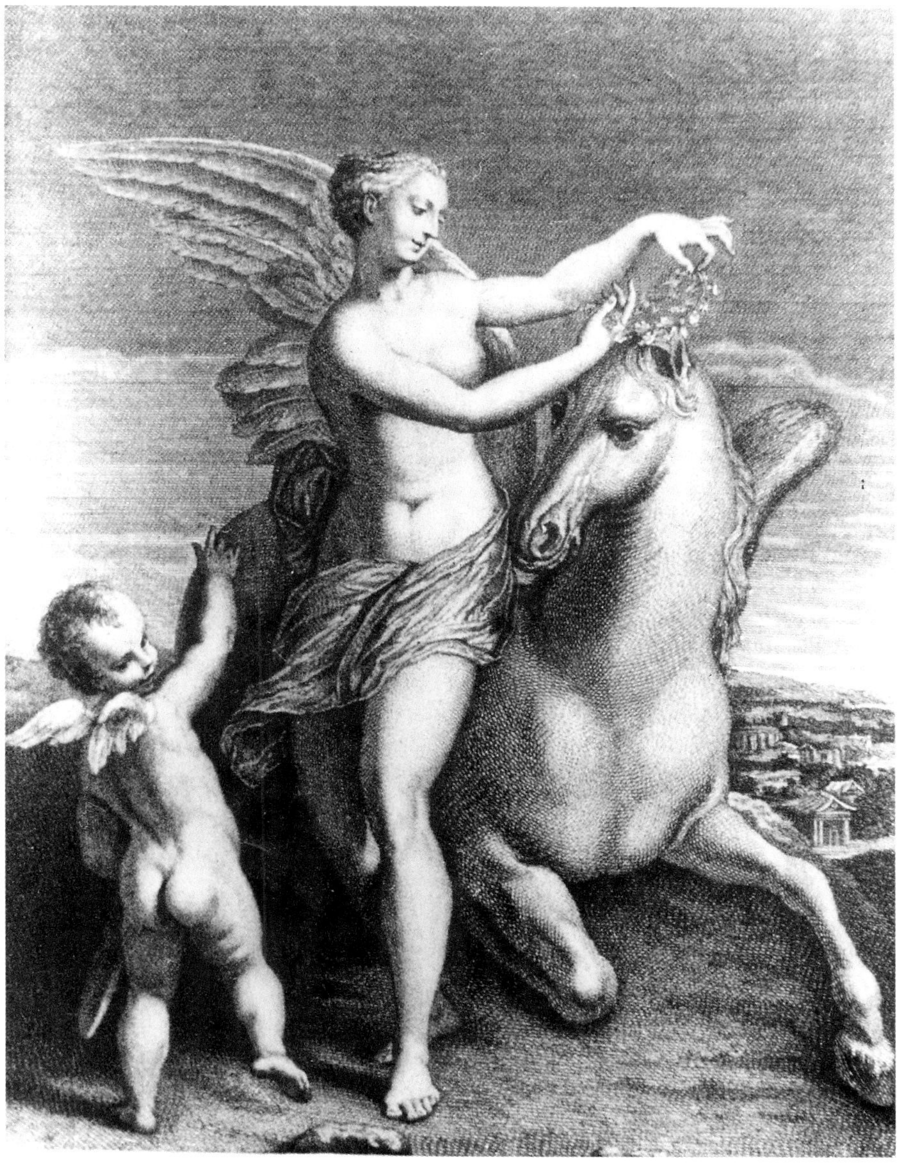

40. BERNARD LEPICIÉ (AFTER PARMIGIANINO)
Saturn and Philyra, 18th century
Engraving

The technique of the Doria *Madonna* is less sketchy than that of the *Holy Family.* It is a tender little picture, and the design is ingenious. The book from which the Madonna reads is bent backward on the Christ Child's knee. This is unusual, but it harmonizes with the rest of the composition. And here I fancy I see an echo of paintings in a building that, like the Cremona frescoes, would have been a recent artistic sensation in Lombardy during Parmigianino's adolescence. This was Mantegna's funerary chapel at Mantua. In all four of the pendentive frescoes (fig. 44), sometimes ascribed to the young Correggio, the Evangelists are shown resting their books on their elbows on balustrades that are semi-circular in plan, but which, being seen from below, are foreshortened to a form that is

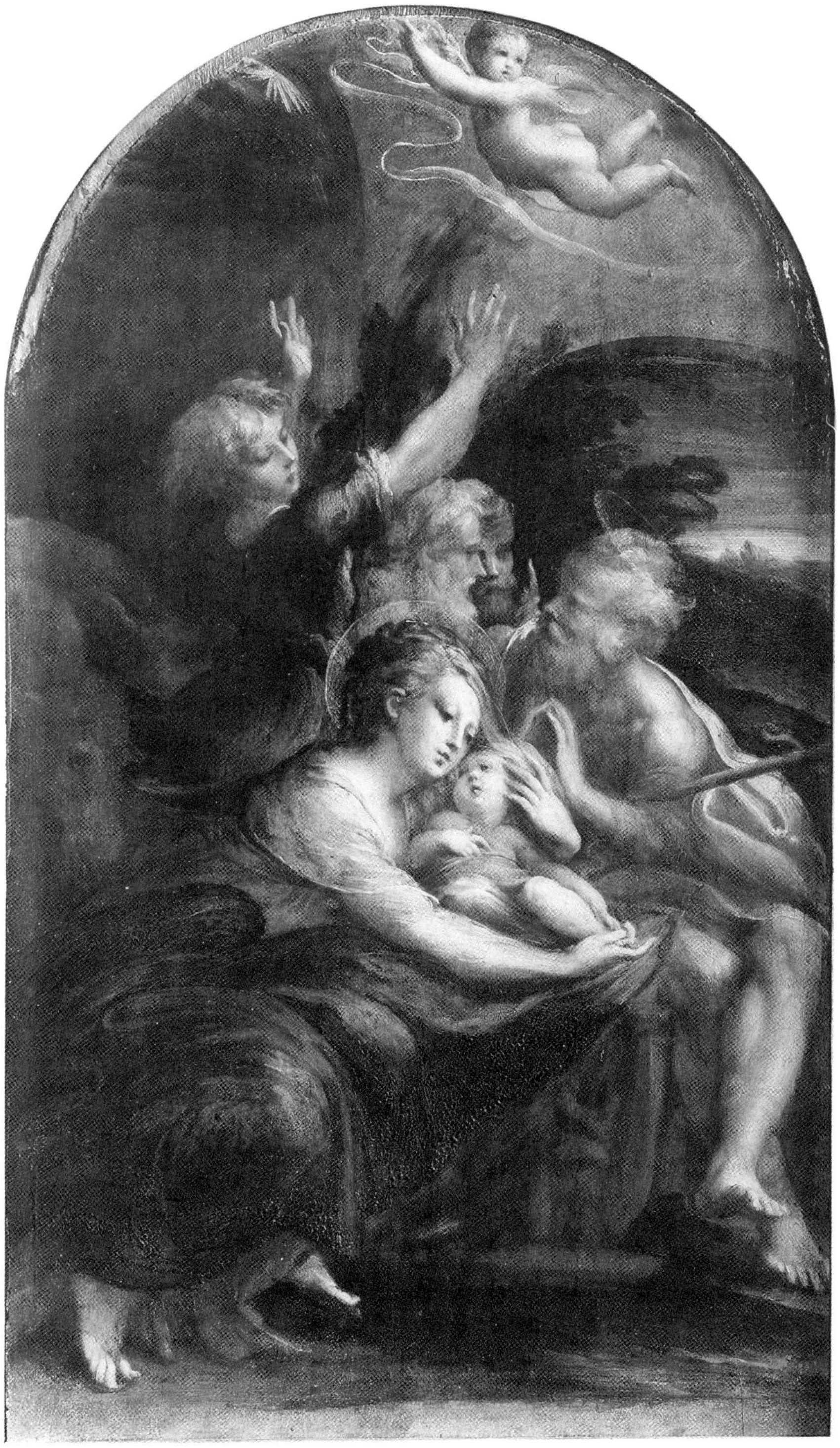

42. PARMIGIANINO
Holy Family (Adoration of the Shepherds),
c. 1524–25
Oil on panel, each panel:
$23\frac{1}{4} \times 13\frac{3}{8}$ in. (59 × 34 cm)
Galleria Doria, Rome (cat. A44)

curved upward like the Madonna's book in the Doria *Madonna.* The artist's visual memory has transformed the bookrest into the book.

Parallel with the shortage of commissions for painting in Rome was the development of Parmigianino's interest in the fascinating new process of graphics. It may have been now, or it may have been later, that he himself started to practice etching. In either case, however, it is certain that it was during his Roman years that he let a number of his designs be engraved on copper by others. Only a few years previously the Bolognese draftsman Marcantonio Raimondi, fired by the sight of Albrecht Dürer's prints and by their artistic and commercial success in Italy, had started to copy and in effect forge them.

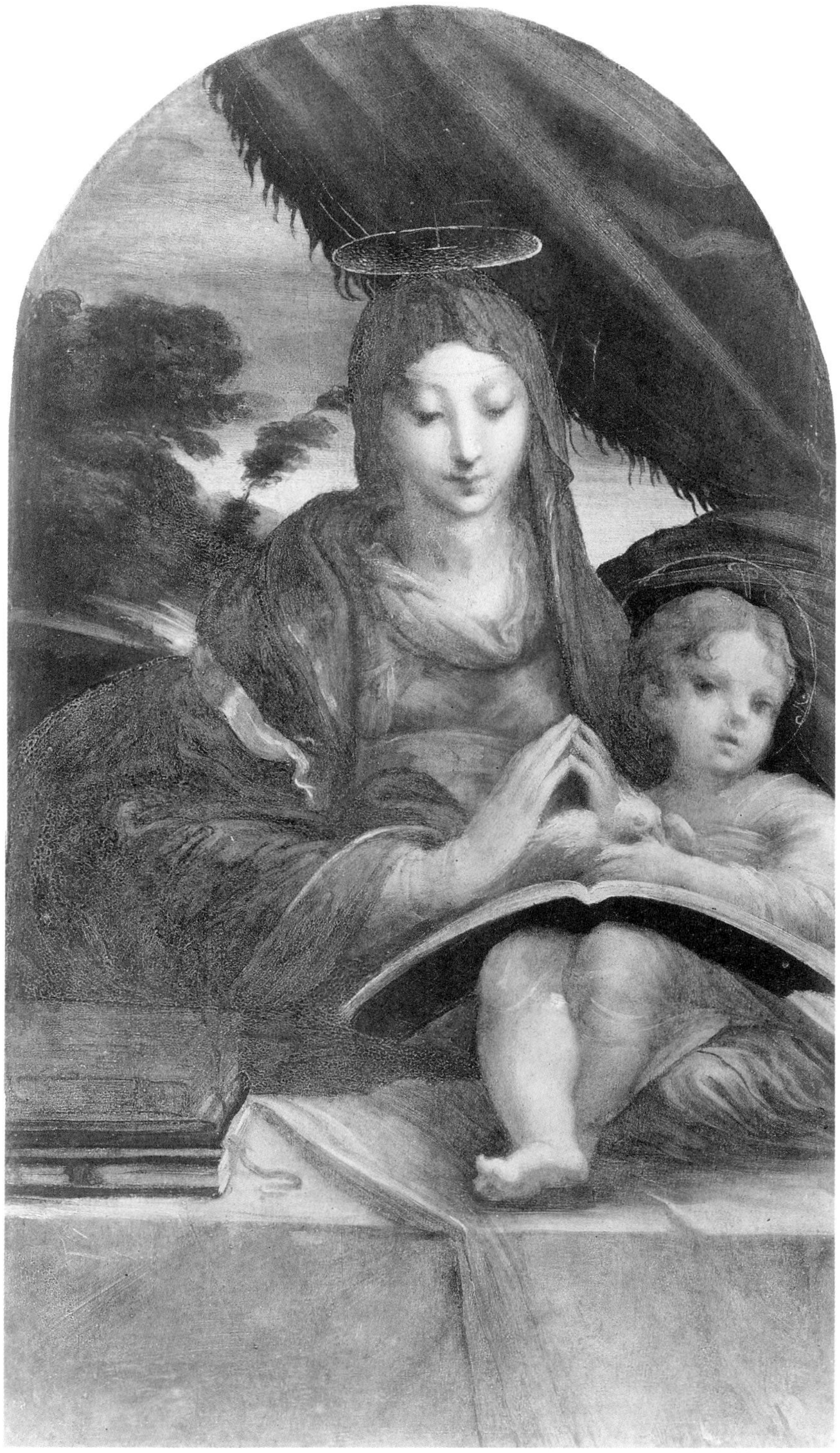

43. PARMIGIANINO
Madonna and Child, c. 1524–25
Oil on panel, each panel:
23¼ × 13⅜ in. (59 × 34 cm)
Galleria Doria, Rome (cat. A43)

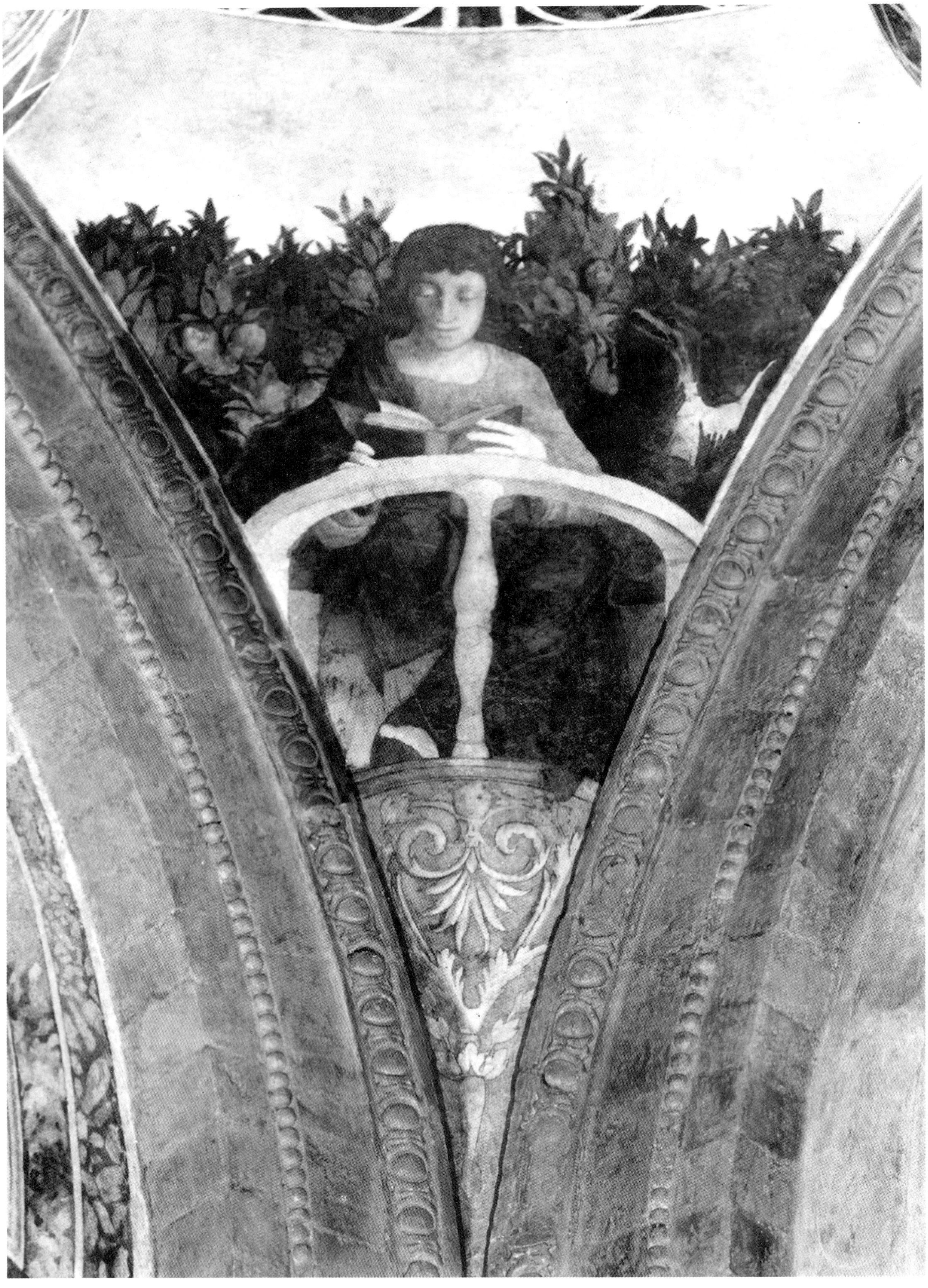

He had then set out to evolve an Italian substitute, with the difference that, unlike Dürer and unlike Italian pioneers of metal engravings such as Andrea Mantegna or Antonio Pollaiuolo, the designs that he engraved were the work of other artists. Chief of these was Raphael, who was quick to realize the possibilities of the new medium for increasing his fame and perhaps his income. Like Pollaiuolo and Mantegna again, what Marcantonio engraved in the early stages were not paintings but drawings. The idea of engraving as a means of reproducing paintings was a later development.

Marcantonio himself did not make prints after designs by Parmigianino. He was indeed in no position to do so at this time since he had been arrested, soon after Parmigianino arrived in Rome, and put in prison on the orders of the pope for having circulated engravings of indecent drawings by Giulio Romano. Giulio himself, by this time, had retired to Mantua. Instead, Parmigianino turned to a younger engraver, Giovanni Jacopo Caraglio, who was currently working for Perino del Vaga and for Rosso—another link between them and Parmigianino. There are four prints by Caraglio after Parmigianino—a *Marriage of the Virgin,* a *Martyrdom of Saints Peter and Paul,* an *Adoration of the Shepherds,* and a *Diogenes.* The last of these is the only one for which Parmigianino's model drawing no longer survives. The head of Diogenes recalls that of Raphael's depiction of the same philosopher in the *School of Athens,* but the posture, and the massive, Michelangelesque proportions, may be a development from one of the discarded ideas for the Saint Jerome in the London altarpiece (fig. 49) on which Parmigianino was working concurrently (a drawing in the Uffizi [P107] includes studies for both Diogenes and Saint Jerome, and an elaborate sketch in the Louvre [P504] might be for either). These four prints are all likely to date from before the sack of 1527, but the only one that bears a date—1526—is the *Adoration.*

It is not certain which of these designs were made with engraving in view and which were originally intended to be painted and were engraved later, after the project for painting them had fallen through. One possibility for the latter category, it has been claimed, is the *Martyrdom of Saints Peter and Paul.*[7] The suggestion has been made that this composition, which evidently derives from Raphael's *Martyrdom of Saint Cecilia,* as engraved by Marcantonio, was intended for the Sala dei Pontefici of the Vatican. Against this theory is the fact that in Parmigianino's original drawing (P190) the characters are shown operating left-handedly, thus allowing for reversal in printing. In any case, however, it seems likely that Parmigianino tried, and evidently failed, to obtain various public commissions at this time, since there are drawings for other oblong compositions in the grand manner of the late Raphael for which there are no corresponding paintings. In addition to the *Martyrdom of Saints Peter and Paul,* for example, there is a finished sketch (P690) for *Christ Healing the Lepers* (subsequently engraved as a chiaroscuro) and sketches for a *Christ Healing the Sick* (P5) and for a scene with the worship of Jupiter (P193) as well as several others.

It would be possible that some of these designs were for projects that may have been still under discussion at the time of the sack, after which all activity of this kind was

44. SCHOOL OF MANTEGNA
Pendentive of Sant'Andrea, c. 1505–16
Fresco
Sant'Andrea, Mantua, Italy

suspended for several years. But a different explanation for the failure would also be a possibility. For these drawings show that the Raphaelesque grand manner was not Parmigianino's forte. He could not beat the big drum. And of the various compositions, paintings, and drawings that he produced during his years in Rome, only one seems to me to be entirely successful and to show him at his best and most characteristic. This is the magical wash drawing (P631; fig. 45) of the *Adoration of the Shepherds.* Caraglio's print of it (fig. 46) is one of his best, but it is less atmospheric than Parmigianino's drawing, partly because the engraved line, though capable of great delicacy, is less suggestive than shading done with the brush. In particular, Caraglio is likely to have experienced difficulty in translating Parmigianino's extraordinary device of actually obscuring to some extent the features of both the Madonna and the Christ Child by means of a combination of dramatic foreshortening and heavy shadow.

The comparison of Rosso's painting *Marriage of the Virgin* (fig. 47) with Parmigianino's adaptation of it (P692; fig. 48), together with Caraglio's print after Parmigianino's adaptation, illustrates another aspect of the way in which his visual sense was working at this time. Though Rosso's picture shows his usual tendency to facial grimace and a highly individual system of draperies, the design as a whole is monumental. But Parmigianino's drawing minimizes the monumentality by reducing the scale of the three main figures and thereby leaves more room for picturesque accessories such as gesticulating spectators and prominent architecture. Some of the differences, however, are probably due to the differ-

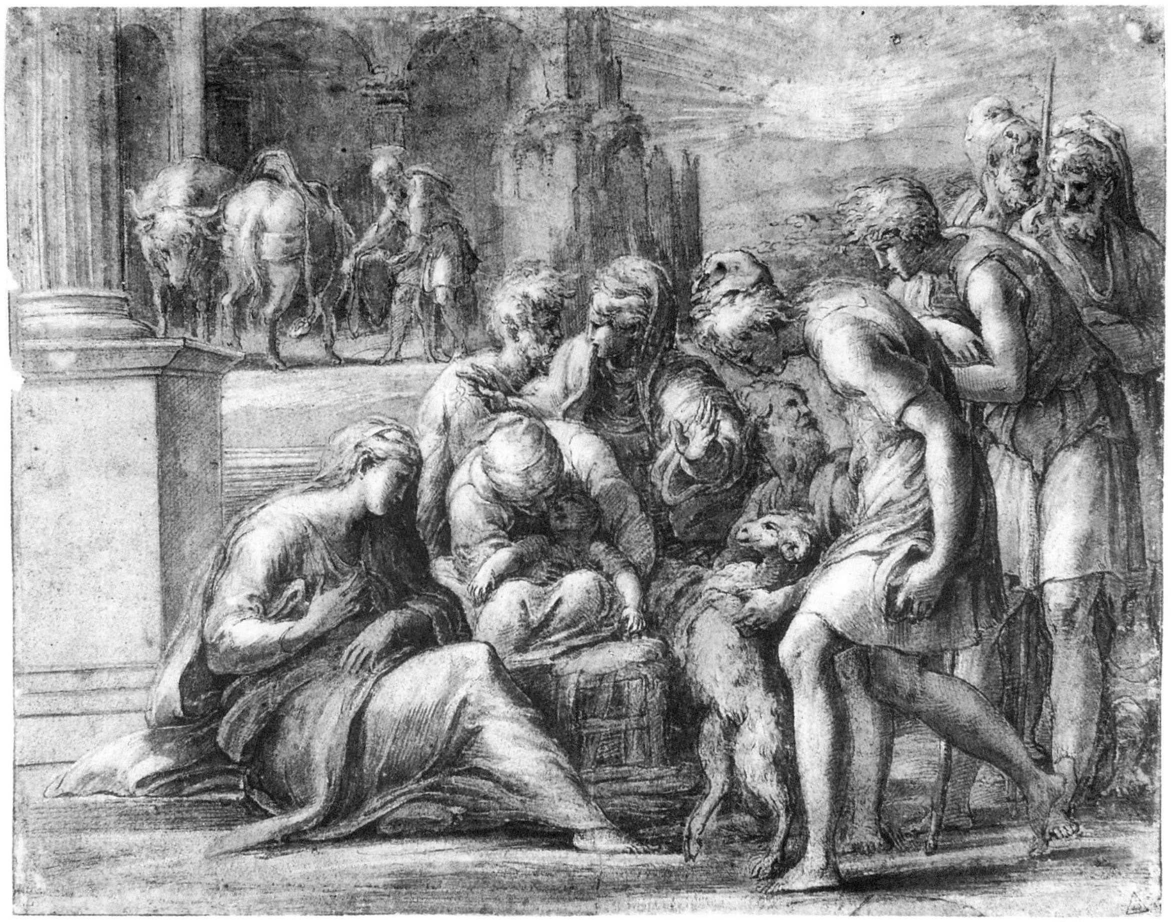

45. PARMIGIANINO
Study for the *Adoration of the Shepherds,* n.d. P631
Pen and ink and wash, heightened with white on paper, 7⅜ × 9⅝ in. (18.8 × 24.5 cm)
Graphische Sammlung, Weimar, Germany

ent shape of the two compositions. Rosso's painting has normal proportions for an altarpiece. But Parmigianino's model drawing adumbrates a highly unusual format—very tall and narrow, and with an arched top. As a result, the three main figures—the bridal couple and the priest—are higher up in Parmigianino's composition than in Rosso's, and in his wish to fill the resulting vacuum Parmigianino inserted two extra figures who are seated and out of scale with the others.

An even more attenuated shape is found in the only altarpiece that Parmigianino actually painted during his Rome years, the *Madonna and Child with the Baptist and Saint Jerome,* now in London (fig. 49). Here the proportions are probably unique in an altarpiece other than the center of a polyptych. Even Titian's *Assunta* at the Frari in Venice is not quite so high in relation to its width, and the events that attended the making of Titian's picture may be relevant to Parmigianino's. For we know, in the case of the Frari picture, that the frame, an enormous architectural affair in marble, was ordered at the same time as the painting; and we can see that the form of the frame, which was conditioned by the proportions of the church, evidently affected in its turn the design of the picture. Thus, the great height of the Gothic vault of the Frari church brought about the huge relative height of the architectural frame, and the latter was responsible for the picture's being designed in three superimposed zones instead of the two that had been normal in an Assumption. The church in Rome for which Parmigianino's altarpiece was intended, San Salvatore in Lauro, was burned at the end of the sixteenth century, and its appearance at the relevant

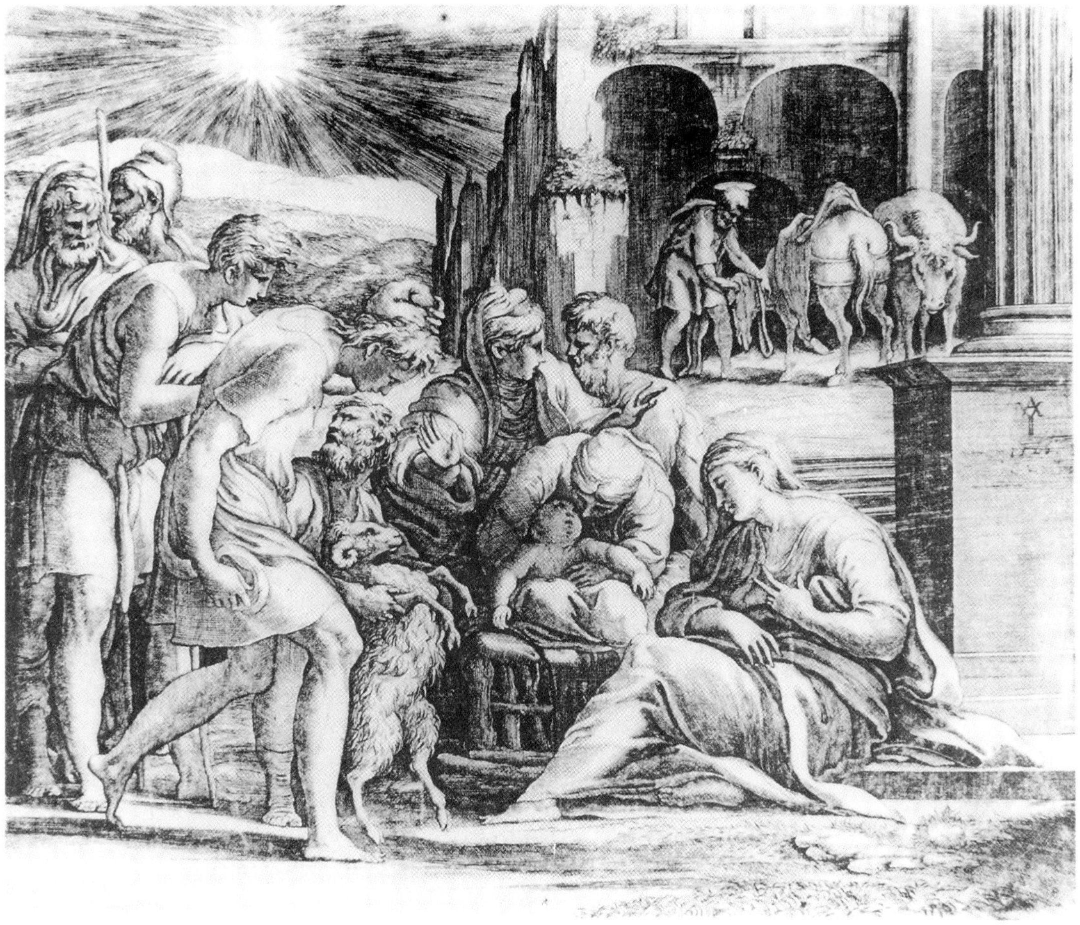

46. GIOVANNI JACOPO CARAGLIO (AFTER PARMIGIANINO)
Adoration of the Shepherds, 1526
Engraving (cat. G3)

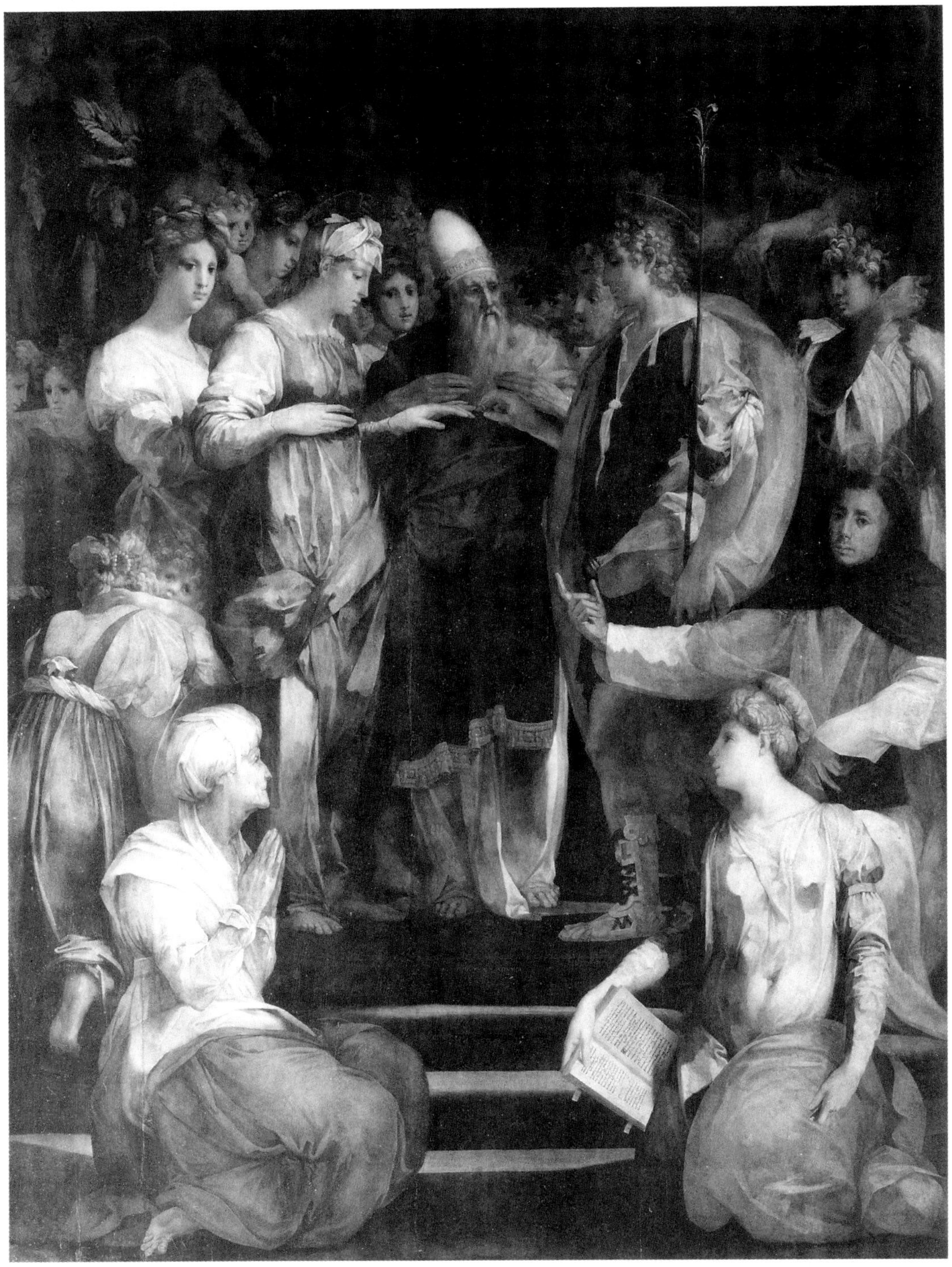

47. ROSSO FIORENTINO
Marriage of the Virgin, 1523
Oil on panel, 127⅞ × 98⅜ in. (325 × 250 cm)
San Lorenzo, Florence

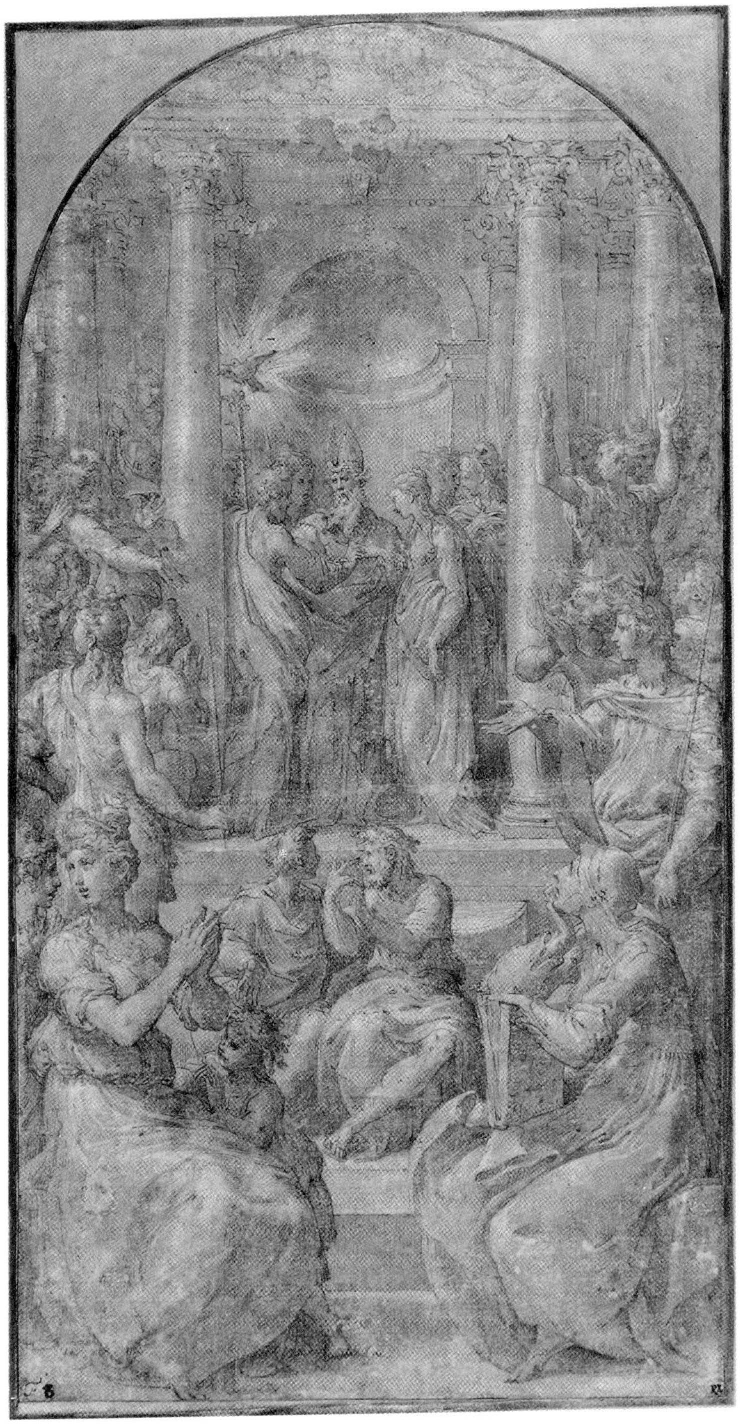

48. PARMIGIANINO
Study for the *Marriage of the Virgin,*
c. 1523(?) P692
Pen and brown ink and brown wash,
heightened with white on paper,
17⅞ × 9⅛ in. (45.3 × 23.2 cm)
Chatsworth, Derbyshire, England

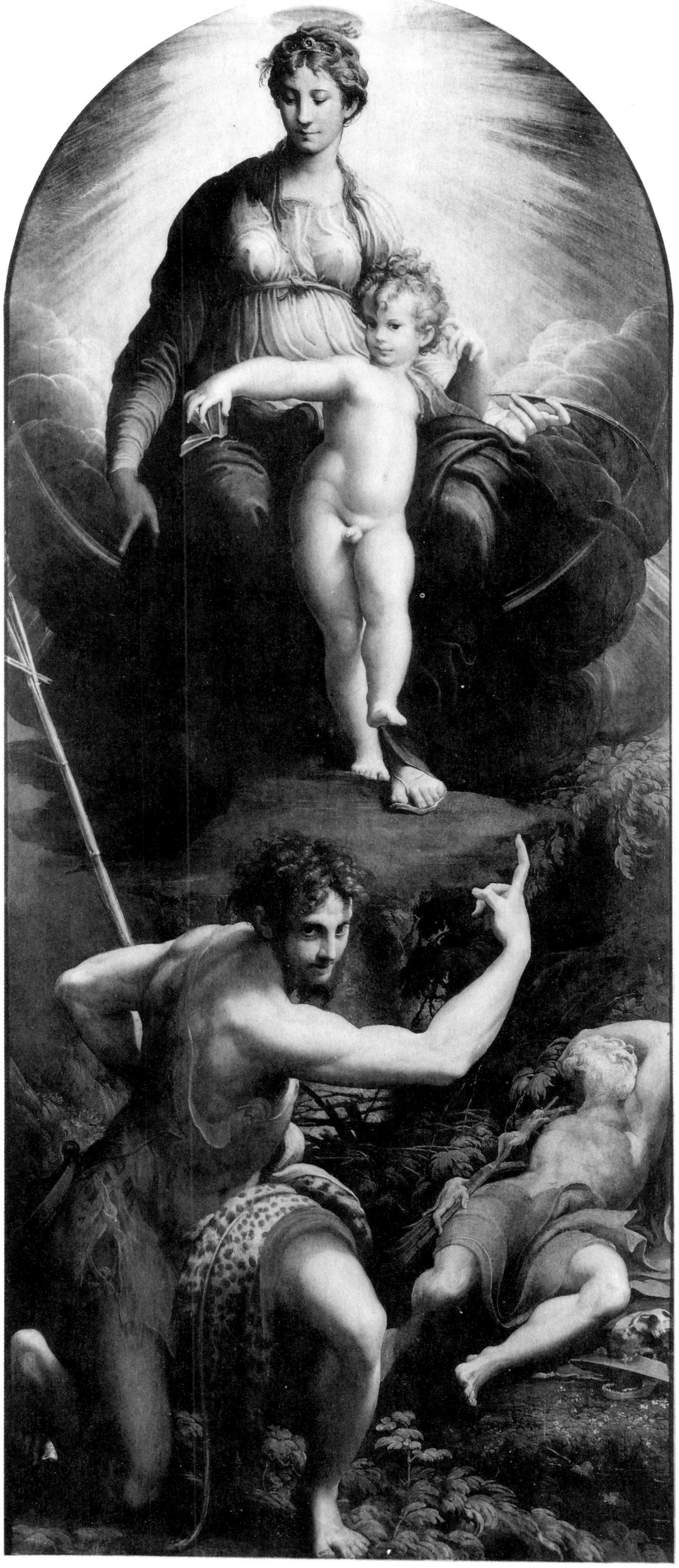

49. PARMIGIANINO
Madonna and Child with the Baptist and Saint Jerome, after 1526
Oil on panel, 135 × 58⅝ in.
(343 × 149 cm)
National Gallery, London (cat. A17)

time is not known.[8] But an architectural drawing by Parmigianino (P273) in his earlier style (Victoria and Albert Museum) shows a niche with a painting, evidently intended to be in fresco, of the *Presentation of Christ,* in the half-dome (fig. 50). Underneath it is a pillared frame with the proportions of the London altarpiece. The frame is flanked by large figures probably intended as sculpture. The interior of the frame is blank.

That such a very unusual format for an altarpiece should thus occur in three separate instances, all dating from the same period—the *Marriage of the Virgin* drawing, the empty frame in the Victoria and Albert sketch, and the London painting itself—suggests that all three may refer to the same undertaking, at San Salvatore in Lauro. A connection between the Victoria and Albert sketch and the London altarpiece was suggested tentatively by A. E. Popham. The contract for the London picture is dated January, 1526, and specifies the subject as it was actually executed, but this might have been preceded by a different project (the blank frame in the Victoria and Albert sketch could mean that a final decision had not yet been reached). The first idea would therefore have been for an altarpiece of the Marriage of the Virgin, surmounted by a fresco of the Presentation of Christ. At the next stage the subject of the altarpiece was changed to the Madonna and Child with Saints, and no more was heard of the fresco. The unexecuted design for the Marriage of the Virgin was then preserved in a print by Caraglio. It is clear from the contract of 1526 that Parmigianino's painting was intended as an element in the context of the Doctrine of the Immaculate Conception, but that it was not itself intended to illustrate it, as this was to be a separate work of art (see appendix 3).

Whether or not the proportions of the London picture were forced on Parmigianino in this way, there can be no doubt that they were closely related to the design of the painting. In the orthodox composition of the Madonna in Glory, as for example in Raphael's *Madonna of Foligno,* the Madonna, being in the air, is relatively isolated, while the saints on the ground below take up the full width of the panel. The triangular arrangement that results is eminently logical in an altarpiece of normal format, but is not practical within the narrow proportions of the London picture. This favored the upper zone, with the Madonna and Child, at the expense of the lower. In a sketch in the British Museum (P181; fig. 51) the artist was still trying to follow the orthodox arrangement. But even though the space was at this stage relatively wider than in the painting, the two saints could only be shown abreast by being drawn on a much smaller scale than the Madonna.

It was evidently at this point that Parmigianino reconciled himself to the fact that the exceptionally narrow format did not permit of more than one figure in the foreground. Saint Jerome was therefore relegated to an awkward and asymmetrical place in the middle distance. In the process this involved a discord of scale and also another of Parmigianino's iconographic modifications in the interests of the design. To show Saint Jerome upright in his new position would be even more difficult visually. Therefore he had to be recumbent, and therefore asleep. In ignorance of this it was assumed in the nineteenth

50. PARMIGIANINO
Study for a niche, n.d. P273
Pen and brown ink, 9¼ × 7¾ in.
(23.5 × 19.6 cm)
Victoria and Albert Museum, London

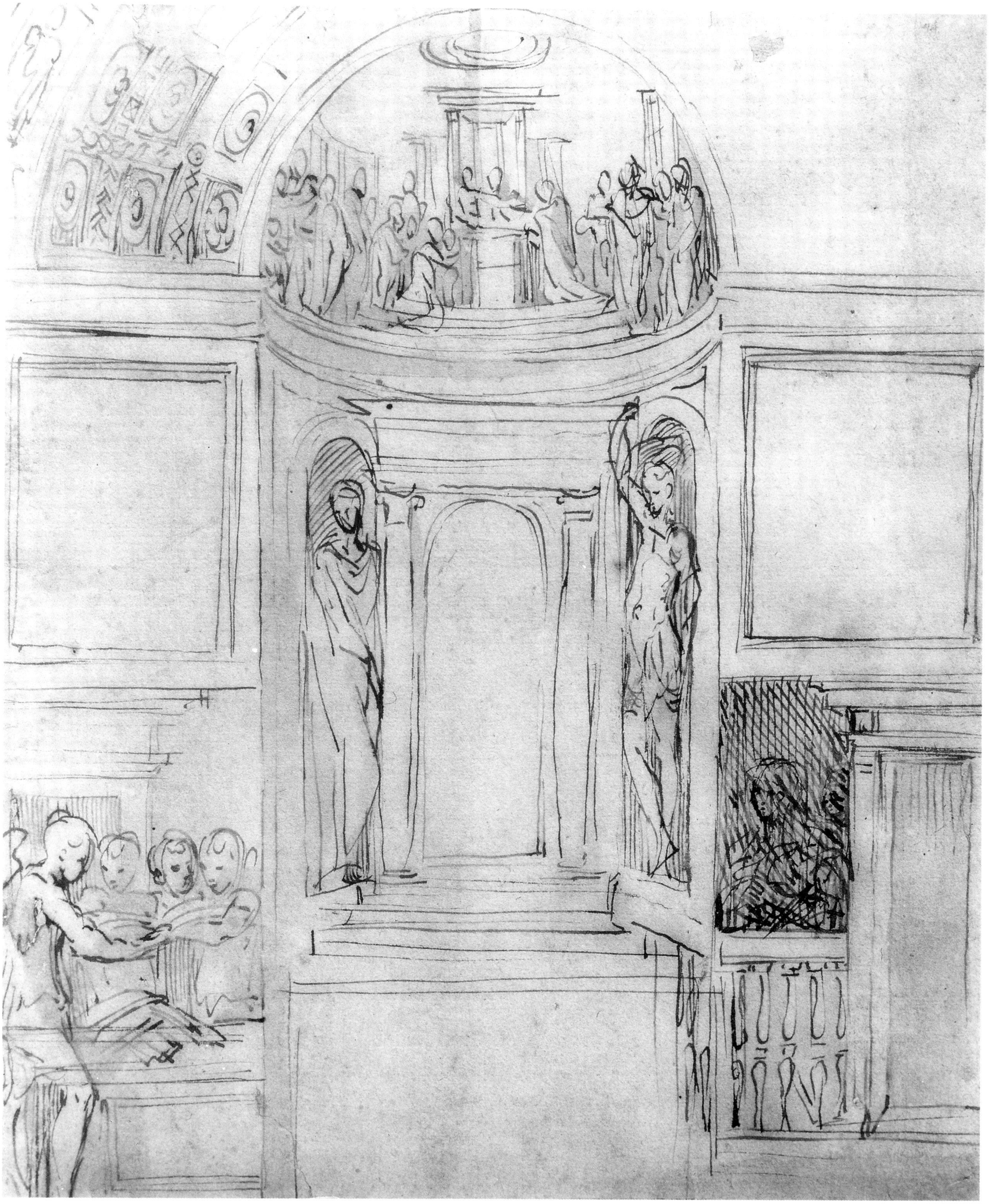

century that he was undergoing a religious experience, and the picture entitled in consequence *The Vision of Saint Jerome*—regardless of the fact that he is not recorded as having had such a vision.

Parmigianino's adaptation of the Madonna in Glory includes another unusual feature, this time not due to the exceptional proportions, and not entirely of his own invention. Instead of being airborne, the Madonna's clouds have been lowered so that they lap the earth, thereby suggesting easier access to her on the part of penitent spectators. This idea had been realized by Correggio in his *Madonna with Saint Sebastian* (Dresden; fig. 52)—a picture that Parmigianino had evidently seen, perhaps unfinished, before leaving Parma.[9] But in that work the Child was still on the Madonna's lap, as in Parmigianino's sketch in the British Museum. The logical sequel—to bring him down so that

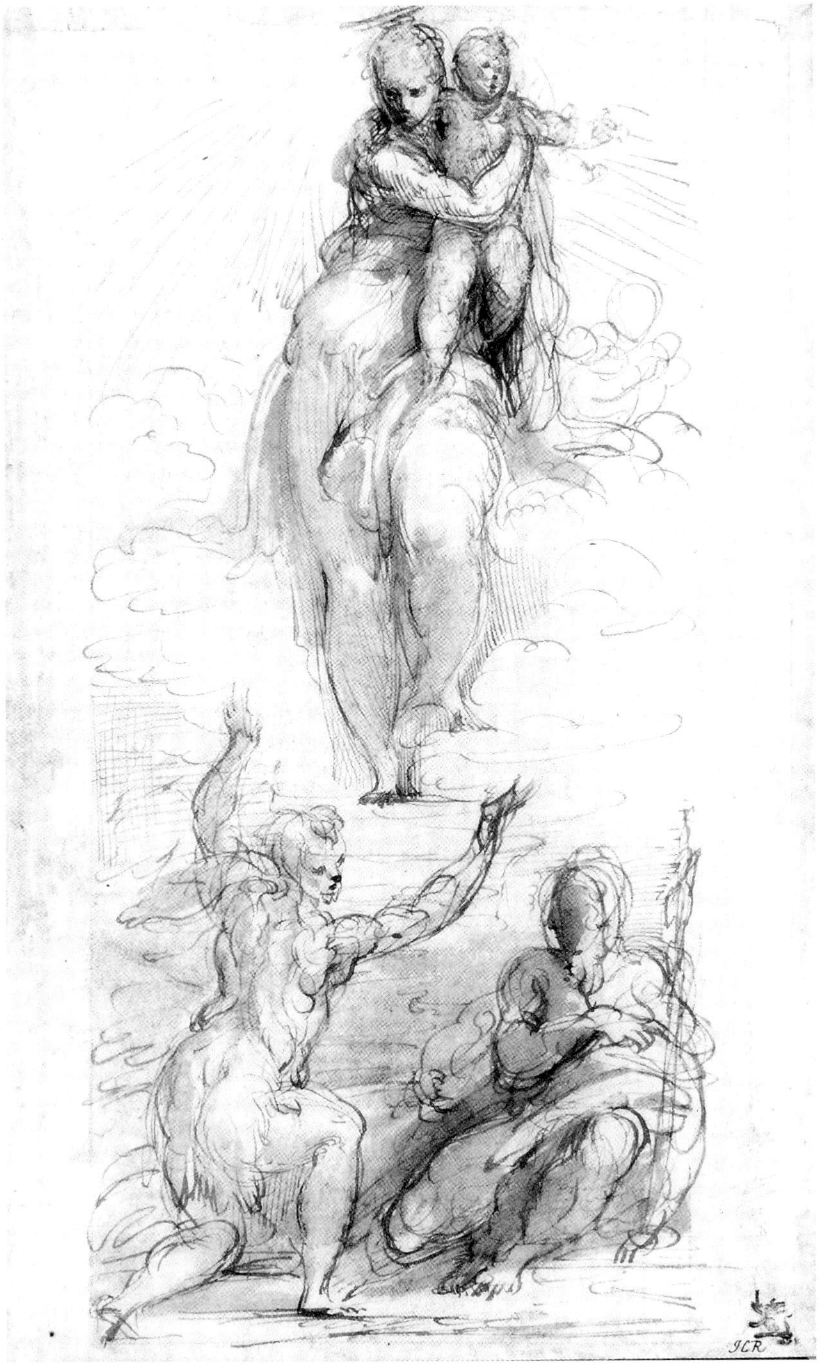

51. PARMIGIANINO
Study for *Madonna and Child with the Baptist and Saint Jerome*, n.d. P181r
Pen and brown wash over red chalk on paper, 10¼ × 6⅛ in. (26 × 15.7 cm)
British Museum, London

his feet touch the ground—was a development of Parmigianino's that he did not evolve until a late stage in the preliminary drawings. In other features of the London picture, Parmigianino did not look to Correggio. The derivation of the design of the Madonna group from Michelangelo, for instance, has been generally acknowledged. The main source was no doubt the marble *Madonna of Bruges* (fig. 53), which was already there in Parmigianino's time, but of which he could have seen casts or drawings at Florence or elsewhere. But two separate elements in Parmigianino's group derive from other works by Michelangelo through channels that are different in the two cases and also interesting in themselves.

First, the shrinking attitude of the Christ Child in the *Madonna of Bruges*—a motif to which Parmigianino was to revert, surprisingly but unequivocally, in his last altarpiece

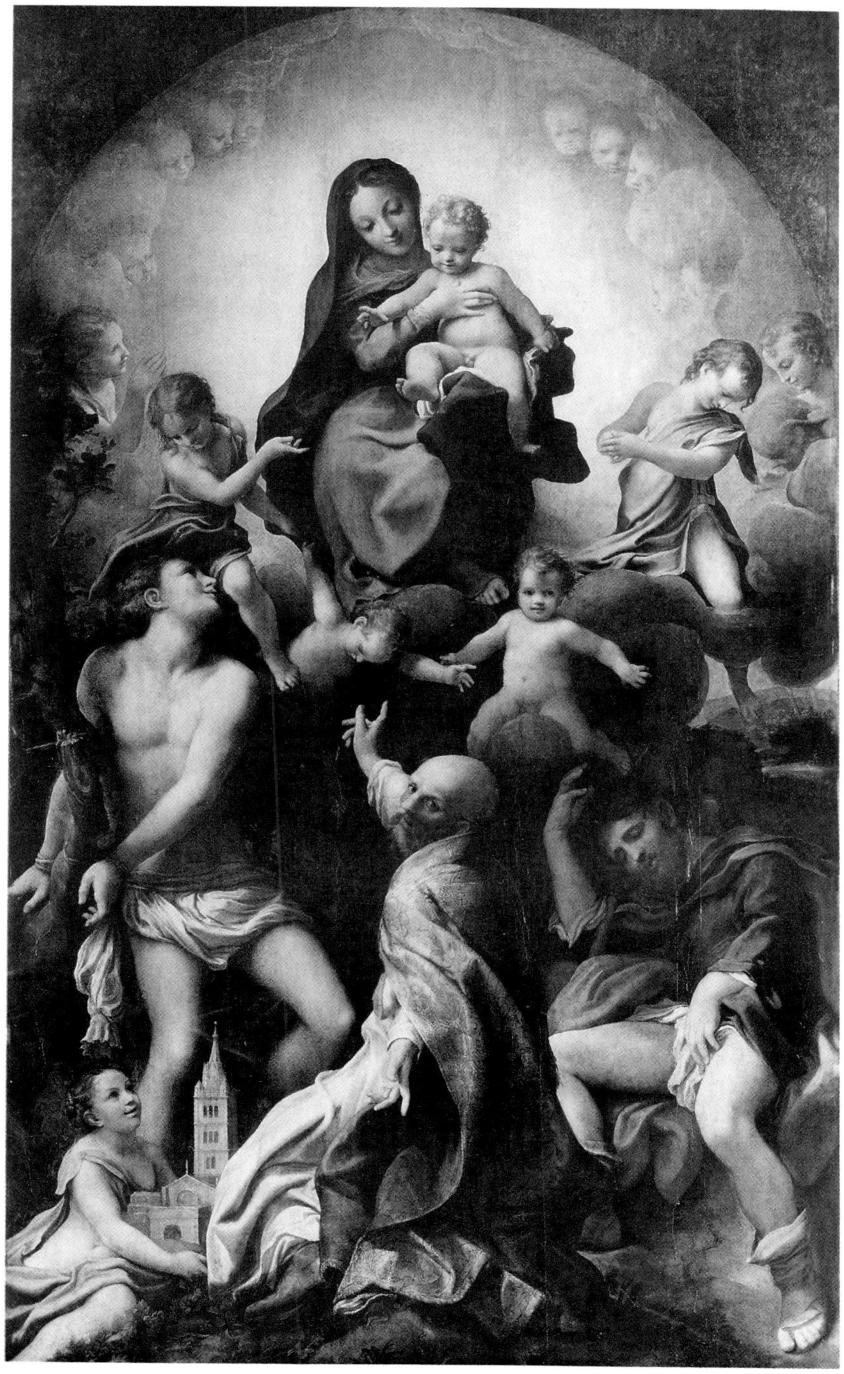

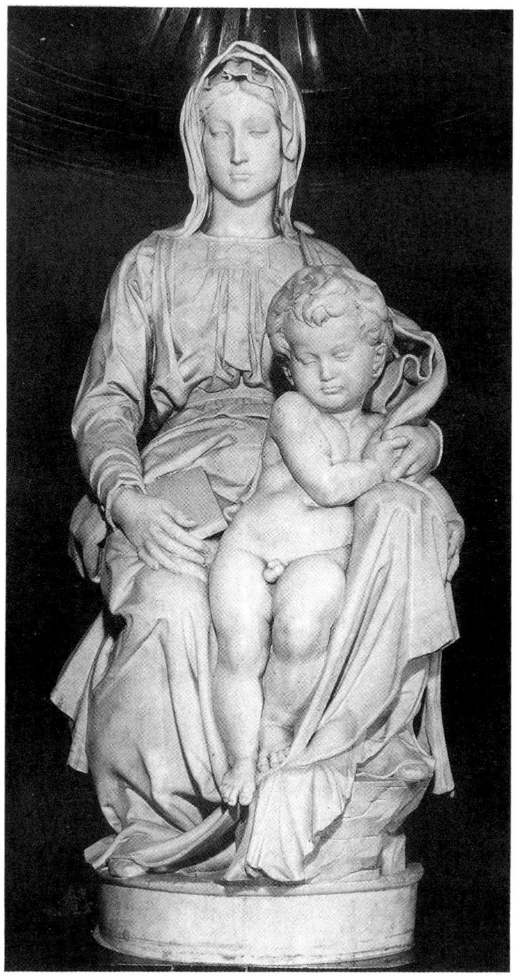

53. MICHELANGELO
Madonna of Bruges, c. 1501
Marble, height: 50½ in. (128.3 cm)
Nôtre Dame, Bruges, Belgium

52. CORREGGIO
Madonna and Child with Saint Sebastian, c. 1525
Oil on panel, 104⅜ × 63⅜ in. (265 × 161 cm)
Gemäldegalerie, Dresden

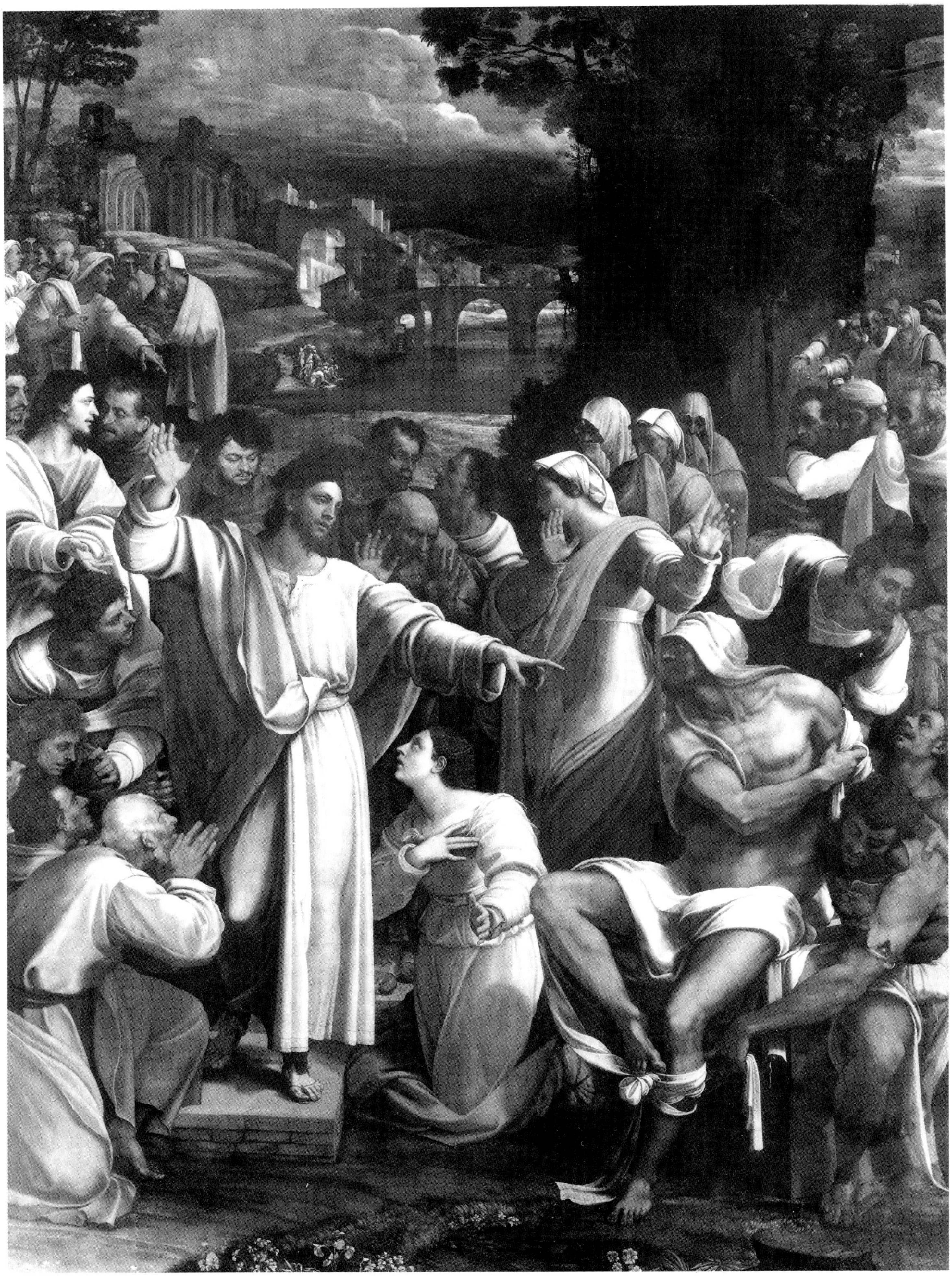

(the Dresden *Madonna and Saints*)—is quite different from the form in the London altarpiece, where Christ, no longer an infant but a self-conscious child, is shown in an imperious pose, his right arm extended, the left raised aloft from the elbow. This gesture is unusual and probably unique in a group of the Madonna and Child, and it has a fascinatingly intricate and hitherto disregarded provenance. In the preliminary drawings Parmigianino had toyed with different arrangements of the Christ Child's arms. The resulting pose is a literal quotation, in reverse, from Sebastiano's adult Christ in his *Raising of Lazarus* (fig. 54). By a strange coincidence both pictures have hung in the same place, the National Gallery in London, for more than a century and a half. This pose was not one of Sebastiano's own invention. Vasari tells us that it was Michelangelo who designed parts of the composition of Sebastiano's painting—certainly the two main figures. Michelangelo's drawing for the Christ is lost, though one of his studies in the British Museum for Lazarus includes what may be the left foot of it.[10] The essential feature of the pose consists of one arm's being extended horizontally, while the other starts horizontal and is then raised vertically from the elbow. The essentials of this pose were later used by Michelangelo himself for the Christ in his *Last Judgment.* It may, before either of the other instances, have been incorporated in his short-lived, colossal bronze statue of Julius II for Bologna, and probably derives ultimately from an antique *Jupiter tonans.* In Michelangelo's drawing for Sebastiano the figure of Christ would have been naked. This complex provenance led to what is probably the most successful of all Parmigianino's depictions of the Christ Child, facilitating, as it did, the solution of a problem that had become more and more difficult with every advance in technical skill—how to make a child look divine and in this case also imperious, but at the same time still childlike. The reason for the elongation of his body may be practical as much as stylistic—to allow for his height above the group.

We do not know precisely when Sebastiano's *Lazarus* left Rome for Narbonne, for which it was always destined. If, as seems almost certain, it had already done so before Parmigianino reached Rome, we must assume that he was in personal touch with Sebastiano, who would doubtless have retained Michelangelo's drawings. This would have given Parmigianino the additional and considerable benefit of the chance to study the technique of Michelangelo as draftsman. In this case, therefore, there would be no need to postulate a meeting between Parmigianino and Michelangelo. But Parmigianino's *Madonna* suggests a different explanation. Though the general derivation is from Michelangelo's marble *Madonna of Bruges,* the prominent motive of the Madonna's right arm in the London picture is different. In the Bruges *Madonna* this arm is brought around onto the Madonna's right knee, instead of falling downward, as it does in the London picture, in order to allow her to grasp something (her cloak) with her hand. And this motif figures in what would have been Michelangelo's latest and current work at the time when Parmigianino was in Florence, namely the *Medici Madonna* (fig. 55).[11] This is the indication that the two may have met at this time.

Opposite:
54. SEBASTIANO DEL PIOMBO
Raising of Lazarus, c. 1516–18(?)
Oil on panel transferred to canvas, 149⅝ × 112⅞ in. (380 × 287 cm)
National Gallery, London

55. MICHELANGELO
Medici Madonna, 1520–30
Marble, height: 89 in. (226 cm)
San Lorenzo, Florence

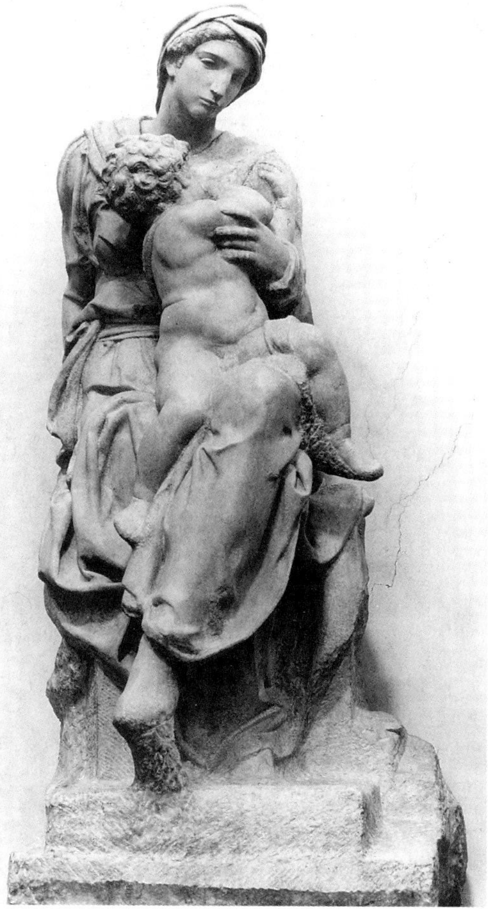

The dress of Parmigianino's Madonna is so thin as to reveal both her nipples and her navel. Its wine-red color contrasts effectively with her yellow aureole, but clashes with Saint Jerome's scarlet. As to the Baptist in the London picture, he also represents a complex and composite derivation. The pointing hand and arm was a motif closely associated with Leonardo. But the curious, starfishlike splaying of the fingers is an evident legacy from Correggio, and the massive bodily proportions from Michelangelo.

Vasari's extraordinary account of the Orpheus scene that occurred during the final stages of Parmigianino's work on the London altarpiece is well known—how, during the ghastly events of rape and destruction of the sack of 1527, some German troops entered the house and found what would have seemed an angelic child at work, heedless of them, on the huge picture; how they watched him paralyzed in amazement as though by an enchanter, and how they left him in peace for the price of some of his drawings. Later Parmigianino was briefly arrested by other soldiers and finally sent on his way by his uncle.

The use made by Parmigianino during his residence in Rome of ideas derived from works by Rosso and Michelangelo in Florence indicates, as we have seen, that he had stopped there on his way to Rome. He may then have halted at Siena. Anselmi

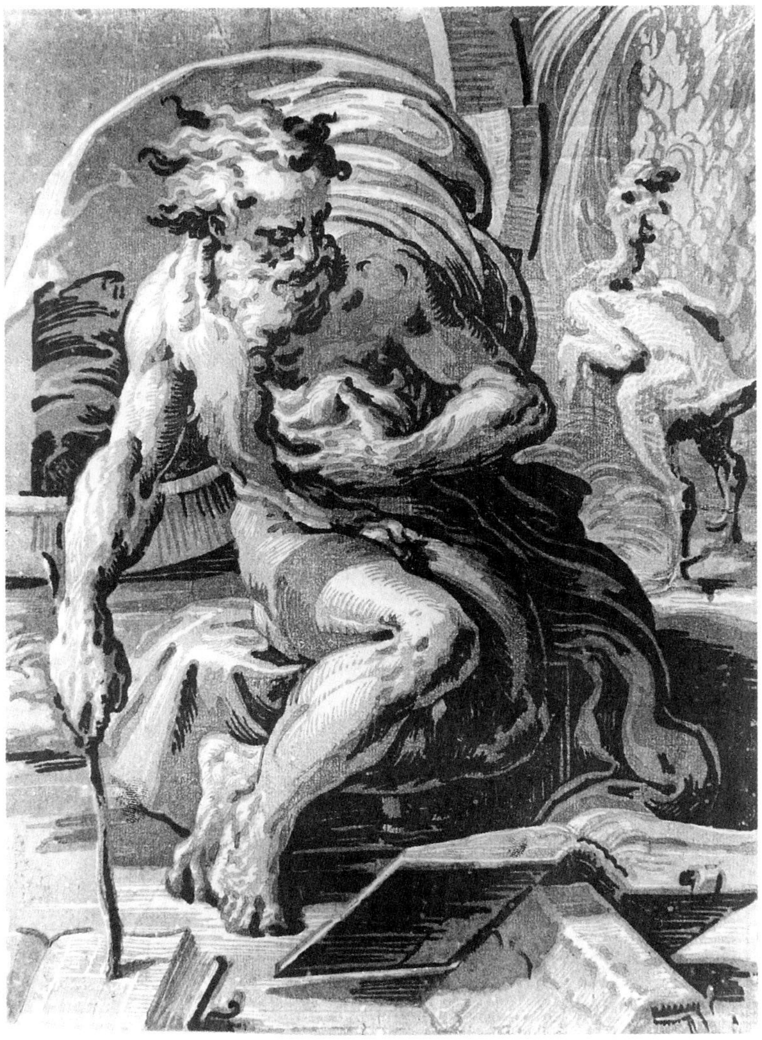

56. UGO DA CARPI (AFTER PARMIGIANINO)
Diogenes, n.d.
Chiaroscuro (cat. F1)

would certainly have told him of what had been done there by Beccafumi, some knowledge of whose exploration of the effects of torchlight may perhaps be traced in Parmigianino's frieze at the Steccata, painted after his return to Parma. Like Parmigianino, Beccafumi was interested in alchemy.[12] On the return journey as far as Bologna, Parmigianino could have taken the route via Ancona, where there was a major Titian of the Madonna in Glory. But if, as is more probable, he returned by the route that he is likely to have taken on the outward journey, that is, via Florence, he could hardly fail to have been interested in the amazing innovations of Pontormo, who had been working at the Certosa di Galluzzo and at Santa Felicita during the intervening three years since Parmigianino passed through the city. These paintings were revolutionary, showing a deliberate negation of traditional Renaissance perspective, modeling, and coloring alike. There are in fact suggestions of interaction between the art of Pontormo and of Parmigianino at this period. Parmigianino's *Diogenes* design, as known through Caraglio's engraving and Ugo da Carpi's chiaroscuro (fig. 56), bears a tantalizing resemblance to Pontormo's *Saint Jerome* (Hanover; fig. 57).[13] Yet it is difficult to see how one could have affected the other. Though neither is precisely dated, both are likely to date from the mid or later 1520s. But Pontormo's picture would have been painted in Florence, while Parmigianino's

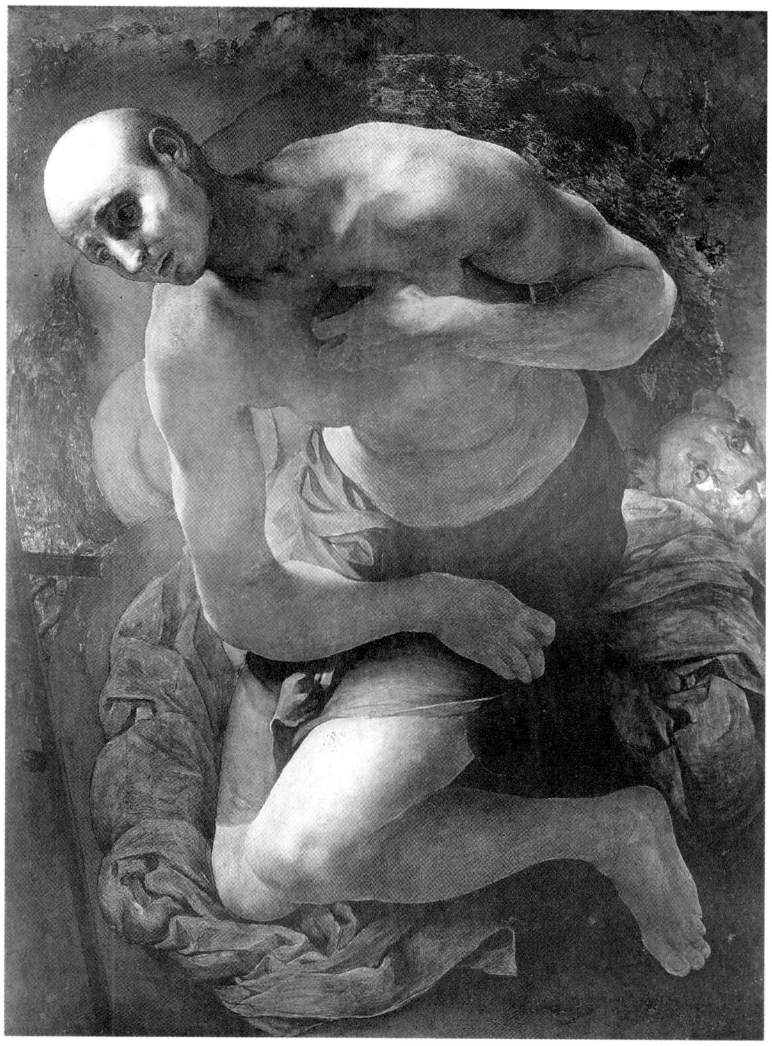

57. PONTORMO
Saint Jerome, c. 1527–28
Oil on panel, 41⅜ × 31½ in.
(105 × 80 cm)
Niedersächsisches, Hanover, Germany

Detail of fig. 58
PONTORMO
Visitation

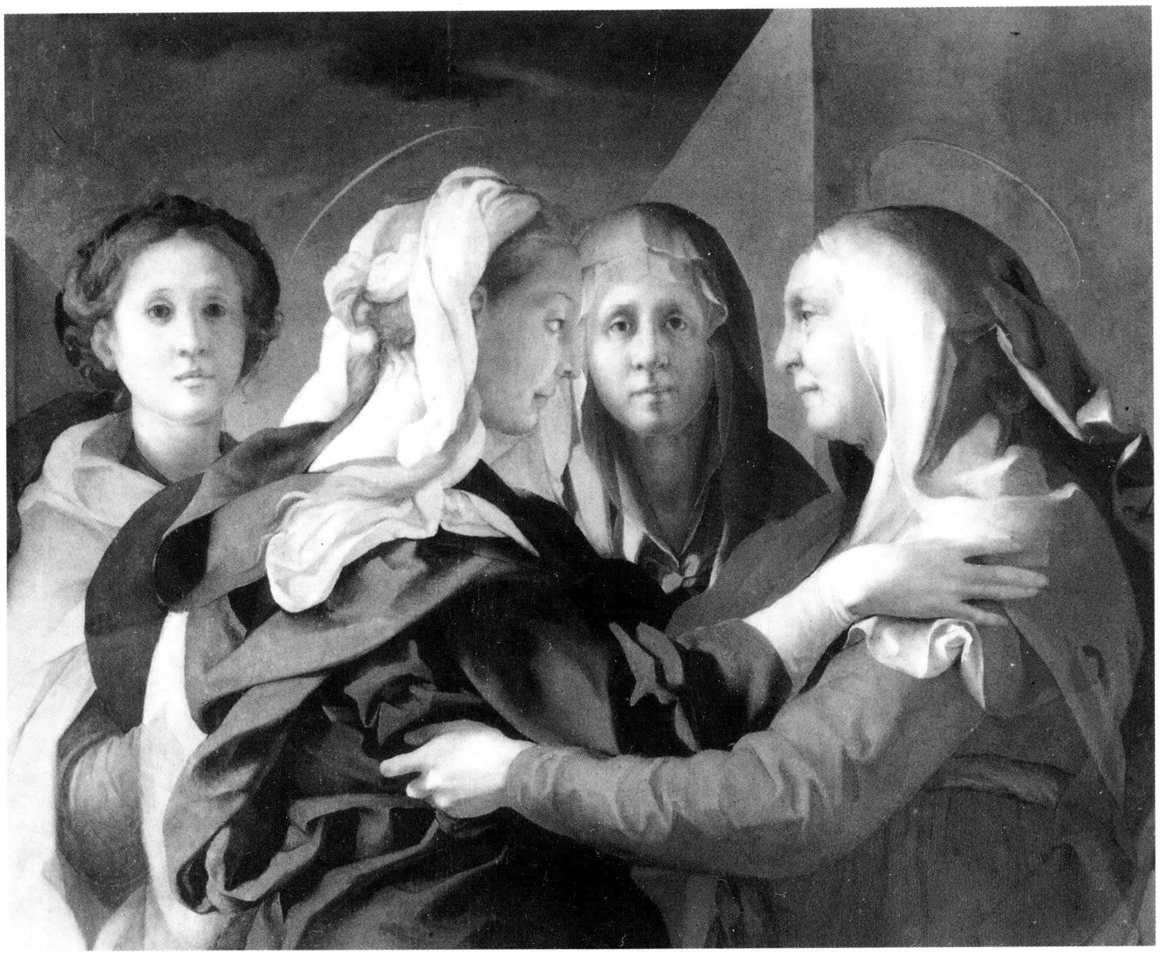

Detail of fig. 59
PARMIGIANINO
Study for the *Visitation*

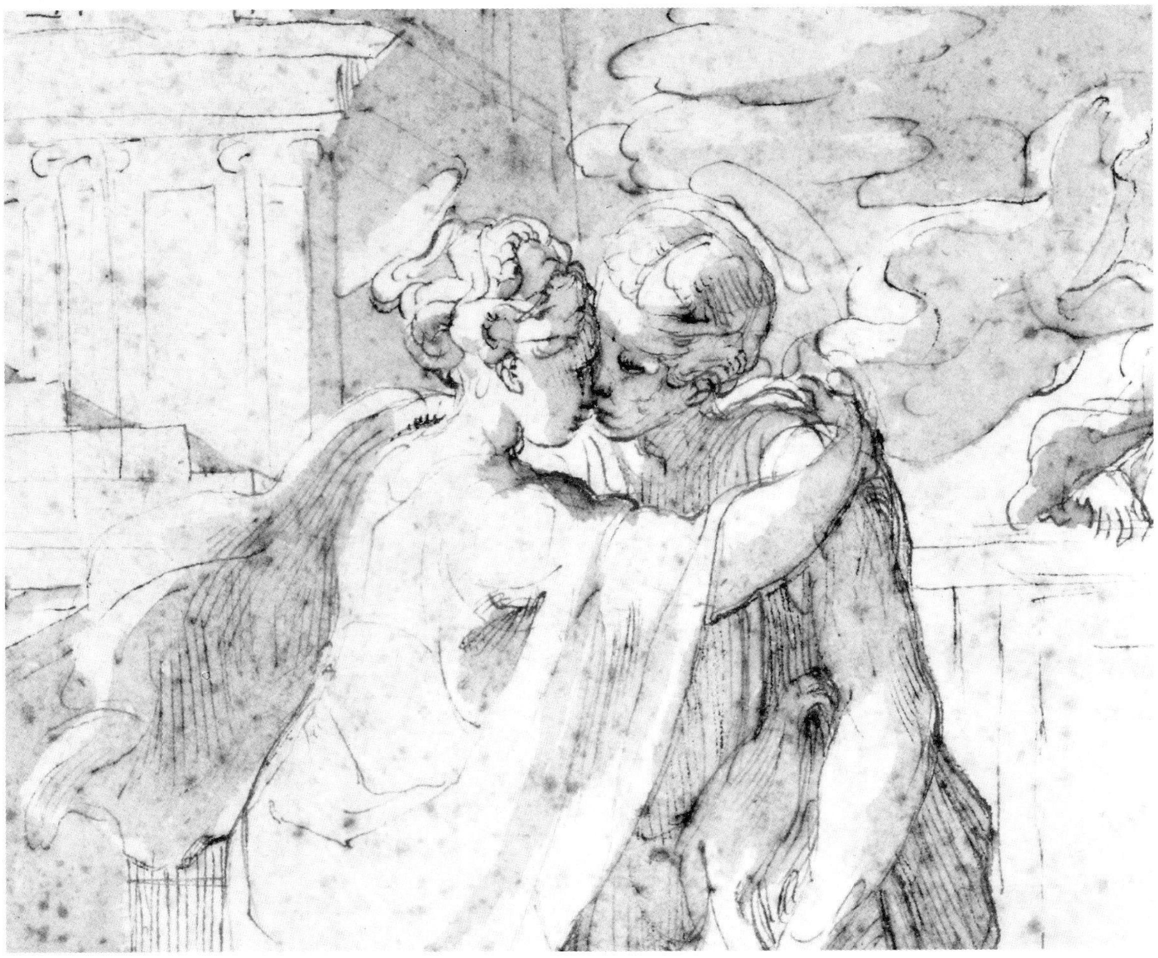

design dates from his Rome years (one of his drawings, P107, combines studies for it and for the London altarpiece). Conceivably an impression of the print or the chiaroscuro had already reached Florence. In another apparent instance of interaction, the sequence of events is less puzzling. This concerns Pontormo's marvelous painting the *Visitation* (fig. 58). It has long been in the parish church of Carmignano (Tuscany) but its original location is not known. It is not dated but probably dates from the later 1520s. Parmigianino's drawing of the same subject (P550), one of his most beautiful (fig. 59), almost certainly postdates this since the architecture is virtually the same as in the small Courtauld *Madonna* (fig. 72), which is datable to the Bologna years from 1527. The relation of the figures in this drawing to the architectural background seems to presuppose knowledge of Pontormo's painting. When, in addition, note is taken that the almost surrealist drop in the level of the middle distance in Pontormo's picture recurs in a very similar form in Parmigianino's *Madonna dal Collo Lungo* (fig. 110), which was not commissioned until December, 1534, it is difficult to resist the conclusion that Parmigianino did indeed return from Rome via Florence, and that there was personal contact there at this time between the two most talented of the post-peak painters. The degree of interaction was nevertheless limited. Pontormo, by this time, was too much committed to his revolutionary innovations to be seriously deflected by what little he could have seen of the art of the younger man; and he, Parmigianino, was to show that these innovations were only one element in his Pandora's box, which was to contain, in addition, his Roman impressions and, for the second time, his impressions of Correggio.

58. PONTORMO
Visitation, c. 1528
Oil on panel, 79½ × 61⅜ in.
(202 × 156 cm)
Pieve di San Michele, Carmignano
(Florence), Italy

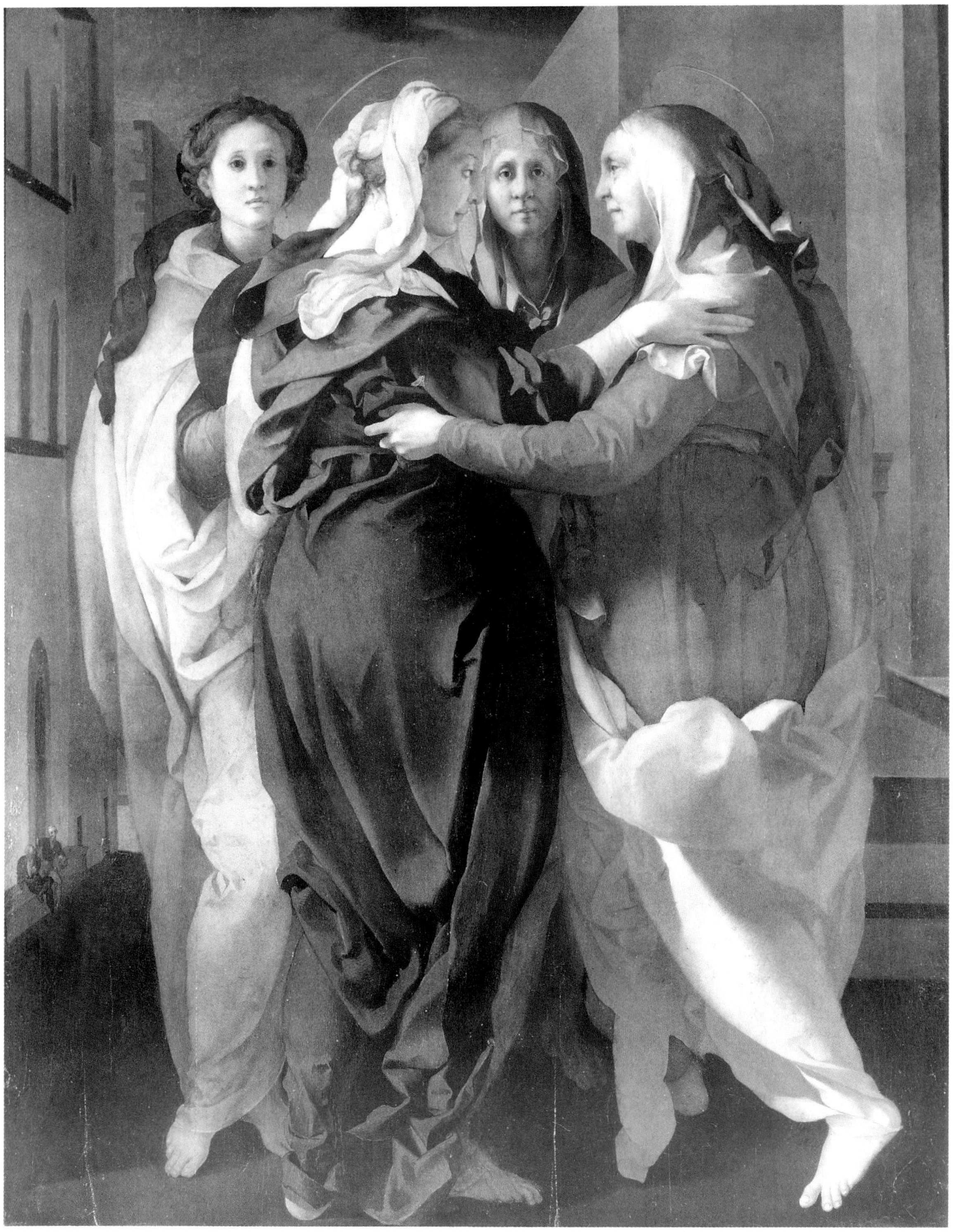

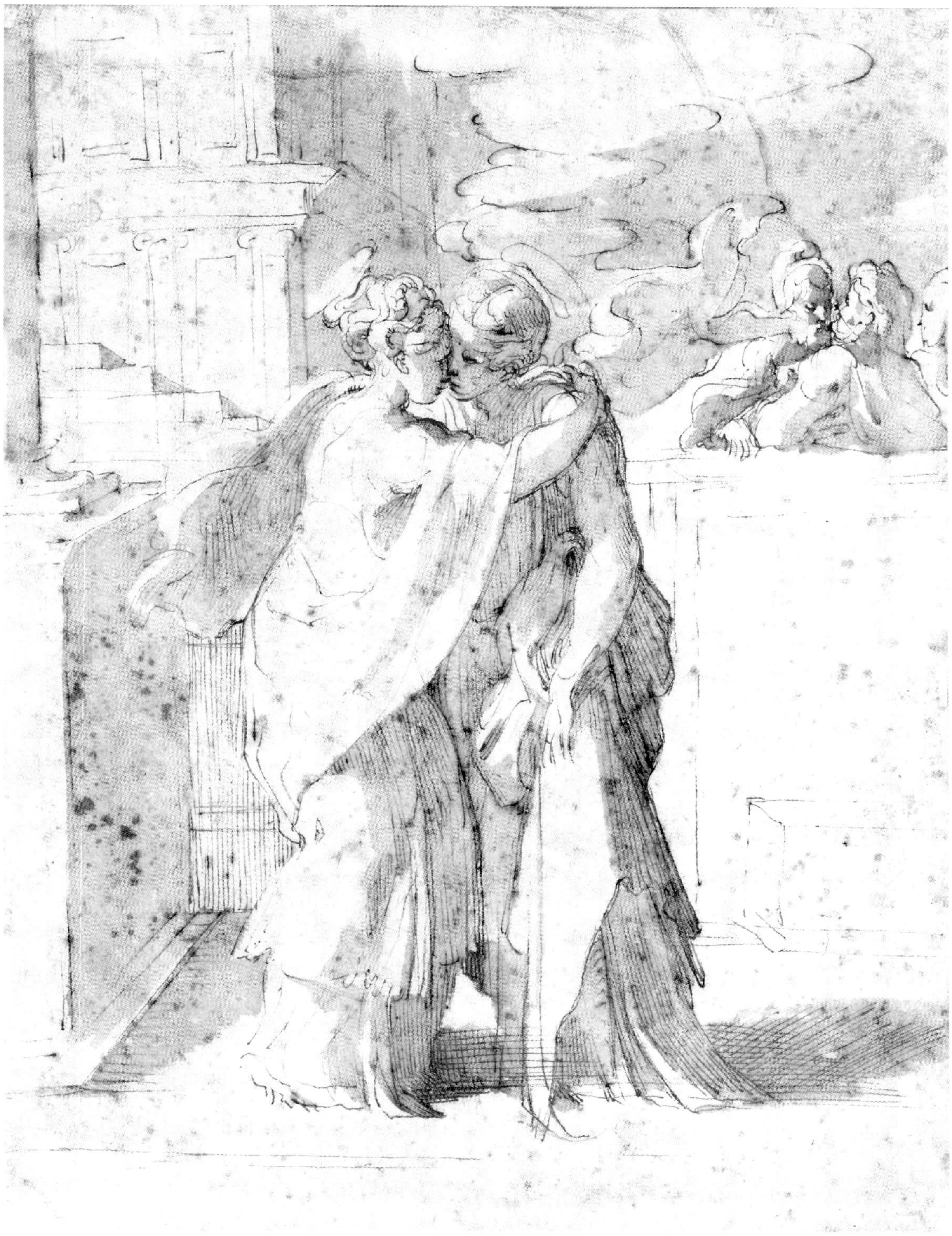

59. PARMIGIANINO

Study for the *Visitation,* n.d. P550

Pen and light brown ink and wash on paper, 7⅝ × 5⅞ in. (19.3 × 15 cm)

Galleria Nazionale, Parma, Italy

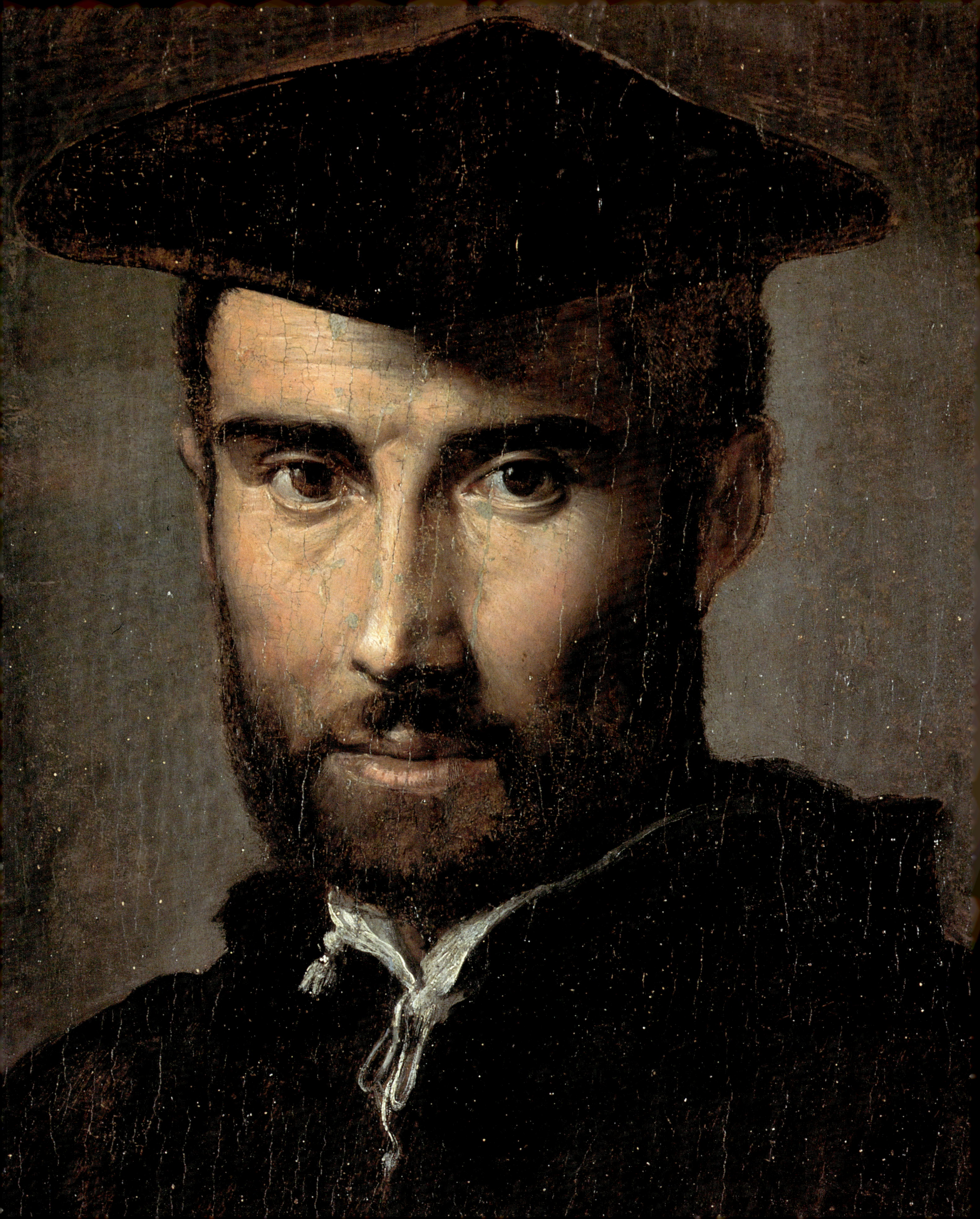

III

Bologna

When he eventually reached Bologna after his escape from Rome in 1527, Parmigianino would have found himself in a similar situation to that which had confronted Leonardo on arrival at Milan from Florence in the early 1480s. In both cases a young artist who had hitherto been one of many, and somewhat frustrated accordingly, now found himself the star turn. Bologna at this time was politically stable under the papacy, but it was as short of conspicuous native talent in the arts as Parma had been in the generation before Parmigianino's, or as Milan before Leonardo arrived. On the other hand, there were examples within the city of Bologna of the work of major masters from other centers, above all Raphael's *Saint Cecilia,* which had been sent from Rome around the year 1514. There was another, smaller Raphael, the *Vision of Ezekiel* (Pitti) in a private collection, the Hercolani, which also had a Correggio, the *Noli Me Tangere,* now in the Prado. Vasari implies that Parmigianino had not intended to stop in Bologna on his way home to Parma, that he did so because he found that the place and the people pleased him. But instead of remaining there "for some months," as Vasari says, he stayed there for three years or more—until Correggio left Parma.

After Parmigianino's early success as a prodigy at Parma, these years at Bologna were the most prosperous in his short and hectic career, but at first he worked mainly in graphics. Vasari says that at this time Parmigianino had woodcuts made in the process called chiaroscuro, in which the use of more than one block for the same design was intended to simulate contrasts of light and shade. The pioneer of this process in Italy was Ugo da Carpi, who had been in Rome when Parmigianino was there. His large and splendid print of Parmigianino's *Diogenes* (fig. 56) may indeed have been made at that time, though it could, alternatively, have been made not from Parmigianino's drawing but from Caraglio's metal engraving.

One of the cutters whom Parmigianino used at this time was Nicolò Vicentino. He is a shadowy figure, and only one chiaroscuro definitely by him and definitely after Parmigianino is known—the *Christ Healing the Lepers,* after a Raphaelesque design by Parmigianino at Chatsworth (P690). In this he fails to translate the majesty of Parmigianino's figure of Christ. Another of Parmigianino's Raphaelesque designs, the fine wash-drawing (P137) *Adoration of the Magi,* was also reproduced in a chiaroscuro reasonably attributed to Nicolò, and at this time or later Giulio Bonasone engraved several of Parmigianino's paintings on copper. A more substantial wood engraver with whom Parmigianino collaborated at

Detail of fig. 87
PARMIGIANINO
A Prelate

Bologna, and who later stole from him, was Antonio da Trento. Vasari names four chiaroscuro prints by him after Parmigianino—the *Martyrdom of Saints Peter and Paul* (which had already been engraved on metal by Caraglio), *Augustus and the Sibyl* (in which the figure of the Sibyl more or less repeats that of Judith in one of Parmigianino's own etchings), a *Naked Man Seen from the Back,* and finally a *Madonna* in an oval format. These prints, and others not named by Vasari, are conspicuously beautiful in themselves and also convey much of the subtlety of Parmigianino's drawings. In particular, the one of the naked man—and another, similar print not cited by Vasari but vouched for by several authentic drawings, representing the young Baptist in the wilderness—are of a type—nude figures seen against forest vegetation—in which Parmigianino excelled. His own etching *Lovers in a Wood* (fig. 60) is of this kind.

Parmigianino's reputation as the first major Italian artist to practice etching can hardly be disputed. The idea of magic—of transmutation of one substance into another—that was inherent in the process would have had an obvious appeal. Another is less obvious. If his etching, already mentioned, *Lovers in a Wood,* is compared with his preliminary drawing for it (P612; fig. 61), the point is made. Not only are the contrasts of light and

Below, left:
60. PARMIGIANINO
Lovers in a Wood, n.d.
Etching (cat. D4)

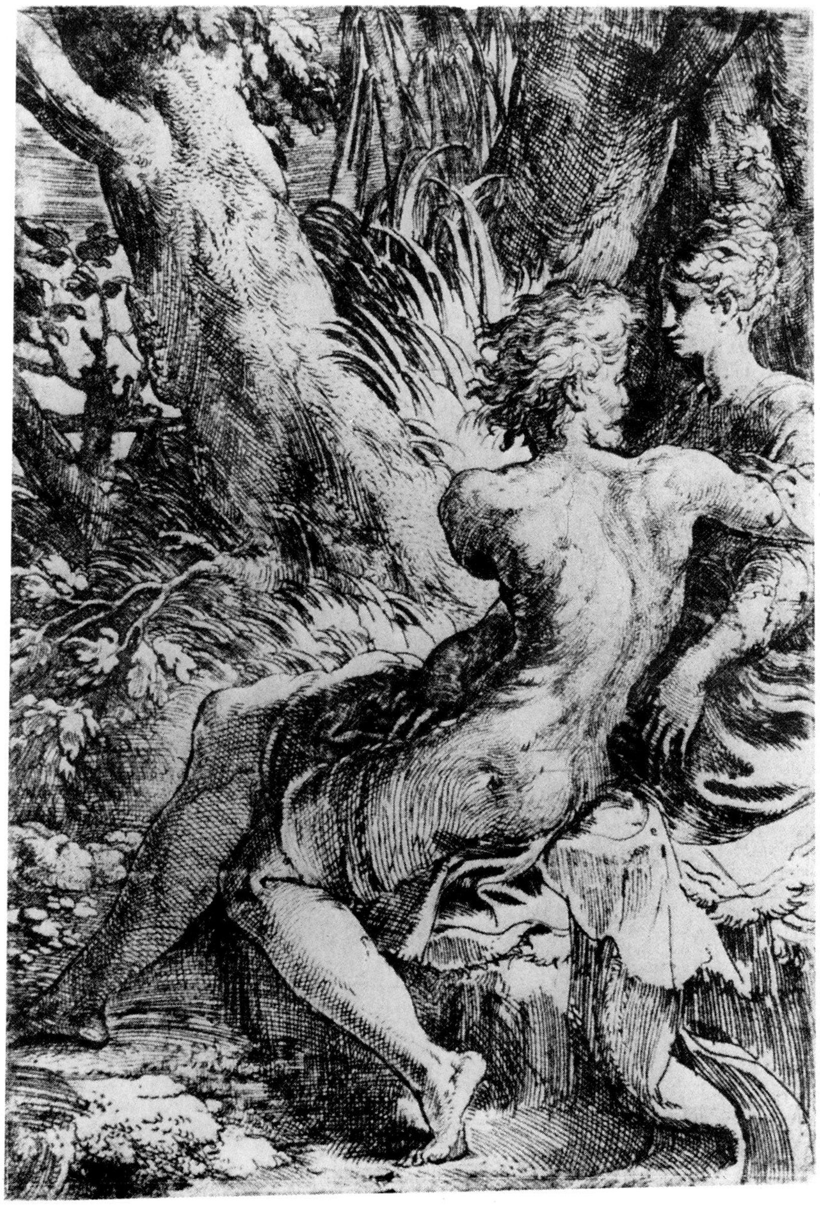

Below, right:
61. PARMIGIANINO
Study for *Lovers in a Wood,* n.d. P612
Black chalk over stylus, heightened with white on paper, 4½ × 3¼ in. (11.5 × 8.2 cm)
Graphische Sammlung Albertina, Vienna

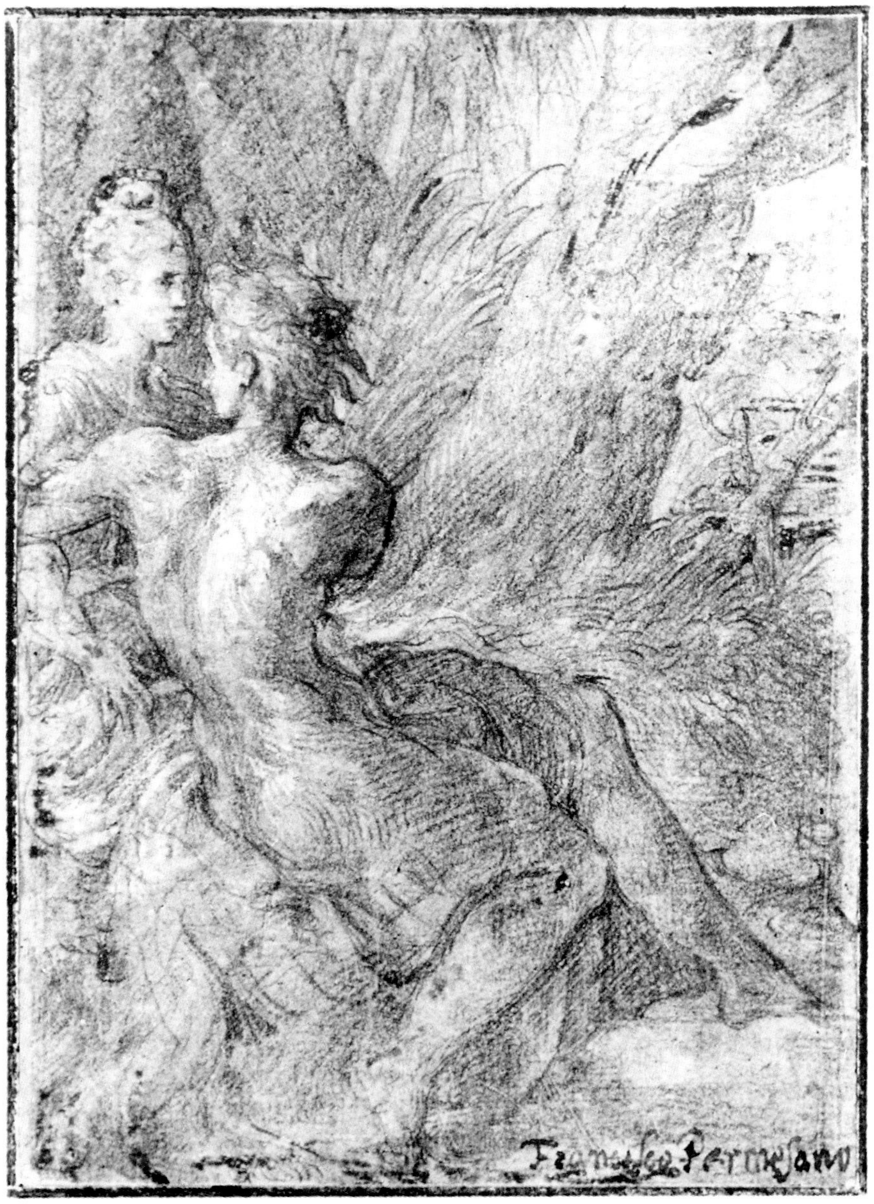

shade greater in the etching than the drawing; the etching also has more refinement of detail, since the etcher's needle, expertly handled, is capable of giving a finer line than chalk or even pen and ink.

Vasari is not very informative on the subject of Parmigianino's etchings. He names three—a *Nativity,* a *Lamentation,* and one after an unspecified tapestry by Raphael. The latter may, as we have seen, have been either the *Paul Preaching at Athens* or the *Healing of the Lame Man.* Vasari adds that there were "many others." In fact, nine existing etchings are vouched for as Parmigianino's own by authentic drawings, and about half a dozen others are currently attributed to him. None of them can be dated precisely, but for the two most elaborate and ambitious—the *Resurrection* (fig. 62) and the *Entombment* (fig. 63)—there may be a terminus a quo. In the *Resurrection* the figure of the soldier on the right repeats the Saint George in Correggio's altarpiece painted for Modena and now in Dresden (fig. 64). We know that this was finished by 1530. It is true that at this stage of his life Correggio seems to have undergone some degree of influence from Parmigianino, his junior by several years.[1] But in the case of this figure the priority was probably Correggio's, and therefore Parmigianino's etching is likely to date from after his return to Parma. The idea that he includes in the etching of one of the soldiers' using his shield to protect his eyes against the light from the risen Christ had been included by Raphael in designs for a major altarpiece of the Resurrection, which he never carried out in paint.[2] Parmigianino's design is masterly, and also unique in type among his work. It is almost Baroque in its swagger, and no previous graphic artist, not even Dürer, had achieved the force of the blinding light that surrounds the risen Christ.

For the other major etching—the *Entombment*—Parmigianino did a preliminary version in the opposite sense. The most striking figure in it, the ecstatically swooning Virgin Mary, who sets the emotional tone of the scene, recalls the same figure in Correggio's painting of the *Pietà* (Parma), which is datable around the year 1524, and this serves again as a terminus a quo for the etching. But it was the figure of the dead Christ extended sideways, which itself derives ultimately from the antique relief *The Death of Meleager,* which was to be the most influential. Echoes of Parmigianino's figure recur not only in painted versions of the Entombment such as Tintoretto's or Prospero Fontana's, but also in the relief representations of sculptors as much separated in time and place as Jacopo Sansovino, Giambologna, and Jean Goujon.[3]

The industry—for it can hardy have been less—that seems to have grown up within Parmigianino's lifetime and that continued without his supervision, for propagating his designs—and his influences—in the form of etchings, engravings, and chiaroscuro prints, included a series of etchings of small figures of apostles; and a further series of classical deities and heroes was perhaps intended, it has been suggested, for playing cards. These are inscribed with Parmigianino's initials—"F.P."—but were evidently not etched by Parmigianino himself. The identity of the artist who signed "F.P." is not established. The name of Antonio da Trento, already mentioned, has been suggested, and also Antonio Fantuzzi.

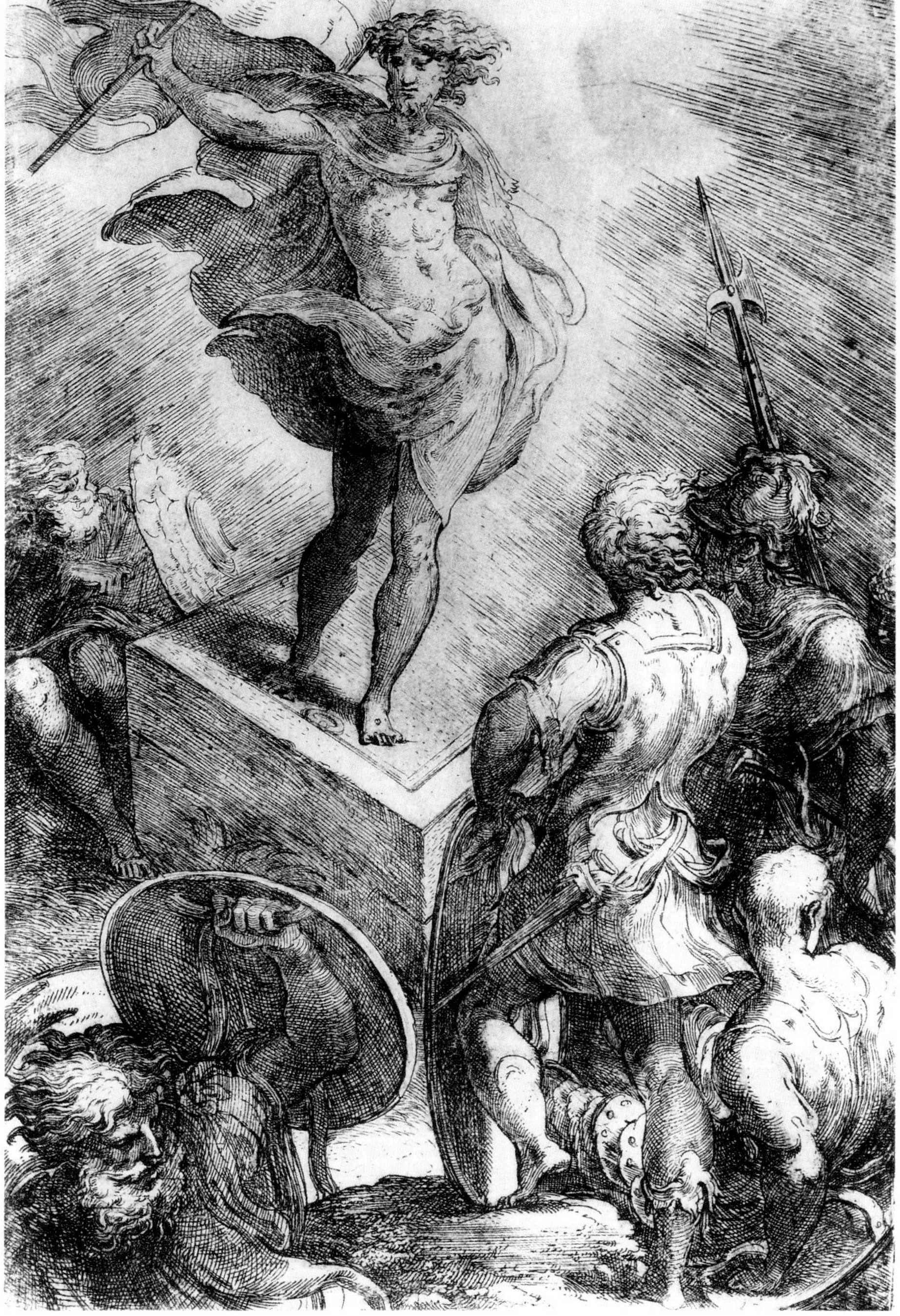

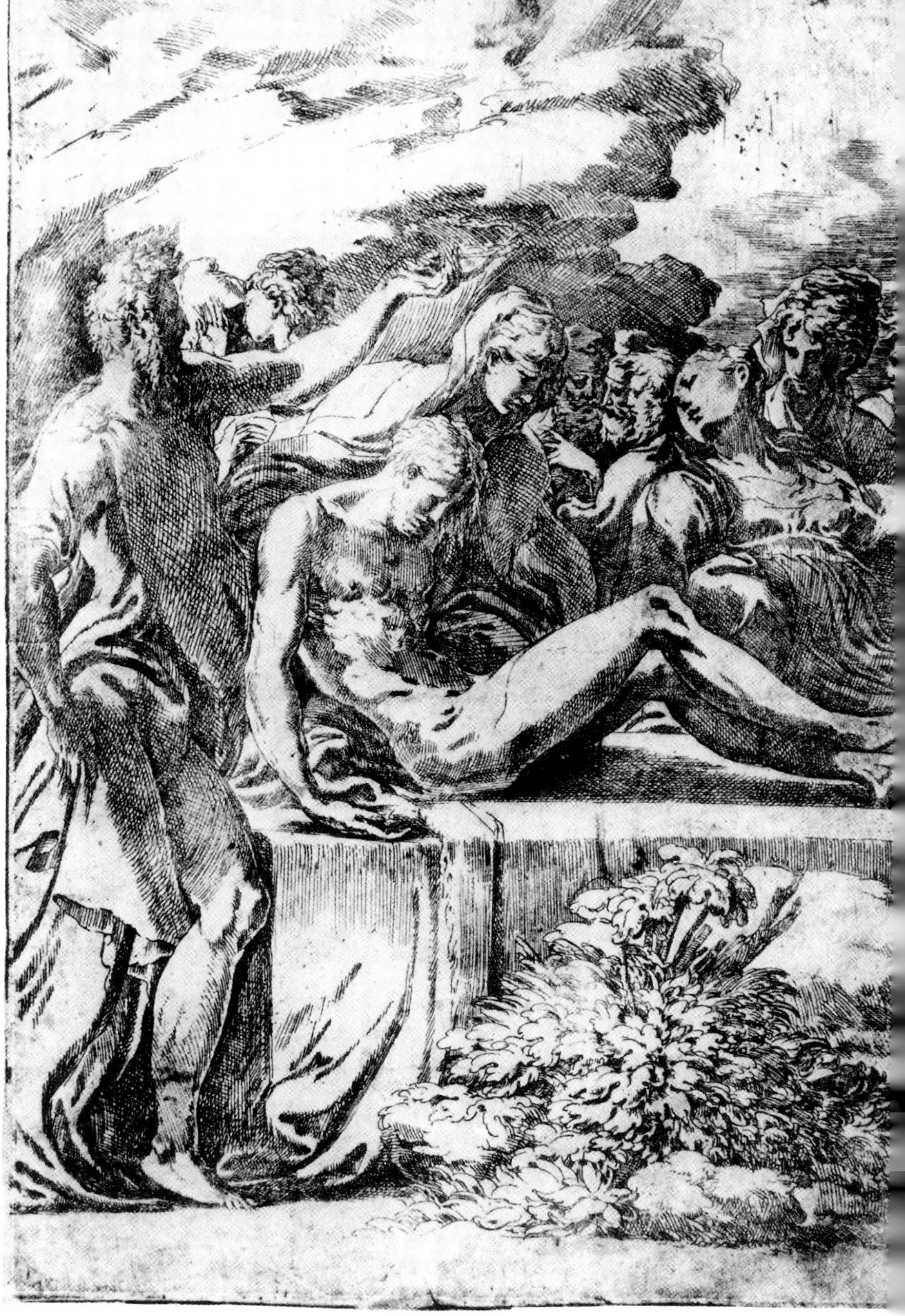

62. PARMIGIANINO
Resurrection, n.d.
Etching (cat. D6)

63. PARMIGIANINO
Entombment of Christ, n.d.
Etching (cat. D2)

Opposite:
64. CORREGGIO
Madonna with Saint George and Others,
c. 1530–32. Oil on panel, 112¼ × 74¾ in.
(285 × 190 cm)
Gemäldegalerie, Dresden, Germany

62. Parmigianino
Resurrezione
Acquaforte
(Cat. D6)

63. Parmigianino
Deposizione nel Sepolcro
Acquaforte
(Cat. D2)

Nella pagina a lato:
64. Correggio
Madonna con S. Giorgio e altri personaggi
Gemäldegalerie, Dresda

Both of these identifications are no more than speculative, and to increase the confusion it has been suggested (and denied) that Trento and Fantuzzi were the same person. Such of Parmigianino's drawings for the second series—of classical figures—as have survived are among his most marvelous feats. No more than ten centimeters high, they provide a total illusion of fascinating beauty. A philosopher sits sideways in the Michelangelesque posture of the Madonna in the London *Marriage of Saint Catherine.* Minerva is shown at full length, her profile in shadow, the light on the draperies that flutter behind her. The muscular form of Mutius Scaevola is seen from the back, a long curved sword at his hip and an elaborate helmet shielding his averted face (P726v; fig. 65).[4]

After speaking of Parmigianino's work in graphics, on his arrival at Bologna Vasari adds, that before long he [illegible] His first

l'acquaforte. Ma è la figura del Cristo morto, che si allunga da una parte all'altra dell'opera e che deriva fondamentalmente dal bassorilievo classico della *Morte di Meleagro*, a esercitare poi la maggiore influenza. Echi della figura del Parmigianino non solo si trovano nelle versioni dipinte della Deposizione nel sepolcro, come quelle di Tintoretto o di Prospero Fontana, ma anche nelle rappresentazioni in bassorilievo di scultori distanti nel tempo e nello spazio come Jacopo Sansovino, Giambologna o Jean Goujon.

L'industria, perché non può essere definita in modo diverso, che sembra essersi sviluppata all'epoca del Parmigianino e che pare sia continuata anche dopo, senza la sua supervisione, con l'intenzione di diffonderne i disegni e l'influenza tramite incisioni, acqueforti e stampe a chiaroscuro, comprendeva una serie di incisioni di piccole figure di apostoli ed un'altra serie dedicata a divinità ed eroi classici che forse, come qualcuno ha suggerito, erano state ideate come carte da gioco. Fontano

86

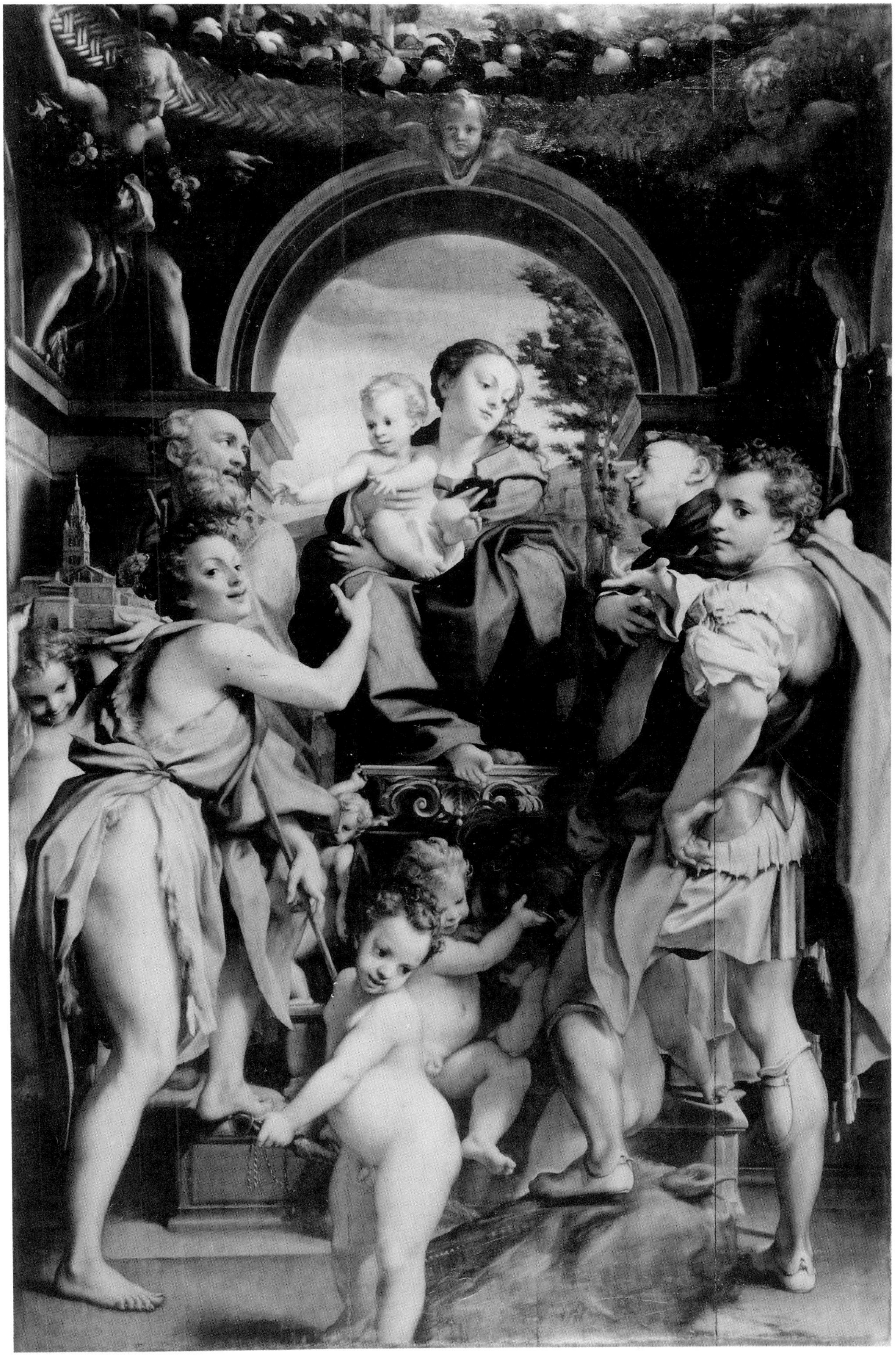

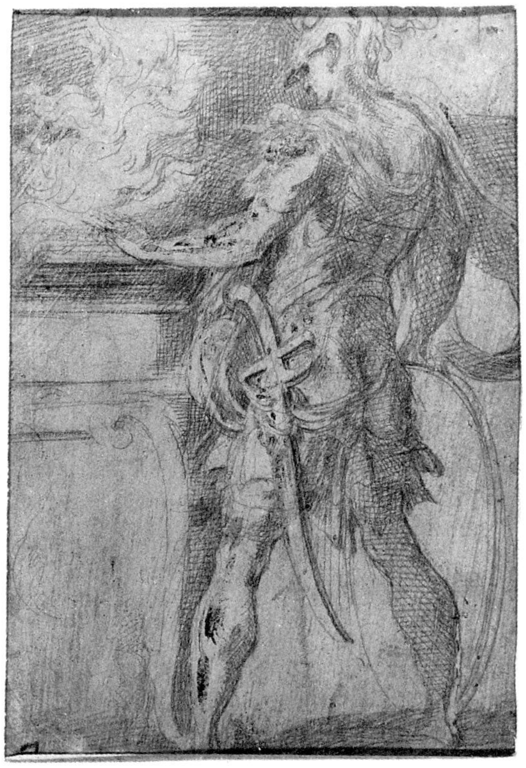

65. PARMIGIANINO
Mutius Scaevola, n.d. P726v
Metalpoint on yellowish ground, heightened with white on paper, 4 × 2⅞ in. (10.3 × 7.3 cm)
Chatsworth, Derbyshire, England

commission of this kind, again according to Vasari, was the altarpiece *Saint Roch,* which, unique among Parmigianino's altarpieces, is still in its original place in San Petronio (fig. 66); next, still following Vasari's chronology, a *Conversion of Saul* that, after much discussion, it is now generally agreed is the picture in Vienna; then a Madonna with other figures—probably the *Marriage of Saint Catherine* (London; fig. 74). At some stage of the Bologna period Vasari specifies a *Saint Margaret* for the nuns of the convent of that name (fig. 67), and finally two paintings that evidently dated from the end of Parmigianino's residence in Bologna, that is, from 1529–30. These are a Madonna and Child with a globe —the *Madonna della Rosa,* now in Dresden (fig. 88)—and a portrait of the Emperor Charles v, now in New York (fig. 91).

Vasari's wording leaves no doubt that he thought the San Petronio altar was Parmigianino's first commission in Bologna for a painting, and stylistic considerations offer no objection to this view. But it may be necessary to depart from Vasari's sequence in some other instances, since he, and later critics, have assumed that all the pictures that Parmigianino painted for residents of Bologna dated from the years of the artist's own residence in that city, and that the same principle applied to Parma. But in this case stylistic considerations suggest that this was not always true. Bologna and Parma are only about one hundred kilometers (sixty-five miles) apart, and the country between them, being entirely flat, would make for an easy journey. Furthermore there is evidence, as well as inherent probability, that Parmigianino maintained some degree of contact with friends in one city while resident in the other. And in the case of two of his paintings support may be found for the assumption that crosscurrents of this kind do occur.

The Vienna *Conversion of Saul,* for instance, was described by Vasari in the context of pictures painted in Bologna, but the panoramic landscape and the high finish of its handling ally it with the Uffizi *Madonna with Saint Zachariah* (fig. 107), a picture that, on documentary indications, was painted for the most part after Parmigianino had returned to Parma, though the patron was a native of Bologna. Conversely, the Vienna *Cupid* (fig. 93), though originally belonging to Parmigianino's loyal friend, the Cavaliere Baiardi of Parma, shows a different and softer touch, and I suspect it dates from an earlier period. These two paintings will be discussed later.

The *Saint Roch,* being for a private chapel (of the Monsignori, according to Vasari) dedicated to that saint in the city's largest church (and one of the world's largest), namely San Petronio, was a commission of some importance. Preliminary drawings show the artist toying with different attitudes for the saint, at one time striding, at another kneeling, before settling for the indeterminate, ecstatic, and ultimately Correggesque posture of the painting. The huge figure of the saint looms over the altar in the chapel and almost touches the frame of the picture on three sides. The result is perhaps not the most successful of Parmigianino's religious pictures, though it is the largest. The saint's statutory dog and the donor are fitted into the pattern formed by the saint's splayed legs and left arm with no consideration of recession—possibly a legacy from Pontormo. The donor

Opposite:
66. PARMIGIANINO
Saint Roch and Donor, 1527
Oil on panel, 106¼ × 77½ in. (270 × 197 cm)
San Petronio, Bologna, Italy (cat. A4)

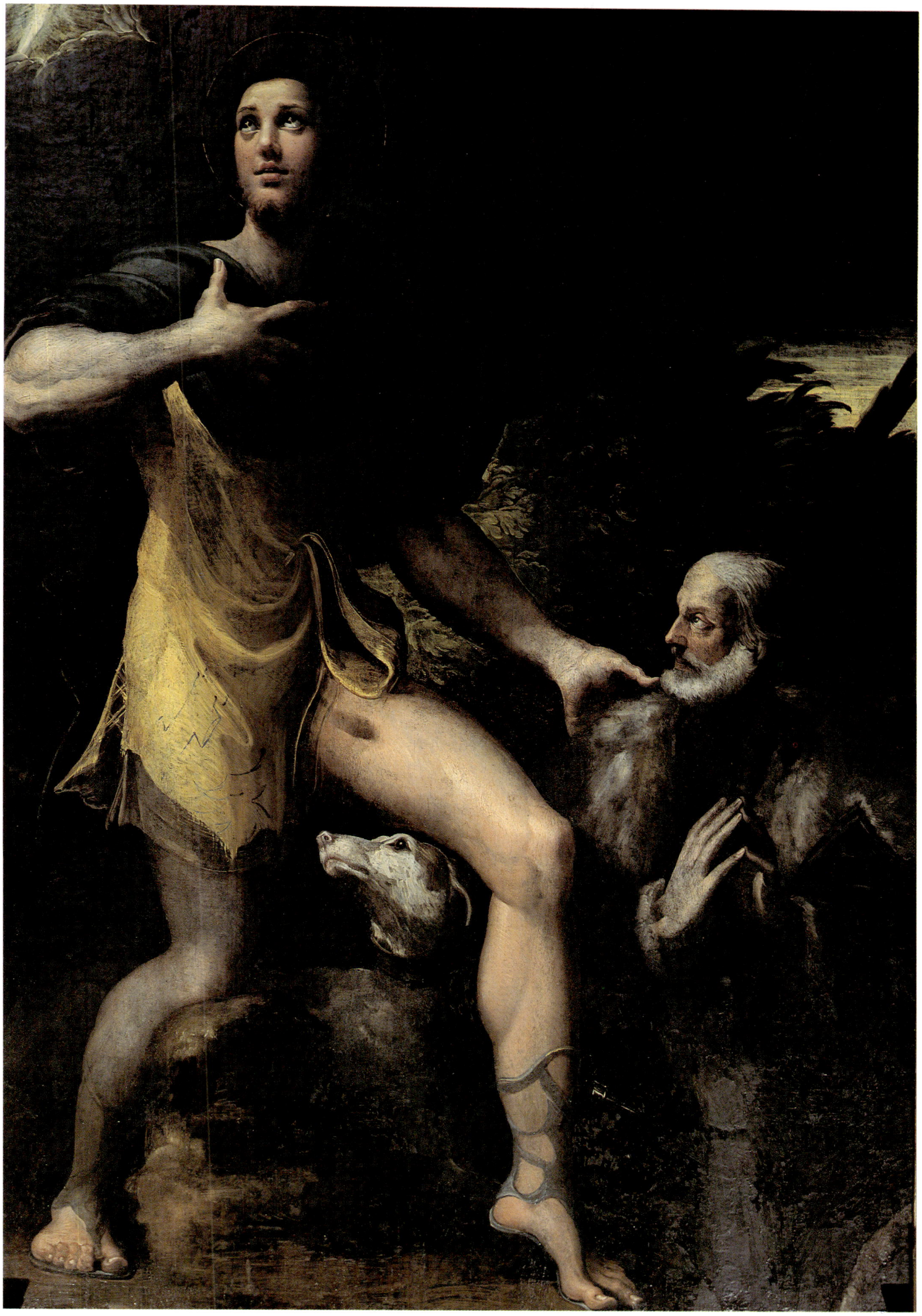

67. Parmigianino
Madonna col Bambino, i Santi Margherita e Girolamo, un Santo Mitrato e un Angelo, 1529 ca.
Tavola, cm 204x149
Pinacoteca Nazionale, Bologna
(Cat. A3)

(ill. 108), un dipinto che, secondo i documenti, fu realizzato per lo più dopo che il Parmigianino era tornato a Parma, anche se il committente risiedeva a Bologna. Il *Cupido* di Vienna (ill. 93), al contrario, anche se originariamente apparteneva al fedele amico del Parmigianino, il Cavalier Baiardi di Parma, mostra un tocco diverso e più leggero e ho il sospetto che sia stato realizzato in un periodo precedente. Ma di questi due dipinti parleremo più avanti.

Il *S. Rocco* destinato ad una cappella privata (la cappella Monsignori, secondo il Vasari) dedicata a quel santo nella più grande chiesa della città (ed una delle più grandi del mondo), cioè S. Petronio, costituiva una commissione piuttosto importante. I disegni preparatori mostrano come l'artista si sia dilettato a studiare diverse posizioni per il santo (una volta in movimento, una volta in ginocchio) prima di decidere la posa vaga, estatica e, in ultima analisi correggesca, del dipinto finale. L'enorme figura del santo appare in lontananza sopra l'altare della cappella e sfiora quasi la cornice del quadro su tre lati. Anche se è il più grande, il dipinto non è il più riuscito tra quelli a carattere religioso del Parmigianino.

L'immancabile cane del santo ed il donatore sono inseriti nello spazio formato dalle gambe divaricate ed il braccio sinistro, senza considerare l'effetto dovuto ai piani di profondità, probabilmente secondo lo stile del Pontormo. Il donatore viene variamente identificato con Baldassarre da Milano (da Lamo) o con Fabrizio da Milano (dal Vasari). E' stato anche suggerito un terzo candidato, il poeta Giorgio Anselmi.

Più significativa è l'altra pala d'altare di Bologna, la *Madonna col Bambino e S. Margherita*. Anche se poteva sembrare una commissione di poco conto (la chiesa delle monache di S. Margherita per la quale fu dipinta e che fu soppressa durante il periodo napoleonico, viene descritta dallo Scaramuccia come «piccola»[5]), il risultato dell'opera è tra i più pregevoli del Parmigianino. A differenza della pala d'altare precedente, la *Madonna e Santi* (quella di Londra), e di quella seguente (la *Madonna dal Collo Lungo*), questa volta non si nota alcuno sforzo di elaborare una composizione originale, ma l'impressione può anche essere sbagliata perché solo pochi dei disegni preparatori sono arrivati fino a noi.

Il Parmigianino, comunque, sembra aver guardato, e con buoni risultati, all'evento artistico più sensazionale della zona: la pala d'altare della *Madonna con S. Girolamo* (ill. 68) del Correggio, che era stata ordinata da un committente privato a Parma parecchi anni prima che il Parmigianino andasse a Bologna e dove era stata finalmente installata nel 1528. La conoscenza del quadro del Correggio da parte del Parmigianino è un indizio che egli abbia visitato Parma mentre era a Bologna. Nella sua prima edizione il Vasari dice che il Parmigianino trascorse qualche tempo a Parma dopo aver lasciato Roma e prima di stabilirsi a Bologna. C'è persino una possibilità che egli abbia fatto domanda per ottenere la commissione di una pala d'altare per Parma perchè uno dei suoi disegni (P99) rappresenta lo stesso soggetto – la *Madonna in Gloria con i Santi Rocco e Sebastiano* – di una pala d'altare dipinta in quello stesso periodo dall'Anselmi per la cattedrale di Parma[6].

Come nella *Madonna con S. Girolamo* del Correggio, il Parmigianino ambienta la sua *Madonna con S. Margherita* all'aperto, privando così la Madonna del suo trono. In tutti e due i casi, inoltre, il santo più importante, S. Maria Maddalena nel Correggio e S. Margherita nel Parmigianino, si inginocchia difronte al Bambino. E ancora, in tutti e due i casi questo particolare può essere visto come un adattamento della posa tradizionale di S. Caterina in uno Sposalizio di S. Caterina che il Vasari, nella prima edizione, erroneamente, ma comprensibilmente, attribuisce al Correggio. Nel caso del Parmigianino il rapporto tra i due soggetti è anche sottolineato (Vasari

67. PARMIGIANINO
Madonna and Child with Saints Margaret and Jerome, a Mitred Saint, and an Angel, c. 1529
Oil on panel, 80¼ × 58⅝ in. (204 × 149 cm)
Pinacoteca Nazionale, Bologna, Italy (cat. A3)

himself is variously identified as Baldassare da Milano (by Lamo) and as Fabrizio da Milano (by Vasari). A third candidate, the poet Giorgio Anselmi, has also been suggested.

More significant is the other Bologna altarpiece—the *Madonna and Child with Saint Margaret*. Though this may not have seemed a very important commission—the church of the nuns of Saint Margaret, for which it was painted and which was suppressed in the Napoleonic period, is described by Scaramuccia as "small"—the result was one of Parmigianino's greatest achievements. Unlike his previous *Madonna and Saints* altarpiece (the London one) and his next (the *Madonna dal Collo Lungo*) there is no evidence this time of striving for an original design, though this may be a false impression, since only a few of the preliminary drawings survive. In any event, Parmigianino seems to have turned, and to good effect, to the latest sensation in the region—Correggio's *Madonna with Saint Jerome* altarpiece (fig. 68), which had been ordered by a private patron in Parma several years before Parmigianino reached Bologna, and which had finally been installed in 1528. Parmigianino's knowledge of Correggio's picture is one indication that he visited Parma from Bologna. In his first edition Vasari said that Parmigianino spent some time at Parma after leaving Rome and before settling at Bologna. There is even a possibility that he applied during the Bologna years for a commission for an altarpiece for Parma, since one of his drawings (P99) is of the same subject—the Madonna in Glory with Saints Roch and Sebastian—as an altarpiece painted at about this time by Anselmi for Parma cathedral.[6]

As in Correggio's *Madonna with Saint Jerome*, Parmigianino sets the scene of his *Madonna with Saint Margaret* in the open air, thereby depriving the Madonna of her throne. In both cases, also, the most conspicuous saint—Correggio's Saint Mary Magdalene, Parmigianino's Saint Margaret—kneels to the Christ Child. In both cases again this can be seen as an adaptation of the traditional pose of Saint Catherine in a Marriage of Saint Catherine—which Vasari, in his first edition, mistakenly but understandably thought was actually the subject of Correggio's picture. The interconnection of the two subjects in Parmigianino's case is also indicated by the fact that a study in the Uffizi (P79; fig. 69) for the whole composition of the *Madonna with Saint Margaret* shows the head of Saint Margaret as more like that of Saint Catherine in the *Marriage of Saint Catherine* (London; fig. 74) than her eventual form in the Bologna altarpiece.

The most striking difference between Correggio's and Parmigianino's altarpieces is in the lighting. Where Correggio bathes his figures in sunlight, Parmigianino's are lit by a mysterious pale glow. This pervades the Bologna picture to such an extent that the sleeve of the Madonna's dress, though actually pale pink, absorbs some of the gold from the surrounding colors. As to the general effect, the spontaneous, almost hedonistic mood of Correggio's picture is replaced in Parmigianino's by a mystical, otherworldly, almost trancelike effect. The expression on Saint Margaret's face is ecstatic, her eye itself almost glaucous.

In some ways the most interesting feature of the Saint Margaret altarpiece is the technique. The three most prominent heads in the center of the picture, those of Saint Margaret, the Madonna, and the Christ Child, are highly finished (

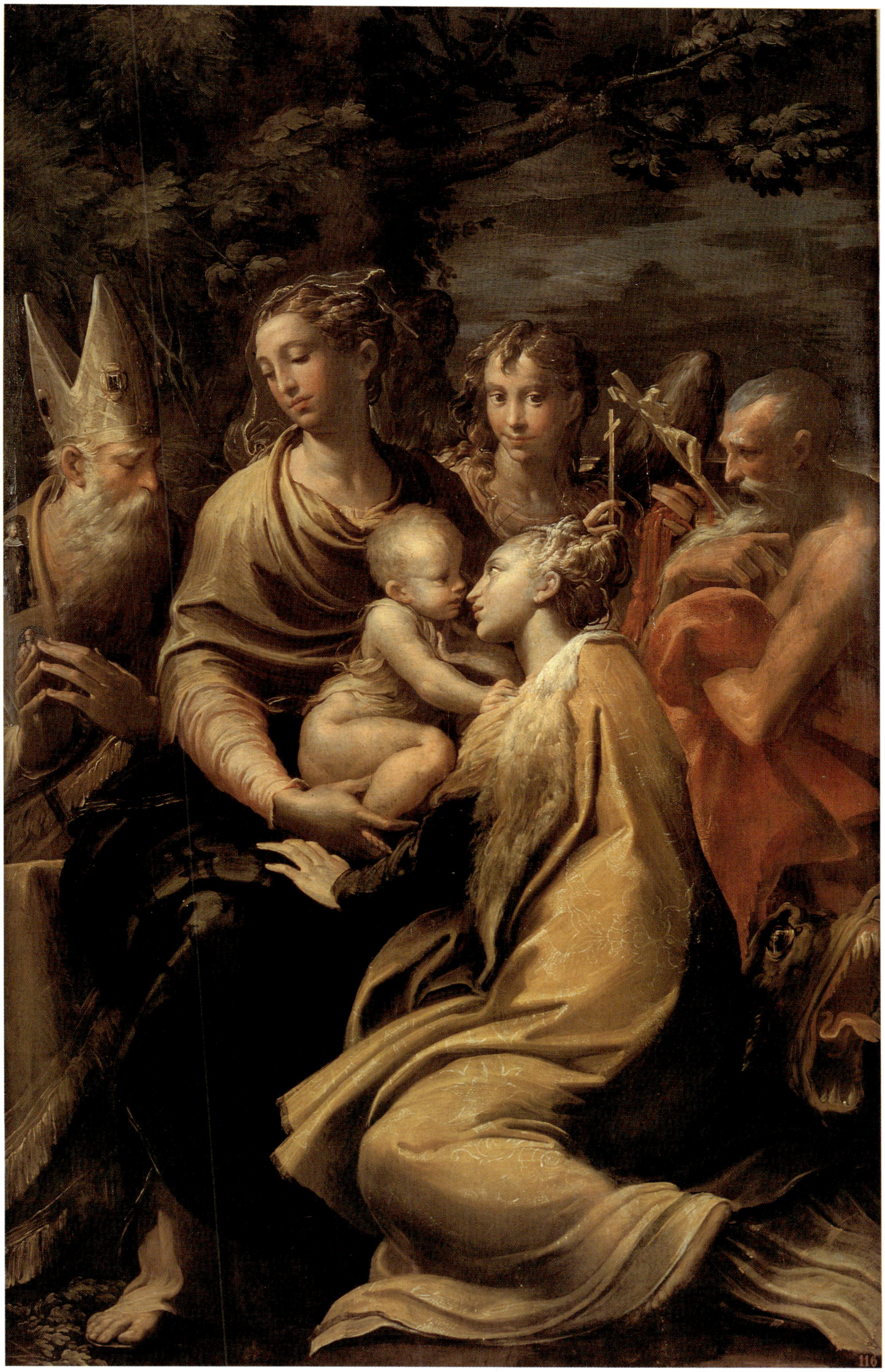
116

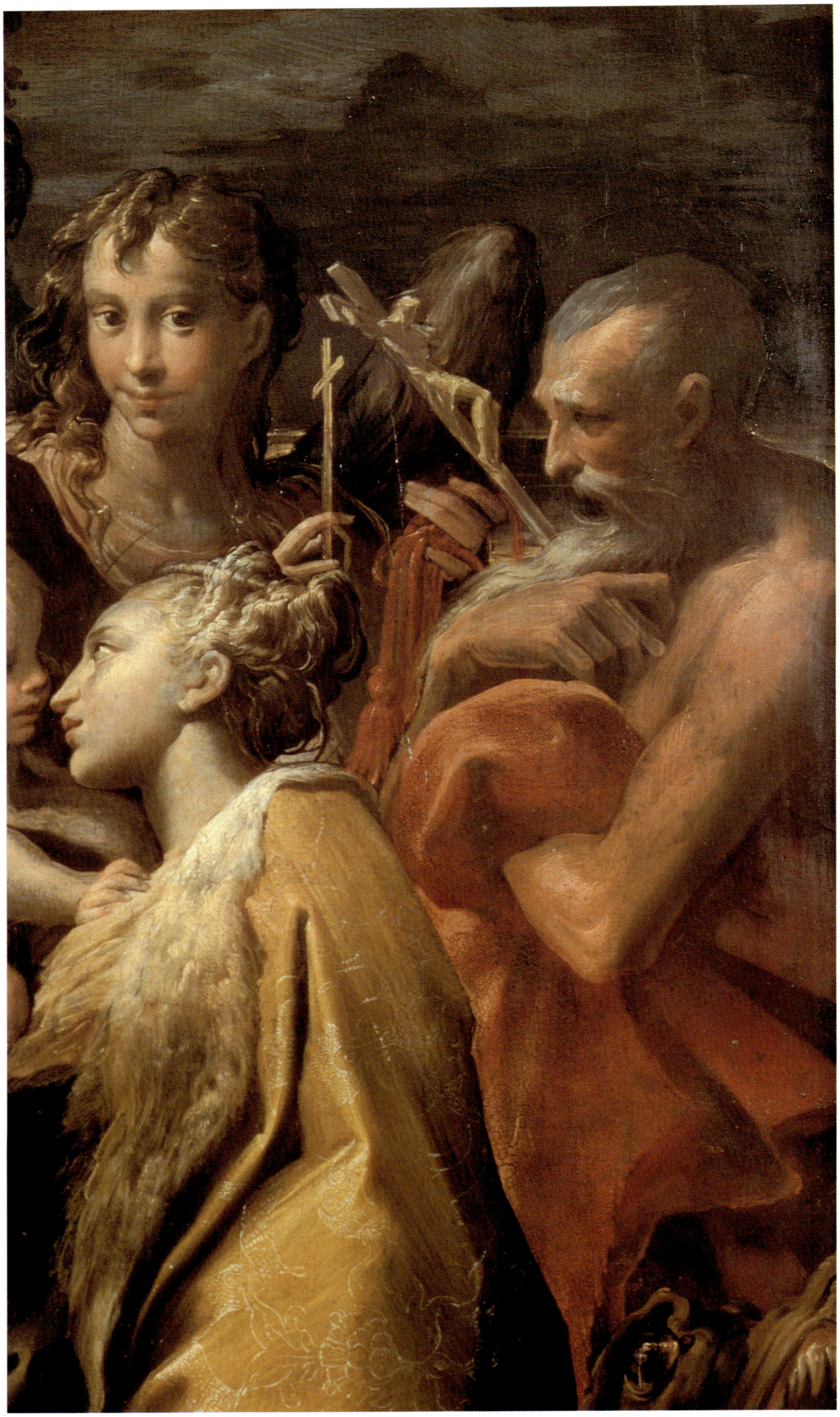

Detail of fig. 67
PARMIGIANINO
Madonna and Child with Saints Margaret and Jerome, a Mitered Saint, and an Angel
(Saints Margaret and Jerome, and an Angel)

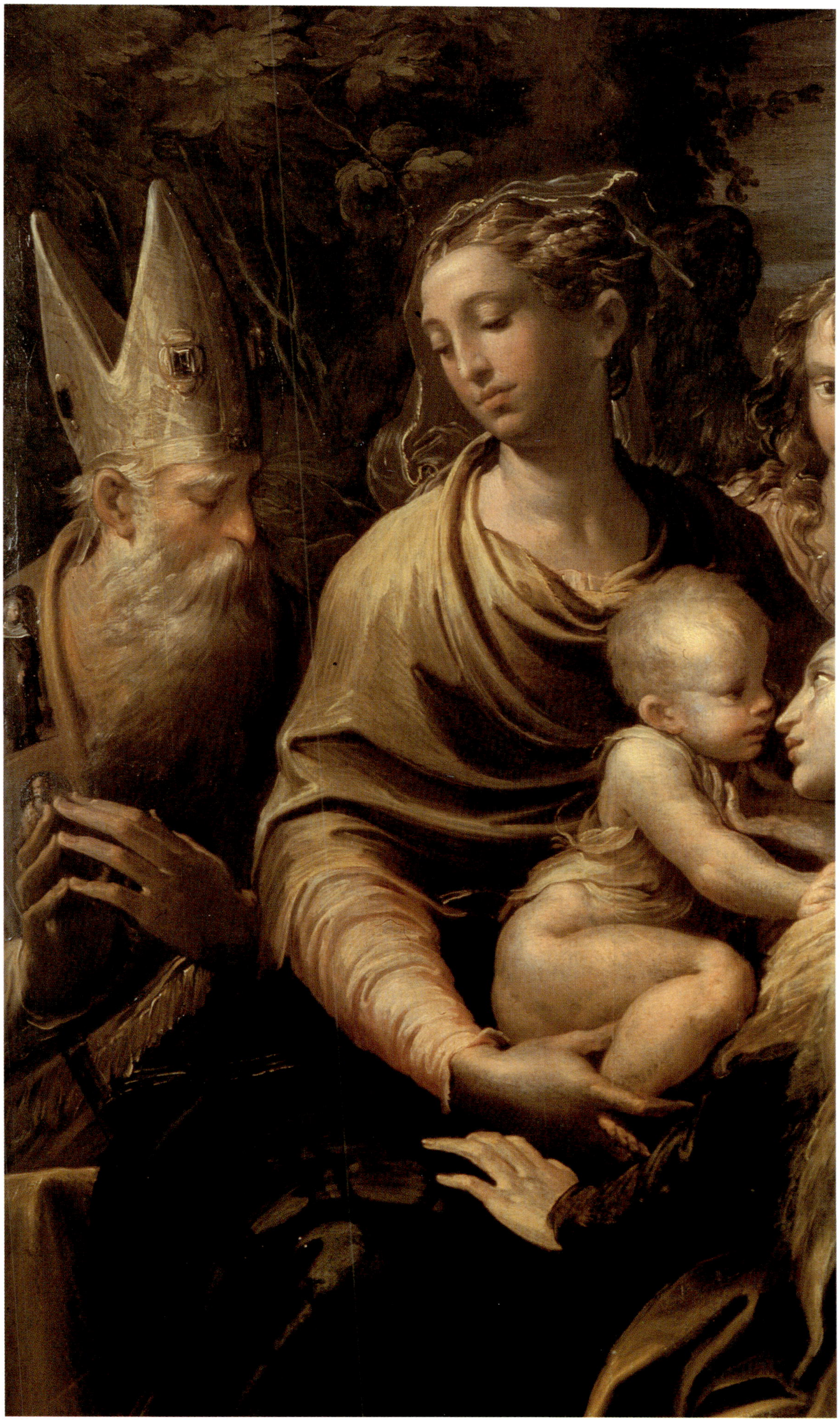

Detail of fig. 67

PARMIGIANINO

Madonna and Child with Saints Margaret and Jerome, a Mitered Saint, and an Angel

(Madonna and Child with a Mitered Saint)

68. Correggio
Madonna col Bambino,
S. Girolamo e altri personaggi
Galleria Nazionale, Parma

68. CORREGGIO
Madonna and Child with Saint Jerome and Others, c. 1528
Oil on panel, 80¾ × 55½ in.
(205 × 141 cm)
Galleria Nazionale, Parma, Italy

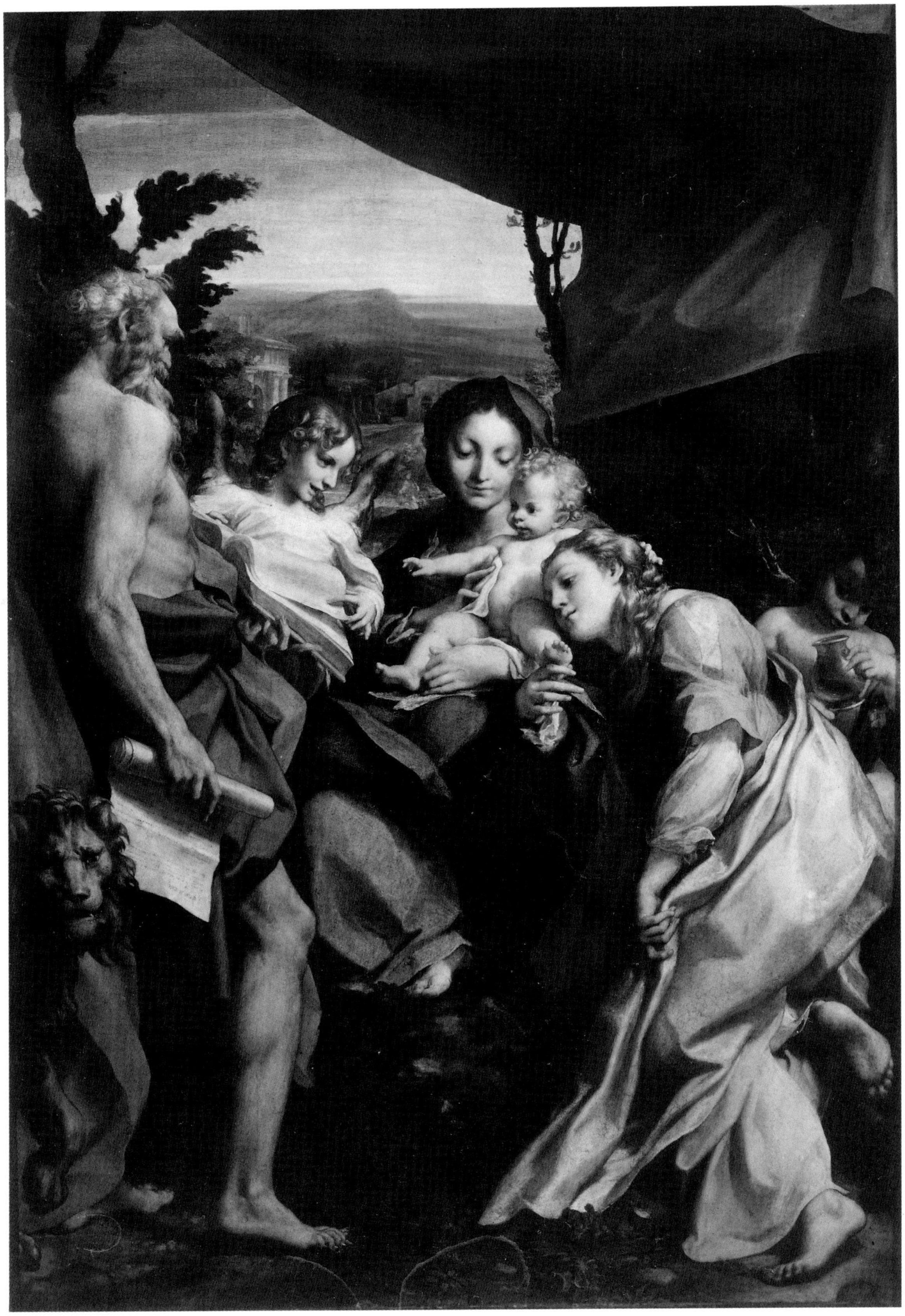

69. PARMIGIANINO
Study for *Madonna and Child with Saints Margaret and Jerome, a Mitered Saint, and an Angel*, n.d. P79
Red chalk, heightened with white on paper, 11⅛ × 8⅛ in. (28.3 × 20.7 cm)
Galleria degli Uffizi, Florence

69. Parmigianino
Studio per *Madonna col Bambino,*
i Santi Margherita e Girolamo,
un Santo Mitrato e un Angelo
Disegno (P79)
Galleria degli Uffizi, Firenze

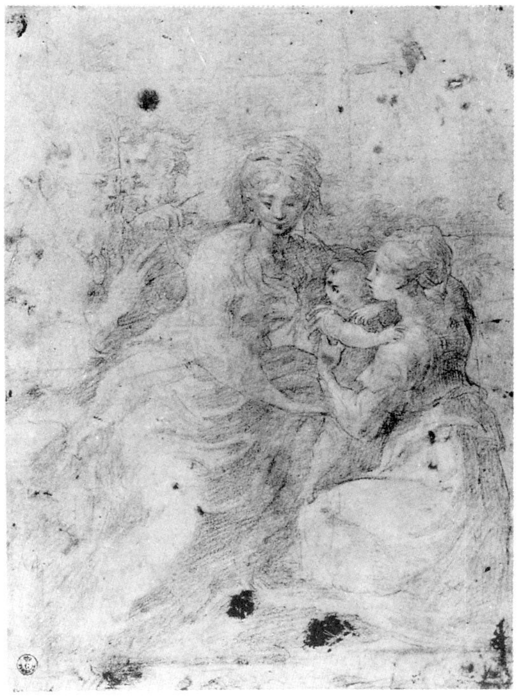

Preceding page:
70. PARMIGIANINO
A Young Man with a Book, n.d.
Oil on panel, 26⅝ × 20⅞ in.
(67.5 × 53 cm)
Kunsthistorisches Museum, Vienna
(cat. A47)

refers to the angel as "Saint Michael," but the picture's dependence on Correggio's altarpiece, which has an undoubted angel, is some argument against this.) The farther the forms recede from this focal point the sketchier the treatment. Some of this effect—for instance, in the Christ Child's body and in Saint Margaret's outstretched left hand—is now accentuated by damage, some of the top paint being evidently missing. But Saint Jerome on the right is well preserved. His face, beard, and hand, and the crucifix he holds, are painted in a kind of brilliant shorthand, with the forms defined by dragging a broad brush across the surface, loaded with thick pigment and relatively little medium—a process that calls for absolute confidence and which in this case shows no sign of correction or hesitation. It was evidently intended as a means of preventing the figures on the perimeter from detracting attention from those in the center. Raphael had also deployed more than one technique in his *Saint Cecilia* (fig. 7), but his distant celestial vision is realized by means other than the shorthand technique of Parmigianino's peripheral figures.[7]

This shorthand technique may also be recognized throughout the surface of a number of smaller, more informal pictures, some of which were probably uncommissioned. Their essential relationship to the *Madonna with Saint Margaret* has not always been admitted in the past, and in consequence they have been wrongly dated to the Rome period, or Parmigianino's authorship doubted. One of this group is the small portrait at Vienna of a young man in very plain clothes, seated with one hand to his face and the other on an open book (fig. 70).

He sits hunched up, his right arm cramped and his cloak slung over his left shoulder. The informality of the effect, and the sitter's everyday dress, suggest a friend of the painter's rather than one of the great of the world. Is he perhaps that saddler from Parma in whose house, according to Vasari, Parmigianino lodged while at Bologna and for whom, Vasari added, he painted a *Marriage of Saint Catherine*? The flashing brushstrokes on the book and on the sitter's doublet, and the quick jabs of paint on his face and hand, are highly characteristic of this phase. Further examples are the small Madonnas at Kedleston and the Courtauld Institute (figs. 71 and 72). In both of the Madonnas the Christ Child is almost a repetition of the one in the Saint Margaret altarpiece. In general the Kedleston *Madonna* seems to anticipate the much bigger *Madonna della Rosa* (Dresden; fig. 88).

The technique of the Courtauld *Madonna* is particularly close to that of the figure of Saint Jerome in the Saint Margaret altar. The Madonna's profile and the architecture on the left are defined by means of broad but unerring sweeps of a heavily charged brush. The composition of this little panel represents Parmigianino's nearest approach to antiquity. The relieflike Madonna, more Greek than Roman, faces a building that recalls the Septizonium, which still stood on the Palatine during Parmigianino's residence in Rome. We have already seen such a building in the background of Parmigianino's *Visitation* drawing (fig. 59).

A further and more considerable work in this group is the *Adoration of the Magi* at Taggia on the Italian Riviera (fig. 73).[8] This shows many analogies both with the informal paintings and with the *Madonna with Saint Margaret,* and these are conclusive enough to refute

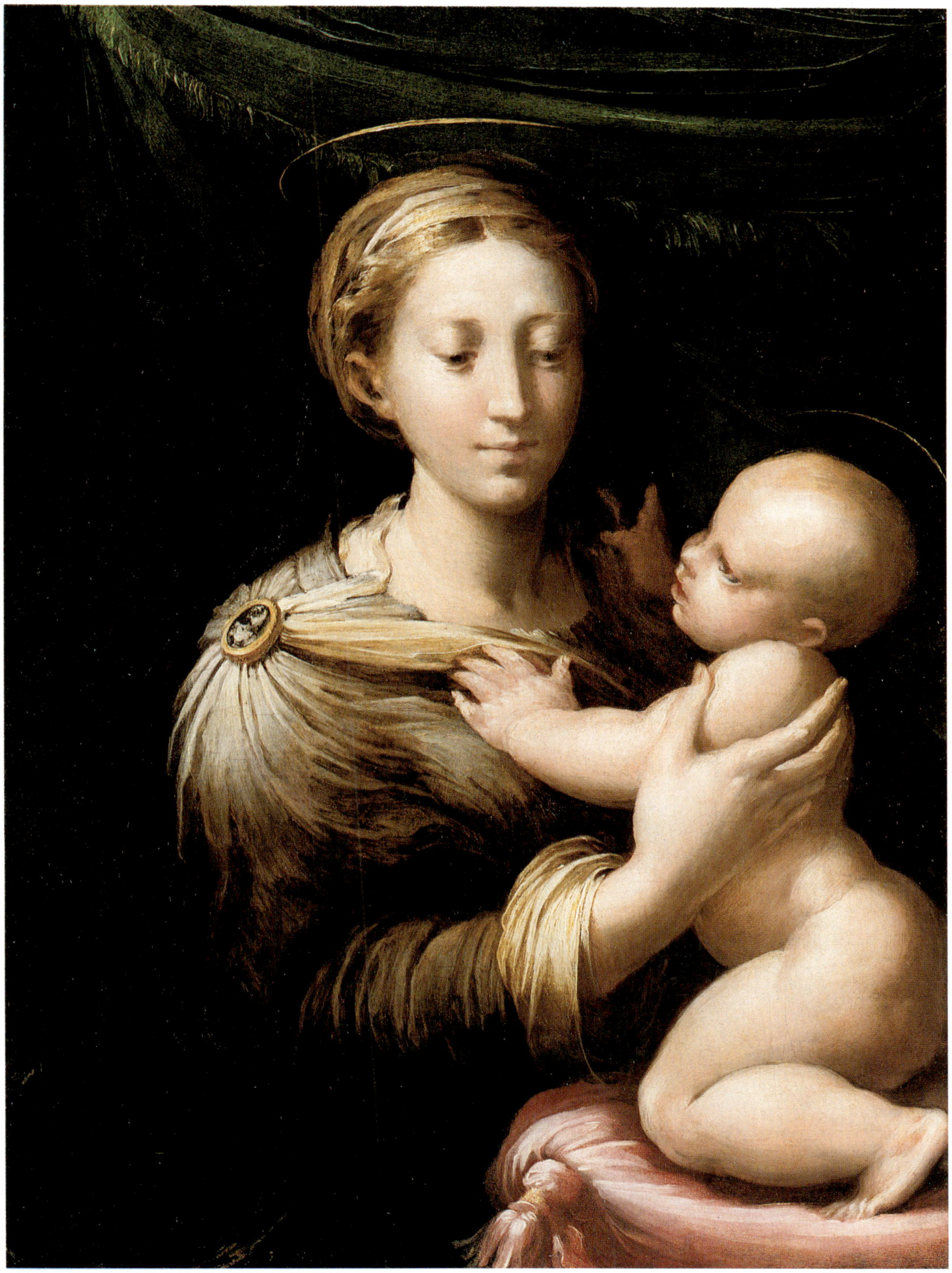

71. PARMIGIANINO
Madonna and Child, c. 1527–30
Oil on panel. Original painted surface
19⅛ × 14 in. (48.5 × 35.5 cm)
(subsequently enlarged)
Kedleston Hall, Derbyshire, England
(cat. A16)

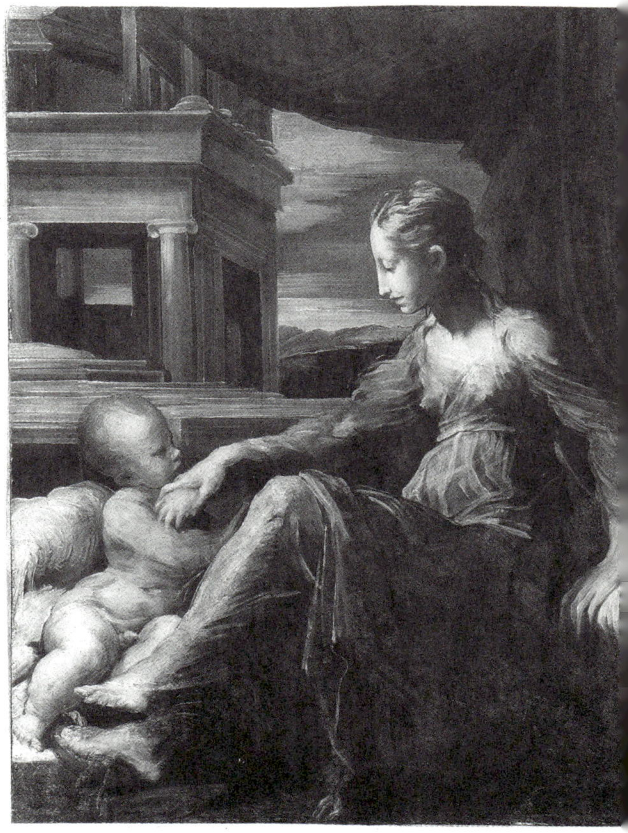

72. PARMIGIANINO
Madonna and Child, c. 1527–30
Oil on panel, 25 × 20 in.
(63.5 × 50.7 cm)
Courtauld Institute, Seilern
collection, London (cat. A21)

an old attribution to Perino del Vaga that has surfaced again recently. In the Taggia picture the Christ Child is of a piece with those in the *Saint Margaret* and the Kedleston and Courtauld Madonnas, while the Saint Joseph and the Madonna herself closely echo the mitred saint and the Madonna respectively in the *Saint Margaret* altarpiece. The king in the foreground is similar to the Saint Jerome in the Bologna picture, and the charged horizontal strokes of the impasto in the architecture and in the clouds are almost identical with those features in the Courtauld *Madonna.* As we shall find in the *Marriage of Saint Catherine* (London), great play is made in the Taggia *Adoration* with the juxtaposition of hands (here no fewer than six) in the center. Finally, the fact that the kings' offerings take the form of amphoras almost constitutes a signature of Parmigianino.

The final painting in this group, already mentioned more than once, is the London *Marriage of Saint Catherine* (fig. 74). It is also the most successful of the smaller ones. The dating of this work to the Bologna period is clear from the affinity between its technique and that of the others in the group. And it is confirmed by the connection, as shown by the Uffizi drawing (P79; fig. 69), between its design and that of the *Madonna with Saint Margaret;* also, as we shall see, with that of another Bolognese commission—the *Madonna with the Baptist, the Magdalene, and Saint Zachariah* (Uffizi; fig. 107). The unusual attitude of the Madonna in the London picture, seated sideways, is the feature that probably identifies it, as Affò already suggested in the eighteenth century, with Vasari's reference, already quoted, to one that he says Parmigianino painted at this time for his friend and host in Bologna, the saddler.[9] Vasari's description of this painting—a "Madonna turned toward the side [*volta per fianco*] in a beautiful attitude with several other figures"—is a fair one.

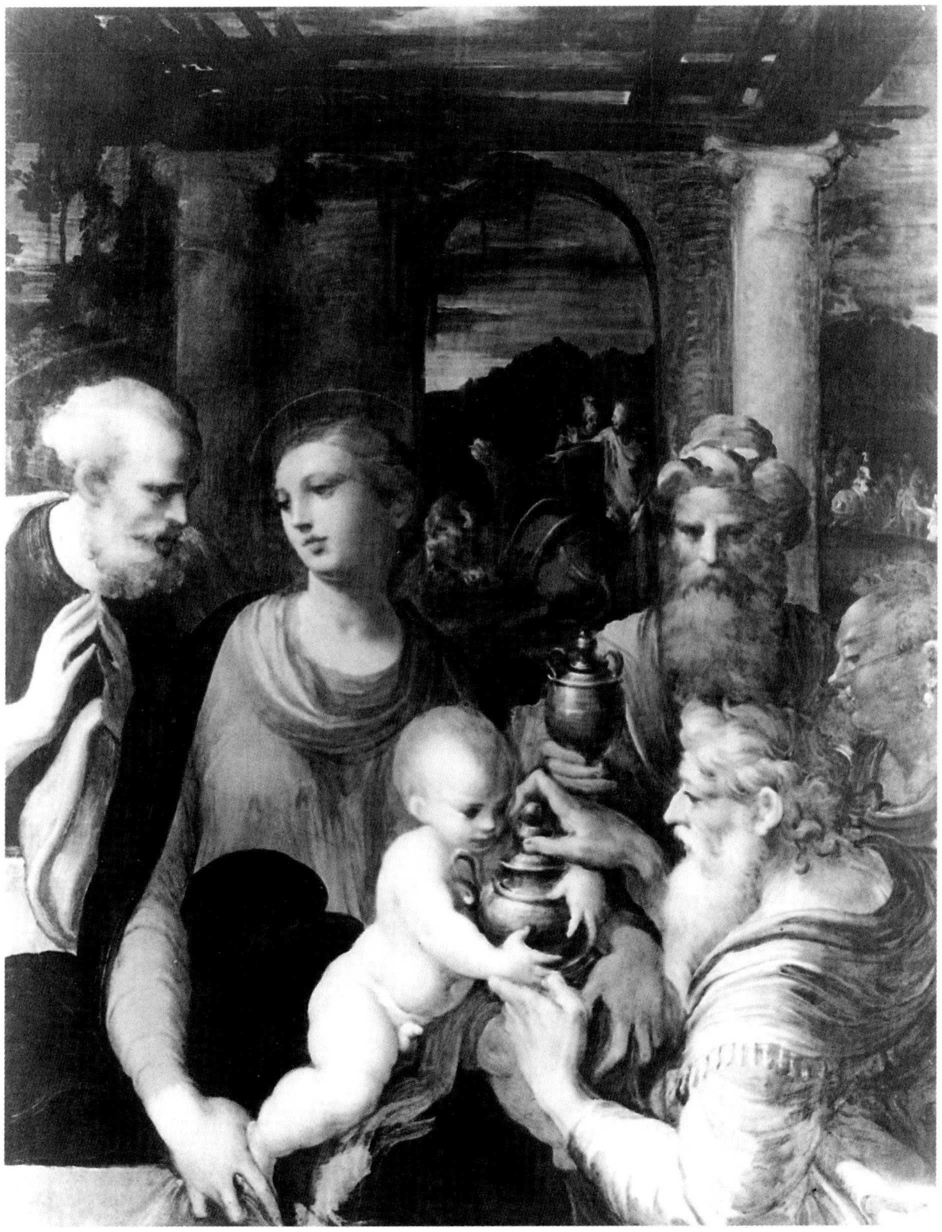

73. PARMIGIANINO
Adoration of the Magi, n.d.
Oil on panel, 47¼ × 37 in.
(120 × 94 cm)
San Domenico, Taggia (Imperia), Italy (cat. A46)

Opposite:
74. PARMIGIANINO
The Mystic Marriage of Saint Catherine, n.d.
Oil on panel, 29¼ × 22½ in.
(74.2 × 57.2 cm)
National Gallery, London (cat. A18)

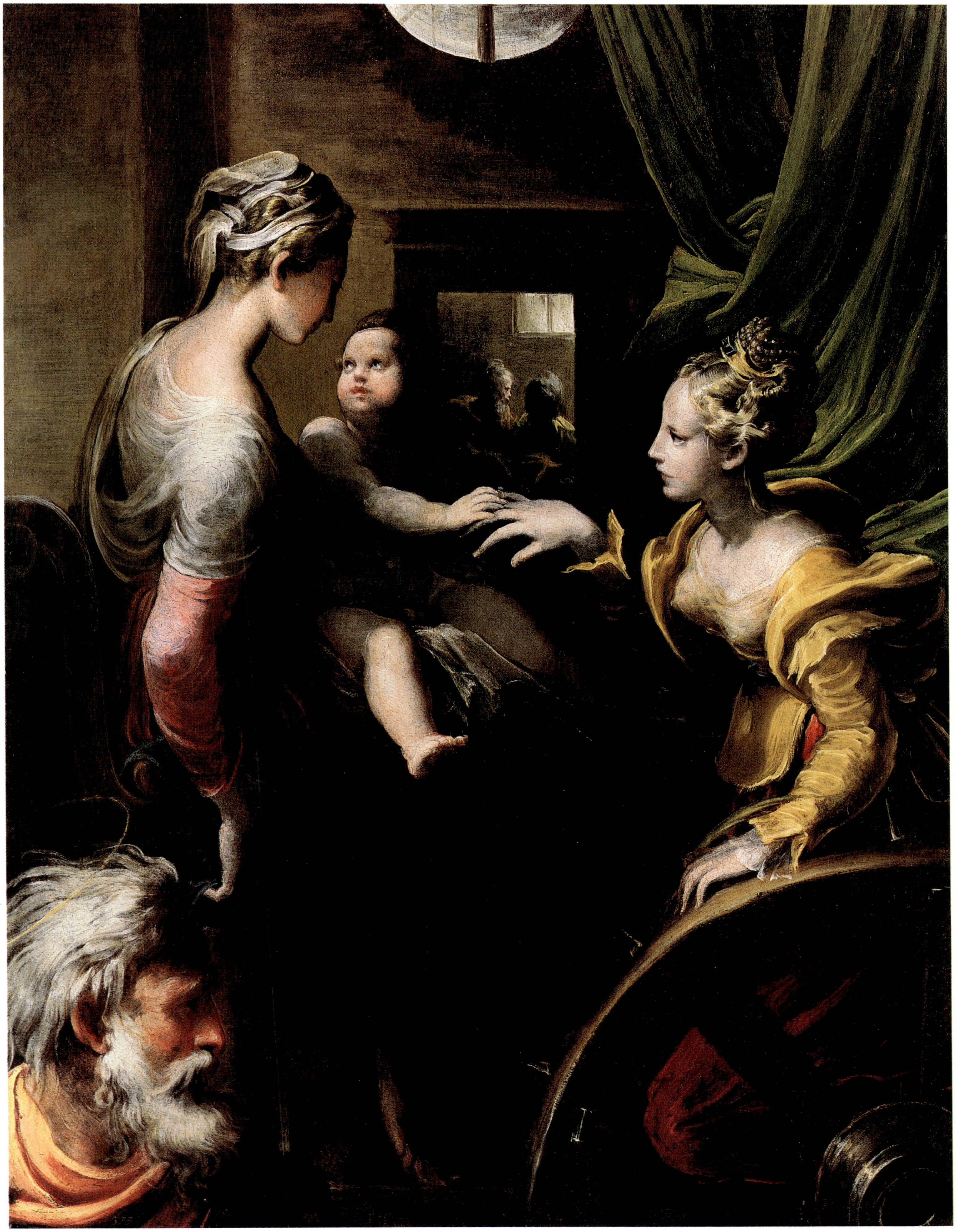

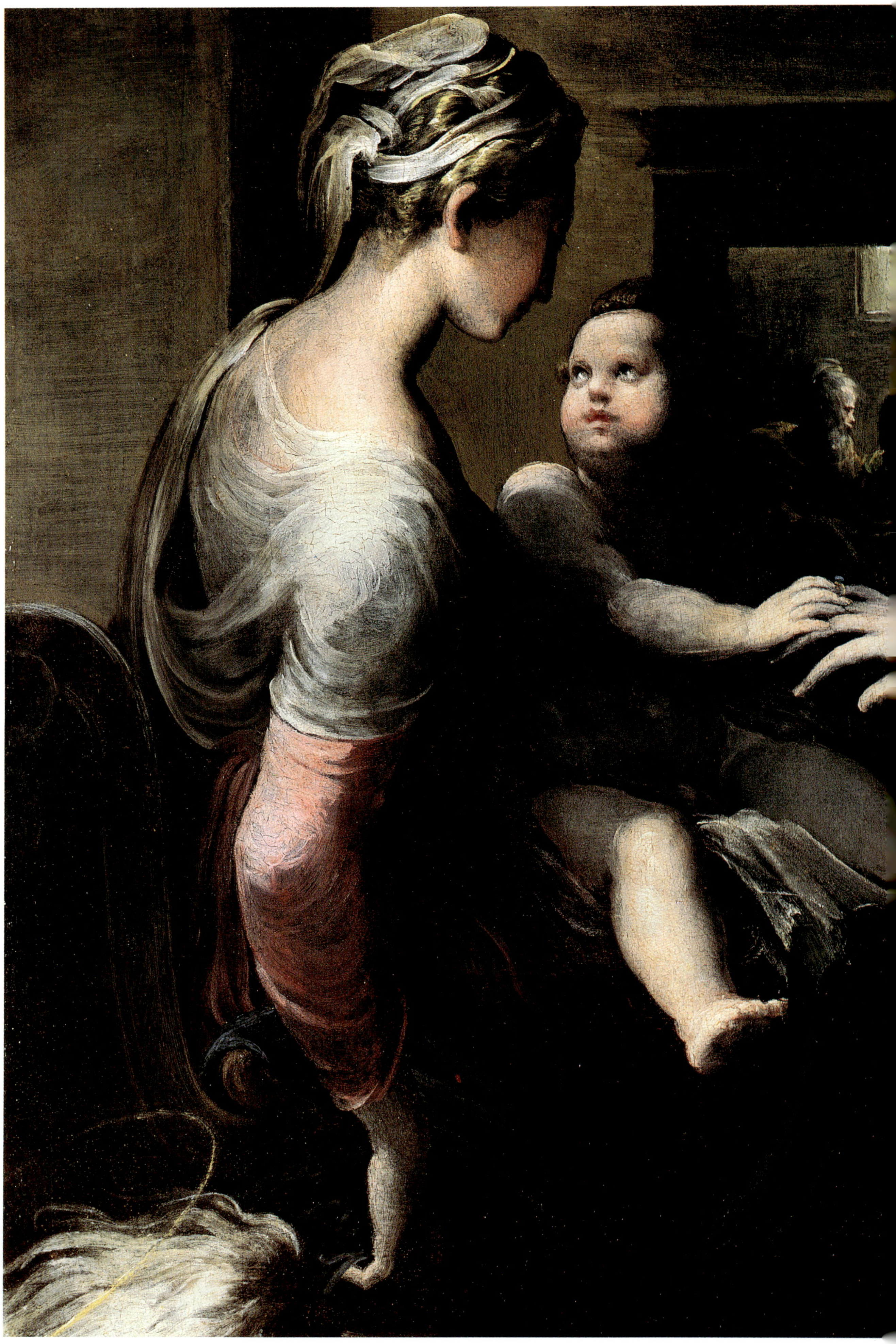

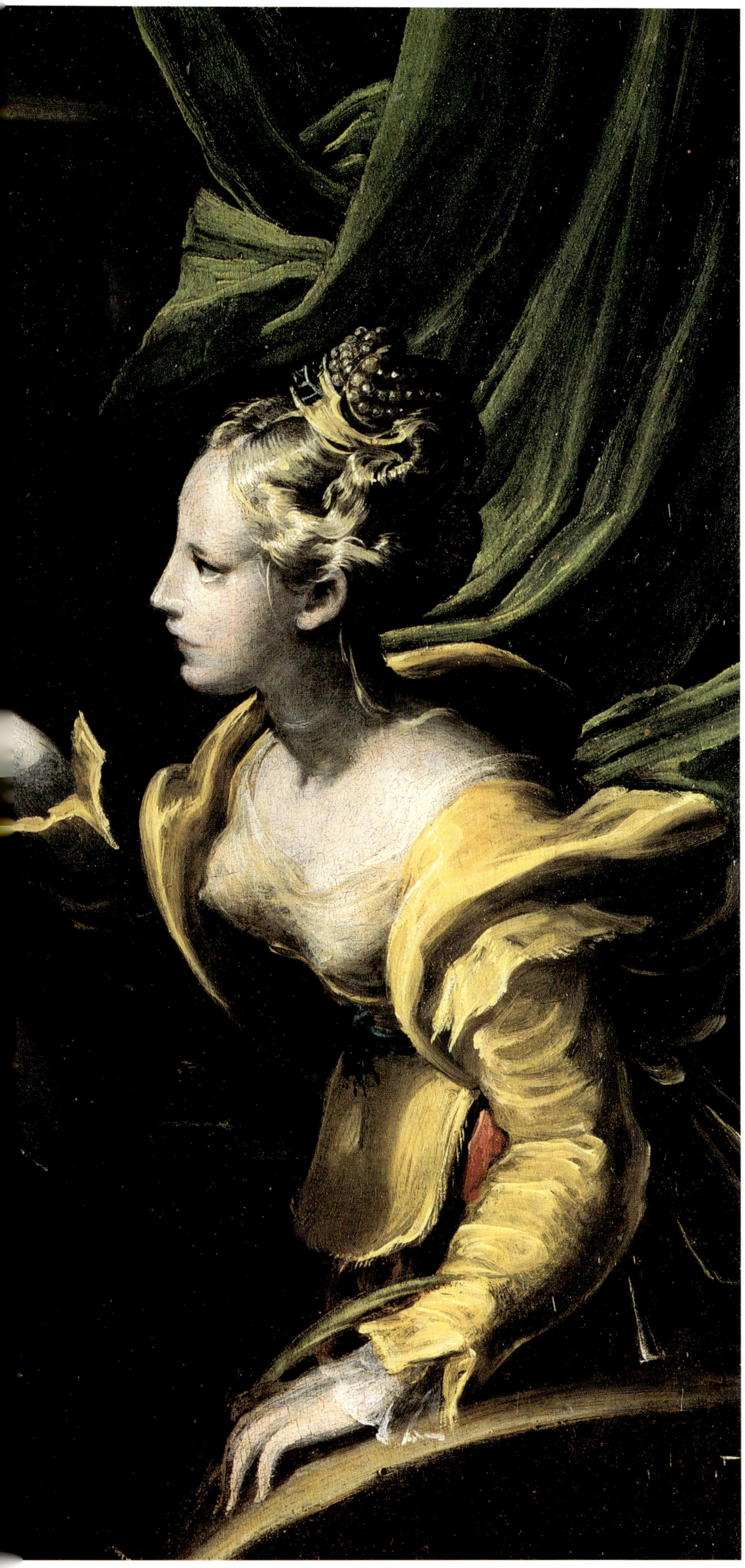

Detail of fig. 74

PARMIGIANINO

The Mystic Marriage of Saint Catherine
(Madonna and Child with
Saint Catherine)

In this picture the desire for elegance begins to result in noticeable simplification of the outlines, and thence in some distortion. The *Marriage of Saint Catherine* is highly eclectic in detail. The Madonna's attitude, which Vasari admired—that strange, immobile figure, which, looked at through half-shut eyes, seems to resemble some root vegetable, and whose lower limbs taper in the form of a triangle with the point downward—derives from Michelangelo. He had evolved the pose and had used variations on it for both the Libyan and the Persian sibyls on the Sistine ceiling, and Parmigianino himself had used it in an early drawing (P413) and in two later ones (P483 and P515V). The Christ Child repeats the form that Correggio had given him in his small picture of the same subject now in Naples (fig. 75), while the truncated male saint in the lower left corner of Parmigianino's paintings echoes the bearded figure on the left of Correggio's *Holy Family* at Hampton Court (fig. 76). Finally, the dim, indoor lighting and the two ghostly, half-lit figures in the background, both of whom wear Parmigianino's obsessive Phrygian caps and who resemble the two in the Doria *Holy Family,* derive from the late Raphael and Giulio Romano (fig. 77).

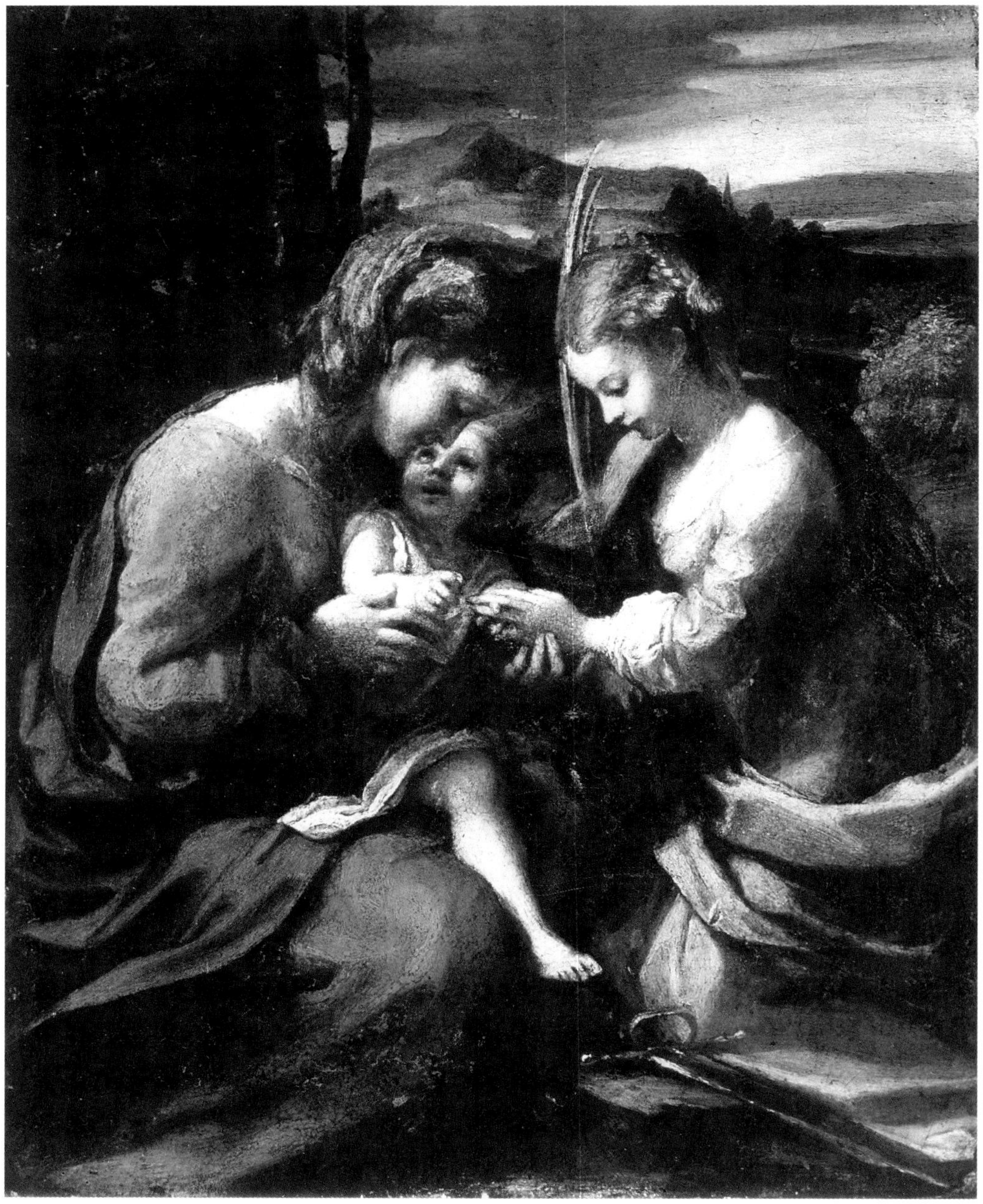

75. CORREGGIO
Marriage of Saint Catherine, c. 1517–20
Oil on panel, 11 × 9½ in. (28 × 24 cm)
Galleria Nazionale di Capodimonte, Naples

Yet these multiple borrowings are somehow welded into a whole that is unlike any of its components and is intensely personal.[10] The picture hangs together so perfectly that the eye may not immediately perceive subtleties such as the way the green curtain, curving downward, and Saint Catherine's yellow draperies, curving upward, accentuate her alert and intelligent beauty, or how the doorway in the center of the background frames both the mysterious figures in front of it and also the central event of the picture—the exchange of the ring. The original of a smaller, oblong painting of the same subject, previously only known in a copy and a variant, has recently come to light in France (fig. 78). In this, the half-length Saint Catherine takes over the position, on the left, and much of the pose, of the Madonna in the London picture.

Altogether in keeping with the mood of technical experiment shown in this group of oil paintings is the Naples *Holy Family with the Infant Baptist* (fig. 79), but in this case the bold brushstrokes are executed, like the rest of the picture, in tempera. The fact that the Madonna evidently derives from a design by Raphael (represented by a drawing in Oxford,

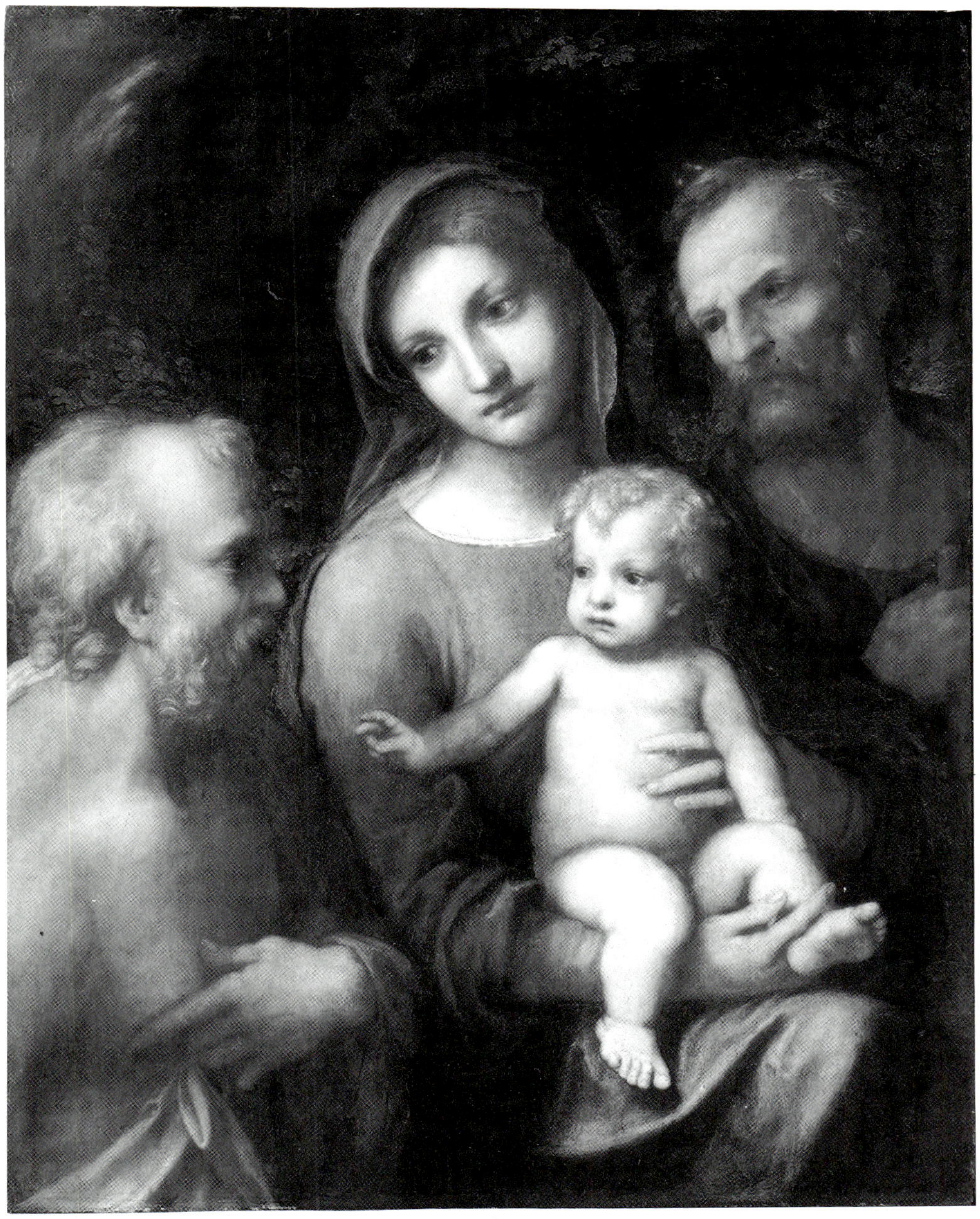

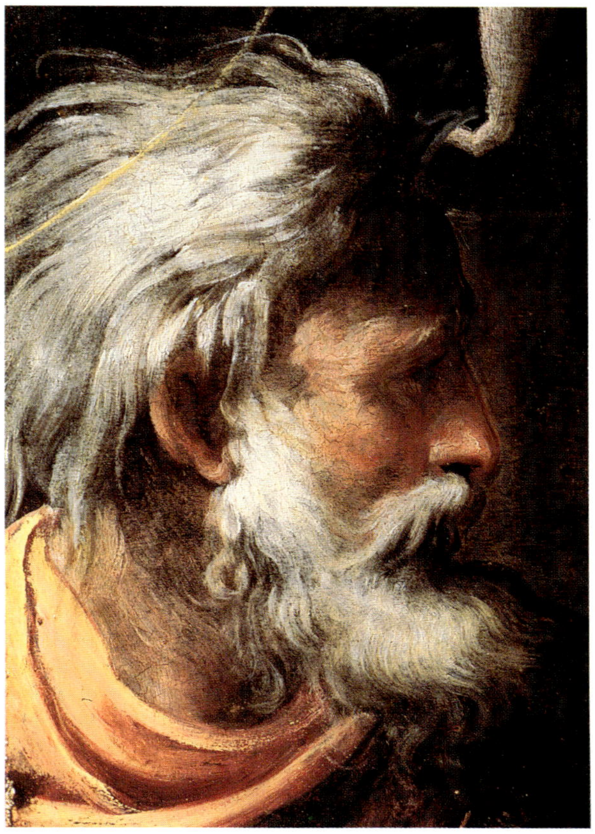

Detail of fig. 74
The Mystic Marriage of Saint Catherine
(Saint Joseph)

76. CORREGGIO
Holy Family, c. 1516–18
Oil on panel, 26¾ × 22 in. (68 × 56 cm)
Hampton Court Palace, Hampton Court, England

77. GIULIO ROMANO
Madonna del Gatto, after 1520
Oil on panel, 63 × 55⅞ in.
(160 × 142 cm)
Galleria Nazionale di Capodimonte,
Naples

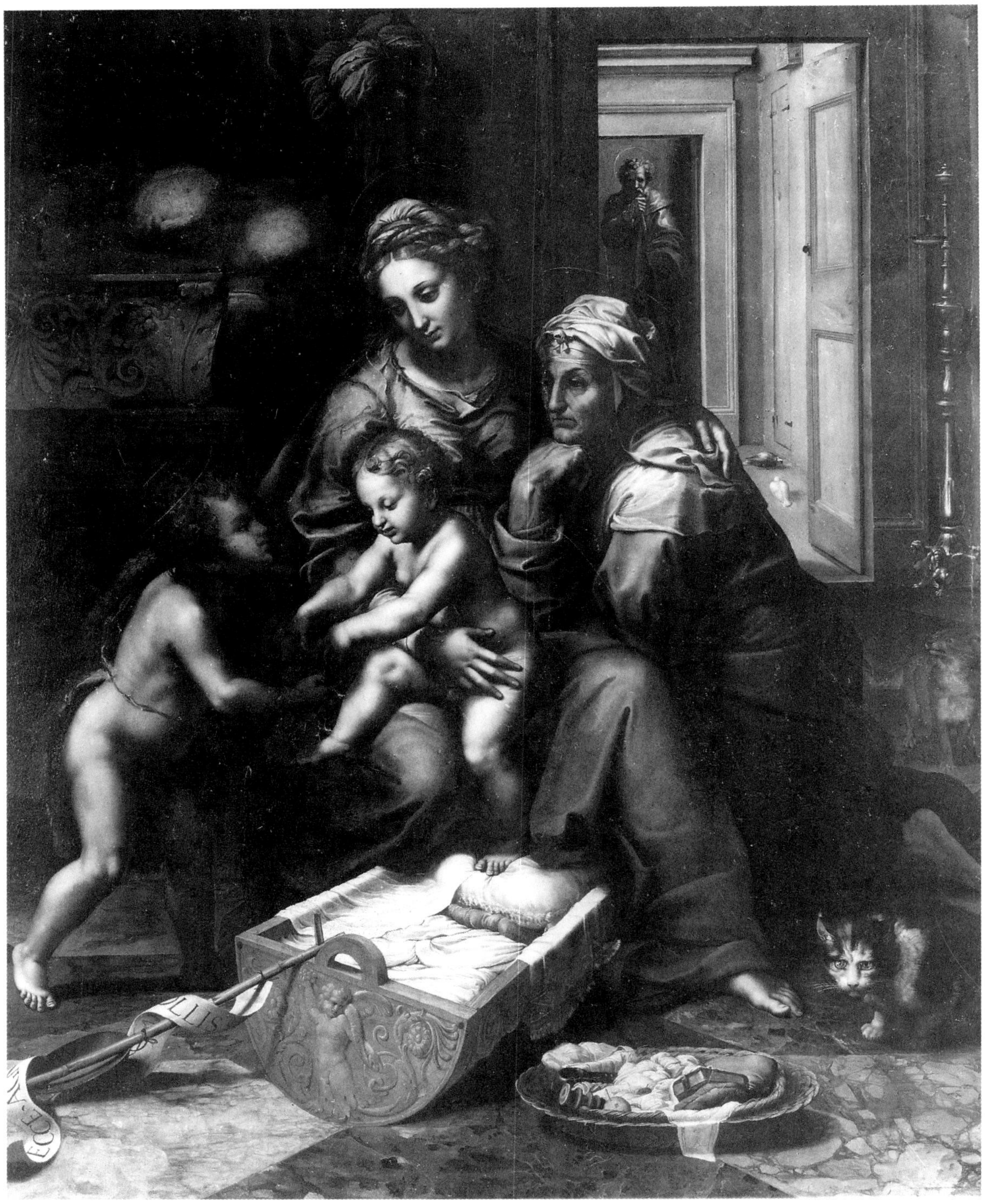

Ashmolean no. 564) and the Christ Child from Michelangelo has led to the assumption that the picture dates from the Roman years. But this need not follow, and considerations of two different kinds point to Bologna. The first is the technique, which aligns the picture with the group just discussed. Secondly, the only pictures that Vasari specifies as painted by Parmigianino in gouache (a word sometimes used as interchangeable with tempera) dated from the Bologna period ("due tele a guazzo per maestro Luca dai Leuti con certi figuretti"). It may be no accident that at this very time—the late 1520s—Correggio was also experimenting in tempera. A related drawing at Parma (P534) for the Madonna shows at this stage an architectural background.

A small painting of Saint Roch in the Desert (private collection, Parma; fig. 80) is so exactly like, both in style and technique, the Saint Joseph in the background of the Naples picture as to support the theory that it is a fragment cut from the other picture, which was specified by Vasari as painted in tempera.

After these fascinating technical exercises Parmigianino seems to have abandoned except on rare occasions his shorthand, or soft-touch, technique. From now on—and this is fundamental to his development as painter—the touch in the panel pictures becomes progressively harder, the finish more minute, the contrasts of color rather more marked, and the effect even more elegant. The same choice of Hercules seems to have had the same outcome in the case of Raphael during the preceding decade. The soft Venetian touch of the *Donna Velata* (Pitti) is contrasted with the hard outlines of the Fornarina portrait (Galleria Nazionale Barberini, Rome).

Concurrently there were more portraits, though only two are specified by Vasari as from this period. On the strength of costume or on other grounds the *Portrait of a Youth* at Hampton Court is one that may be assigned to this time (fig. 81).[11] It has similar lighting

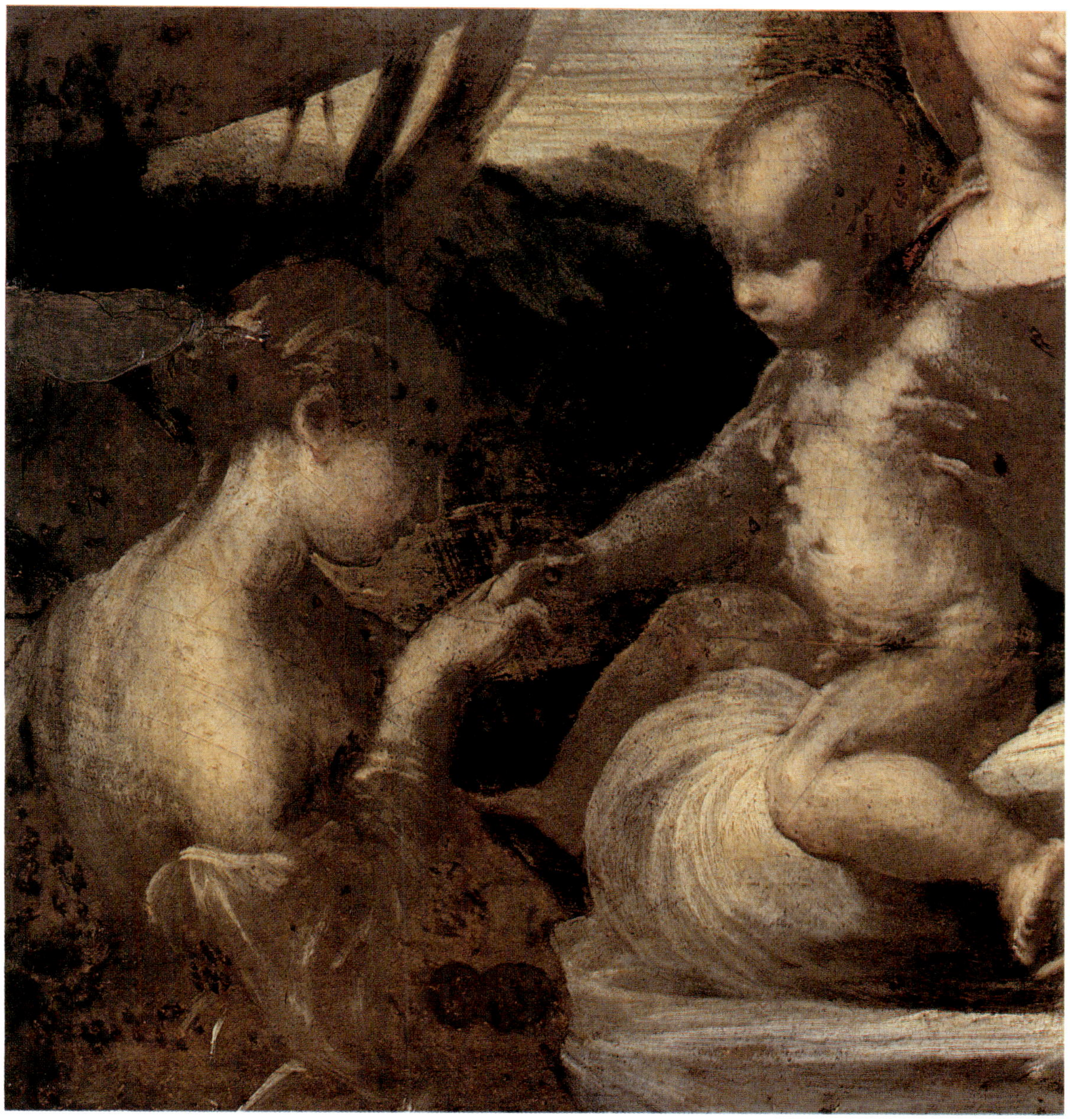

Detail of fig. 78
PARMIGIANINO
The Marriage of Saint Catherine, and a Male Saint
(Christ Child and Saint Catherine)

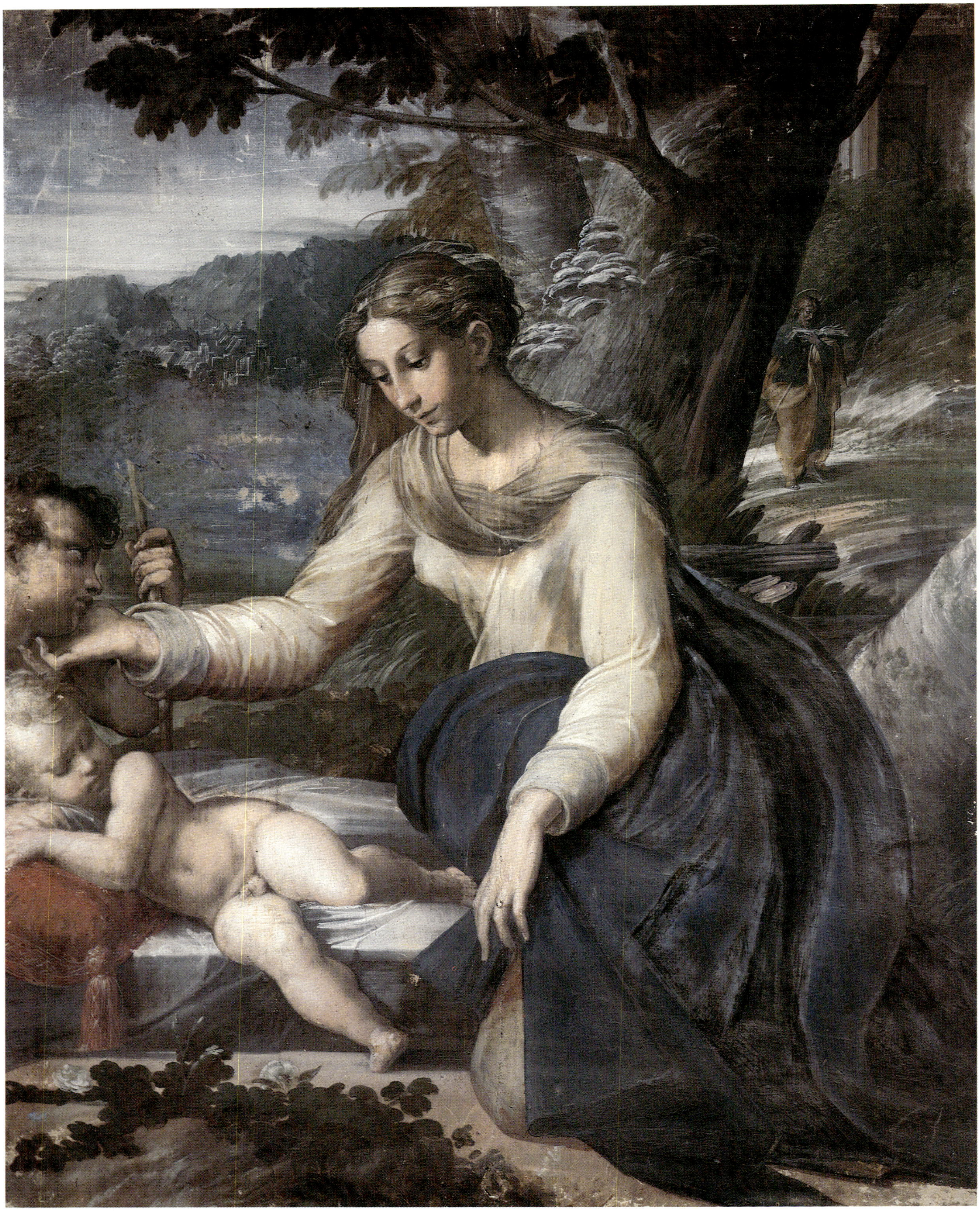

to the London *Marriage of Saint Catherine,* and the doorway in the background of the two pictures is almost identical. It shows an odd feature in that one of the sitter's shoulders appears slightly elongated in a way that helps the composition while violating anatomy. We shall see this peculiarity repeated in some of the later portraits, notably the so-called *Antea.* Several other famous and marvelous portraits also fit more easily into the Bolognese period than any other. One of them is the so-called *Self-Portrait* in the Uffizi (fig. 82). Here the true identity of the sitter is best left in suspense. The identification as a self-portrait does not extend back as far as the sixteenth century, while the fact that the picture was acquired by the Medici as a component in their collection of self-portraits argues a measure of wishful thinking on this point. As to the facts of the matter, there are undoubted likenesses of Parmigianino, both in youth—the Vienna tondo (fig. 36)—and toward the end of his life—the profile drawing in the Albertina (P600; fig. 83), which was evidently the model for the woodcut in Vasari's second edition. The pudding-faced youth in a drawing at Windsor (P635) and the shadowy head in the Louvre (P431) accord well enough with the Vienna picture; and three other drawings—in the British Museum (P256), in the Louvre (P406), and at Chatsworth (P719r)—with the later one. The little oil sketch at Parma (fig. 84) also goes with the second group. It is not easy—though it is necessary—to reconcile these two groups: to accept, that is, the transformation within about twenty years of the beautiful, round-cheeked youth into the aquiline, hirsute man of the later group. The difficulty of such an equation would, however, be diminished by assuming that for the two early drawings (P635 and P431) use was made of the same convex mirror as for the Vienna portrait—that the face at that time was really longer, as in the Louvre portrait, now attributed to Correggio, of the youth with one hand to his face (fig. 37). This would, of course, support the view that the latter represents the adolescent Parmigianino. But even if this is the case, as I am inclined to think, it would not make the Uffizi picture more acceptable as a self-portrait.

Another portrait probably dating from this period—this time on the evidence of the fashionable costume—is the so-called *Turkish Slave* (Parma; fig. 85). So far from being a slave, the costume unequivocally indicates a lady of high fashion. This time the glance is coquettish, as though she were daring the spectator to ask her to move the fan that she holds to her bosom. The "*Turkish Slave*" is the first surviving portrait by Parmigianino of a woman. In almost all of his portraits of men to date—the London *Collector,* the *Sanvitale,* the *Cybo,* or the Hampton Court *Youth*—the elaborate adjuncts or backgrounds are an element in the composition and also contribute to the mood of the picture. The same applies to later male portraits such as the so-called *Castaldo,* the *Malatesta Baglione,* or the *Conte di San Secondo.* There are only four acceptable portraits of women—the present one, the "*Gozzadini,*" the "*Antea,*" and the *Contessa di San Secondo*—and none of them shows the elaborate backgrounds of the male portraits. In these paintings the portrayal of the sitter's character and the degree of communication between her and the spectator are such as to stand in no need of adjuncts.

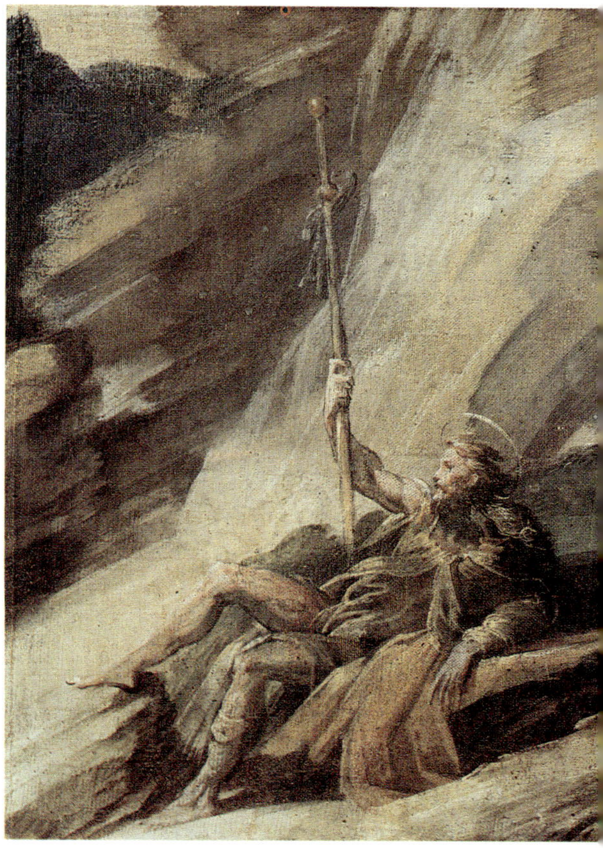

80. PARMIGIANINO
Saint Roch in the Desert (fragment), n.d.
Tempera on canvas, 11 × 8½ in.
(27.8 × 21.5 cm)
Private collection, Parma, Italy
(cat. A40)

Opposite:
79. PARMIGIANINO
Holy Family with the Infant Baptist,
c. 1535–39
Tempera on canvas, 62⅝ × 52 in.
(159 × 132 cm)
Galleria Nazionale di Capodimonte,
Naples (cat. A30)

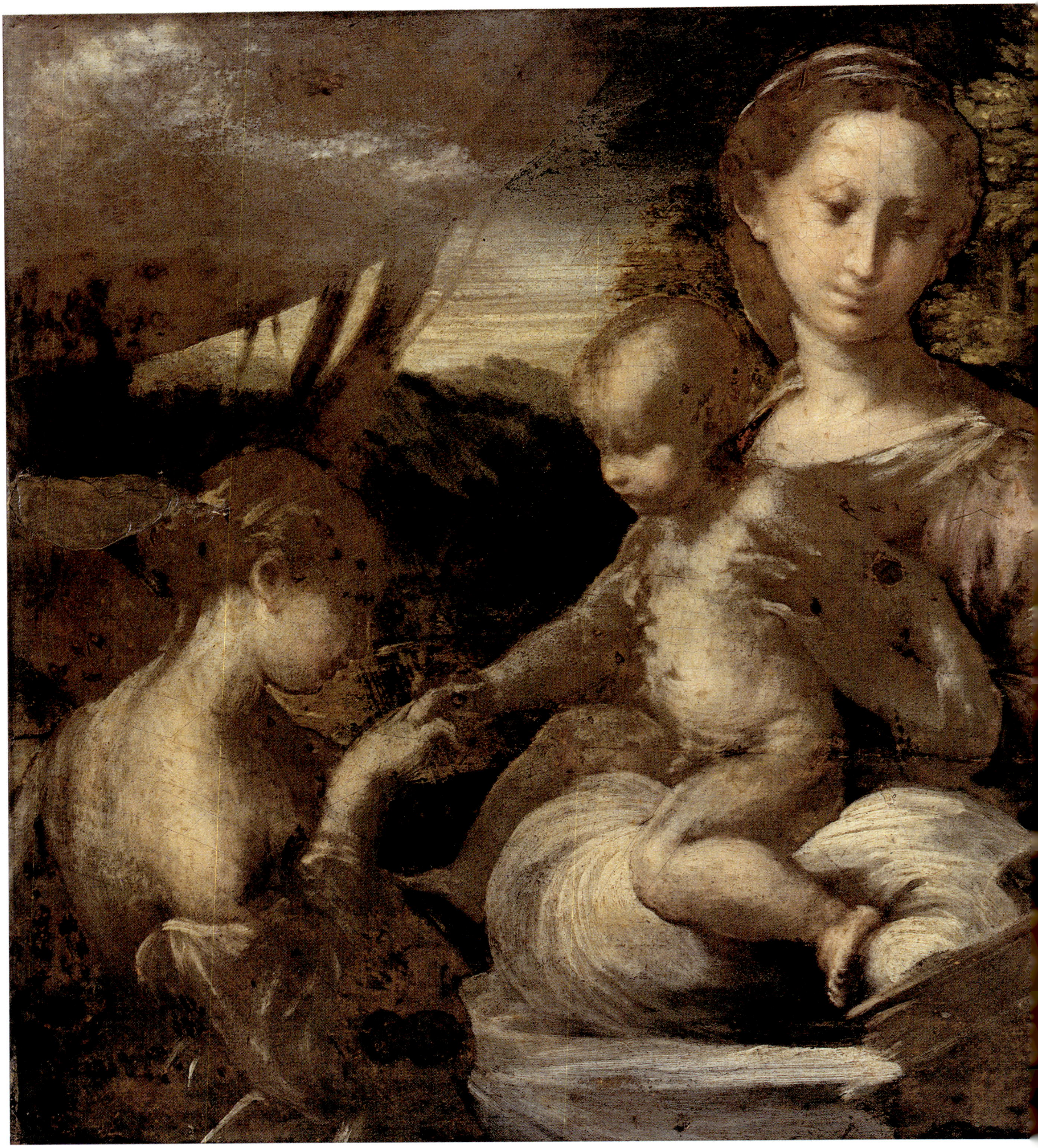

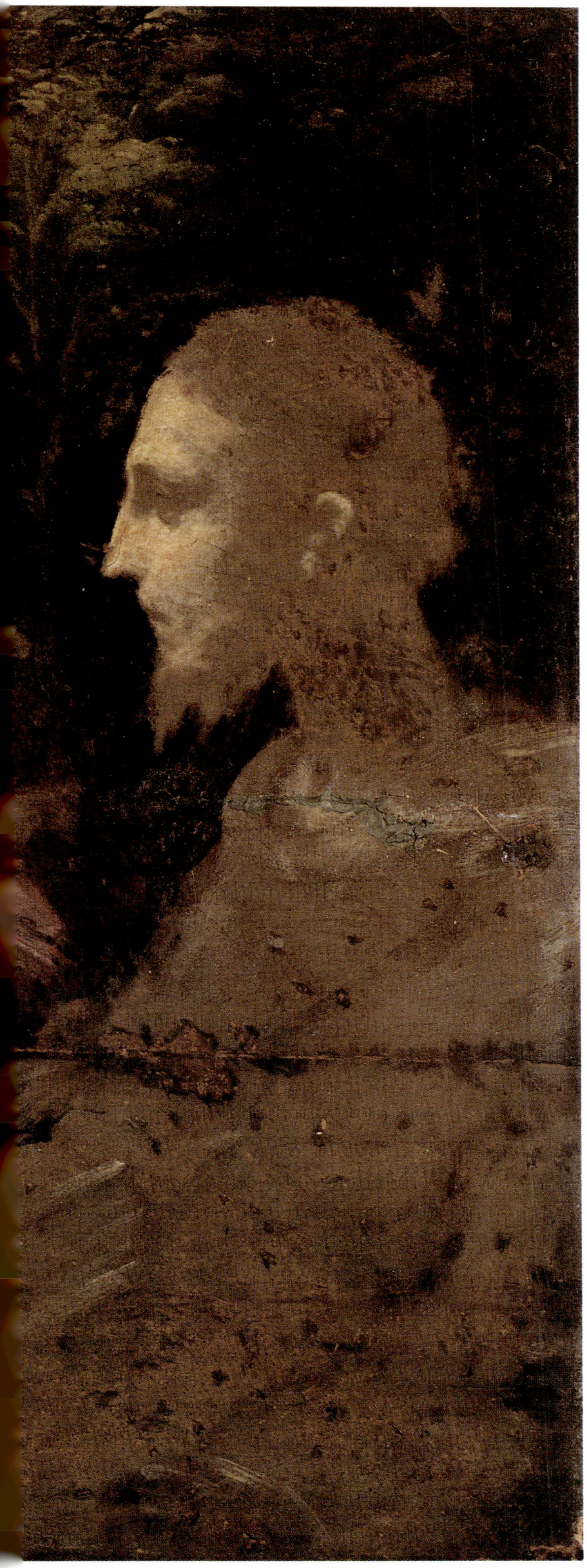

78. PARMIGIANINO
The Marriage of Saint Catherine, and a Male Saint, n.d.
Oil on panel, 7⅞ × 10⅝ in.
(20 × 27 cm)
Musée du Louvre, Paris (cat. A32)

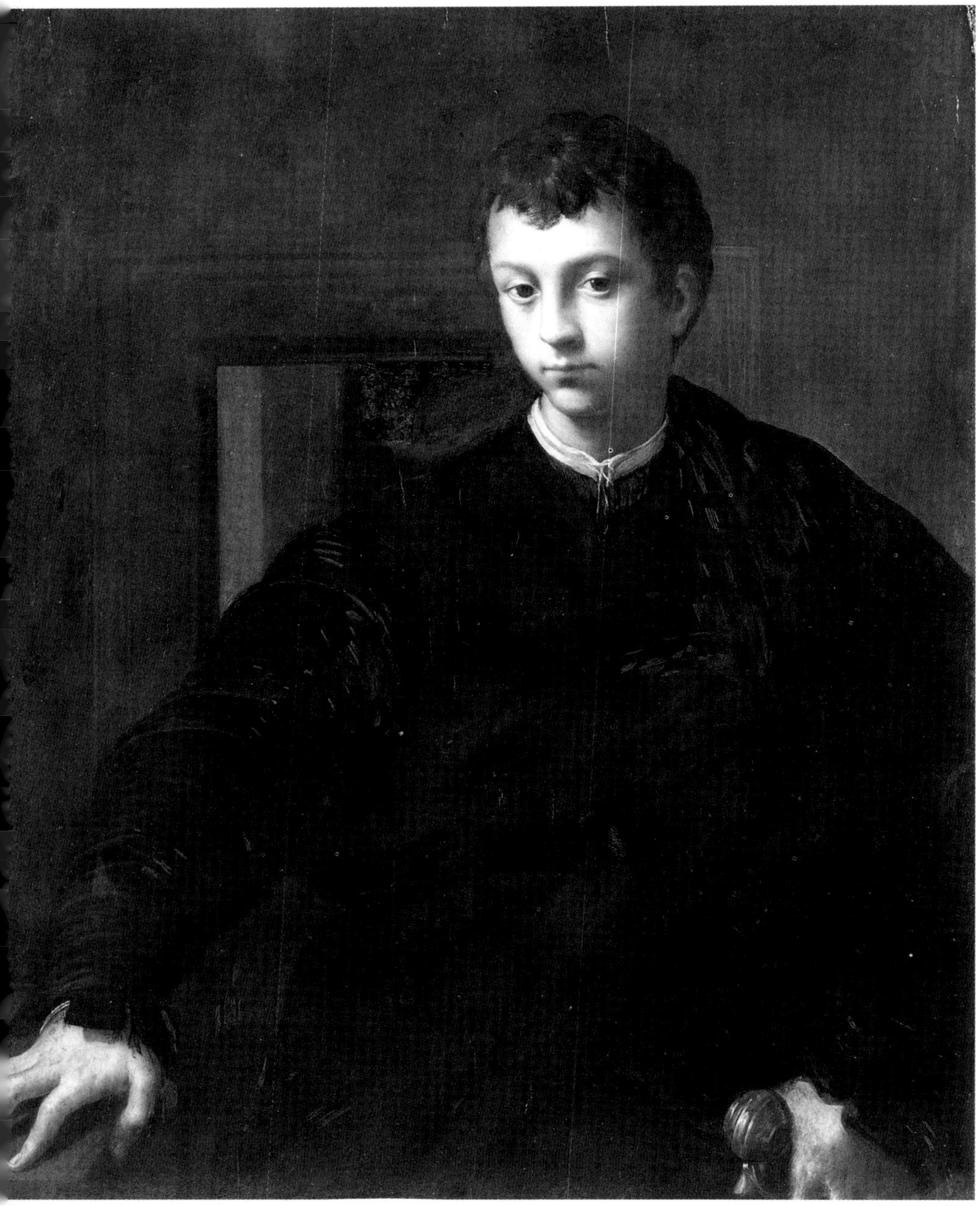

81. PARMIGIANINO
A Young Man, c. 1527–30
Oil on panel, 38¾ × 32½ in.
(98.5 × 82.5 cm)
Hampton Court Palace, Hampton Court, England (cat. A14)

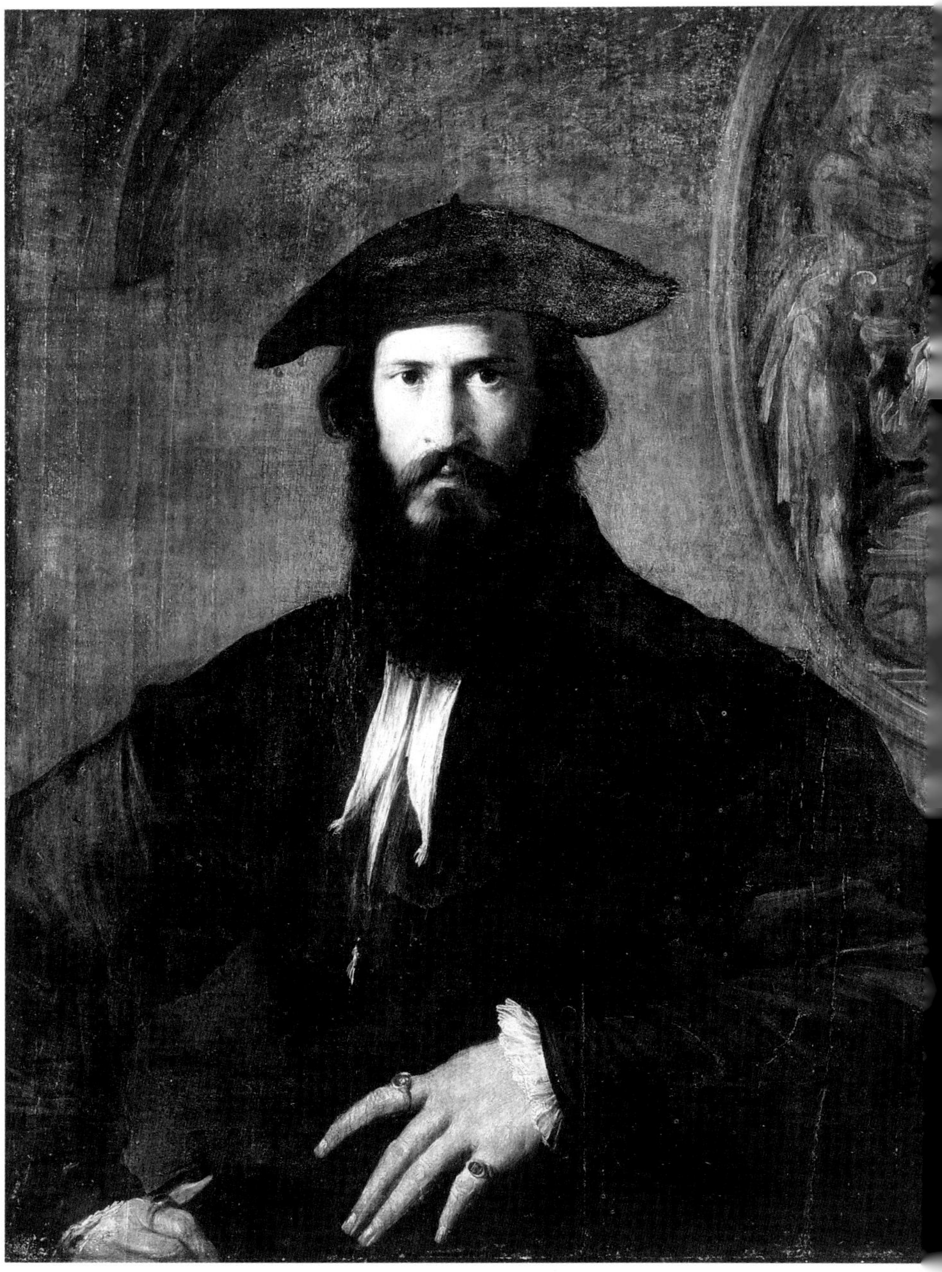

82. PARMIGIANINO
Portrait of a Man ("Self-Portrait"), c. 1530
Oil on panel, 39⅜ × 28 in.
(100 × 71 cm)
Galleria degli Uffizi, Florence (cat. A11)

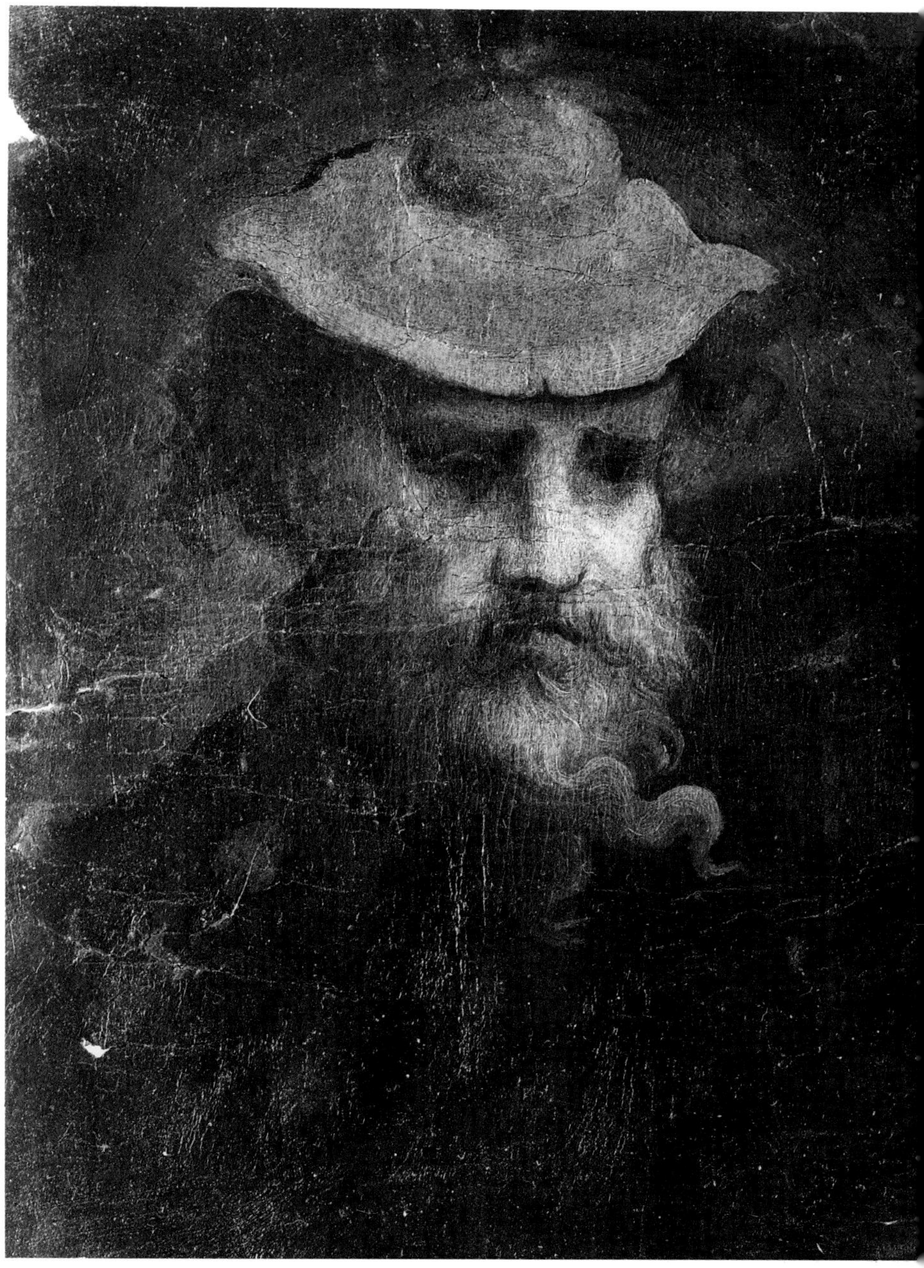

84. PARMIGIANINO
Self-Portrait, c. 1540
Oil on paper, mounted on canvas,
8¼ × 6⅛ in. (21 × 15.5 cm)
Galleria Nazionale, Parma, Italy
(cat. A39)

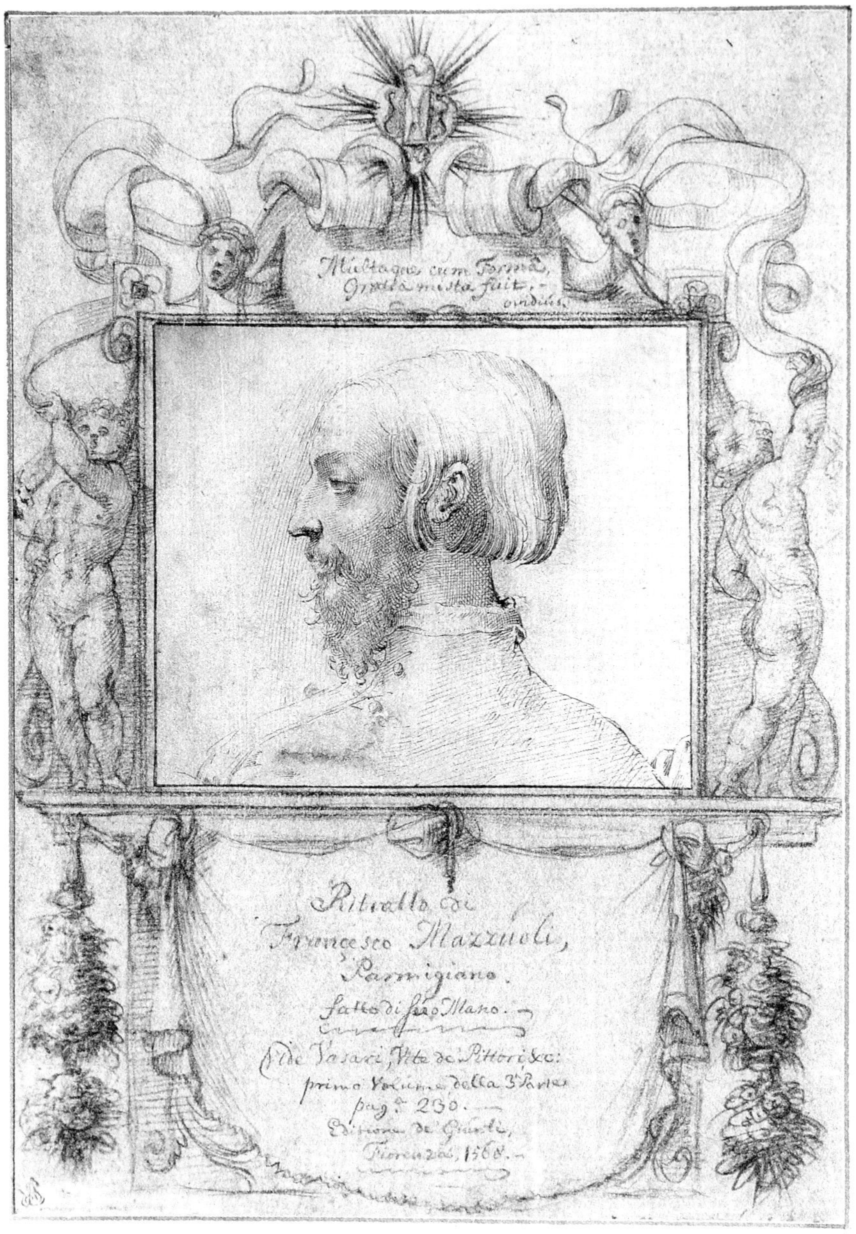

83. PARMIGIANINO
Self-Portrait, n.d. P600
Pen and brown ink on paper,
4⅝ × 4 in. (11.7 × 10.3 cm)
Graphische Sammlung Albertina,
Vienna

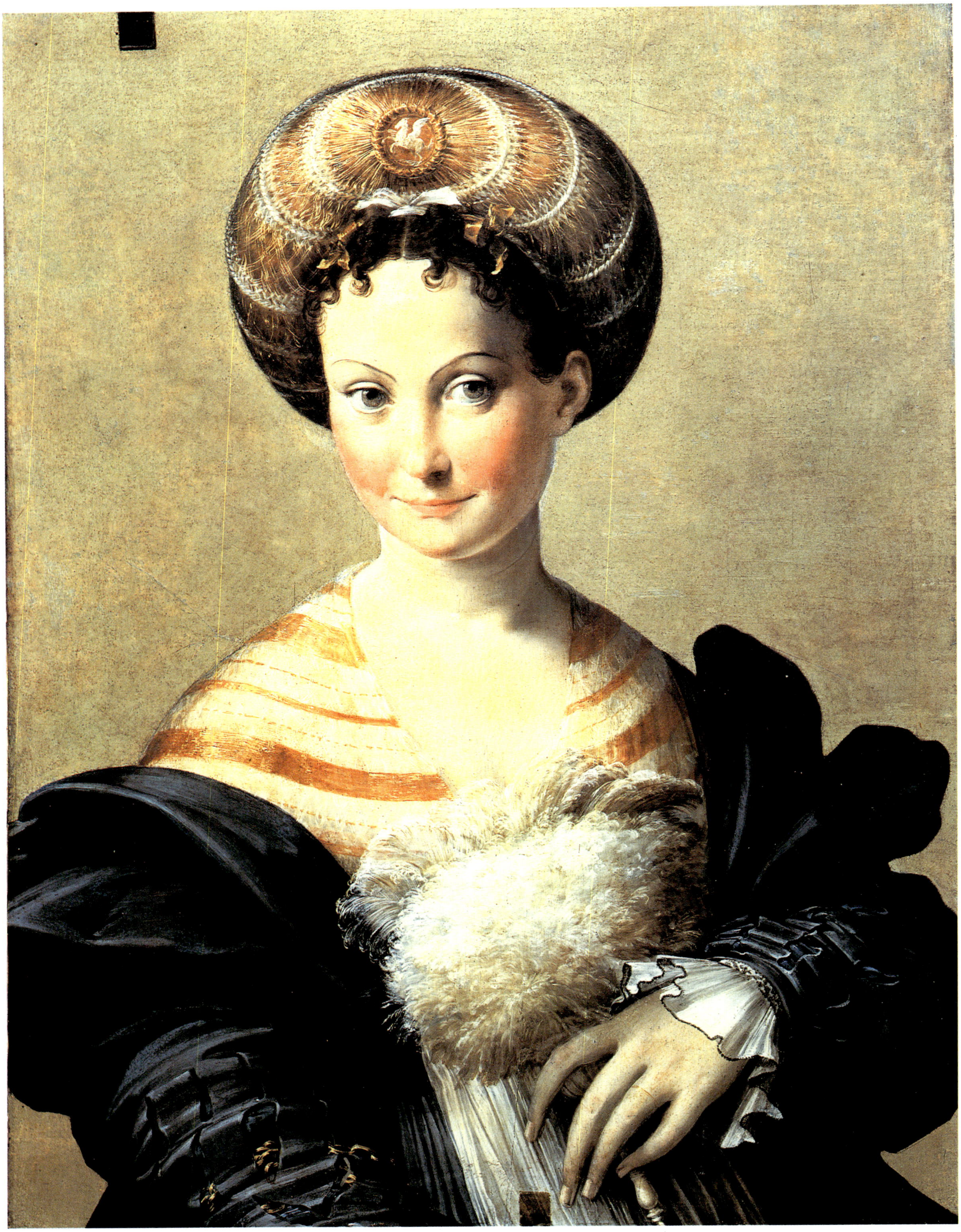

The *"Castaldo"* at Naples (fig. 86) and the little portrait of a prelate in the Borghese gallery in Rome (fig. 87) have the same intensity of gaze from a frontal angle, together with a rather more finished technique. In the case of the Borghese picture the restricted format may perhaps have been chosen (if the panel has not been greatly cut down) to correspond with the sitter's ascetic image. But the loss that it involved of the usual picturesque details of costume and background make it the least characteristic of Parmigianino's male portraits to date, though the quality of the execution is very high. Despite the strictly frontal viewpoint the projection of the tip of the nose and of the underlip appear fully three-dimensional.

The much more elaborate *"Castaldo"* is similar to the Uffizi portrait in design. The casual rejection of the attribution of this picture to Parmigianino was one of the most perverse of Roberto Longhi's utterances, but as with others from the same stable it had for a time deplorably widespread influence. Longhi's alternative suggestion of Girolamo da Carpi can now be seen to be untenable and is generally rejected. The Naples portrait would be a possible candidate for the portrait of a Bolognese count mentioned by Vasari. The alternative identification with Giovanni Battista Castaldo is speculative and modern. It would be difficult to equate Parmigianino's young, aristocratic scholar with Titian's portrait of Castaldo as a grizzled soldier some twenty years later.[12] Parmigianino's painting depends less on picturesque adjuncts than do the more elaborate of the earlier portraits, but is nevertheless of the greatest subtlety. An effect of spontaneity is communicated to the extent that the sitter has just put down the book on his knee and looked up from it at the request of the painter. And the fact that the book itself is partly open does more than merely point to an interrupted action. From a visual point of view the steep angle from which the book is seen introduces a pattern of diagonals, assisted by the shadows that it casts, which create their own modifications to the design by falling across the sitter's left hand and across the arm of the chair. There are further subtleties in that the sitter's hat just meets the vertical molding of the door, while the drooping feather just avoids touching his hair. And the bands—the long patterned triangles of cloth that hang from his collar—relieve the darkness of the coat and bridge the gap between the light tones of the face and of the book. On the left is an odd feature—apparently the truncated back of someone, presumably a servant, approaching a doorway. The fact that this is more broadly painted than the main figure suggests that it may have been an afterthought, the brighter color (pink) of this person's dress compensating for the somber tones of the sitter.

The growing emphasis at this time on elegance is illustrated by the *Madonna della Rosa* (Dresden; fig. 88). Vasari says that this picture was intended for Pietro Aretino but that Parmigianino switched it instead to Pope Clement VII. Vasari adds significantly that as many as fifty copies of the picture had already been made in his time. His own evident enthusiasm for it goes far to explain this degree of admiration in the sixteenth century. He comments favorably on the suggestion of childlike naughtiness in the young Christ, enthuses over the marvelous treatment of the hair, and pays particular attention to the sleeves of the Madonna's dress, which he describes as of yellowish crepe, seemingly striped with gold.

Opposite:
85. PARMIGIANINO
A Young Woman ("Turkish Slave"), c. 1530–31
Oil on panel, 26⅜ × 20⅞ in. (67 × 53 cm)
Galleria Nazionale, Parma, Italy (cat. A38)

Following pages:
86. PARMIGIANINO
A Man ("G. B. Castaldo"), 1530–31
Oil on panel, 38⅝ × 32⅝ in. (98 × 83 cm)
Galleria Nazionale di Capodimonte, Naples (cat. A28)

87. PARMIGIANINO
A Prelate, c. 1530
Oil on panel, 20½ × 16½ in. (52 × 42 cm)
Galleria Borghese, Rome (cat. A42)

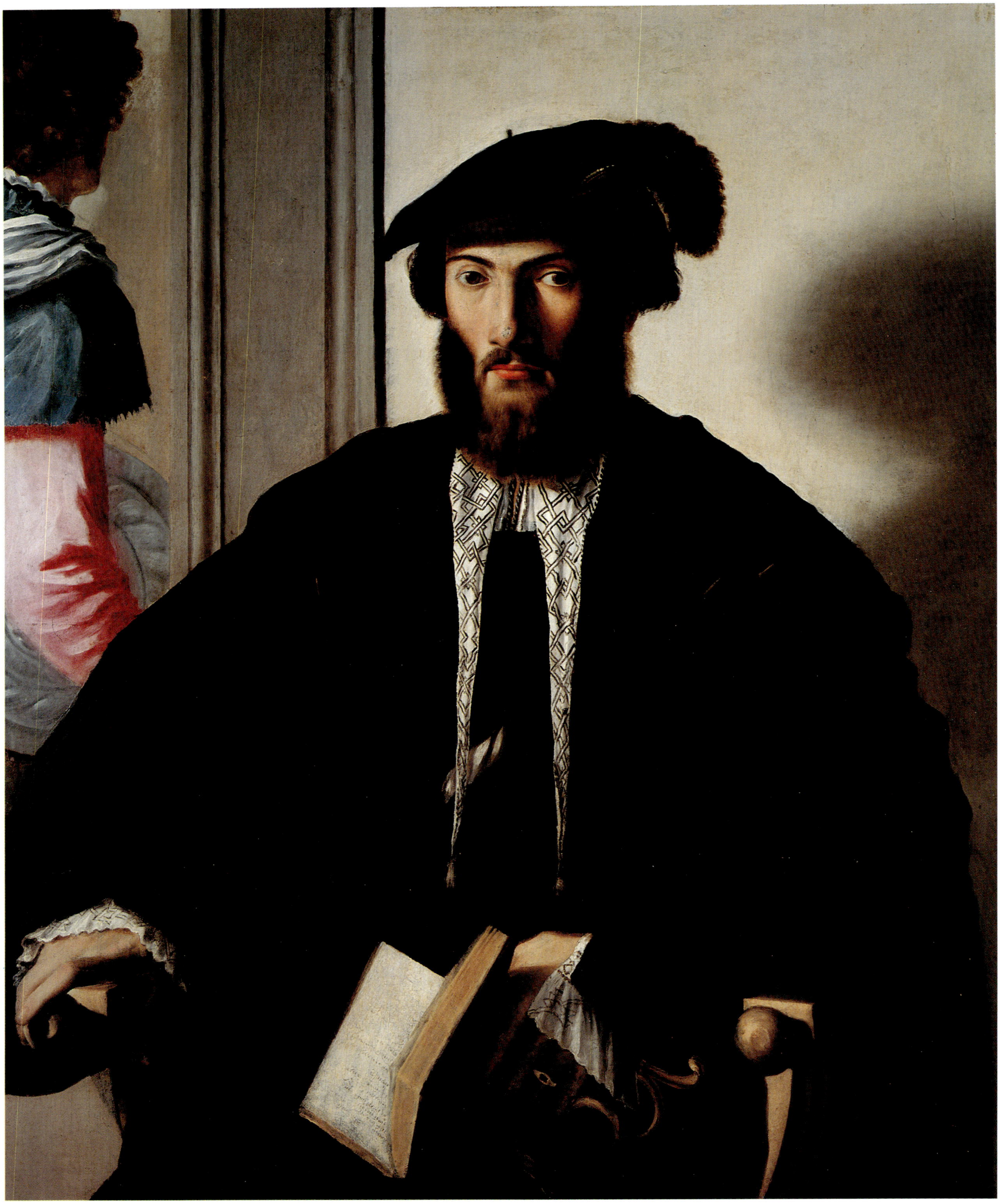

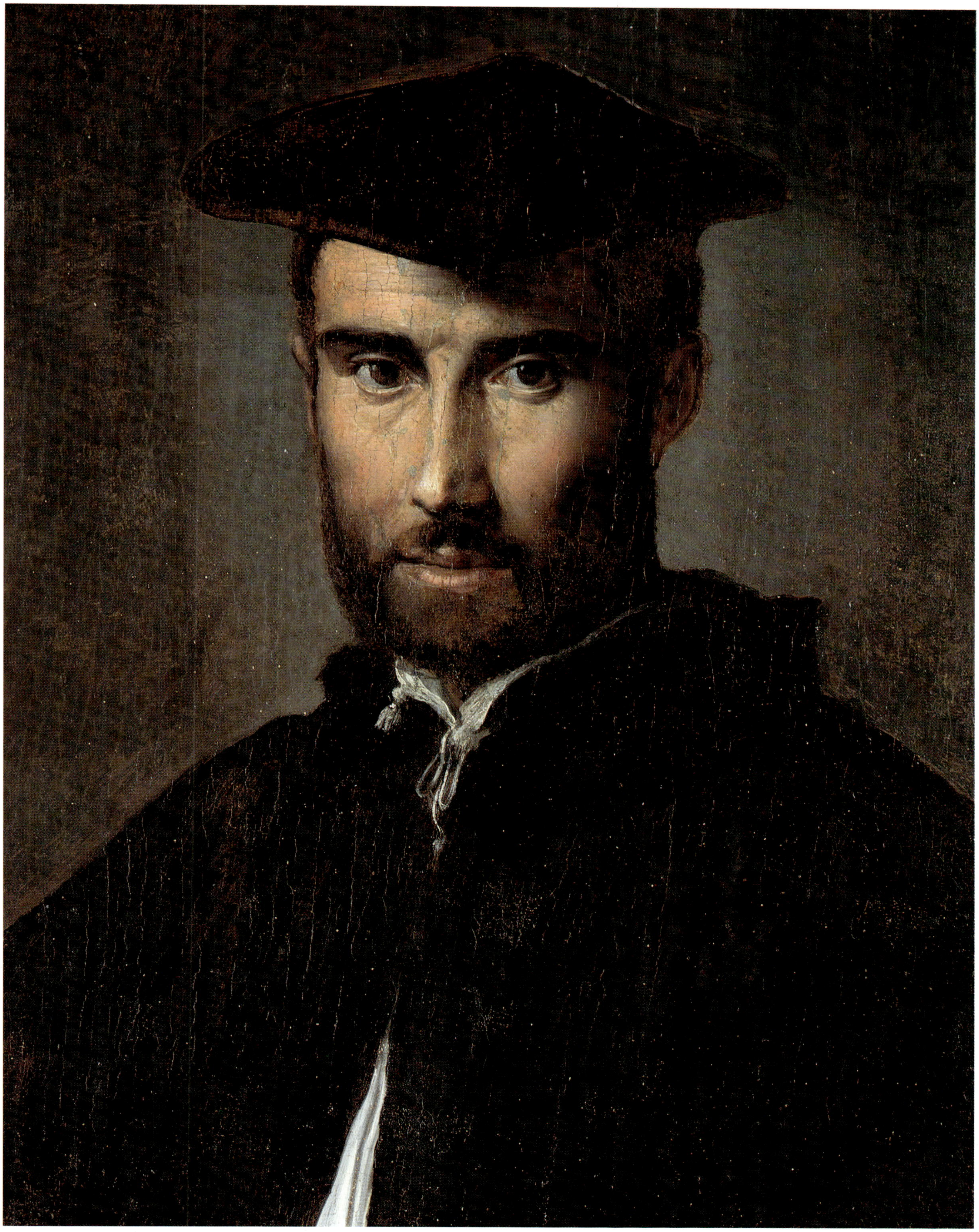

But in modern times the *Madonna della Rosa,* together with the *Madonna dal Collo Lungo,* has incurred the most censure on the ground of affectation. The theory put forward by Affò in the eighteenth century that it was originally intended as Venus and Cupid would be theoretically consistent with the original intended recipient in that he, Aretino, was more addicted to the cult of Venus than to that of the Mother of God.[13] But the surviving drawings offer no confirmation of this theory, and somewhat against it is the consideration that the design seems to have evolved out of that of a famous religious picture by Correggio, the *Madonna del Latte* (Budapest; fig. 89), which had been painted a few years previously.[14] A final anomaly concerning the *Madonna della Rosa* is that, however much it may have chimed with sixteenth-century taste in general, it was not appreciated by its first

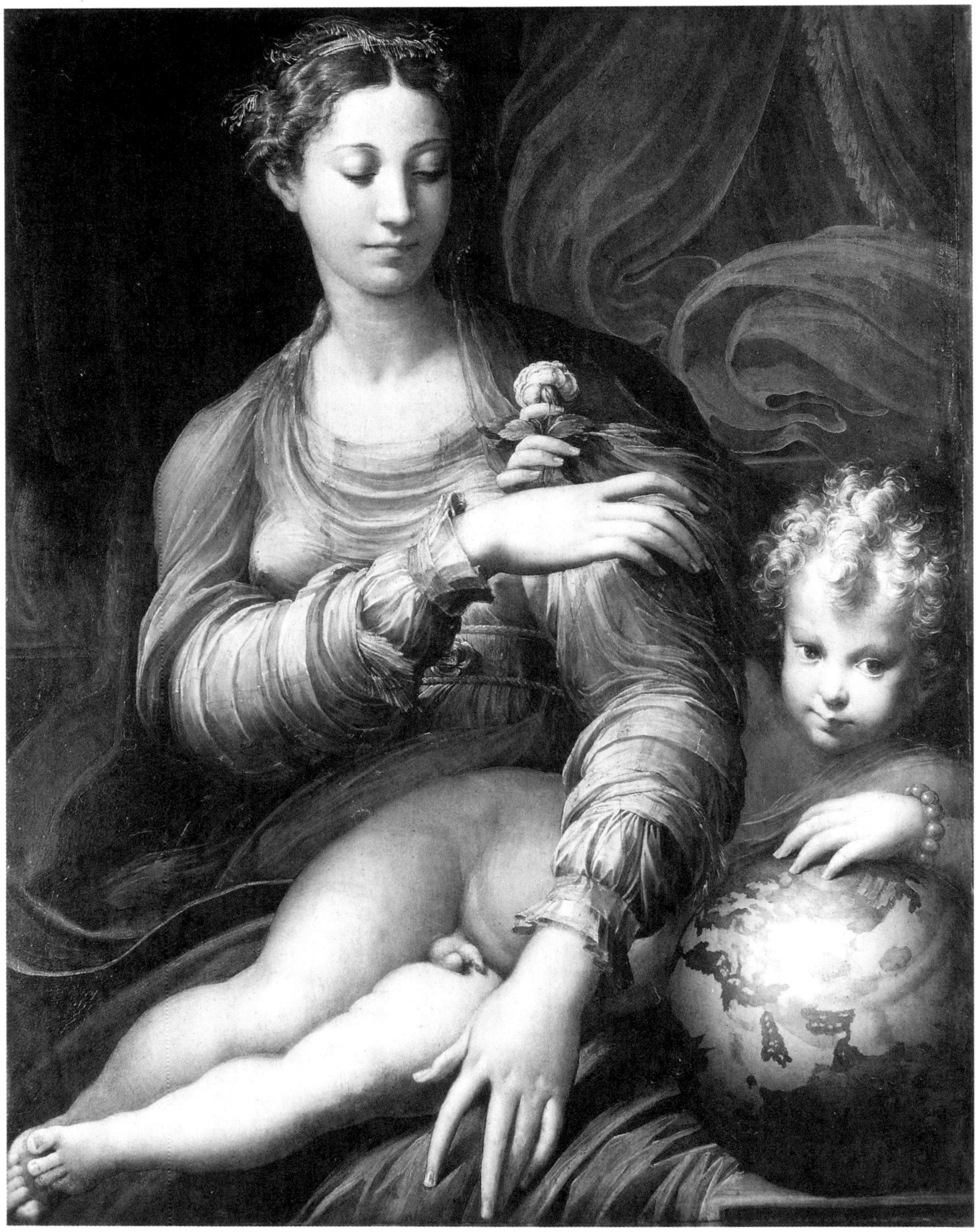

88. PARMIGIANINO
Madonna and Child (Madonna della Rosa),
c. 1529–30
Oil on panel, 42⅞ × 34⅞ in.
(109 × 88.5 cm)
Gemäldegalerie, Dresden, Germany
(cat. A7)

owner, Pope Clement VII. As in Rome six years previously, he seems to have disposed of this example of Parmigianino's art without delay—that is, before leaving Bologna—as Vasari, even in his first edition, notes it as in a private collection there.

The Christ Child, who holds up a flower to the Virgin without looking at her, is unusually big, but no great anatomical liberties are taken. The disturbing impression is due rather to the contrived patterns assumed by the drapery—the whirlpool of red curtains on the right—and above all to the extraordinary attitude of the arms of both figures. The child's right hand and arm curl under the left arm of the Madonna, pressing against her left breast in the process, while her left hand, ostensibly intended to prevent the child from falling, would not in fact be firm enough to do so, and seems only to be

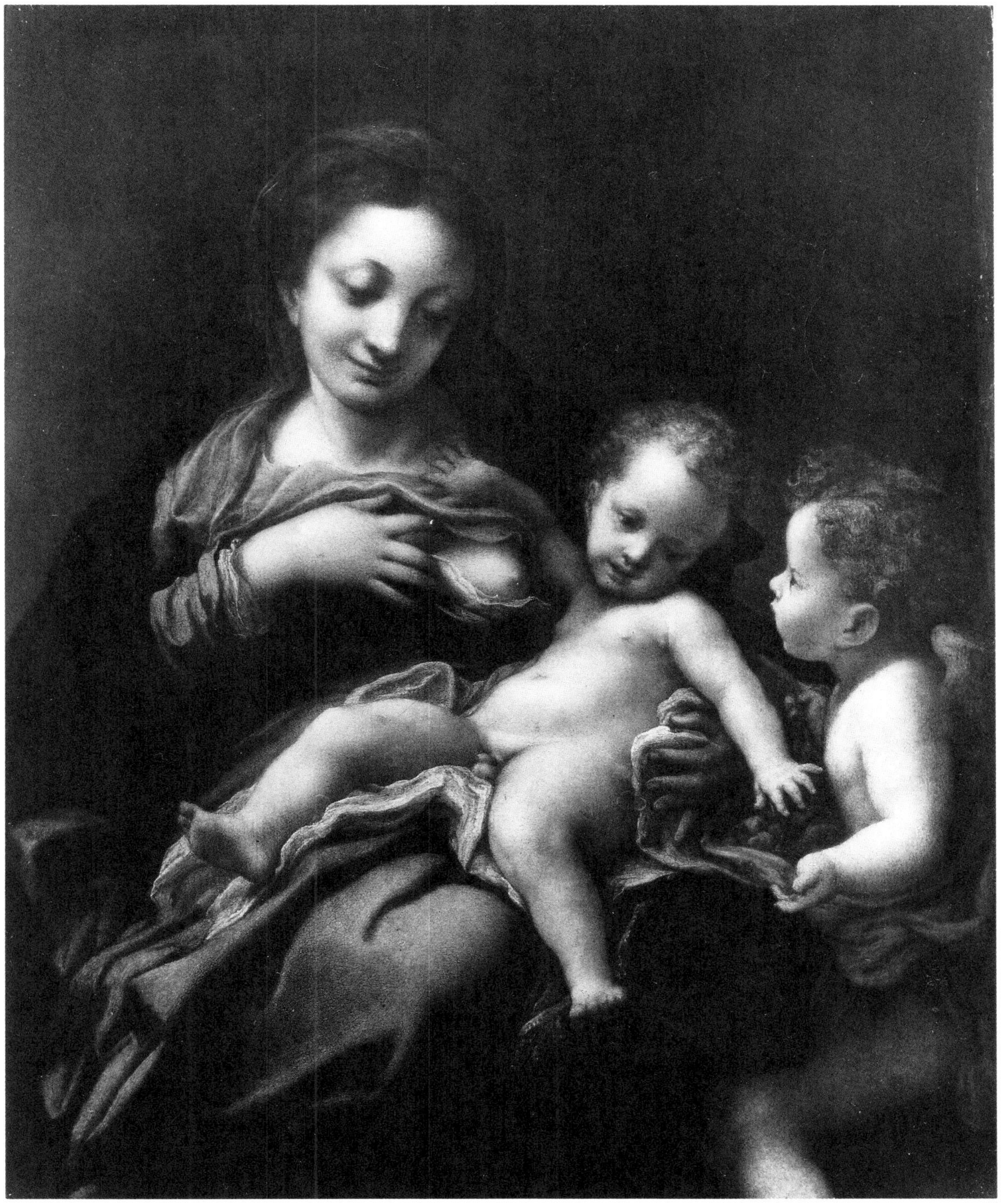

89. CORREGGIO
Madonna del Latte, c. 1522–24
Oil on panel, 27 × 22½ in.
(68.5 × 57 cm)
Szépmüvészeti Múzeum, Budapest

where it is in order to show off the elegance of her fingers. Parmigianino evidently set store by this eccentric idea, as it occurs already in preliminary sketches in which the Christ Child, whose attitude is explored in a series of extraordinary contortions (e.g., P702; fig. 90, or P739), has not yet assumed his eventual posture in other ways.[15]

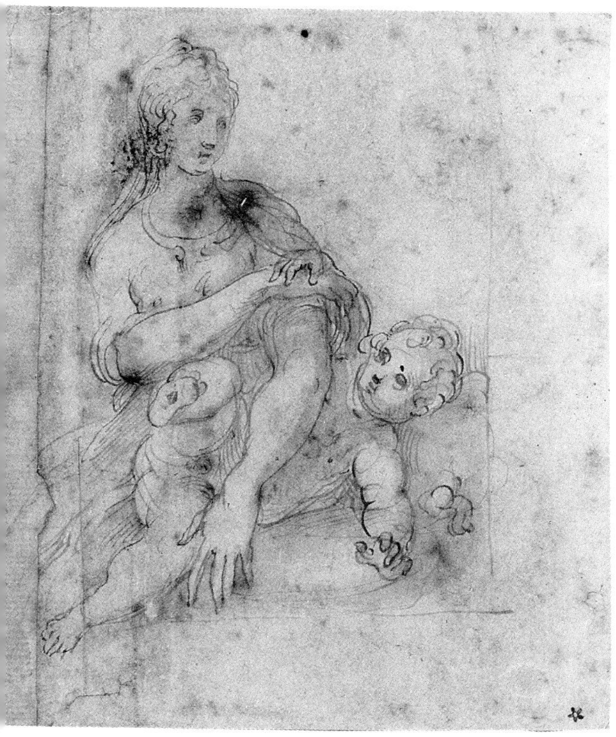

90. PARMIGIANINO
Study for the *Madonna della Rosa*, n.d. P702r
Pen and brown ink on paper, 5⅛ × 4⅝ in. (13.1 × 11.6 cm)
Chatsworth, Derbyshire, England

While still at Bologna, Parmigianino was overtaken by great events for the second time. At the end of the year 1529, two years after the sack of Rome, pope and emperor were reconciled and converged on Bologna where, in February, 1530, one crowned the other. At the age of eighteen the ambitious young Vasari joined half the world at Bologna for the occasion. He notes that he bought, perhaps at a later date, a Madonna that Parmigianino had started ("abbozzò")—perhaps the one now at the Courtauld Institute—but does not claim to have met him. Nevertheless he relates how, having witnessed the emperor at table, Parmigianino painted a large allegorical portrait of him that pleased both the sitter and the pope but which the artist declined to leave with the former. The painting is assumed to be the one now in New York (fig. 91), which includes a globe similar to that held by the Christ Child in the *Madonna della Rosa.* One explanation of the common factor would be the probable presence in Bologna at this time of Pietro Aretino. Parmigianino would have known him in Rome when he was the recipient of the early self-portrait. Many years later, in 1548, Aretino, as is well known, advised Titian (who rejected the advice) to add allegorical figures of Fame and Religion to his portrait of Charles V. A similar allegorical element in Parmigianino's portrait of the same sitter suggests Aretino's involvement, and the factor of outside intervention of this kind, together with the fact that the allegorical portrait, as a genre, was still in its infancy, may explain why, as Vasari implies, the artist was not satisfied with the result. Since Aretino was intended as the original recipient of the *Madonna della Rosa,* the presence in that picture of the globe might also be due to a suggestion from him, though Popham suggested an alternative hypothesis—that the globe in the Dresden picture was an afterthought, added when the picture was switched from Aretino to the pope.

The pope's entourage in Bologna included two notabilities from whose presence Parmigianino was to profit. One was the young Ippolito de' Medici, whose role as enthusiastic patron has already been mentioned. Ippolito was accompanied by Paolo Giovio, the newly appointed bishop of Nocera, who was collecting portraits of famous men for his museum. As we shall see, it may have been as a result of a meeting with Parmigianino at this time that he was commissioned to portray the *condottiere,* Malatesta Baglione; and a further meeting at Bologna may have been with Sebastiano del Piombo, whose presence there on this occasion is attested by his drawing, in the British Museum, of emperor and pope together. As we have seen, Parmigianino would have known Sebastiano in Rome. A meeting at this time would therefore have been virtually inevitable and may be considered confirmed by an extraordinary feature that is common to portraits painted by both at this time. In Sebastiano's portrait of Ippolito de' Medici, the patron of both painters, the fingers of one hand, but not the whole hand, are shown projecting from the far side of

Opposite:
91. PARMIGIANINO
Allegorical Portrait of Emperor Charles V, c. 1529–30
Oil on canvas, 67¾ × 47 in. (172 × 119.4 cm)
Rosenberg & Stiebel, New York (cat. A31)

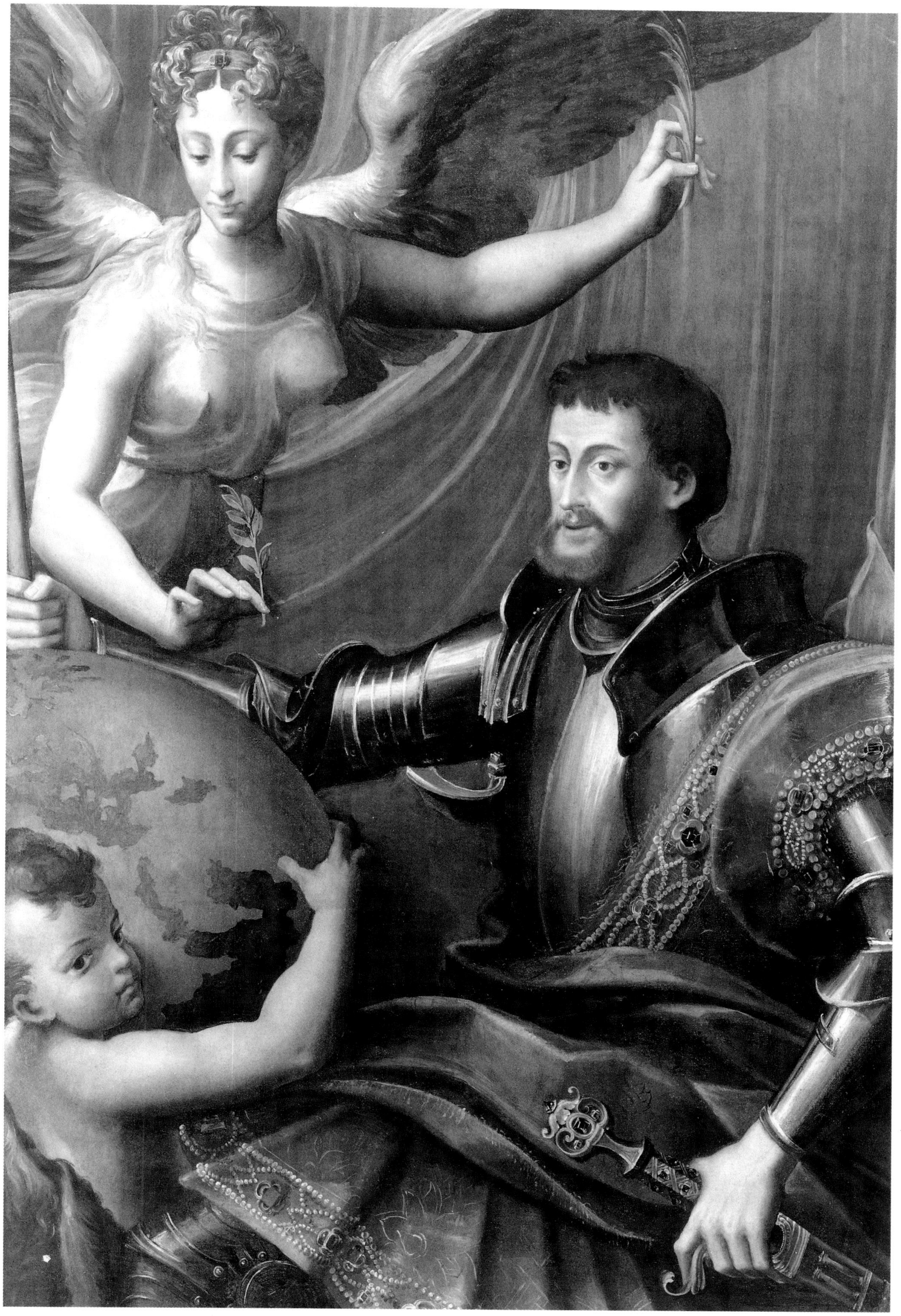

the sitter's body. The same curious feature occurs in a little self-portrait of Parmigianino that has recently come to light (fig. 92).

There remains the problem of the date of the Vienna *Cupid* (fig. 93). I have already suggested that though the original owner, the Cavaliere Baiardi, was a resident of Parma, the painting does not show the hard and brittle touch and the minute finish of the panels painted by Parmigianino after his return to his native city, and for that reason I suspect that it dates from before that time. But how much earlier? It is too accomplished to be pre-Roman, and if painted in Rome it would surely have found a home there. There remain the years at Bologna, and this seems a more valid dating than the usual one, both on technical grounds—the flashing brushstrokes of the hair of the farther child and the thin pigment on her arms where the underdrawing shows through—and in consideration of Parmigianino's plans at this stage. He had traveled to Rome with specimens of his art to show what he could already do. Now, after an absence of six or more years, he was to return home. His habit of painting without commission, together with the spur of wishing to

92. PARMIGIANINO
Portrait of a Young Man (Self-Portrait),
c. 1524
Oil on panel, 11¼ × 8⅞ in.
(28.5 × 22.5 cm)
Location unknown (cat. A55)

astonish his countrymen, would constitute sufficient reason for painting the *Cupid* in Bologna and bringing it with him on his return. Vasari's statement that it was painted for the Cavaliere Baiardi need mean no more than that Baiardi was the original owner—a fact confirmed by the inclusion of a picture of this subject by Parmigianino in an inventory drawn up at Baiardi's death.[16] Baiardi was to come to Parmigianino's rescue as guarantor at Santa Maria della Steccata in Parma. The Baiardi inventory shows that he had a large collection of paintings by Parmigianino and no fewer than 557 of his drawings. These quantities suggest that he had acquired the contents of Parmigianino's studio at his death, while that most of the paintings are specified as small would support the idea that most of them were probably uncommissioned. Many of the drawings are specified as of classical subjects. Baiardi also owned a painting of Venus and Adonis by Titian.

A revealing early study (P543; fig. 94) for the *Cupid,* and two other sketches, were obviously made from life (P500 and P524v). In addition, Parmigianino evidently drew on his recollection of a celebrated antique sculpture, the *Cupid* of the Capitoline museum

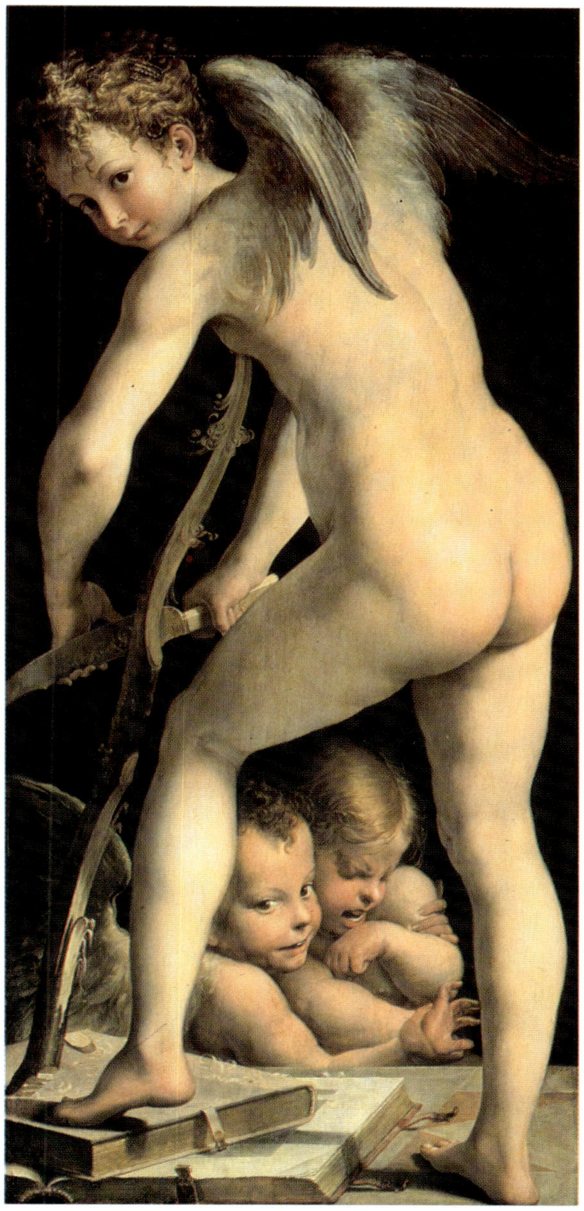

93. PARMIGIANINO
Cupid Cutting His Bow, c. 1531–32
Oil on panel, 53⅛ × 25¾ in.
(135 × 65.3 cm)
Kunsthistorisches Museum, Vienna
(cat. A52)

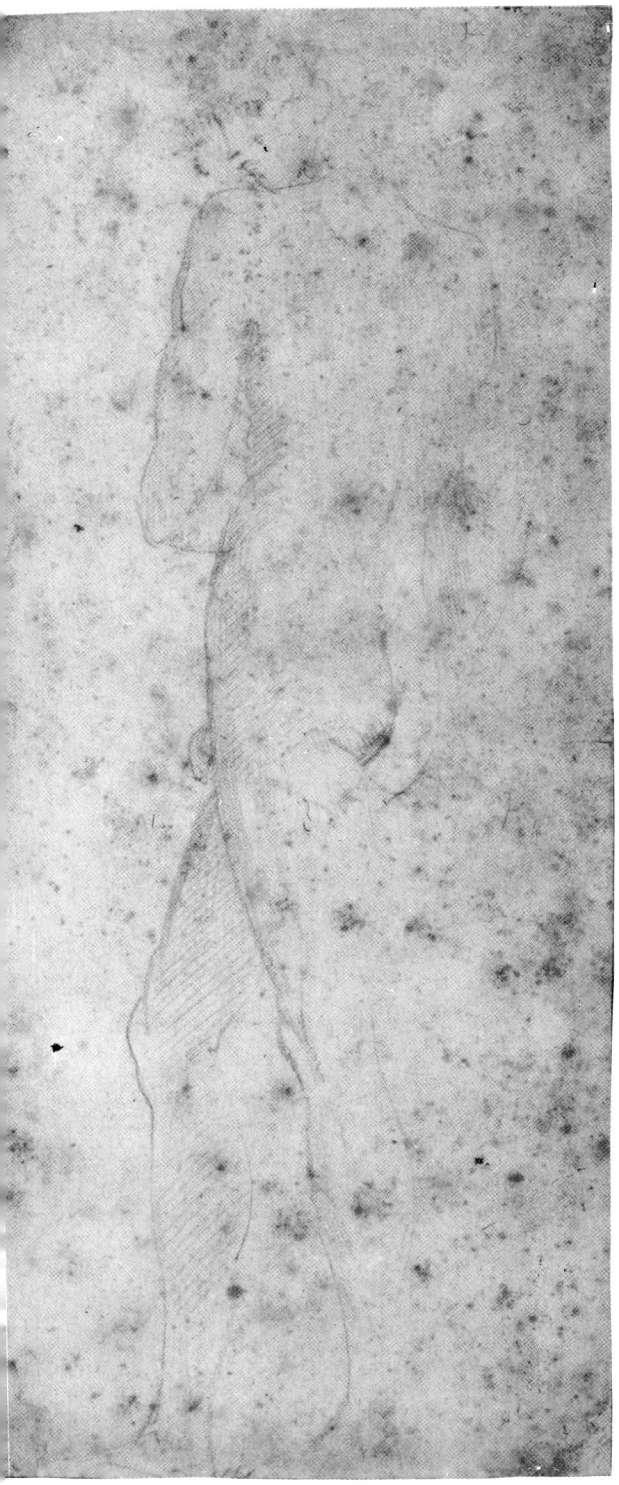

in Rome (fig. 95). Characteristically he elects to depict the figure from the back, and while retaining the bow as a formal element he changes Cupid's action from stringing it to cutting it (upward), thereby adding a new emphasis. The limbs are not unduly elongated, but the boy, with his narrow shoulders, is still very young, and with his ingenious ideas on space Parmigianino would have us believe that the platform on which Cupid stands drops suddenly in the middle distance. This principle had been realized in a late work of Mantegna (the Castello Sforzesco altarpiece), and it was later to be developed by Veronese.

The meaning of the *Cupid* has been much discussed, particularly as regards the relevance of the children who are glimpsed between Cupid's legs. To judge by the partings in the hair the nearer child is a boy, the other a girl. Only the boy has wings visible. He seems, as Vasari says, to have tried to get the girl to touch Cupid's leg, but this has frightened her and she weeps. For the rest the meaning is obscure, and none of the published theories carries conviction. Some connection between the weeping girl and the cutting of wood may exist, as though adumbrating the pain felt by the female on the first experience of physical love. As to Cupid's action in placing his foot on the books, an obvious explanation would be to imply that passion despises intellect. But this would not explain why one book is open, the other closed.

To judge by the large number of copies still extant of the Vienna *Cupid,* it was once, like the *Madonna della Rosa,* enormously admired. Surprisingly, it was attributed in the eighteenth century to Correggio; and there is almost certainly a debt to him both as regards the tall, narrow format of the painting (as in most of Correggio's mythologies) and in the direct contact between the painted figure and the spectator. Two of Parmigianino's figures—the little boy and Cupid himself—look the spectator full in the face. Though by no means confined to erotic art, this device is a feature of it. It occurs, for instance, in nude subjects by Correggio and Titian. Nevertheless, Parmigianino's attitude could hardly be more different from Correggio's, two of whose mythologies—the *Io* and the *Ganymede*—now hang near it in Vienna. While Correggio's approach is uninhibited, Parmigianino's is ambiguous. And the strong contrasts of light and shade, together with the dark background, may be seen as a foretaste of another ambiguously erotic master, Caravaggio.

Parmigianino's contact with the emperor at Bologna led to a mysterious mission to Venice and Verona to buy marble for a projected chapel in San Petronio.[17] Nothing is known of the outcome, but the curious may speculate on a meeting, in the circumstances almost inevitable, between Parmigianino and Titian on this occasion.

94. PARMIGIANINO
Study for *Cupid Cutting His Bow,*
n.d. P543
Red chalk on paper, 7¾ × 3⅜ in.
(19.6 × 8.7 cm)
Galleria Nazionale, Parma, Italy

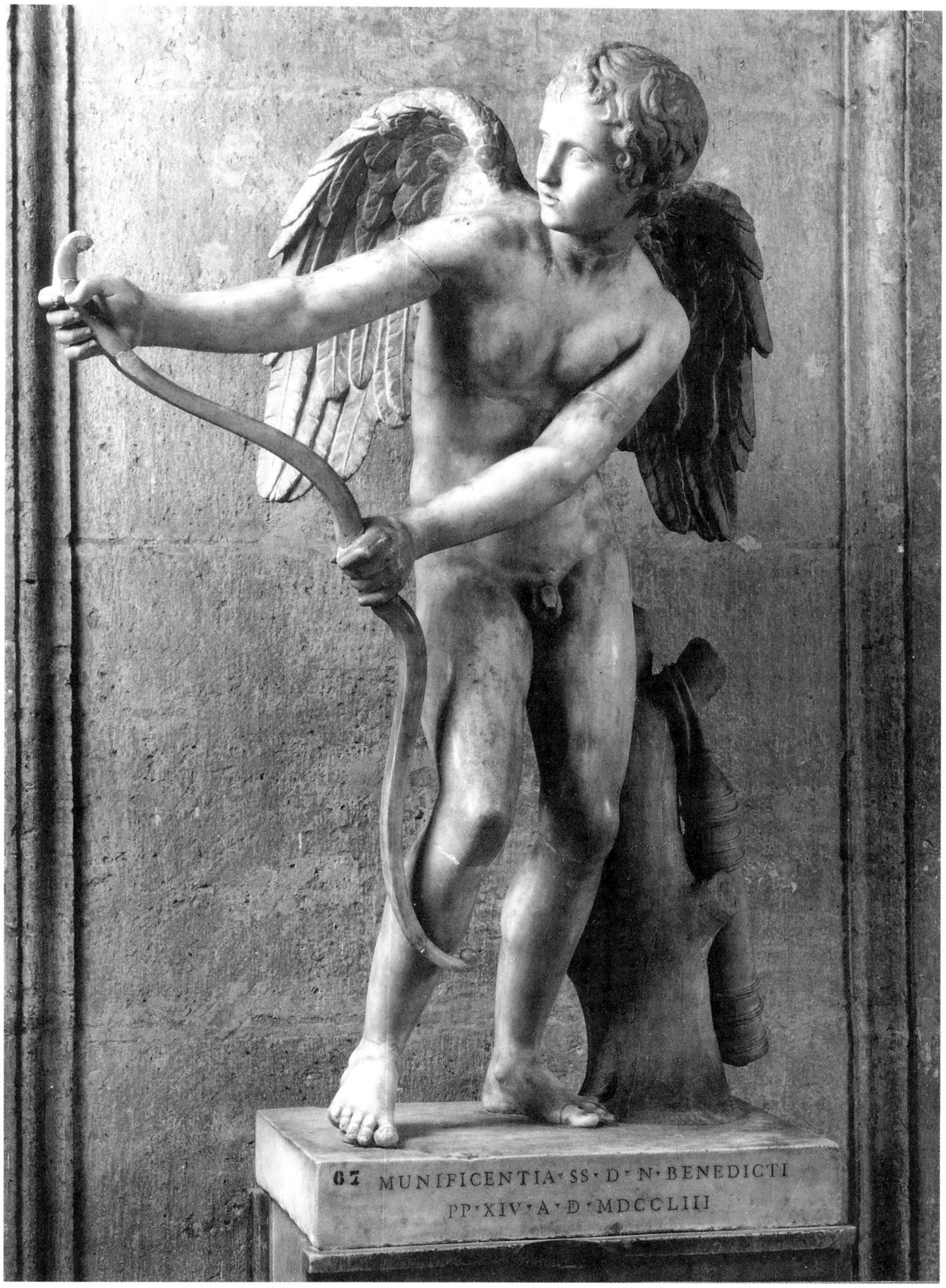

95. *Cupid*
Antique sculpture
Museo Capitolino, Rome

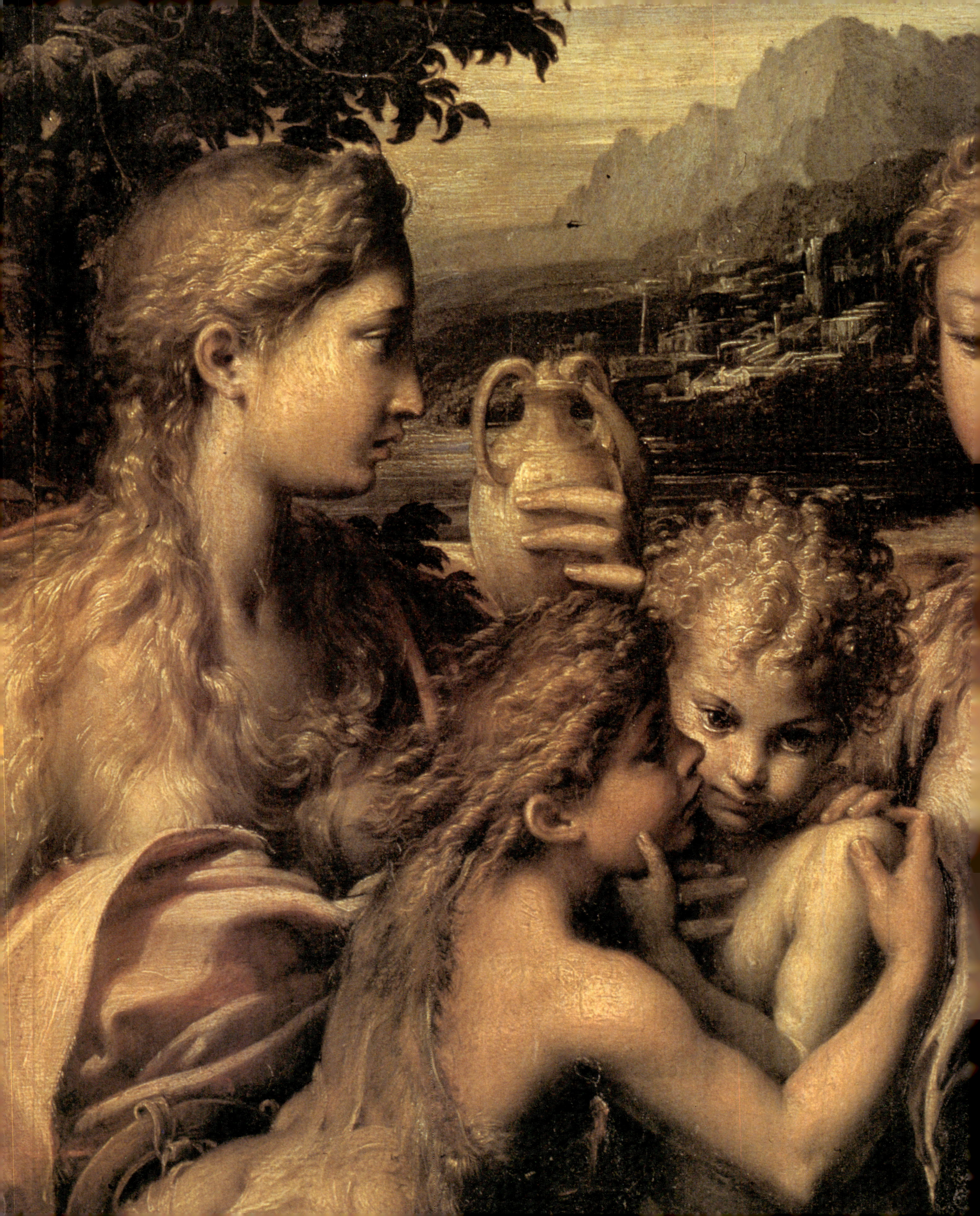

IV

Parma and the End

For the last years of Parmigianino's short life a few personal details are known. On his return to Parma in 1531 he stayed for a time in the family house with his uncle, Pier Ilario, who was to outlive him. During his absence his colleague and childhood friend, Girolamo Mazzola Bedoli, had married Pier Ilario's daughter and seems to have replaced Parmigianino as the favored adopted son. Within a few months, according to research by Copertini (1932) and Dall'Acqua (1984), Parmigianino had moved out of the family house and set up on his own. In all probability this would have marked the turning point in his life, the moment when the alienation and eccentricity of his last years became explicit. Even the fact of homecoming produced its traumas. Though Correggio himself was no longer resident at Parma, there would have been no escaping his painting, nor its fame. The Camera di San Paolo would indeed already have been inaccessible,[1] but his frescoes at San Giovanni and the Duomo and his Saint Jerome altarpiece would have provided matter for constant discussion and a magnet for visitors. Parmigianino's reaction seems to have been a case of "letting 'I dare not' wait upon 'I would.'" At the Steccata, where he was now to work, he wanted to challenge Correggio; and then found, when he tried, that he could not.

As early as 1524 Bartolomeo Montini, a canon of Parma cathedral and prior of Santa Maria della Steccata, had bequeathed a thousand *scudi* for the decoration of the new church, the money being in the hands of his executor, the Cavaliere Scipione della Rosa, a patron of Correggio's. At this time the church was still unfinished. It replaced a small oratory that housed a miraculous image of the Baptist, protected by a palisade (*steccata*). This word was subsequently transferred to an image of the Virgin Mary and then to the new church itself. In April 1530 Parmigianino, then perhaps still resident in Bologna, had been commissioned to paint two altarpieces for the splendid new church, and in May of the following year, 1531, he undertook to decorate the eastern half-dome and the adjoining choir vault. The subject of the fresco in the half-dome was to be the Coronation of the Virgin—the same as Correggio's at San Giovanni.

In the event Parmigianino seems to have made no attempt to paint the altarpieces. Instead he made sketches for the *Coronation*, starting with a symmetrical arrangement, as Correggio had done, and then making others in which Christ was off center, high up on

Detail of fig. 107
PARMIGIANINO
Madonna and Child with Saints Zachariah, Mary Magdalene, and the Infant Baptist
(Mary Magdalene, the Christ Child, and the Infant Baptist)

the right, and the Virgin lower down on the left.[2] This was where his courage failed him. All four half-domes at the Steccata are enormous, much bigger than the one at San Giovanni as it existed then.[3] He therefore delayed painting the *Coronation* and instead turned his attention to a task of a kind that had never faced Correggio—the short, broad stretch of coffered barrel vault between the main dome of the church and the eastern apse (fig. 96). It might be argued that his decision to proceed with the barrel vault, where Correggesque illusionism was hardly practicable, rather than with the half-dome, where it could scarcely be avoided, implied a deliberate rejection of Correggio's legacy rather than an admission of incapacity. More probably the two emotions were inextricably linked.

A reference in the contract of 1531 to "*lacunari*" shows that at the time when Parmigianino was called in, the vault was not a smooth surface but was already coffered. As the choir is so broad and so short, it needs seven of these coffers or cassettes to span the vault but only two in the longitudinal dimension—therefore, fourteen in all (they can be thought of as seven pairs, arranged transversely along the vault). The coffers are square and are sunk back from the surface of the vault. The square cores are framed by two further structural squares, one recessed behind the other between the main surface of the vault and the core in the center of each square. There are therefore four different levels. Frames and centers would have been perfectly smooth and unadorned when Parmigianino started, like the coffers of many Roman buildings, including the dome of the Pantheon in Rome, which was probably the prime source of their inspiration.

The existence of the coffers obviously precluded the possibility of covering the surface of the vault with a unified, illusionist composition, and to that extent they may have seemed to Parmigianino an asset, as decreasing the degree of competition with Correggio. But they presented difficulties of their own. Looking at the Pantheon dome, it would be difficult to imagine how to apply figured decoration to such a pitted surface at all. At one stage, represented by one side of a drawing in the British Museum (P228), Parmigianino was apparently planning a trompe l'oeil colonnade of pilasters along the vault. At another stage, illustrated in a sketch in the Louvre (P450), he toyed with the idea of filling the innermost squares with small illusionist paintings. These ideas were not followed up. In the event, boldly projecting gilt-bronze rosettes, already mentioned in the 1531 contract but not put in hand until 1537, were let into each coffer—another antique motif, and one which had been revived locally for the wooden doors of the Duomo and the Baptistry at Parma.[4] The sunken areas around the rosettes are painted blue. On the top surface the ground color is scarlet. These are the only strong colors on the vault, though there is much gold. There are also twelve much smaller gilt-bronze rosettes, or bosses—five in an arc at each of the central, coffered sections of the vault, and two in the center. Unlike the others, these are not in sunken areas but are applied to the main surface of the vault. Vasari states with surprise that Parmigianino himself worked the rosettes in bronze. According to the documents they were in fact made by

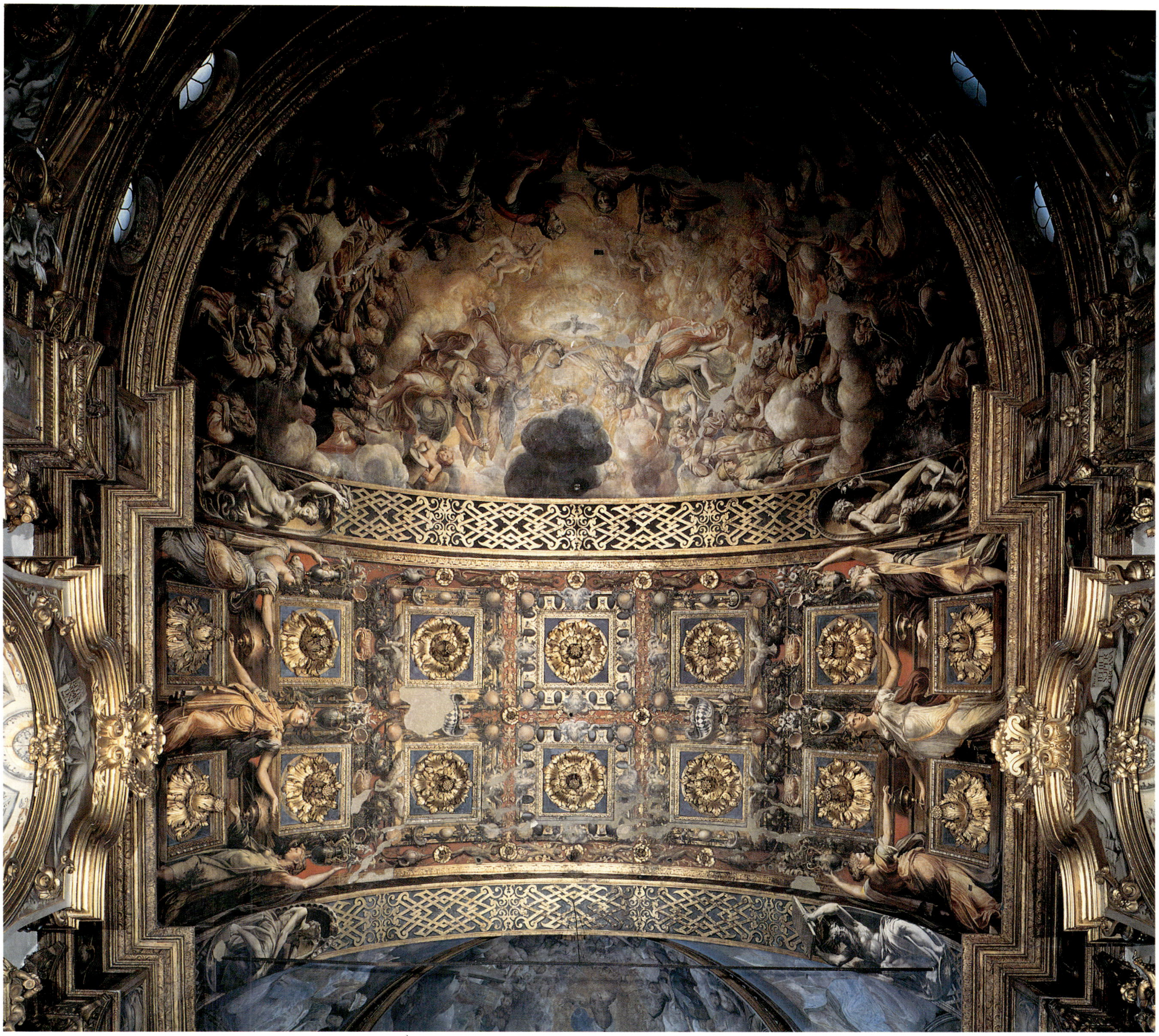

96. PARMIGIANINO
Choir vault of Santa Maria della Steccata, c. 1535–39
Tempera on fresco
Santa Maria della Steccata, Parma, Italy
(cat. A35)

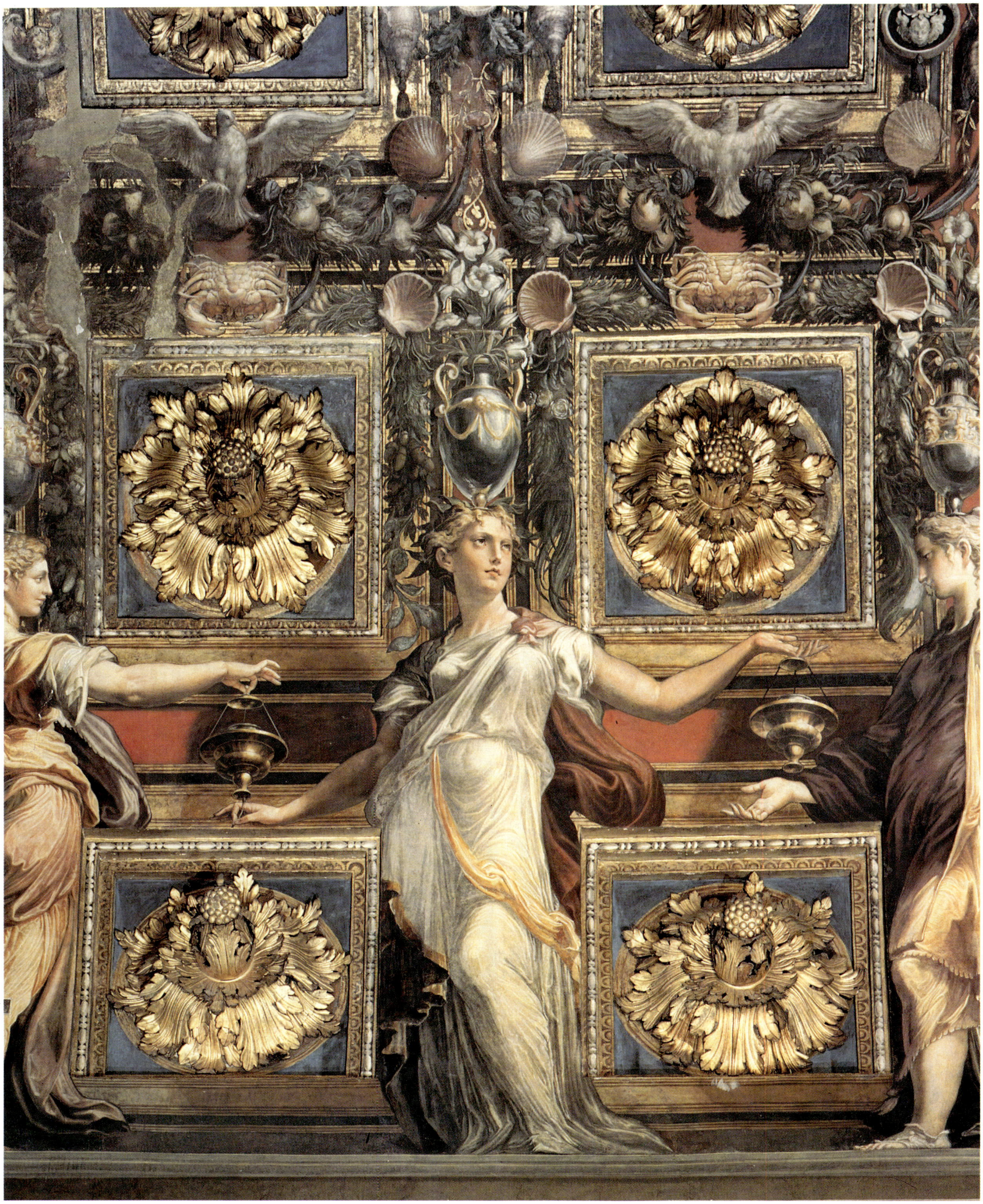

specialists, but in August 1538 he was entrusted with gilding them.[5] Such a process, apparently turning base metal into gold, would have held an obvious appeal for him.

An early phase in Parmigianino's plans for painting the vault is illustrated by its double-sided drawing, already mentioned, in the British Museum (P228; fig. 97). At this stage the raised intersections between the coffers were to receive oval medallions of biblical figures, not in the central, coffered section of the vault but only at the ends, at the base of the supporting arches (*sottarchi*). These arches, which have a smooth surface, not a coffered one, separate the choir vault from the dome over the crossing on the west side and from the half-dome of the apse on the east. Probably on the crown of one of these arches there was to have been a large medallion of Daniel in the Lions' Den, for which several drawings survive.[6]

At this point it evidently dawned on Parmigianino that it would be possible to fit large-scale figures actually into the coffered zone—in the cruciform intersections between the coffers—not, indeed, on the crown of the vault but at the base of both sides. One such figure, the prototype of the existing maidens, is lightly sketched over other forms on the verso of the British Museum drawing. The idea may perhaps have come in principle from recollection of the ingenuity of certain painters of the time—above all, Polidoro da Caravaggio in Rome—in fitting figure painting around the windows on the exterior of palaces. It was in any case a brilliant solution, and it was carried out with consistent skill.

There are three women on each side of the vault. The design of the group of three is basically the same on both sides (figs. 98 and 99). The central maiden is shown frontally. The faces of the flanking ones are in profile, facing inward, but their bodies are contrasted. The one on the right on each side is arranged spirally, while the left-hand maiden is seen from the back, looking over her shoulder. But despite the repetition of the attitudes, the north and south groups are far from identical. As the light is imagined as coming from the east, it strikes the northern group from the right and the southern from the left. There are also considerable differences of color and in the arrangement of the draperies in the corresponding figures on the two sides. For this reason alone the suggestion, which has received a certain currency, that one side was entirely painted by Parmigianino himself and the other not at all is unlikely.[7] And after inspection from a scaffolding, I am of the opinion that both sides are basically autograph.

The women's outstretched hands and arms use up every millimeter of the very restricted space on the top surface of the vault, and they finish at the very edges of the sunken areas. Even then there was not quite enough room. Parmigianino would therefore have us believe, by the use of trompe l'oeil moldings, that the coffers, which are in fact sunk into the depths of the vault, are framed by moldings imagined as projecting out from the surface. Thus, the draperies that fall behind the backs of the women are truncated as though they were being obstructed by projections of this kind. The deception is so effective that it is usually not noticed. From the ground it is, in any case, very difficult to see which parts of the coffers are structural and which are painted.

Detail of fig. 99
PARMIGIANINO
(Three Foolish Virgins)

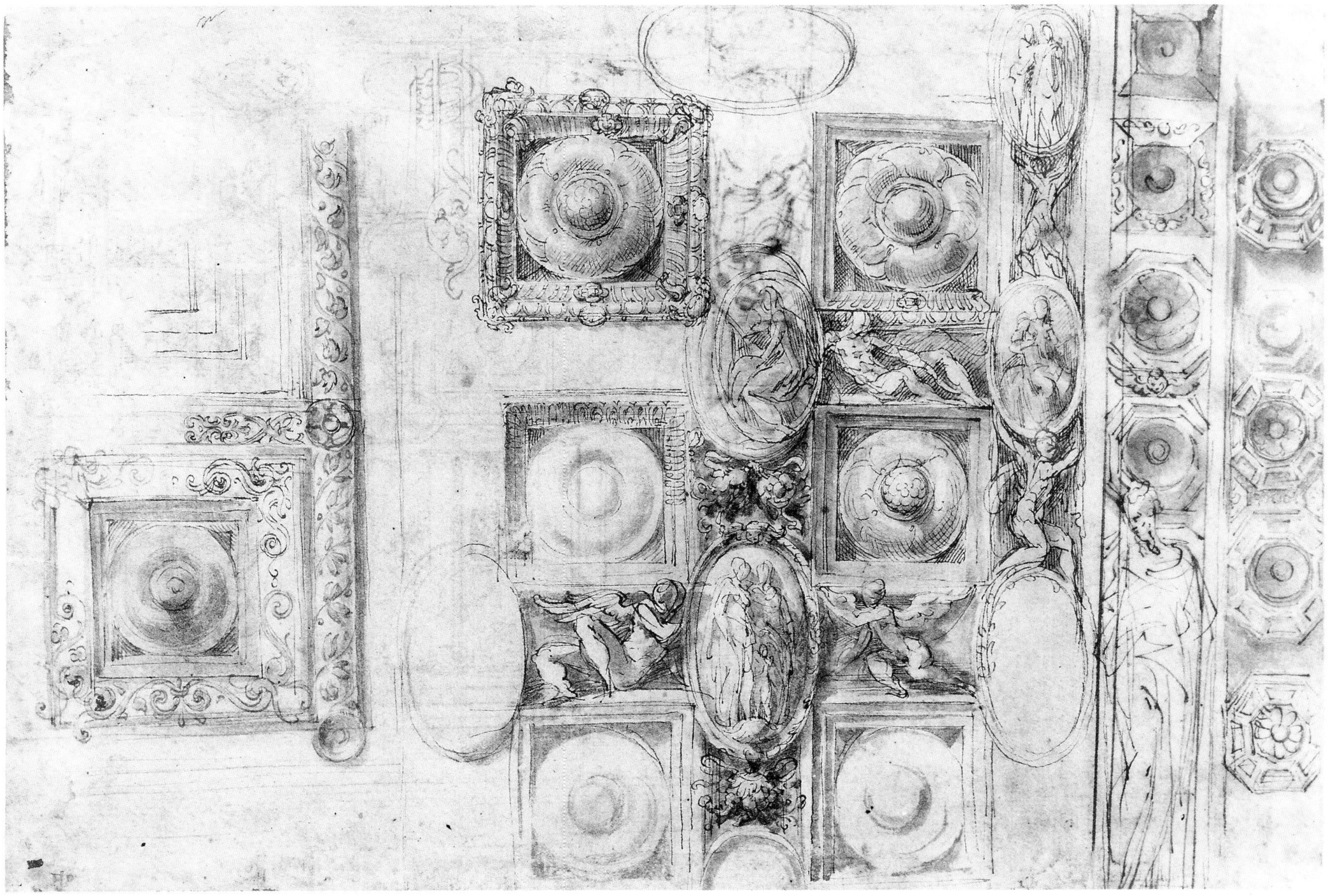

97. PARMIGIANINO
Study for vault of Santa Maria della Steccata, c. 1535–39 P228v
Pen and brown ink and brown and yellow wash on paper, 8 × 11⅞ in. (20.3 × 30 cm)
British Museum, London

These trompe l'oeil features are a major element in the decorative scheme in their own right. The moldings that frame the seven pairs of coffers are all decorated differently, though the two in each pair are the same. The pairs at the base of the vault on both sides are the plainest, so as not to detract from the effect of the maidens at the same level and from the lamps they hold. But higher up, the broad outer frames are ornamented with a fantastic assembly of creatures and objects. The frames of the pair at the apex are the most highly decorated. They have rams' heads in the center of each of their four sides, and seashells at the corners. In the areas of frame between these features (in the pair at the apex alone) are oval reserves filled with the same blue color as the sunken areas around the gilt-bronze rosettes. In the adjoining pairs of frames, that is, the next pairs down on both sides from the pair at the apex, the seashells recur at all four corners, but the rams' heads only on the top sides. The inner sides of these pairs are bridged by coats of arms; the outer ones have a variety of objects suspended on cords. The bases of these pairs have doves in the center, and at the tops of the next pairs, lower still, there are crabs (fig. 100). At this level there are swags of fruit and leaves between the bases of one pair and the tops of the pair beneath them. There are further swags on the tops and sides of the penultimate pairs. As with the livestock, these are painted in natural colors, as though they were actual objects and not carvings. But the lobsters and frogs on the scarlet ground around the pair of frames at the apex are in gold. The complexity of the scheme is extreme, and the result an extraordinary and unique achievement.

Though the effect as a whole is of bewildering originality, the individual elements can be traced to a variety of sources. Most important of these was probably Perino del Vaga's and Giovanni da Udine's ceiling of the Sala dei Pontefici in the Vatican (fig. 101)—

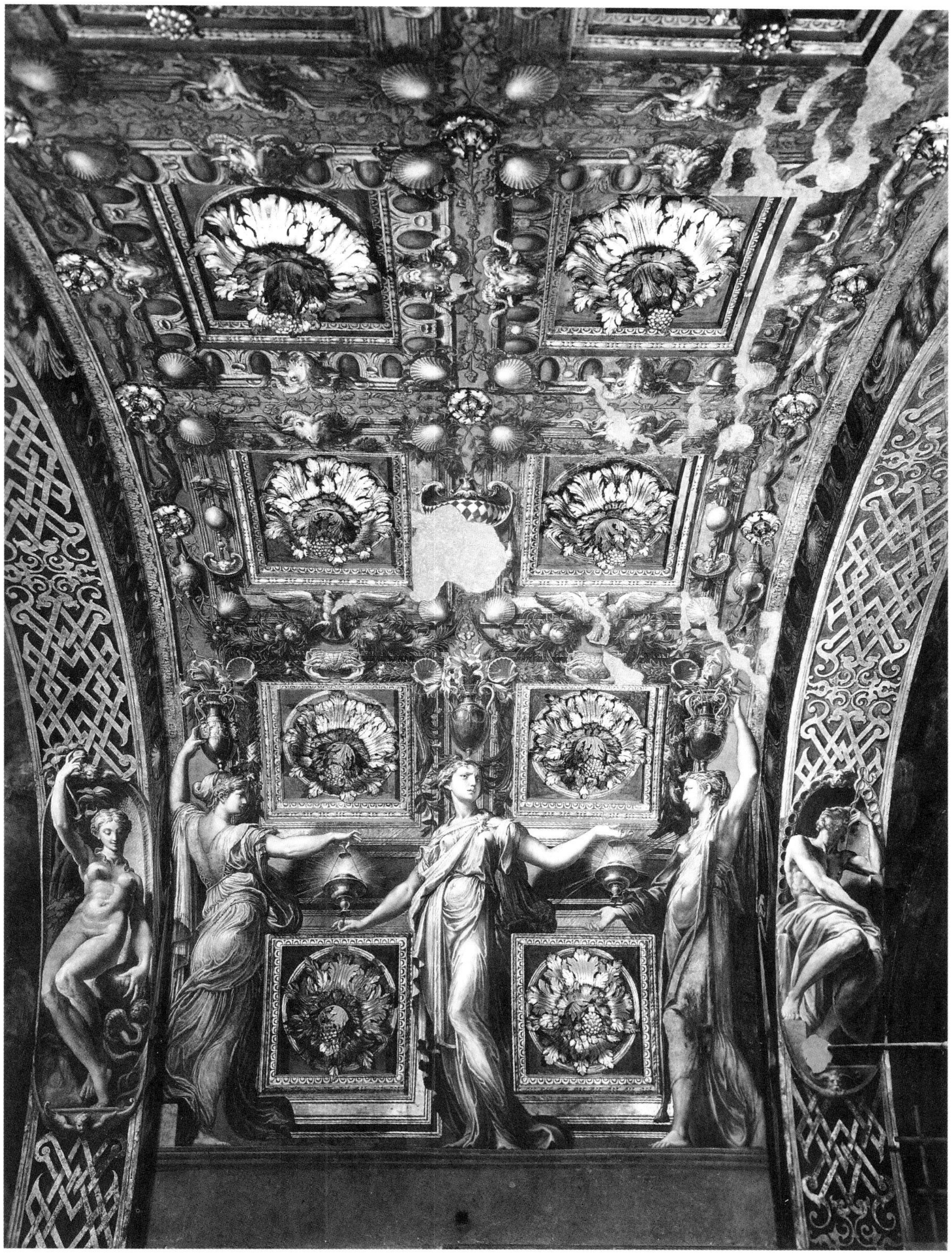

98. PARMIGIANINO
Detail of vault of Santa Maria della Steccata, c. 1535–39
(Three Wise Virgins)
Tempera on fresco
Santa Maria della Steccata, Parma, Italy (cat. A35)

99. PARMIGIANINO
Detail of vault of Santa Maria della Steccata, c. 1535–39
(Three Foolish Virgins)
Tempera on fresco
Santa Maria della Steccata, Parma, Italy
(cat. A35)

that room whose walls Parmigianino might have decorated but that he never did. Deriving, it is assumed, from the Volta Dorata of the Domus Aurea in Rome, this ceiling affected Parmigianino's scheme at the Steccata in two separate ways. One was the deployment of rectangular compartments against a scarlet ground. The other was the inclusion of animals and fish. These were introduced with astrological intent in the Sala dei Pontefici, but by Parmigianino perhaps merely for decorative purposes.[8] In the case of the maidens the ultimate inspiration was probably the antique tradition of caryatids. But a well-known figure in one of Raphael's frescoes in the Vatican—the girl with a pitcher on her head in the *Fire at the Borgo*—would have provided a precedent for the maidens' supporting amphoras (filled in this case with exquisite bouquets of lilies) instead of capitals. A further visual source was perhaps the group of muses in Mantegna's *Parnassus*.[9] Then again, the idea of painting figures against a coffered or cassetted background—in this case a painted rather than a structural one—had been anticipated on a limited scale by Correggio on the crossing arches of San Giovanni Evangelista; and at this time

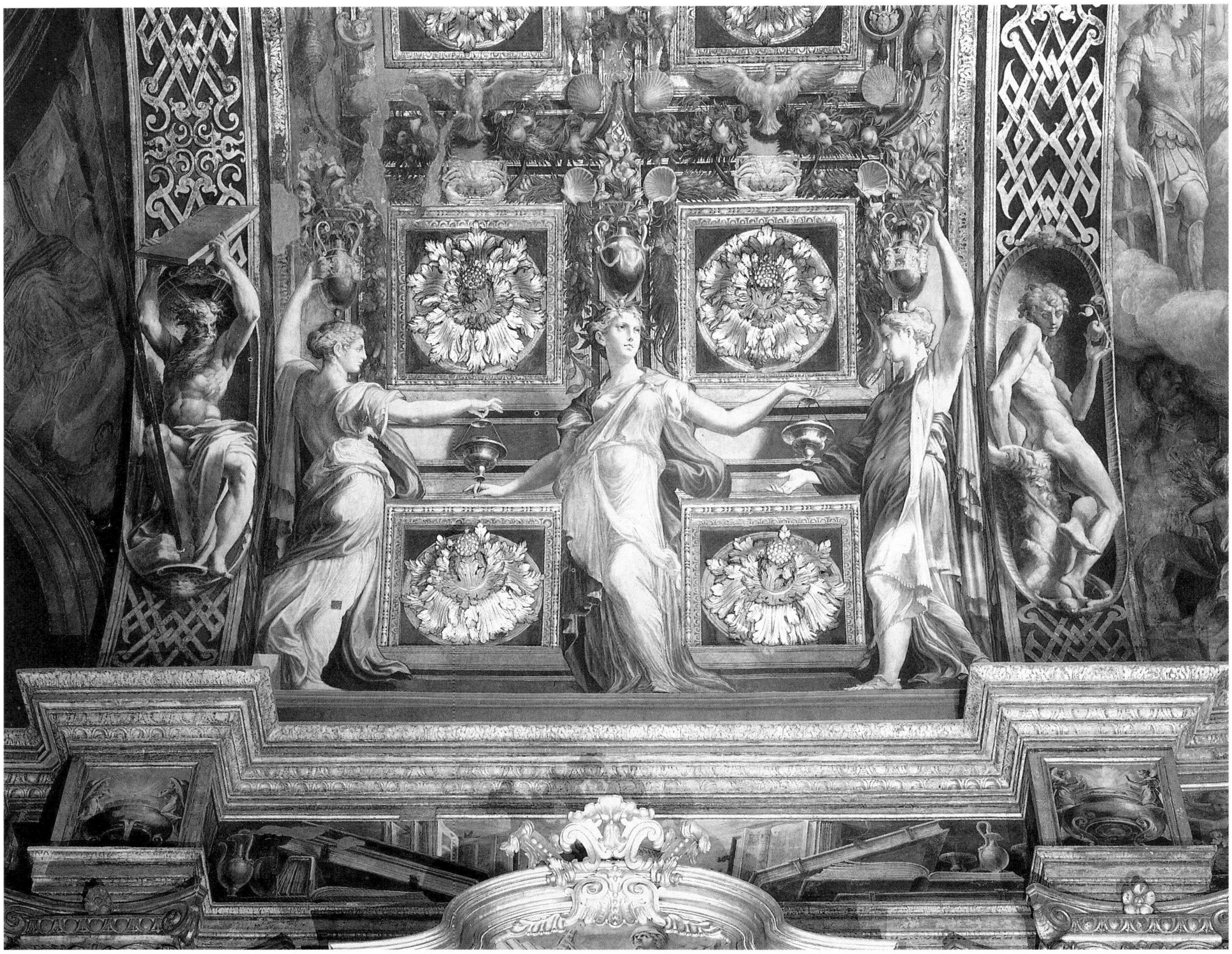

Torbido was doing much the same when executing Giulio Romano's design for the *Assumption* (dated 1534) in the half-dome of Verona cathedral.[10]

The evolution of the maidens provides a clear illustration of the interaction of decorative and iconographic factors in Parmigianino's mentality. In his earlier sketches the women have no attributes and were then evidently purely decorative. Later they were given biblical relevance by being transformed, by the addition of lamps, into Wise and Foolish Virgins—the Wise Virgins, with lamps alight, on the south wall, the Foolish ones, with unlit lamps, on the north. Despite this face-saving improvisation, the effect of the women is still decorative and secular while the fact that there are only three of each, and not five as specified by Saint Matthew, is an indication of the cavalier attitude shown by the artist toward theology throughout the work, and indeed throughout most of his career. When, in addition, it is borne in mind that the spaces that were finally filled by the creatures on the trompe l'oeil moldings were originally to be occupied by medallions of biblical figures, that the relevance of these animals, birds, and crustaceans to the Wise and Foolish

100. PARMIGIANINO
Detail of vault of Santa Maria della Steccata, c. 1535–39
Tempera on fresco
Santa Maria della Steccata, Parma, Italy
(cat. A35)

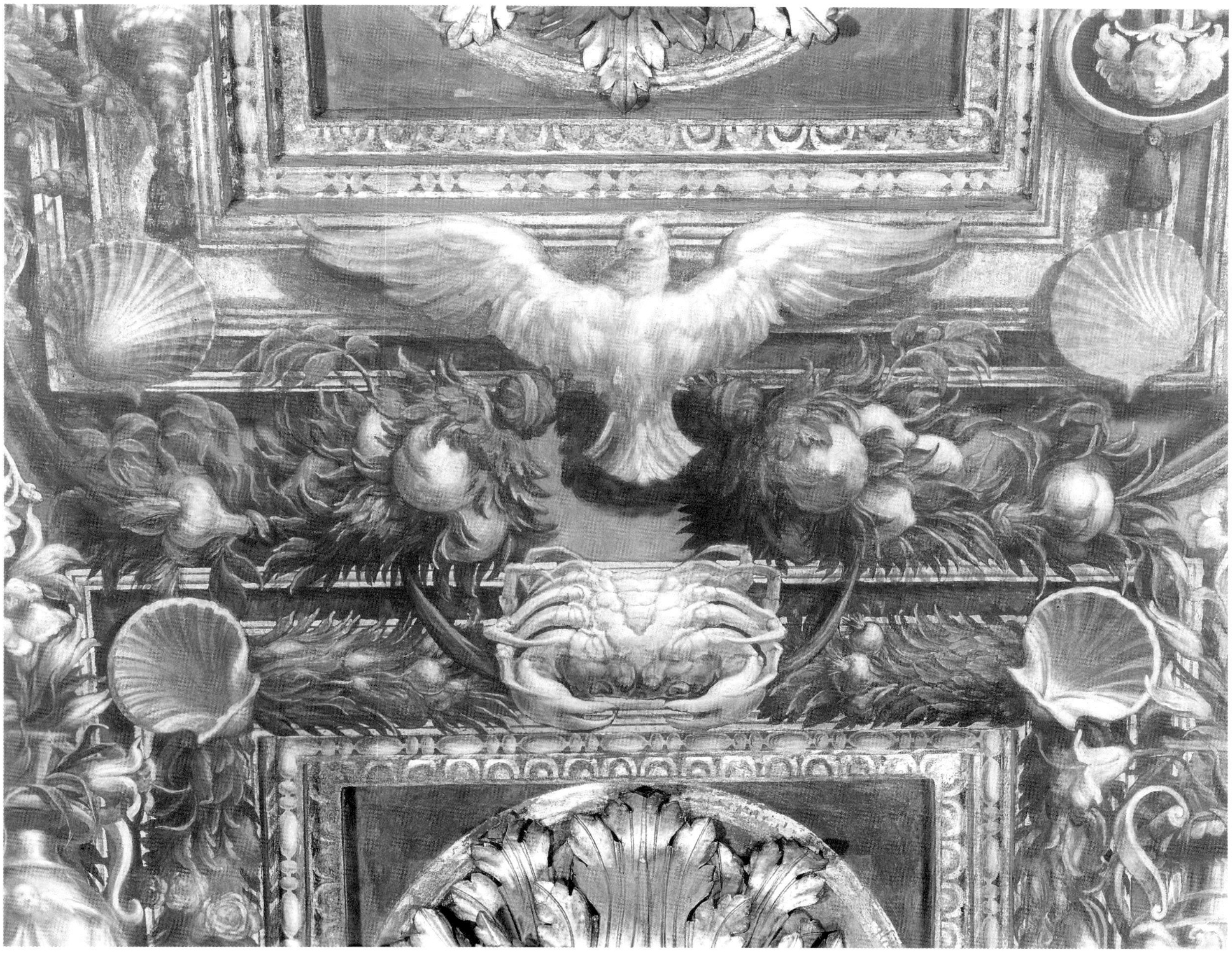

Opposite:
102. PARMIGIANINO
Study for vault of Santa Maria della Steccata, c. 1535–39 P618
Red chalk over stylus on paper, 9 × 4⅜ in. (22.9 × 11.1 cm)
Graphische Sammlung Albertina, Vienna

Virgins is, to put it mildly, not immediately obvious, and finally that no subject for the decoration of the vault is specified in the contract of 1531, the conclusion suggested earlier in this book seems inescapable, namely that Parmigianino was allowed remarkable iconographic liberty, and that he exercised such liberty with striking disregard for theological consistency. Parmigianino's mental processes may be illustrated further by Popham's observation that in certain of the drawings Christ appears to be interchangeable with Jupiter, and the Virgin Mary with Venus.[11]

In their completed form the maidens, and Parmigianino's detailed studies for them, are among his supreme achievements (P618; fig. 102). In particular, I doubt if any other painter has equaled the variety and beauty of the draperies or the virtuosity with which the infinitely complicated reflections and half-lights on the metal surfaces of the lamps have been painted.

In the figures themselves the elongation was not so much a stylistic factor as an

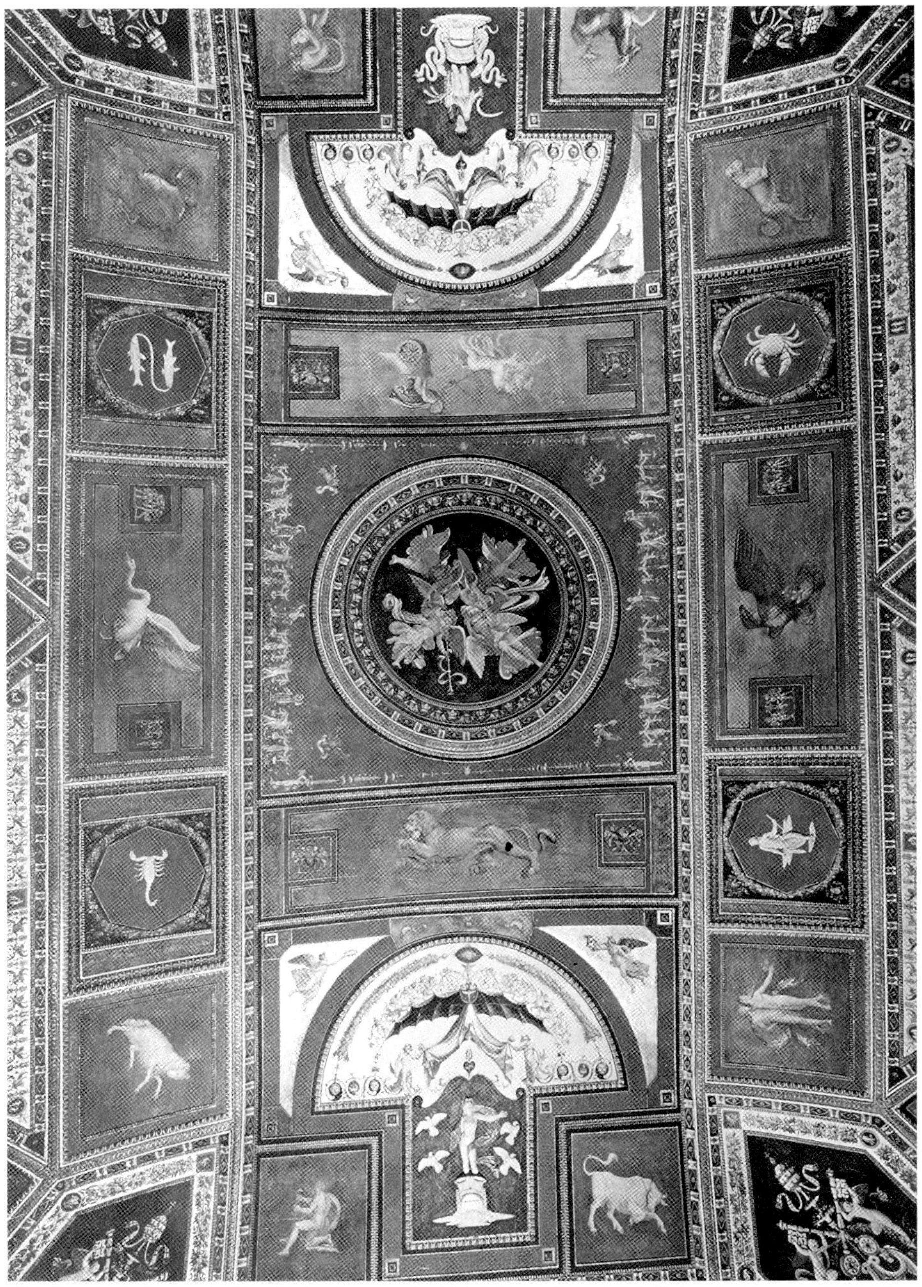

101. PERINO DEL VAGA AND GIOVANNI DA UDINE
Ceiling of the Sala dei Pontefici, n.d.
Fresco
Vatican City

optical one—to allow for foreshortening from the ground. The women combine the restraint and balance of antiquity with an inventiveness of detail peculiar to Parmigianino, and, facilitated by the process of finishing the fresco underpainting in tempera, this elaboration is still more evident in the astonishing objects on the trompe l'oeil moldings. The effect of these various creatures is jewellike, complex, capricious, and exotic, reminding the spectator of goldsmith's work or of an embossed cope. Lower down there is brilliant impressionist painting on the friezes, this time all in fresco. The still life of books and lamps, adorned with winged figures, is of an amazing freedom, the whole of a face being suggested by a single line of light paint.

At the west and east extremities of the vault, on the central section of the curvature and alternating with the small, subsidiary gilt-bronze rosettes, are eight diminutive and very graceful nudes, the survivors from the early stage represented by the British Museum drawing (P228; fig. 97). There are four of these at each end of the vault, alternately male and female, seen from the front and from the back. On the soffits of the supporting arches, the *sottarchi,* are four large grisaille figures, of Adam, Eve, Moses, and Aaron. From certain angles they appear to be juxtaposed with the maidens, who are larger still. But the discord in the scale is not disturbing owing to the projection of the *sottarchi* and to the difference in coloring. These four grisailles can be seen as another illustration of Parmigianino's relationship to Correggio, and as a further instance of the challenge facing the post-peak generation. For they are evidently an attempt to take up where Correggio's grisailles on the soffits of the crossing arches at San Giovanni Evangelista left off (fig. 103). And here for once it may be claimed that in at least one instance Parmigianino surpassed his model. His four figures, being larger than Correggio's, are more elaborately planned, and in the *Moses* (fig. 104) Parmigianino achieves one of his greatest feats. A sheet of preliminary studies in the Metropolitan Museum for this figure shows the artist struggling with a variety of frenzied attitudes (P301; fig. 105) before settling for a simple frontal posture of colossal force and majesty, and one that found even Sir Joshua Reynolds at a loss "which to admire most, the correctness of the drawing, or the grandeur of the conception."[12]

On the reentrant sides of the *sottarchi,* that is, on the inner surfaces, there are painted looped curtains, as in a theater. Higher up, there are shells and ovals, with winged cherubs' heads at the apex. There are smaller cherubs' heads above and below the grisailles of Adam and Eve, and others at the sides of the frames of the two pairs of cassettes immediately below the pair at the apex of the vault. Above and below the grisailles of Moses and Aaron there are heads of bearded figures that suggest a further technical experiment, related to, but not quite the same as, the shorthand technique of the friezes. Here the quick jabs of paint, or blots (fig. 106), do no more than hint at the light and shade on the heads. This seems to me to be an attempt, like that of Polidoro da Caravaggio in the dado of the Sala di Costantino or at San Silvestro al Quirinale, to emulate the technique of antique murals dating from the period of the so-called Fourth

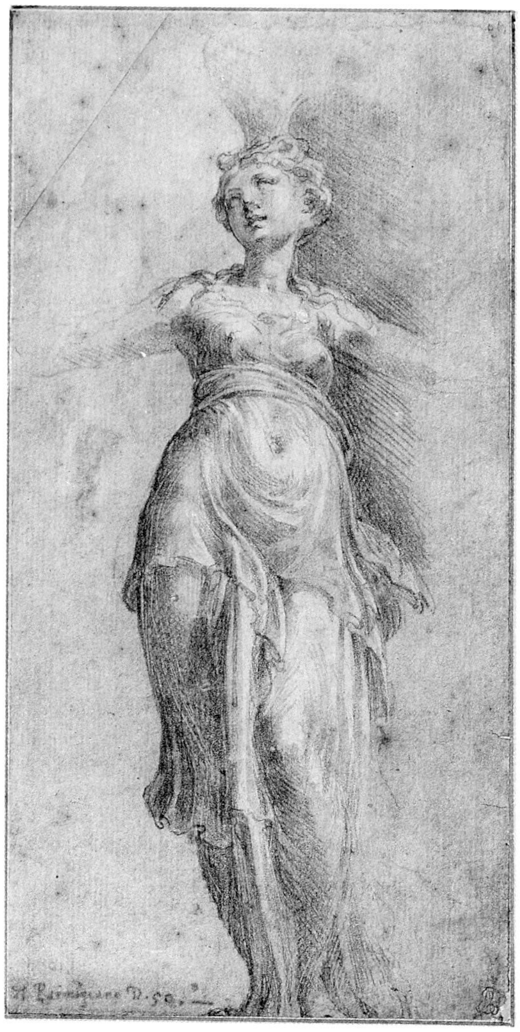

Following pages:

103. CORREGGIO
Detail of the crossing arch of
San Giovanni Evangelista, 1520–22
Fresco
San Giovanni Evangelista, Parma, Italy

104. PARMIGIANINO
Detail of vault of Santa Maria della
Steccata, c. 1535–39
(*Moses*)
Monochrome fresco
Santa Maria della Steccata, Parma, Italy
(cat. A35)

105. PARMIGIANINO
Studies for *Moses,* c. 1535–39 P301r
Ink and black pencil on paper,
21 × 15.4 cm
Metropolitan Museum of Art,
New York

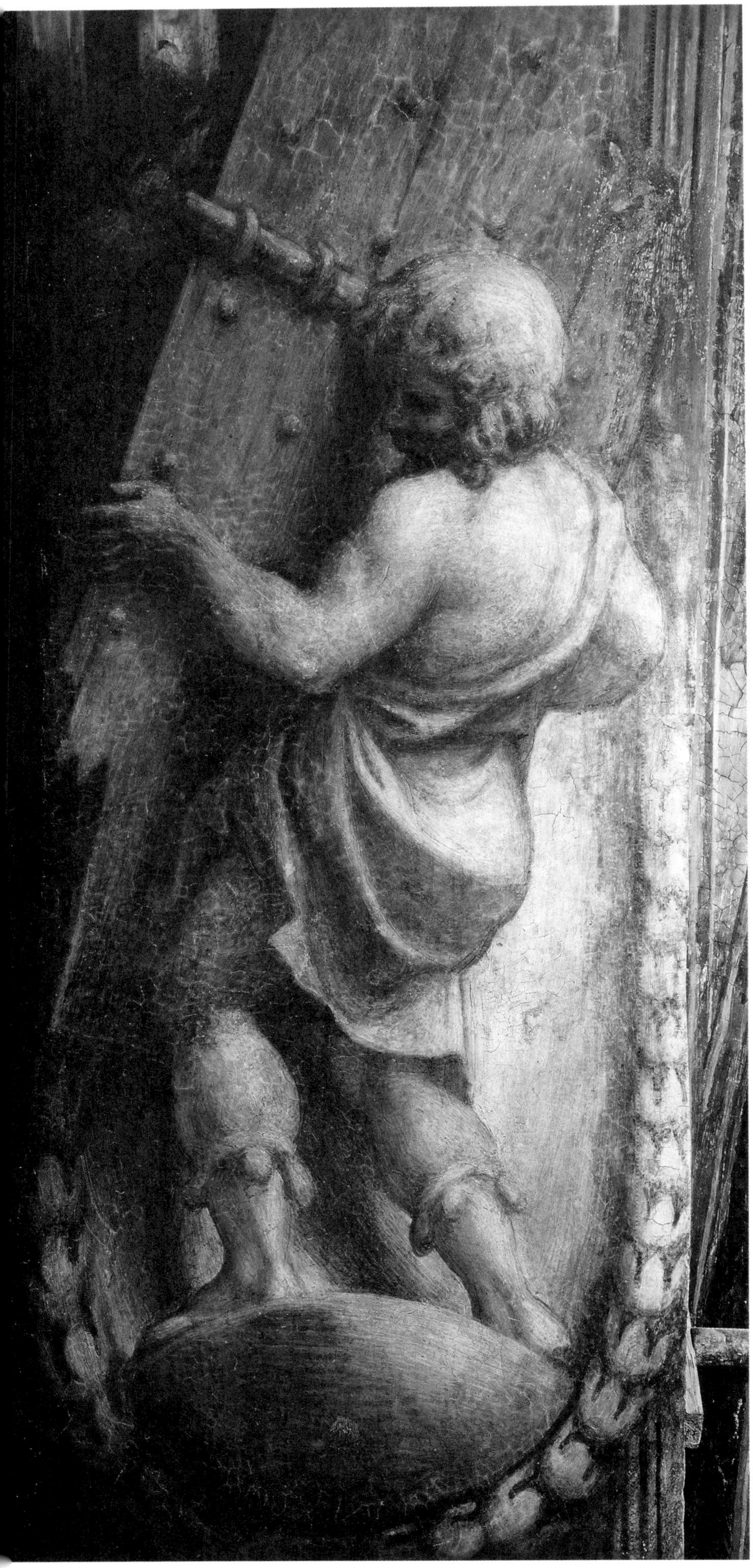
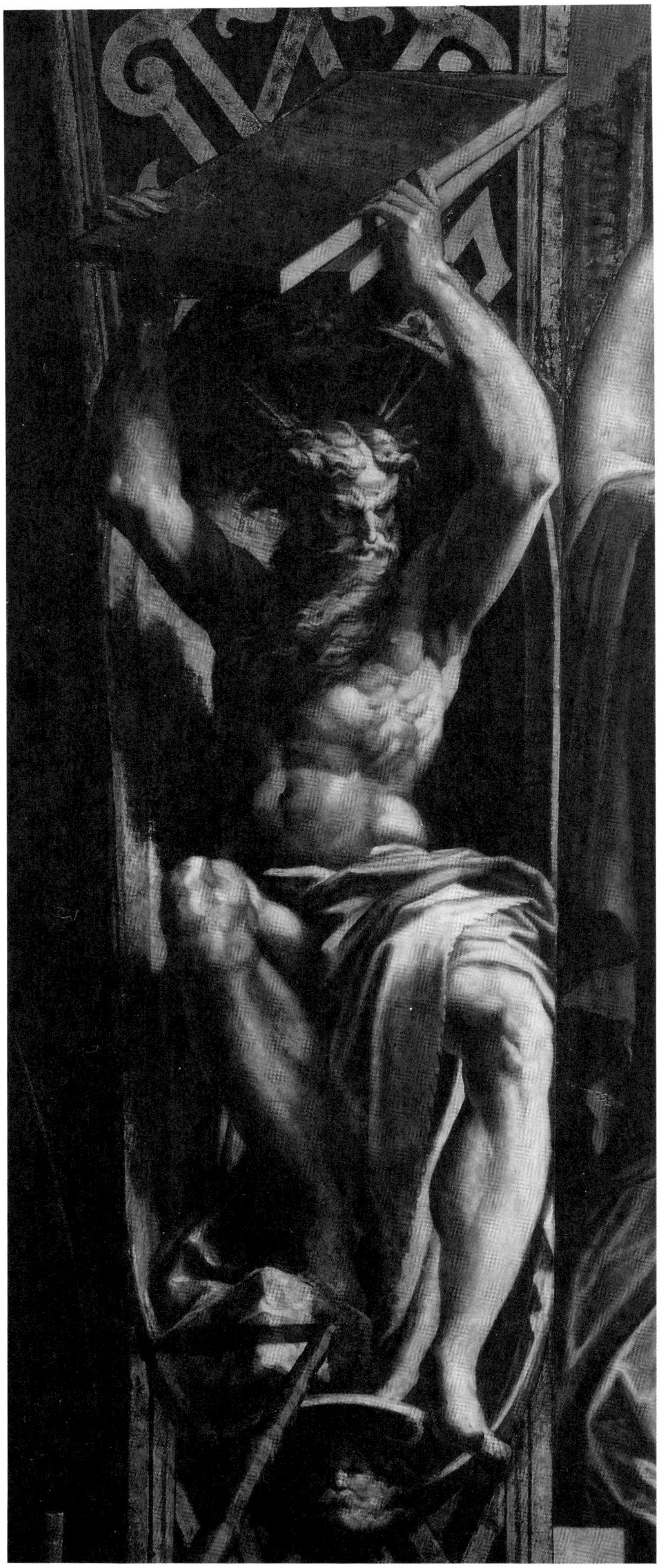

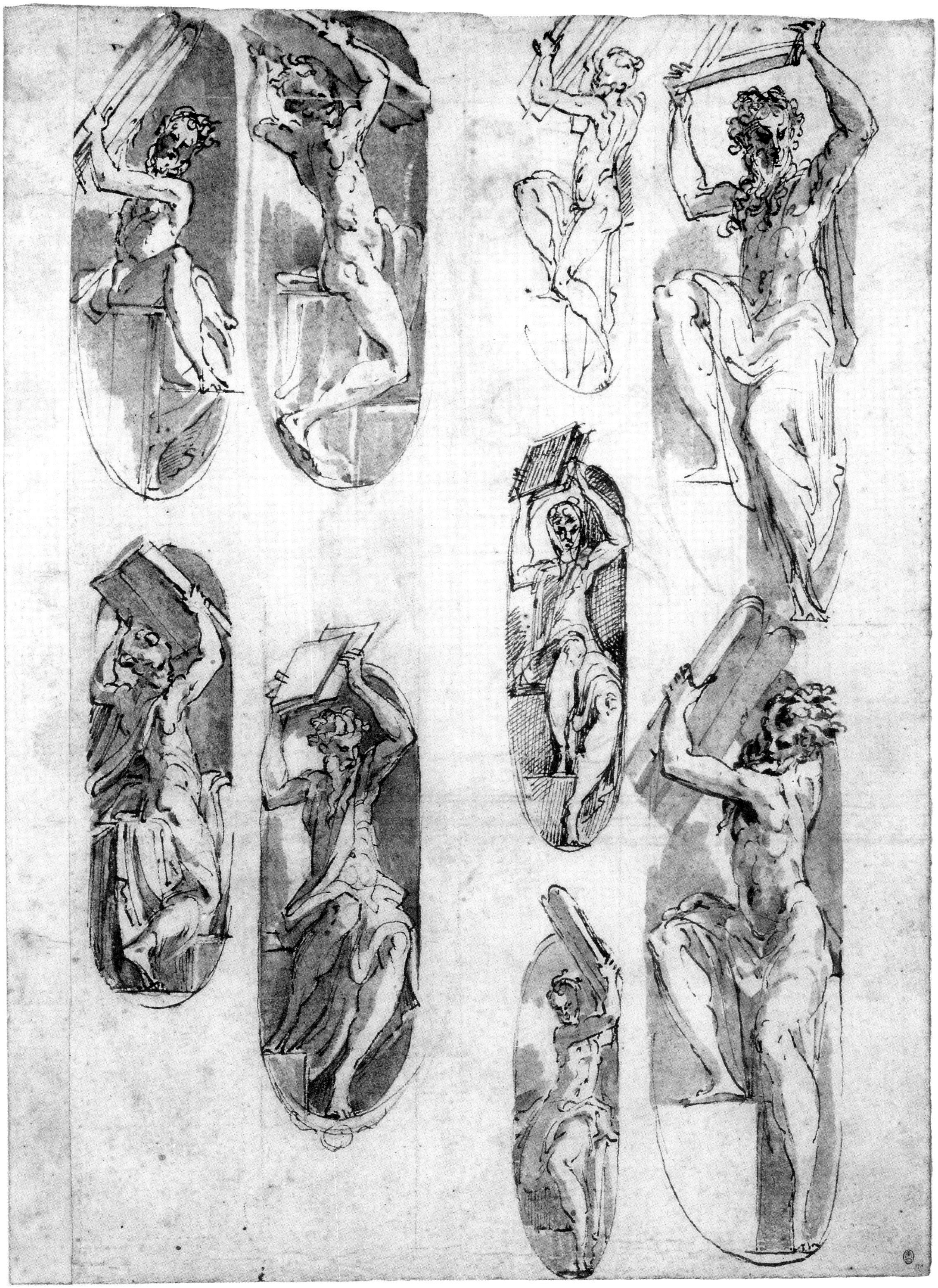

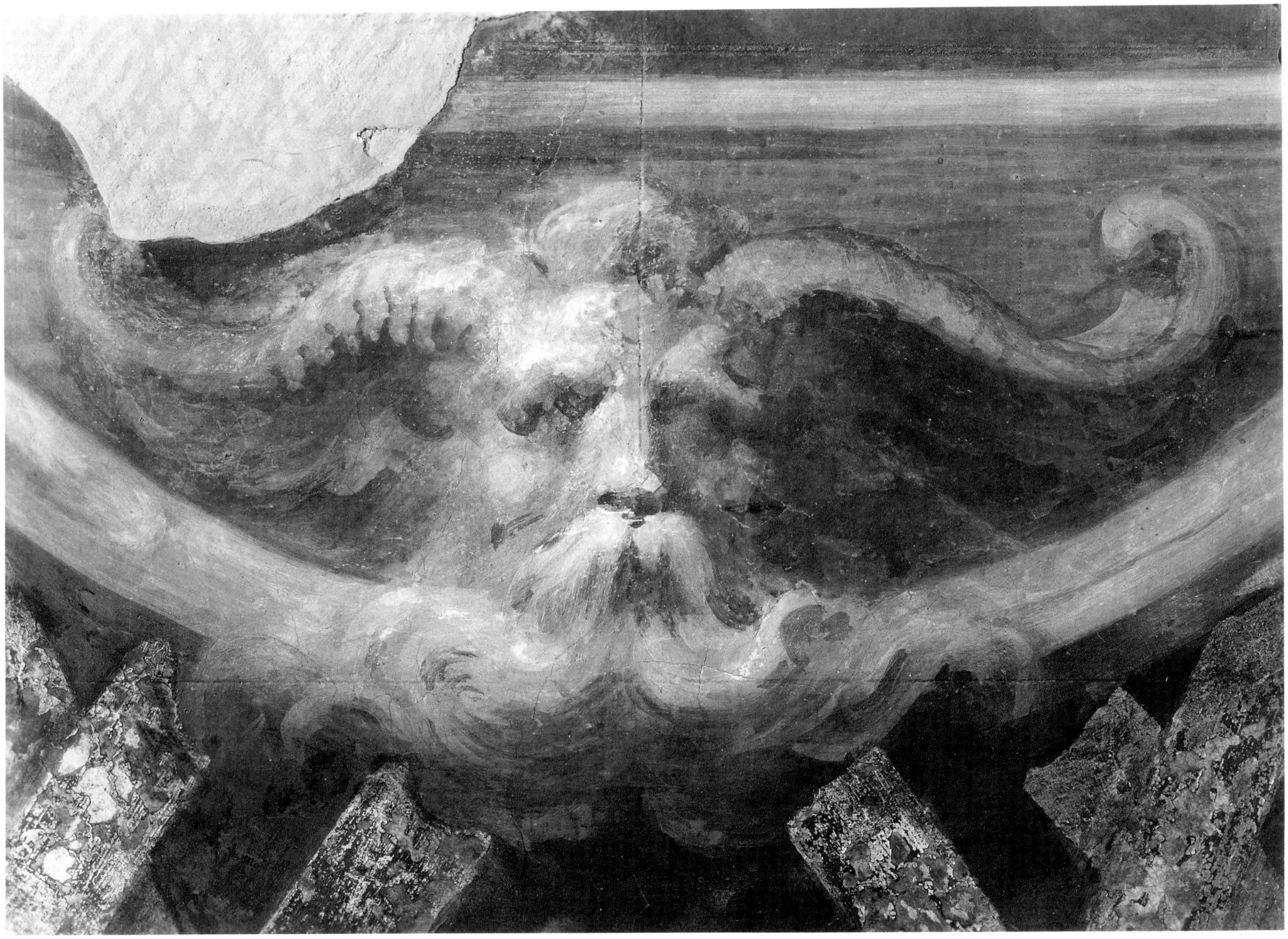

106. PARMIGIANINO
Detail of frieze of Santa Maria della Steccata, c. 1535–39
(Bearded head)
Fresco
Santa Maria della Steccata, Parma, Italy
(cat. A35)

Style. Examples of this would have been known to both artists following the excavation of the Domus Aurea of Nero.

Concurrently with his work at the Steccata, which dragged on throughout the 1530s, to the increasing exasperation of the church authorities, Parmigianino painted a number of panel pictures. One of these, already mentioned, was evidently the Uffizi *Madonna with Saint Zachariah* (fig. 107), which had been commissioned by Bonifazio Gozzadini of Bologna (Parmigianino's portrait of Gozzadini's wife is reasonably identified with an unfinished picture now in Vienna [fig. 108]). The Uffizi *Madonna* seems to have been started in Bologna but to have been finished, and probably mainly painted, after Parmigianino returned to Parma. It emerges from the documents that the picture was delivered to the patron, and therefore finished, in the year 1533. The background includes a remarkably ungrammatical conflation of the arches of Titus and Constantine, as well as a column that, in view of its distance from the foreground, must be gigantic. This is one factor, together with the curiously lurid light and the impassivity of the adult figures, that gives the picture an almost surrealist air. Extensive landscapes of this kind, interspersed with buildings, had figured in late Raphael Madonnas, one of which, *La Perla* (Prado), was probably already at Verona, where it is recorded by Vasari. This picture is likely to have been known to Parmigianino, who, as we have seen, visited Verona before returning to Parma. Raphael's painting includes an Infant Baptist who is as animated as the one in Parmigianino's picture. In other respects the design of the Uffizi painting favors the view of it as a development from that of the London *Marriage of Saint Catherine* (fig. 74). A drawing in Madrid (P279; fig. 109) was even considered by Popham to be a study for the London picture, but two separate factors would seem to exclude this, and both accord with the Uffizi picture. The Madrid drawing shows two children and not one. And the Christ Child in the drawing ignores the female saint in the foreground and is occupied in looking at the large open book on the Madonna's lap. With the female saint transformed into Saint Zachariah, and the transfer to him of the book, the Madrid drawing emerges as the link between the two paintings. Where they differ most is in the technique. Instead of the brilliant shorthand of the London picture, the Uffizi panel has the hard finish of Parmigianino's late style. The similarity of the Christ Child's features, and of his amazing blond curls, to those of his counterpart in the *Madonna della Rosa* (fig. 88) would also be consonant with a dating for the inception of the Uffizi picture at the end of the Bologna period. The attributional jar of ointment, proper to Saint Mary Magdalene, is here transformed into Parmigianino's obsessional amphora. This is one of the most enigmatic in effect of Parmigianino's paintings. The passionate dynamism of the Infant Baptist breaks into the frozen immobility of all three adult figures.

The other picture in this category, the *Conversion of Saul* (Vienna), was formerly attributed to Niccolò dell'Abate but is authenticated as Parmigianino's by three preliminary drawings and reliably identified with Vasari's mention of a picture of this subject that Parmigianino painted for one Albio, a doctor from Parma, then apparently resident

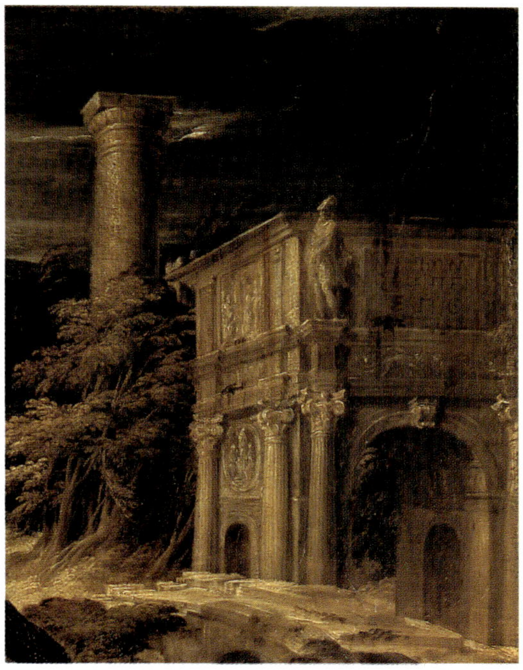

Detail of fig. 107
PARMIGIANINO
Madonna and Child with Saints Zachariah, Mary Magdalene, and the Infant Baptist
(Arch of Titus)

in Bologna. Like the Uffizi *Madonna* it is highly finished and also includes a panoramic landscape. I assume that, like it again, it was largely executed after Parmigianino's return to Parma. Saul's ecstatic expression is almost the same as that of Saint Roch in the San Petronio altarpiece, but more extreme. Indeed, the mood of the picture as a whole is dramatic to the point of melodrama and has something in common with that of Parmigianino's etching of *The Resurrection.* In the preliminary drawings Saul's horse is even less like those in nature than the creature in the painting, where, with perverse ingenuity, the saddlecloth is of almost the same color as the horse, so that the spots on the cloth look at first like the horse's, while the fringes of the cloth are made to look like the horse's mane. The composition evidently owes something to Raphael's *Expulsion of Heliodorus* in the Stanze of the Vatican and the saint's figure to Michelangelo's *Adam* on the Sistine ceiling.

A further altarpiece, the *Madonna dal Collo Lungo* (Madonna with the Long Neck; fig. 110), was commissioned by Elena Baiardi in 1534 for her chapel in the Servite church at

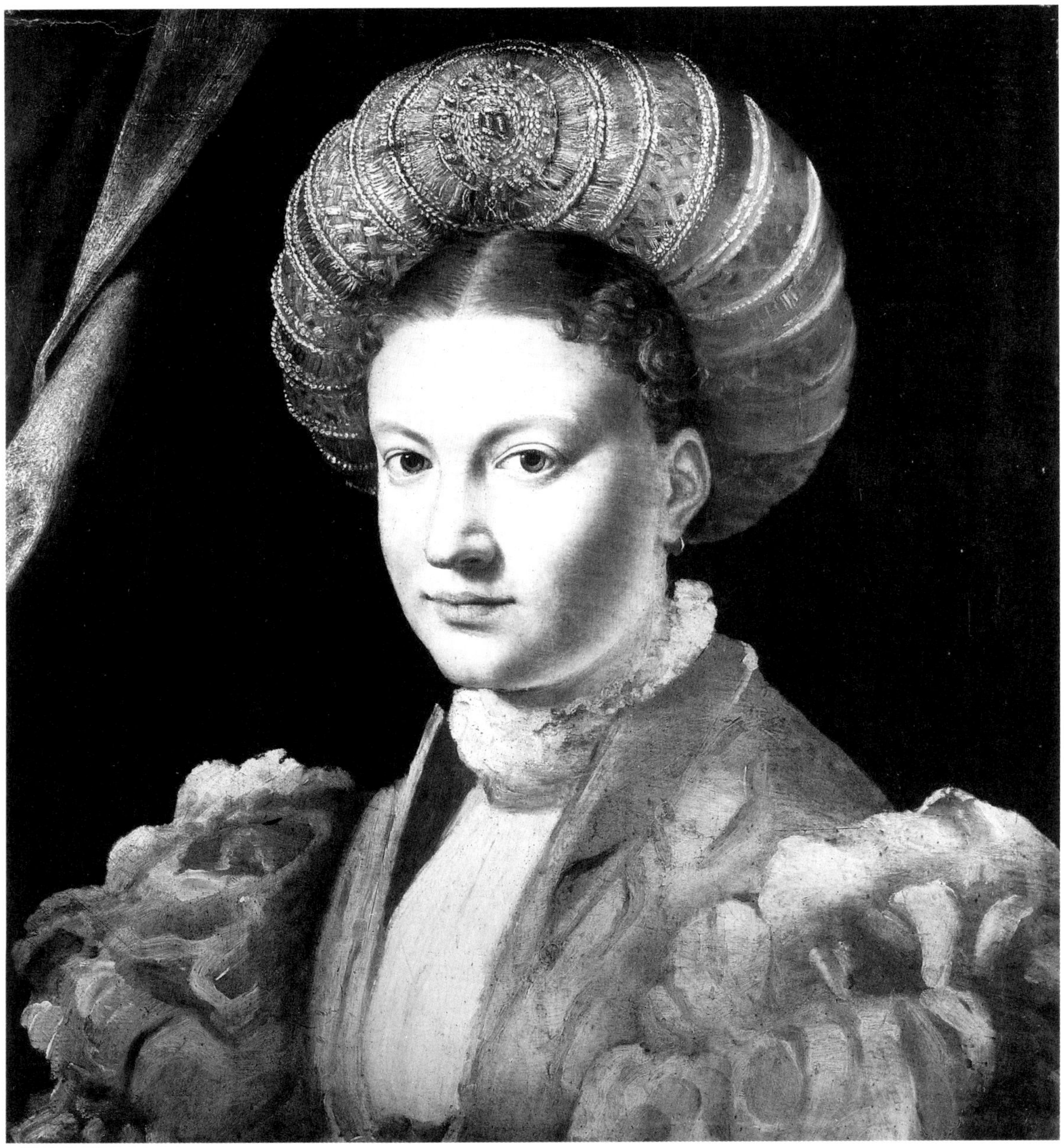

108. PARMIGIANINO
A Woman ("Contessa Gozzadini"), 1530–31
Oil on panel, 19⅝ × 18¼ in.
(50 × 46.4 cm)
Kunsthistorisches Museum, Vienna
(cat. A50)

Opposite:
107. PARMIGIANINO
Madonna and Child with Saints Zachariah, Mary Magdalene, and the Infant Baptist, c. 1530
Oil on panel, 28¾ × 24⅜ in.
(73 × 62 cm)
Galleria degli Uffizi, Florence (cat. A10)

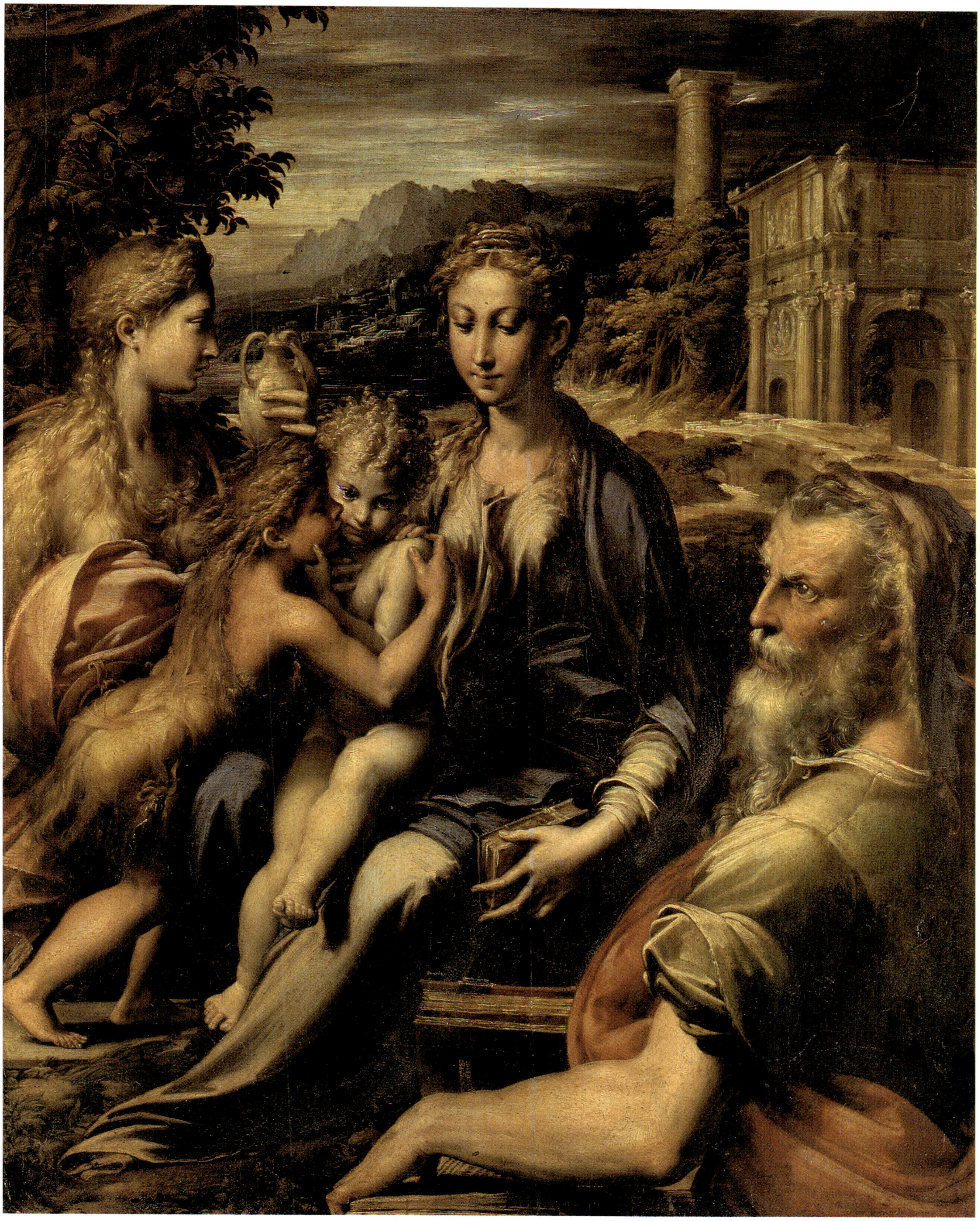

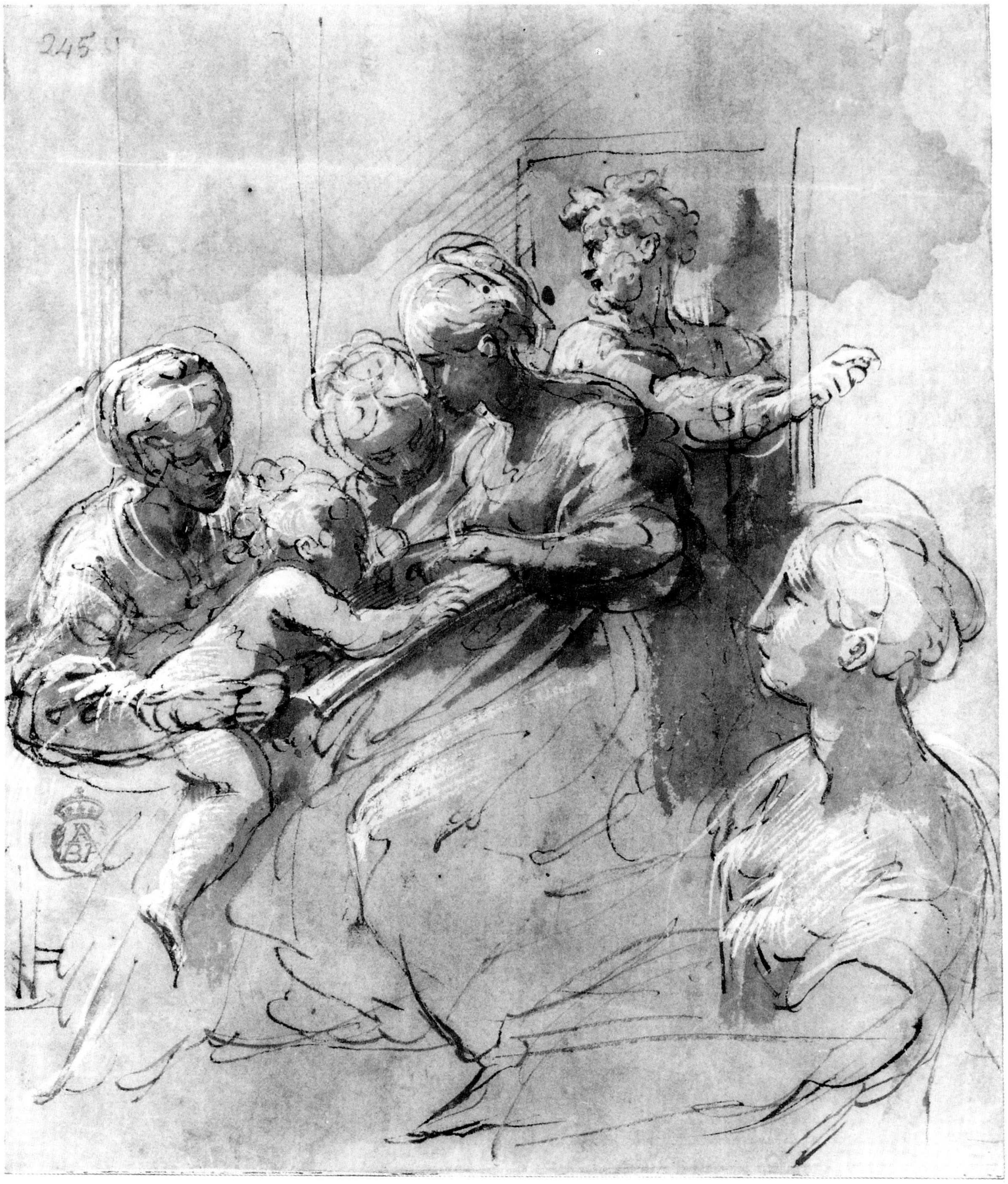

109. PARMIGIANINO
Study for *The Marriage of Saint Catherine,* n.d. P279
Pen and brown ink and brown wash on pink-tinted ground, heightened with white on paper, 8⅝ × 7 in. (21.9 × 17.8 cm)
Academia di San Fernando, Madrid

Parma. The Servites were an order with which Parmigianino, like his patron, evidently felt an affinity, since he was to be buried in another of their churches—at Casalmaggiore. The contract stipulated that the work be finished by Pentecost of the following year—a vain hope, as it proved. The picture is Parmigianino's most famous, also his most characteristic and most extreme. Its frenetic evolution is similar in principle to that of his London altarpiece, *Madonna with the Baptist and Saint Jerome.* As with the latter, the numerous surviving studies for the *Collo Lungo* show that the artist started with an orthodox arrangement. The Madonna was to be enthroned, flanked by the standing figures of Saint Jerome and Saint Francis (B.M. 1978-3-4-6; fig. 111). In another early sketch (P363) intermediate figures are glimpsed between the flanking saints and the throne. Parmigianino seems to have resented the presence of the saints and the symmetry that they imposed. At the next stage he

Opposite:
110. PARMIGIANINO
Madonna dal Collo Lungo, 1535
Oil on panel, 84¼ × 52⅜ in. (214 × 133 cm)
Galleria degli Uffizi, Florence (cat. A9)

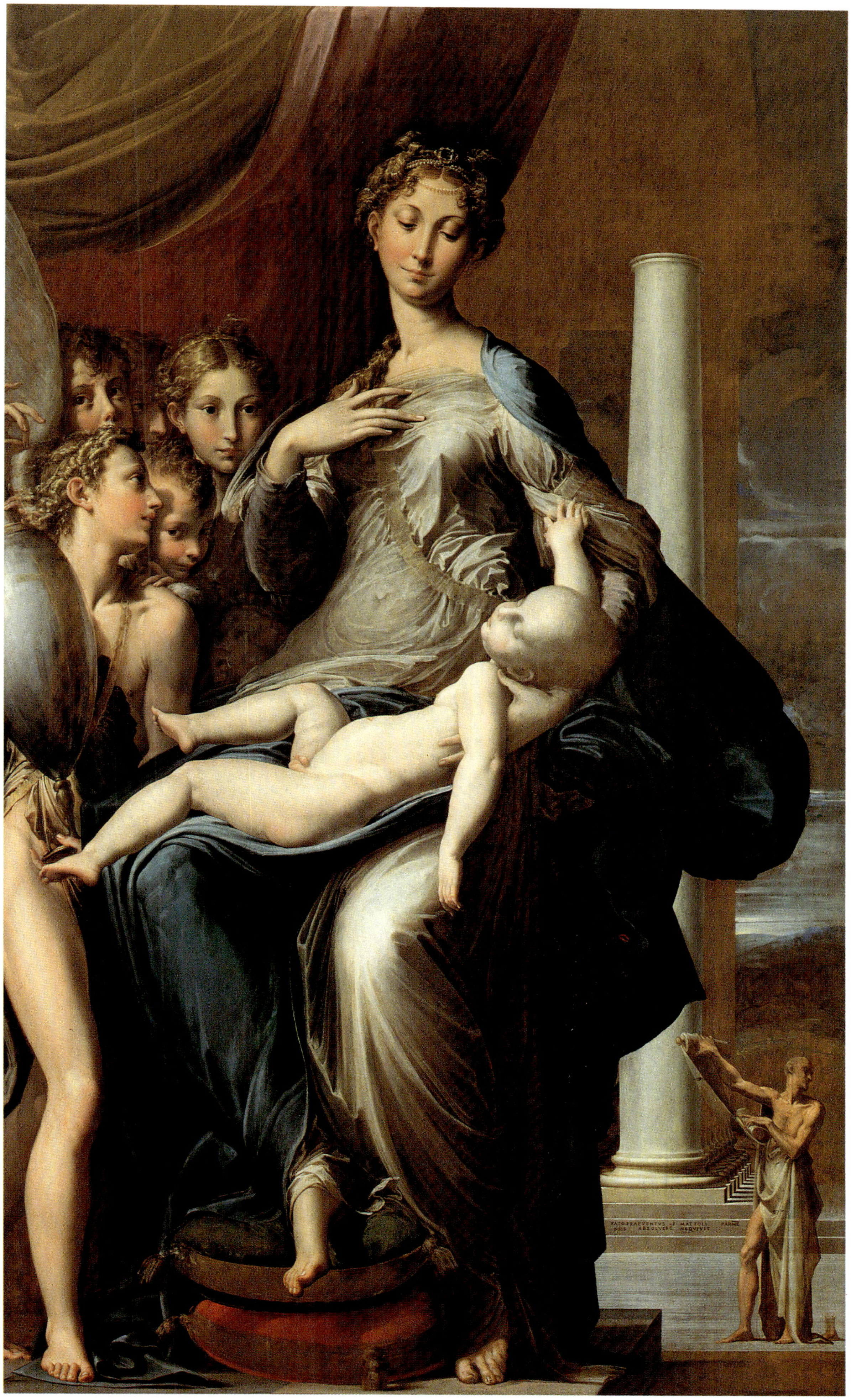

removed them from their place on either side of the throne. At one moment (P553; fig. 112) Saint Jerome is lying on the ground—a posture to which he had finally been relegated in the London picture. As in the lower half of that work the painter toyed, at one stage of the *Collo Lungo,* with a violently asymmetrical arrangement—the Madonna was to be in the left foreground and one saint standing farther back on the right (P327; fig. 113). The other saint, at this time, was banished to a place farther back still. Finally the Madonna was returned to the center, and Saint Jerome reduced to a minute figure who unrolls a scroll (presumably his translation of the scriptures, as in Correggio's famous altarpiece at Parma) in front of a colonnade of giant columns; Saint Francis was never painted, apart from a ghostly token foot (and even this may be no more than an alternative position for one of the feet of Saint Jerome). The resulting composition, showing the Madonna at full

111. PARMIGIANINO
Study for *Madonna dal Collo Lungo,* c. 1535
Pen and ink (?) on paper
British Museum, London

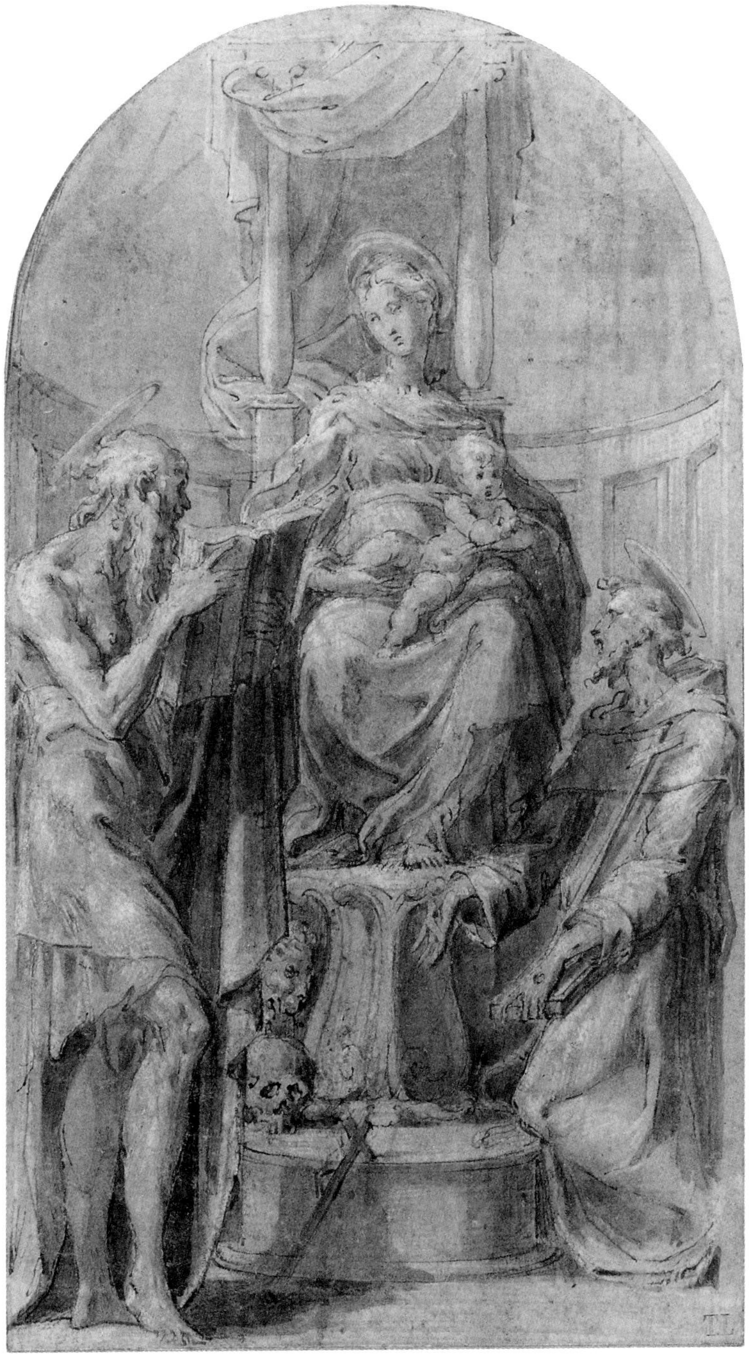

Opposite, left:
112. PARMIGIANINO
Study for *Madonna dal Collo Lungo,* c. 1535 P553
Lead point on prepared white surface, heightened with white on paper, 3⅝ × 2¾ in. (9.3 × 7.1 cm)
Galleria Nazionale, Parma, Italy

Opposite, right:
113. PARMIGIANINO
Study for *Madonna dal Collo Lungo,* c. 1535 P327
Pen and brown ink and brown wash, heightened with white on paper, 7¾ × 4⅜ in. (19.7 × 11.1 cm)
National Gallery of Canada, Ottawa

length without flanking saints, and not as a Madonna della Misericordia, is a rare form for an altarpiece.

As with some other Renaissance painters—for example Raphael and Correggio—a long process of experiment in the design of a picture resulted, by some curious, perhaps subconscious mental process, in a recollection of another artist's work. I have suggested that the composition of the *Madonna dal Collo Lungo* as a whole may be seen as a development on a large scale from that of Correggio's small *Madonna of the Basket* (London; fig. 114), a picture that had been painted a decade previously.[13] As the patron was none other than the Cavaliere Baiardi, there can be no doubt that Parmigianino was well aware of Correggio's painting. Such a derivation may concern the theme as well as the design of the *Madonna dal Collo Lungo.* The shirt that Correggio's Madonna puts on the Christ

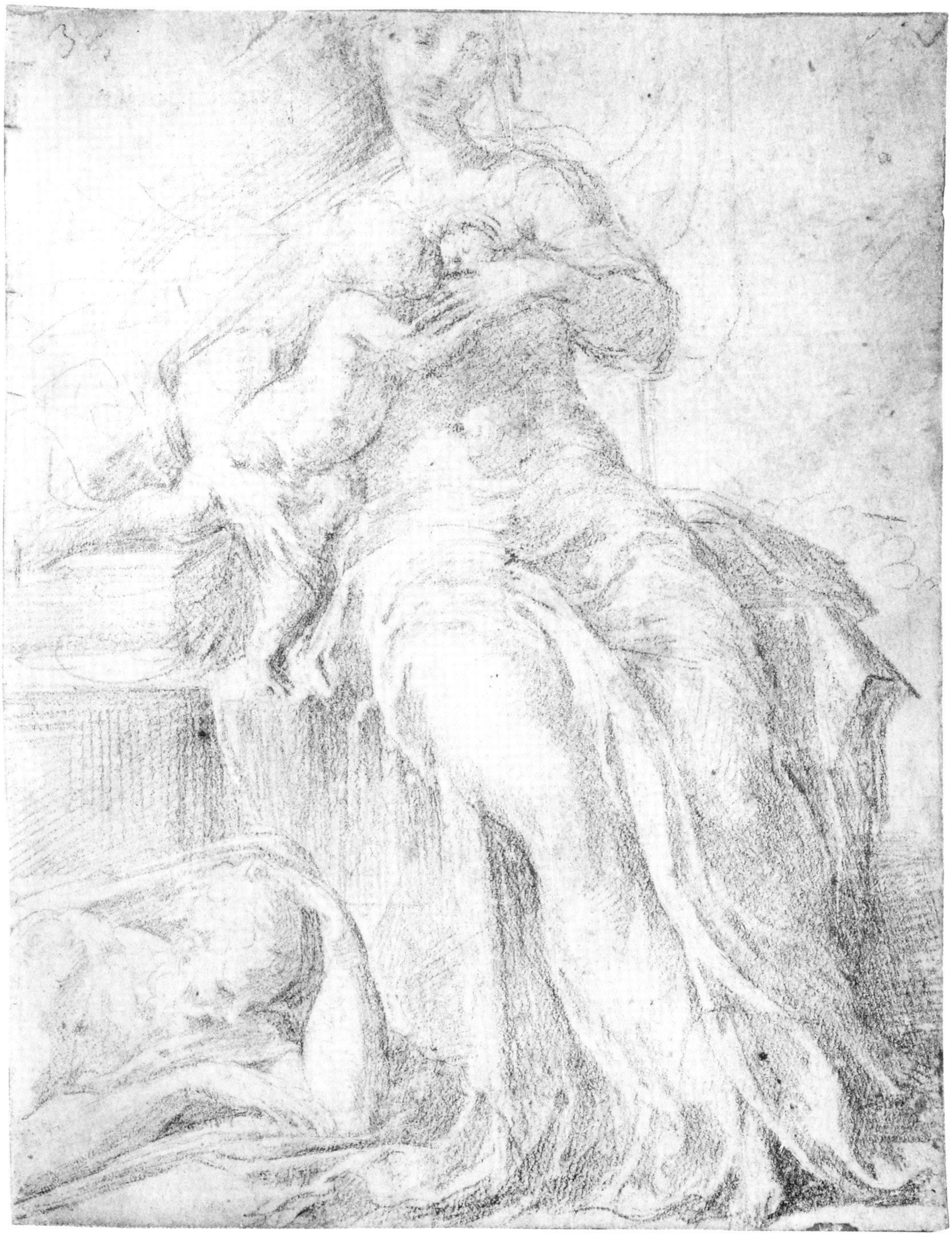

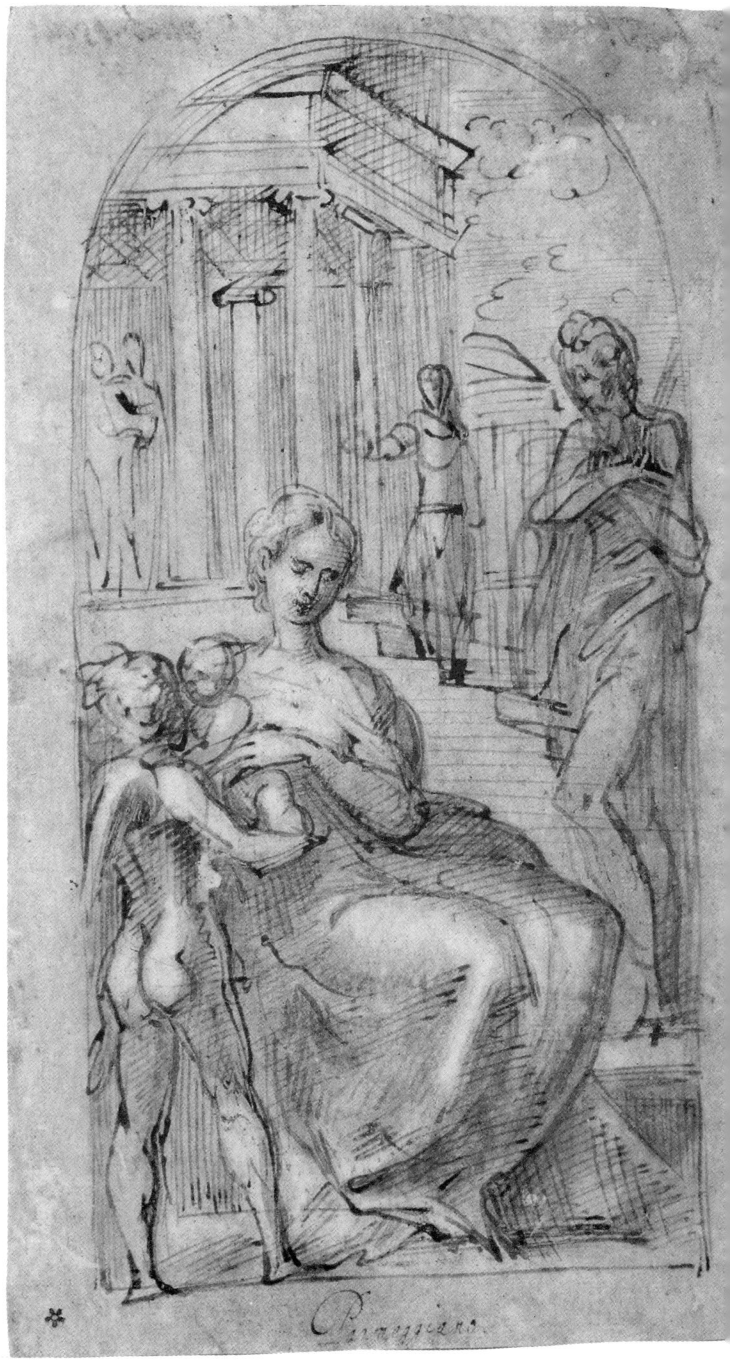

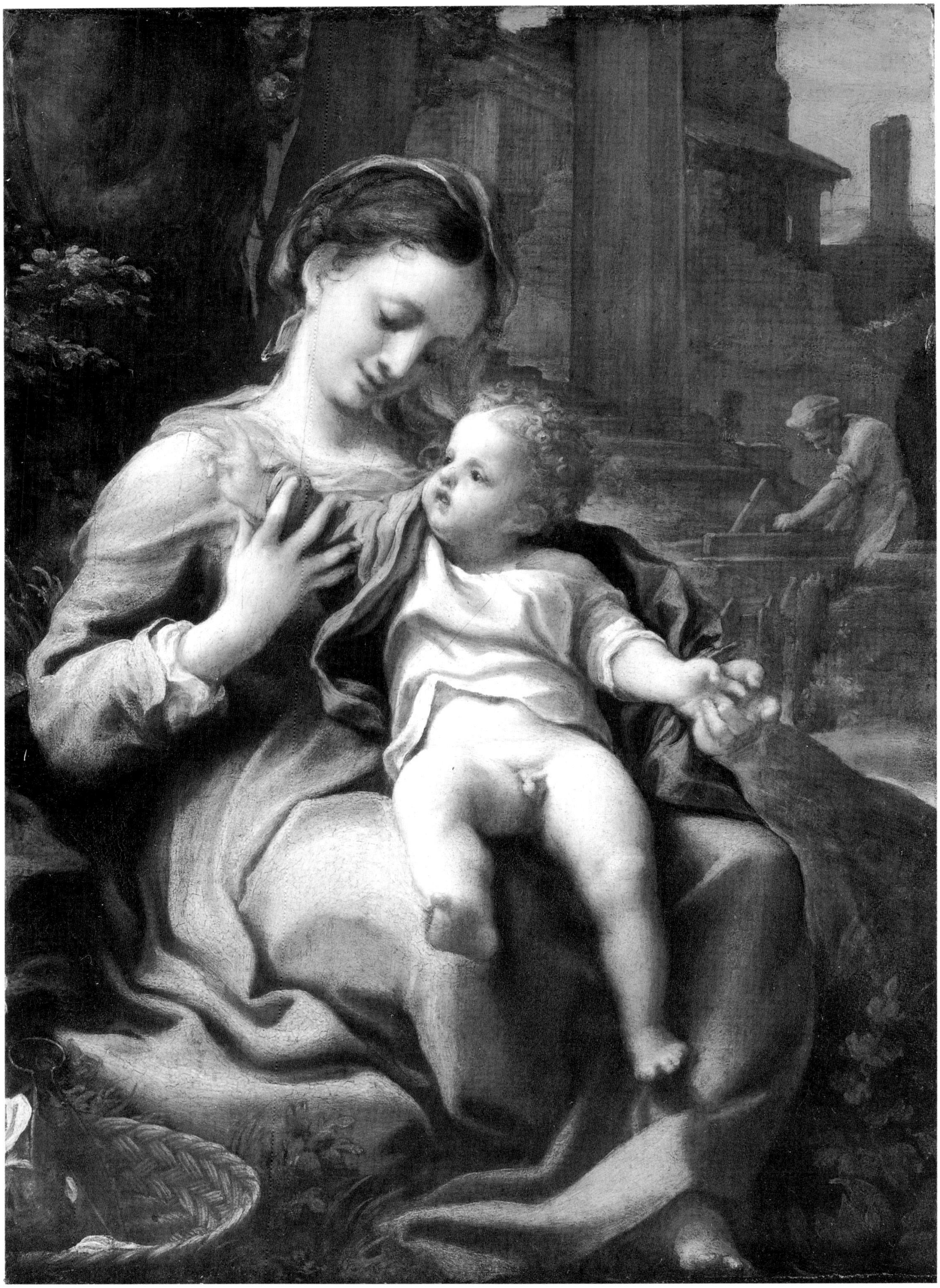

Child—a motif that he, in his turn, had taken from Jacopo della Quercia's sculpture over the main door of San Petronio at Bologna—has been interpreted as a symbol of the Passion. Symbolic allusion of this kind, inexplicit in Correggio's picture, is unequivocal in Parmigianino's. The urn that the angel on the left holds out for the Madonna's contemplation contained a glowing cross. It is now nearly erased but is still just visible in the painting itself, and clearly legible in Petrucci's and Lorenzini's prints. It is also mentioned by Vasari. As so often with Parmigianino, this idea—of considerable thematic importance—was introduced only during the course of the work. The urn does not figure in the earliest sketches for the painting. Another instance of Parmigianino's characteristically flexible iconography is the fleeting appearance of the youthful Baptist at one stage (P359 and P.O.C. 25; see appendix 3).

I have suggested that the popular theory that Parmigianino's work in general is characterized by excessive elongation of the limbs rests on no more foundation than that this picture, in which it is very evident, is also his most famous. The attenuated figure of the Madonna, which was itself to prove immensely influential, is a variant of Michelangelo's spiral pose. More willful is the form and placing of the Christ Child. As with Correggio's Christ in the *Madonna of the Basket,* his form is almost entirely contained within the outline of the Madonna's swelling body and draperies. But his posture is quite different from that of Correggio's Christ Child. Monstrously large and sprawling, his left shoulder foreshortened almost to the point of dislocation, he is the most disquieting feature of all. But there are others. Is the Madonna standing or seated? Is she indoors or out? And if the cushions at the base are as near the edge of the picture as they seem, it would follow that the Madonna's right foot should project through the picture and emerge on the spectator's side. How, again, could there be space for the bodies of the angels if their heads are as close together as they seem? And how could gravity justify the mantle's billowing out behind the Madonna in those fascinating folds? In its particular kind of unreality the *Madonna dal Collo Lungo* has only one true predecessor—in the art of Pontormo. The Madonna's weightlessness recalls that of the Virgin in the Santa Felicita *Deposition* and the surrealist perspective that of the Carmignano *Visitation* (fig. 58).

Unlike Parmigianino's other altarpieces, the source of illumination in the *Madonna dal Collo Lungo* appears to be bright sunlight; whereas the mysterious light in the *Madonna with Saint Margaret* (fig. 67) reduces most of the colors to a golden monochrome, the *Collo Lungo* has contrasts of bright blue and two shades of red. Like those of most of the later Madonnas, the Virgin's dress is not the traditional red but gray.

As in the London altarpiece and the maidens at the Steccata, the dress worn by the Madonna in this painting is of such fine material that the contours of her nipples and even of her navel are visible through it. Her head, like those of the angels, is brought to an amazing perfection of finish. Pearls and a jeweled brooch nestle among the strands of her hair, which, in the variety of its writhing coils, is suggestive neither of human curls nor even of gold wire, but rather of something more exotic and sinister, as if Medusa's serpents had

114. CORREGGIO
Madonna of the Basket, c. 1520–24
Oil on panel, 13⅜ × 9⅞ in. (34 × 25 cm)
National Gallery, London

been turned to a golden color. Such a face was evidently meant to stand as the type of ideal beauty: and very beautiful it is, with a different and less classical cast of feature than that of the Madonna in the London altarpiece. But the beauties of the picture are apt to be overshadowed by the eccentricities, and its strange, intense spirituality misinterpreted, as with Pontormo's Certosa frescoes or Rosso's *Deposition* at Volterra, as frivolity. It is perhaps not surprising that Vasari tells us that it was dissatisfaction with the result that caused the artist to abandon work on which he had lavished so great an amount of thought and skill, while the fact of the abandonment so near to completion is a significant indication that, on this occasion at least, he was unwilling to accept studio assistance.

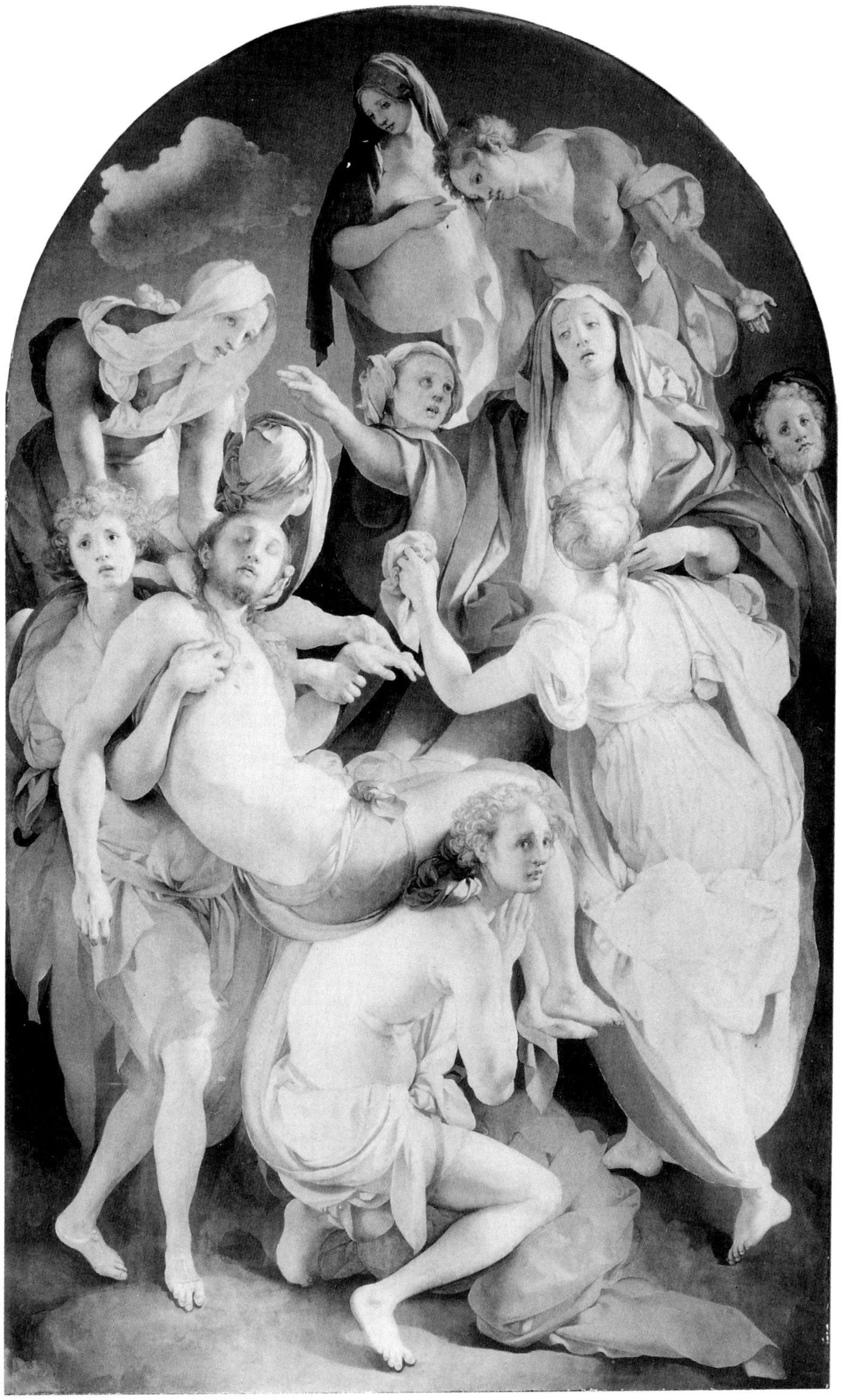

115. PONTORMO
Deposition, c. 1526–28
Oil on panel, 123¼ × 75⅝ in.
(313 × 192 cm)
Santa Felicita, Florence

Of the later portraits the finest is the so-called *Antea* (Capodimonte, Naples; fig. 116), Parmigianino's masterpiece in portraiture. The picture projects an intensity of presence that is almost physical. The sitter is so obviously the same as the angel nearest the Madonna in the *Collo Lungo* that the portrait may be dated to the mid-thirties with confidence. As with the earlier portraits, but with greater intensity, the sitter looks straight at the spectator, and seems to protest her innocence—an impression sustained by the utter simplicity of the pose. There may well be some symbolic allusion to this idea in the choice of fur—a sable or ermine—which distorts her right shoulder and which is arranged as though the creature were still alive (it even looks as though it were about to sink its teeth into her gloved hand).

It is the lack of such communication with the spectator, and the loss of vitality that it brings with it, which may explain why the attribution to Parmigianino of the portrait of Malatesta Baglione (Vienna; fig. 117) has sometimes been unjustly questioned. But the execution is of very high quality and fully typical of Parmigianino's late manner. The explanation of the tepid image is almost certainly that the sitter was not available to sit. The identification with Baglione, a *condottiere* who first defended Florence and then surrendered it to the enemy and died soon afterward (in 1531), can only be traced as far back as the eighteenth century, and for that reason has itself been doubted. But it is almost certainly correct. Making allowance for the crudity of the woodcut portraits in the 1575 (Basel, Switzerland) edition of Paolo Giovio's *Elogia,* the one of Baglione (fig. 118) corresponds well enough with the present painting, from which it presumably derives. I have suggested that the painting may have been commissioned as a result of a meeting between Parmigianino and Giovio in Bologna in 1529–30. Like the "*Antea*" and the other late portraits, the Malatesta Baglione portrait is larger than the earlier ones, showing the sitter at three-quarter length. As in the *Madonna dal Collo Lungo,* the space is treated semisurrealistically. The sitter is framed by a doorway, which is flanked by halberds. The spectator assumes these are of normal size until he notices that the floor appears to be below the level where the sitter is sitting. The doorway and halberds must therefore be of a frighteningly enormous size. The colors in this masterly painting are in restrained shades of red (in the sitter's coat) and pinkish gray (in the background). And the diagonal lines of the sitter's costume are effectively contrasted with the uprights and horizontals of the room.

If the Baglione portrait is accepted, there should be little difficulty in also accepting the portrait of Pier Maria Rossi, count of San Secondo (Prado; fig. 119), and its pendant of the countess (fig. 120). In any case there is early documentation. Like the Sanvitale family, the Rossi of San Secondo were lords of a fief near Parma and had transformed the interior of a medieval castle into a Renaissance palace. In his first edition Vasari says that Parmigianino took refuge at San Secondo when the situation at the Steccata was becoming intolerable. Though the omission of this statement in the second edition suggests that Vasari had come to doubt it, it would accord with the apparent date of the San Secondo

Following pages:

116. PARMIGIANINO
A Young Woman ("Antea"), c. 1535–37
Oil on canvas, 53⅛ × 34⅝ in.
(135 × 88 cm)
Galleria Nazionale di Capodimonte, Naples (cat. A27)

117. PARMIGIANINO
Malatesta Baglione, c. 1537
Oil on panel, 46 × 38⅝ in.
(117 × 98 cm)
Kunsthistorisches Museum, Vienna (cat. A49)

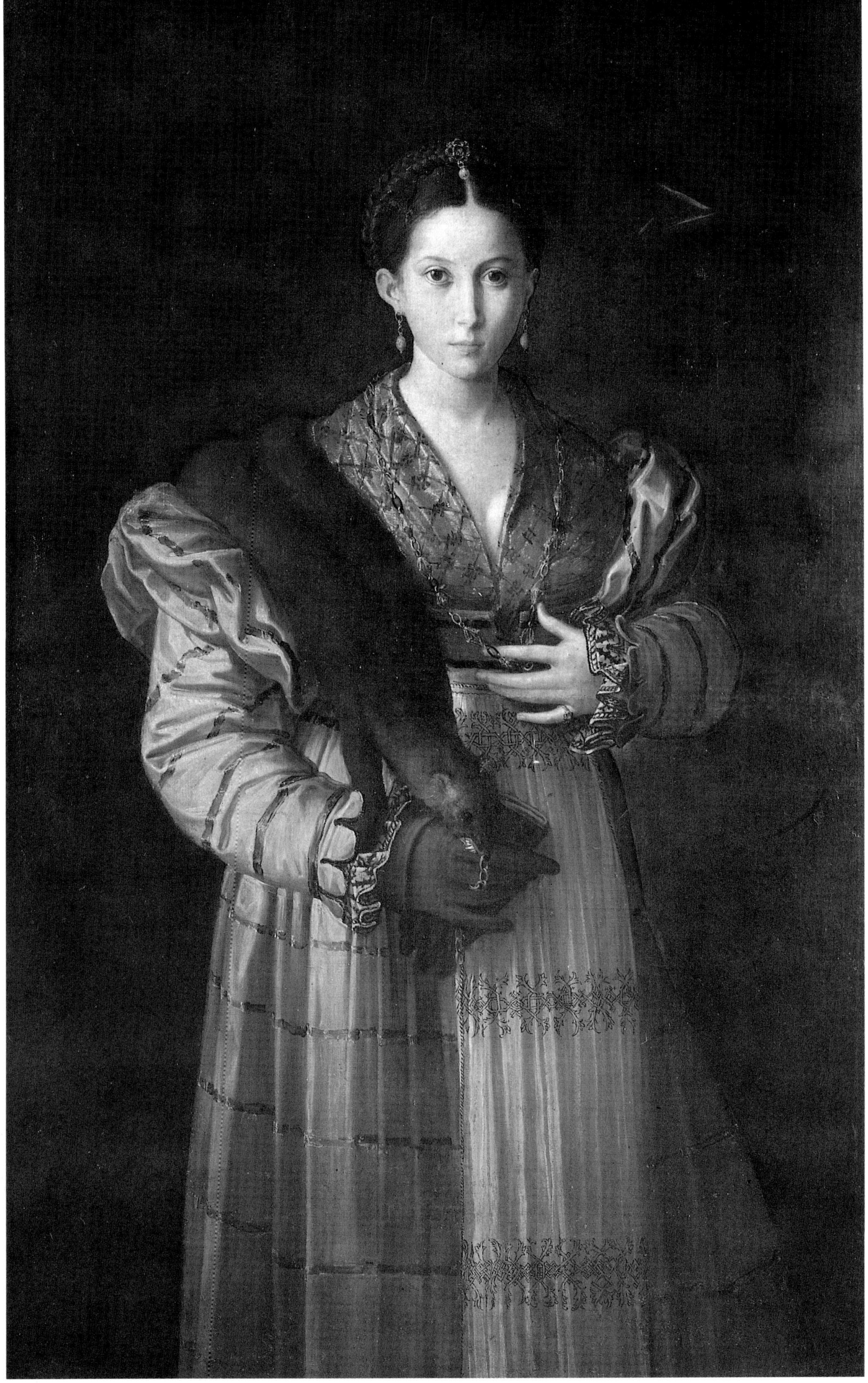

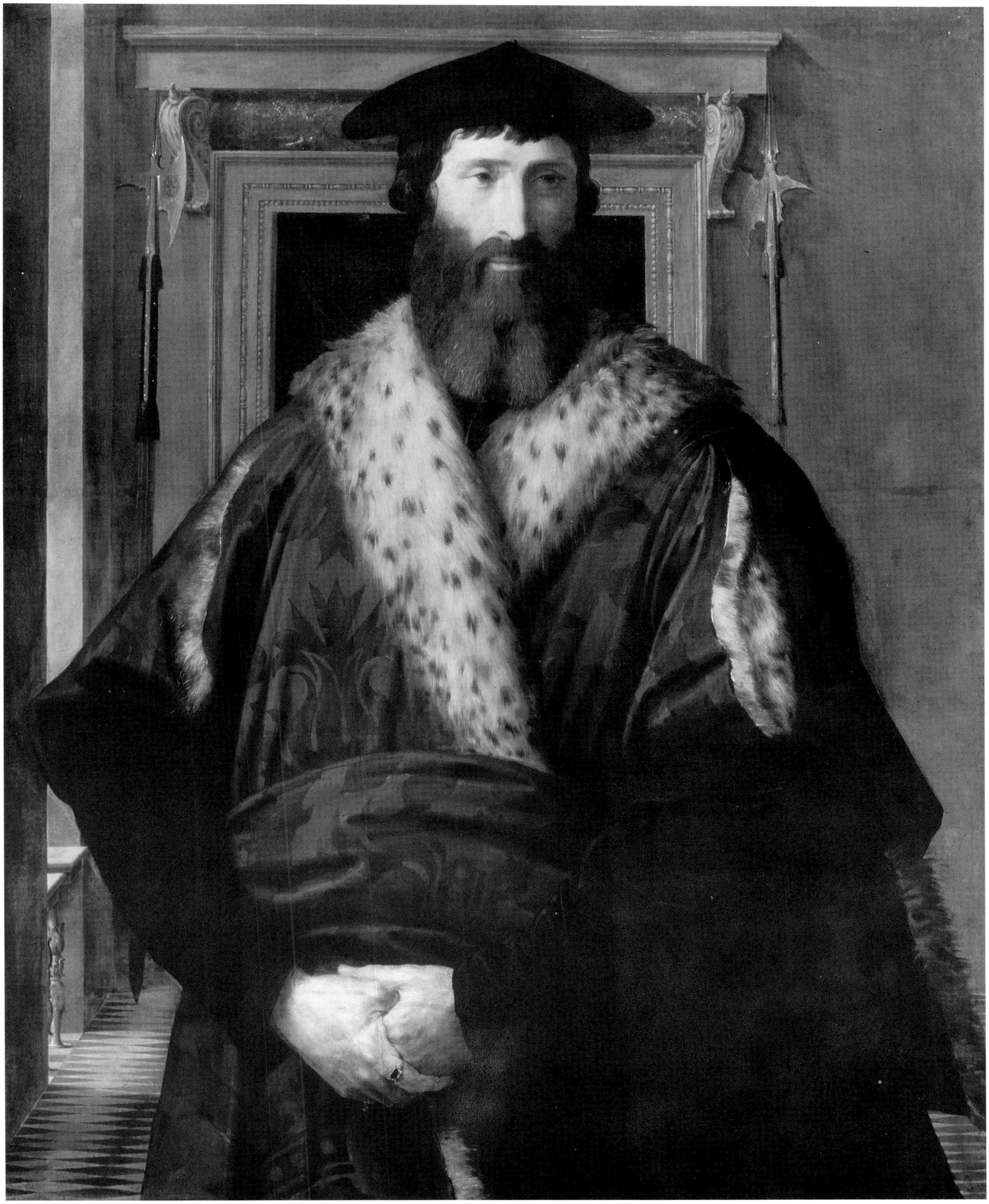

portraits: in particular, the resemblance of the count's excessively thin, spidery fingers to those of Saint Stephen in the Dresden altarpiece (fig. 124) would indicate a late dating. In addition, there are significant resemblances to the Baglione portrait. Here, too, there is some ambiguity in the relation of the background to the foreground. In both cases the sitter averts his gaze, and there even seems to be a certain resemblance in the features. One explanation, and only one, would appear to link these features: the artist did not see the sitter. Like Baglione, the count was a famous soldier, in the service at different times of patrons as diverse as Charles v, François i, and Duke Cosimo de' Medici.

The separate portrait of the sitter's wife and three young children (fig. 120) is more

118. AFTER PARMIGIANINO
Malatesta Baglione
Woodcut from Paolo Giovio,
Elogia virorum bellica virtute illustrium, 1575

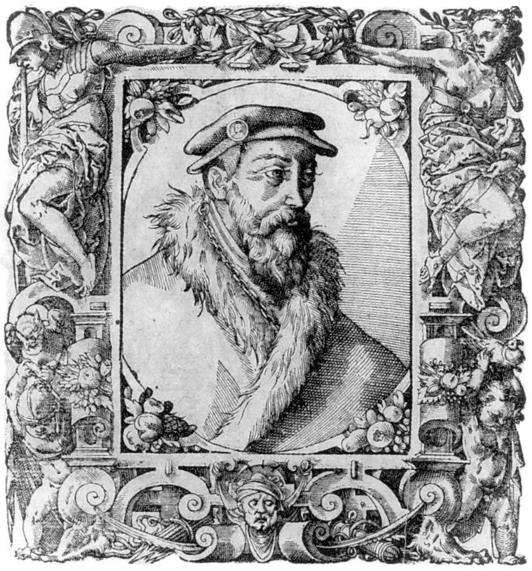

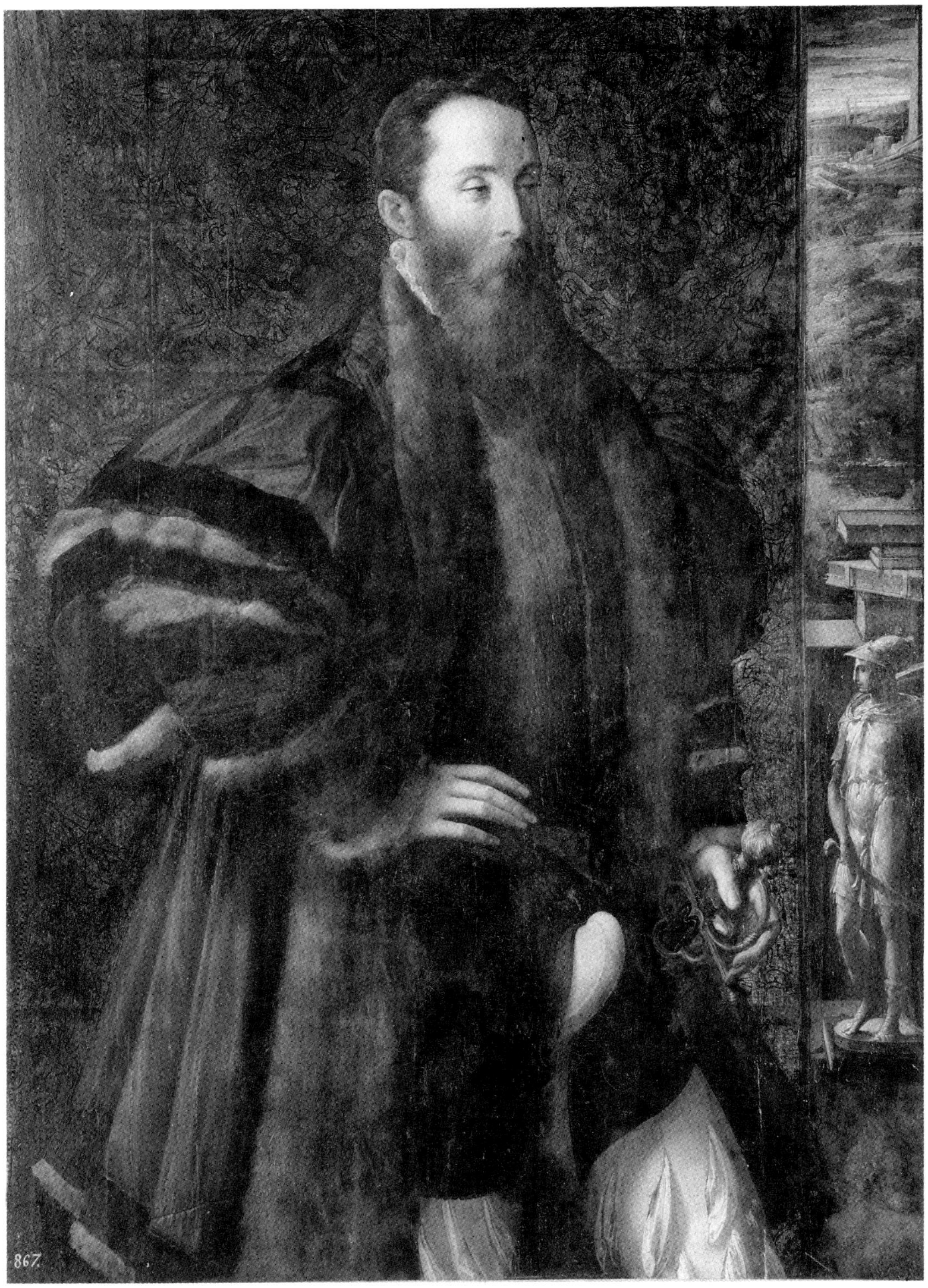

119. PARMIGIANINO
Pier Maria Rossi, Count of San Secondo,
c. 1540
Oil on panel, 53⅛ × 15 in. (135 × 38 cm)
Museo del Prado, Madrid (cat. A24)

lively, and there would be no reason for thinking it was not done from life. The theory that Parmigianino left it unfinished seems less likely since the recent cleaning. But in any case it can be vouched for as the pendant to the male portrait (the denial of this in previous Prado catalogs is now admitted to have been a mistake, due to the fact that for a time the two pictures were separated and came to the Prado from different palaces). There is also a drawing (P704) that is probably for one of the children. The idea of a mother's being portrayed surrounded by her children, as in a personification of Charity, was then new in Italy, though Holbein had painted his wife with their children a few years previously (now in Basel, Switzerland).

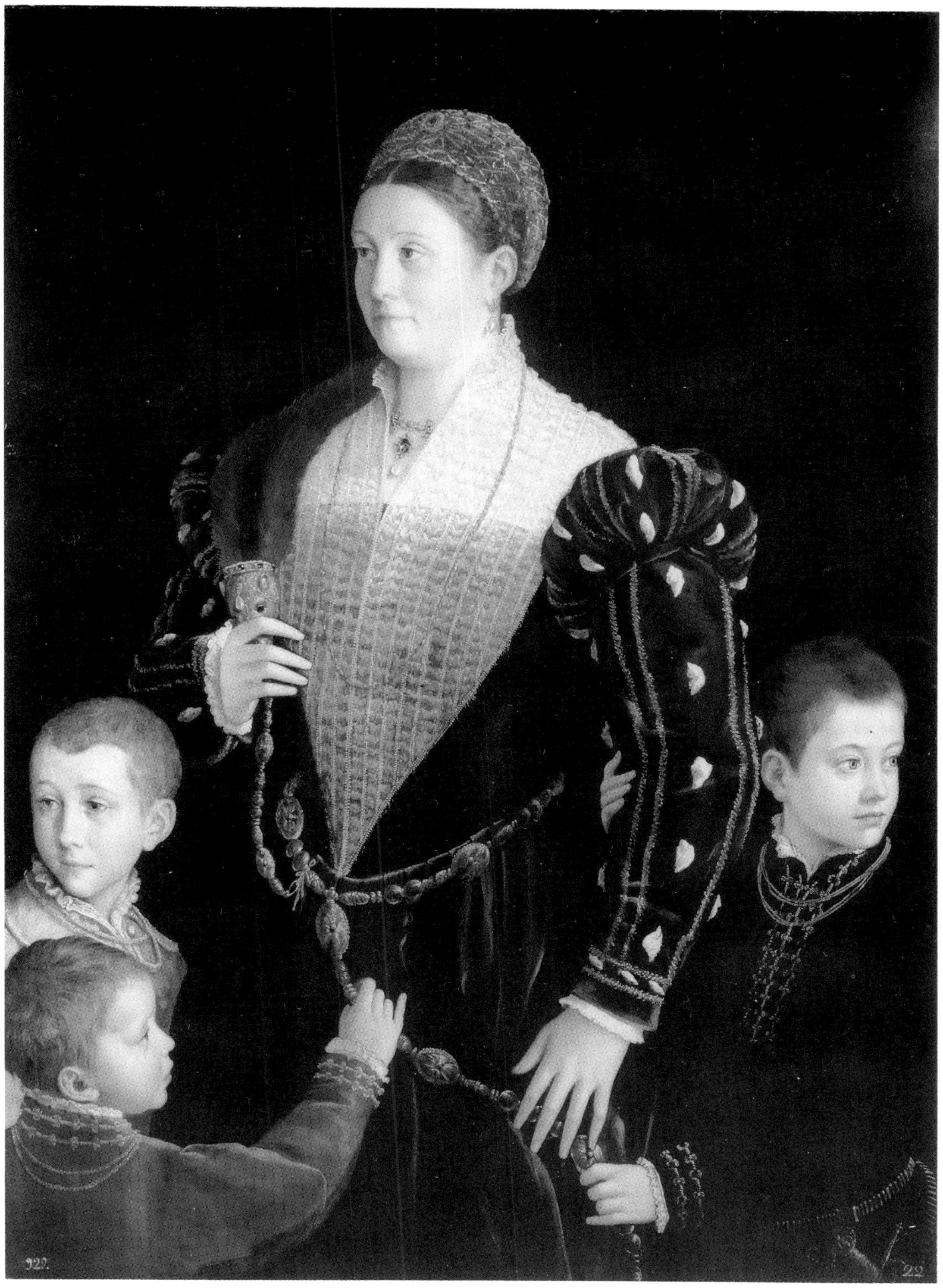

120. PARMIGIANINO
Camilla Gonzaga, Countess of San Secondo, with Three Children, c. 1537–39
Oil on panel, 50⅜ × 38⅝ in.
(128 × 98 cm)
Museo del Prado, Madrid (cat. A25)

The total of paintings dating from the last decade of Parmigianino's life is small, even by his standards, but it is likely that a number of the more elaborate drawings were done at this time. A few of the finest, whether for presentation or engraving, evidently date from an earlier period—the *Diana and Nymphs* (P74; fig. 121), for instance, or the two versions of the *Circe* (P73; fig. 122, and P85; both in the Uffizi). But others of superb quality—the *Venus, Mars, and Vulcan* (P546), the *Visitation* (P550; fig. 59), and the standing *Diogenes* (P551; all three in Parma), the *Standard-Bearer* (P255; British Museum; fig. 123), the *Huntsman* (P282; Melbourne), or the *Saint Christopher* (P528; Ecole des Beaux-Arts, Paris)—are probably datable to this period.

By the summer of 1539, eight years after the contract that was to have been fulfilled within eighteen months, the situation at the Steccata had reached breaking point. The church, at long last, was otherwise finished, and it was in fact consecrated in that year.

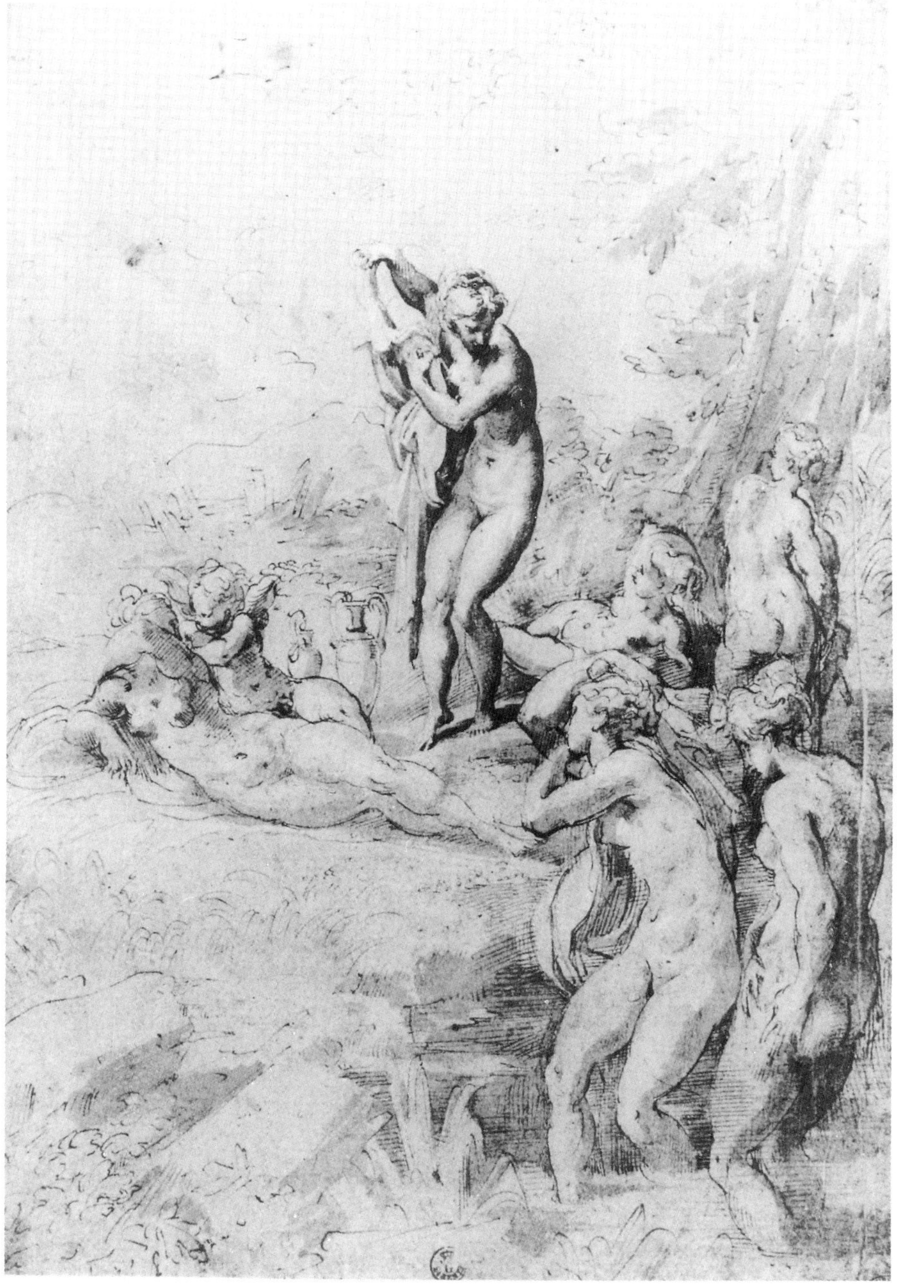

121. PARMIGIANINO
Diana and Nymphs, n.d. P74
Pen and brown ink and brown wash with some white heightening on paper, 11⅝ × 8¼ in. (29.5 × 21 cm)
British Museum, London

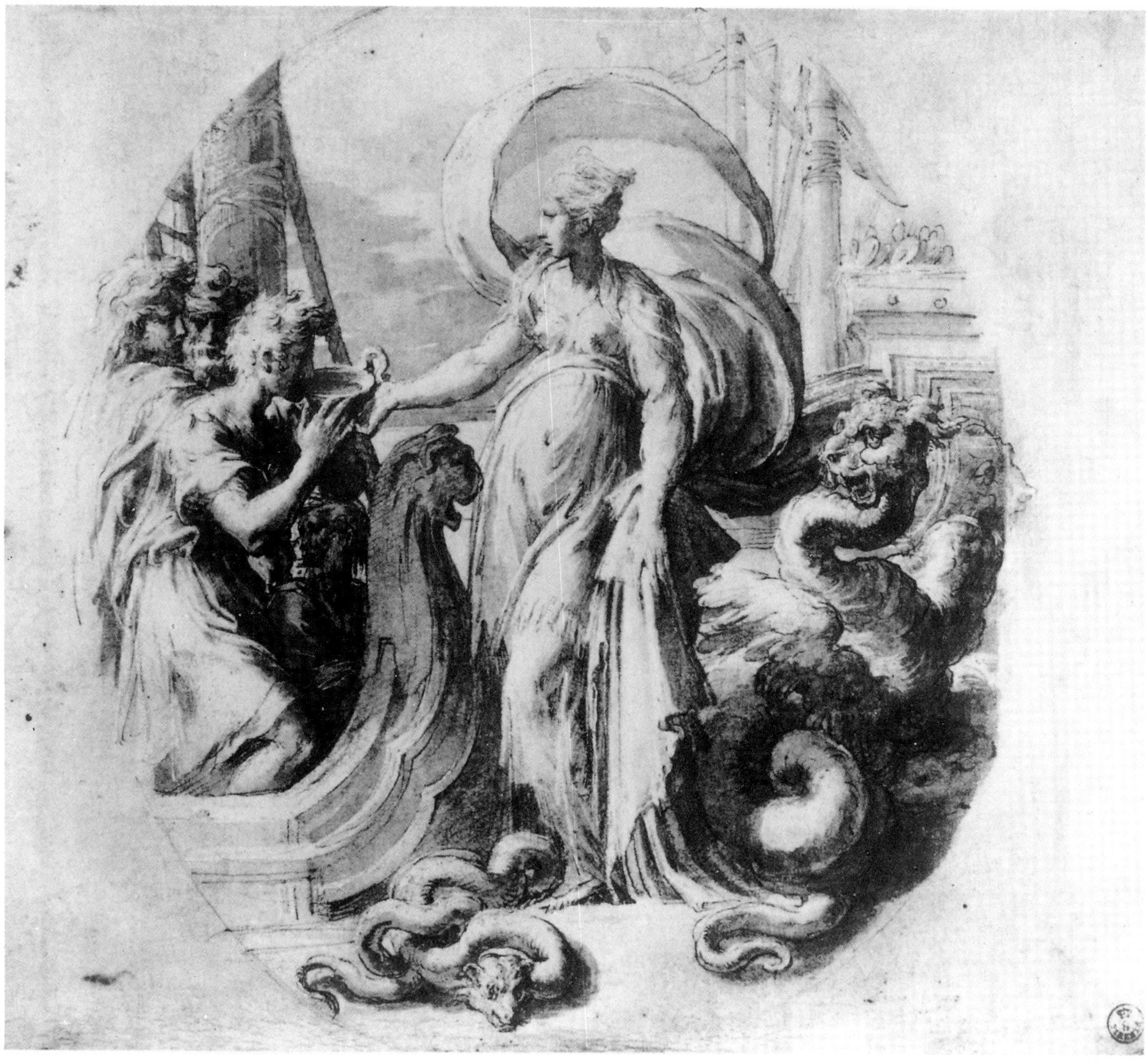

122. PARMIGIANINO
Circe, n.d. P73
Pen and brown ink over black chalk, heightened with white on paper, 9 × 11 in. (23 x 28 cm)
Galleria degli Uffizi, Florence

Documents recording the issue of gold leaf may provide some general indication of the irregular course of Parmigianino's activity at the church. There are only single issues for the years 1535 and 1536, and none in 1537. Then, presumably in connection with the gilding of the bronze rosettes, there were five in 1538 and five more in the first half of 1539. It is likely that the decoration of the barrel vault was virtually finished by 1539, but little else, if anything. The precise reason for the failure is difficult to determine. Vasari would blame it all on Parmigianino's preoccupation with alchemy. In view of Vasari's contact with Girolamo Mazzola Bedoli, who was in a position to know (in his biographies of Garofalo and Girolamo da Carpi Vasari mentions that he met Bedoli at Parma in 1566), this is indeed likely to have been a factor. Another may have been Parmigianino's lack of experience in large-scale mural work in general. But over and above this I suspect that the most cogent explanation lies in the psychology of procrastination: if you delay long enough doing something of which you are apprehensive—in this case, the painting of the half-dome—it is surprising how often the difficulty solves itself. On this occasion it did indeed do so, but not in a manner agreeable to Parmigianino.

Extra time had already been allowed the artist, who had accepted advance payment without completing his obligation. Now the patience of the church authorities was

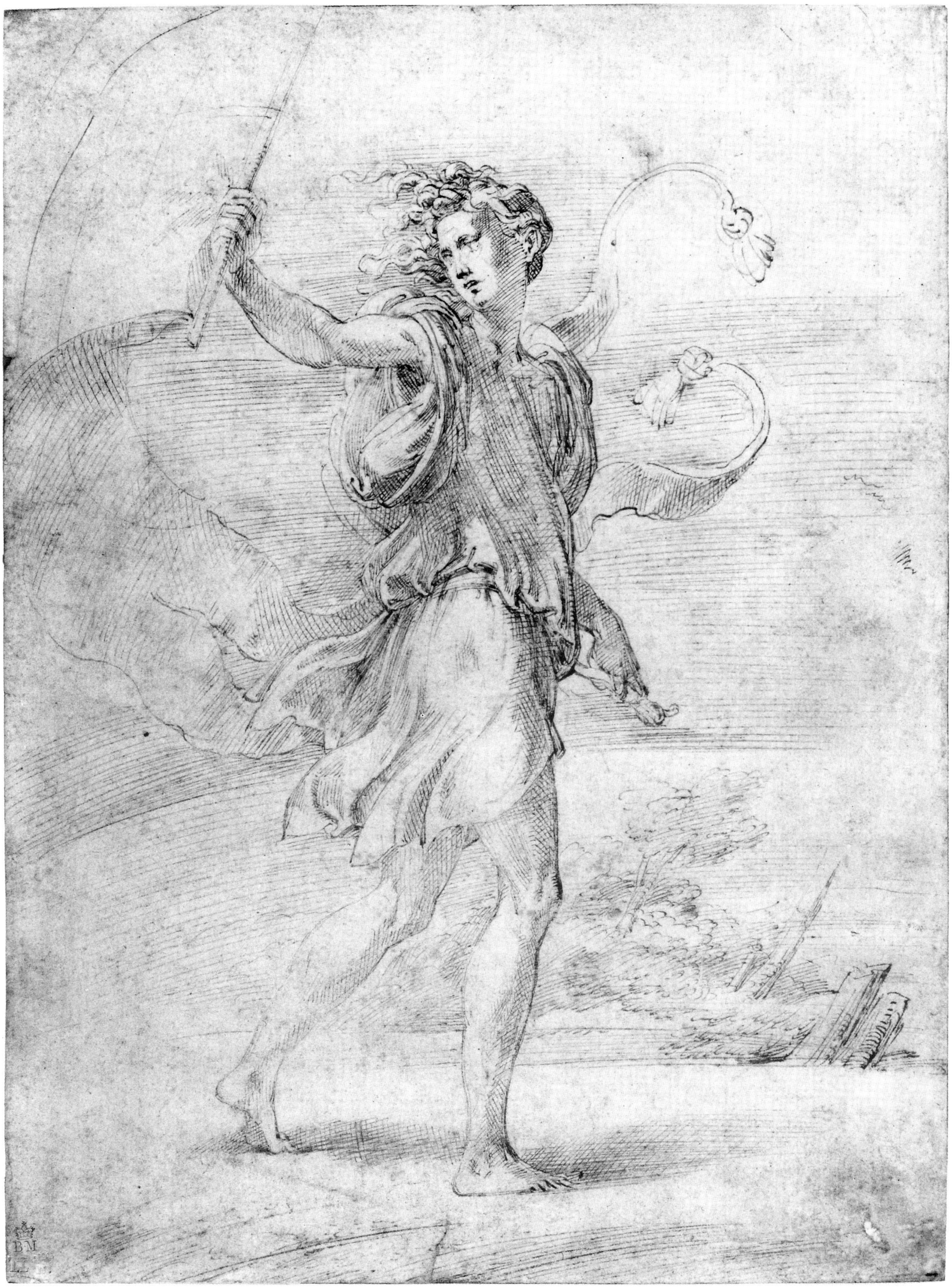

exhausted, and they had him arrested. A document of September 19, 1544 (after Parmigianino's death), indicated that after his release he did some unspecified damage to his work at the Steccata out of spite.

He now fled to Casalmaggiore beyond the Po. Normally so refined-looking, he now appeared, according to Vasari, more like a wild man, with long, unkempt hair and beard, as indeed he shows himself in the little self-portrait at Parma (fig. 84). At this point a new crisis supervened. On hearing that the authorities at the Steccata were calling on Giulio Romano to replace him, he wrote to Giulio in desperation. His letter, the only document surviving from his hand that expresses his feelings, is preserved in the Parma archives.[14] Its strange, convoluted style may be approximately translated as follows:

> *Very splendid Messer Giulio, greeting!*
>
> *Since there has been in the past not a little discord between a certain Company and myself concerning my work at the Steccata in Parma it seems to me best to enlist your help concerning the work which I can get done while remaining here at Casalmaggiore just as if I were at Parma; and there only remains to be done a certain niche which I for my part only lack my fee. The reason for my writing to yourself is that the word in Parma has it that the Company has come to an agreement with yourself that you should make the drawings and they would get them executed by an artist of their choice. This would deprive me of three hundred* scudi. *Please deign to write to me and give me advice on this matter as I know not what to say except that I think you love me as much as I love you . . .*
>
> *Casalmaggiore, 4th April, 1540.* D.V.S. *franco Mausolo.*

In commenting on this letter Giulio gives a vivid picture of Parmigianino's messenger—a very arrogant, beardless youth, who prattled with bizarre obscurity and was evidently devoted to Parmigianino ("un giovane sbarbato molto arrogante con una gran chicchiara e parlaua p' geroglifichi. E molto devoto al detto M. Fra.co"). Though embarrassed at the prospect, Giulio agreed to send a design for the half-dome, which was later painted by Anselmi. Eventually Parmigianino's scheme of decoration was copied, more or less, on the other three barrel vaults. In the case of the north and south arms, Bedoli was specifically enjoined to imitate Parmigianino's work, though the result was virtually a caricature of it.[15]

Despite everything, Parmigianino pulled himself together sufficiently to acquire a local patron at Casalmaggiore and to paint for him his masterpiece in the field of religious art—the altarpiece now at Dresden (fig. 124). Painted for the church of Santo Stefano at Casalmaggiore, it represents the patron saint of the church with the Madonna and the Baptist. It undoubtedly constitutes a measure of reform, probably deliberate. Realizing that in the *Collo Lungo* he had carried originality almost to the point of perversity, he seems to have set out to return to relative orthodoxy—at least to the extent of making the innovations less aggressive. Faced once again with the subject of the Madonna

123. PARMIGIANINO
Standard-Bearer, n.d. P255
Pen and brown ink on paper,
10⅜ × 7¾ in. (26.5 × 19.8 cm)
British Museum, London

and saints, he started with a normal composition of the Madonna in Glory type, shown in preliminary drawings (P276, P664r, P.O.C. 33). In these the Virgin is seated on clouds. At this point he evidently allowed his mind to revert to Raphael's Sistine *Madonna,* a picture that had been in Piacenza, only some fifty-six kilometers (thirty-five miles) from Casalmaggiore, for about a quarter of a century. In it Raphael had shown the Madonna on her feet and approaching the spectator.

In following Raphael, Parmigianino made a change in the posture of the Christ Child. Instead of being cradled in his mother's arms, as Raphael had shown him, he now stands up, and for his attitude Parmigianino reverts, surprisingly, to a much earlier memory. The Dresden Christ Child is a literal and accurate repetition, in reverse, of Michelangelo's Jesus in the *Madonna of Bruges* (fig. 53), that work that Parmigianino never saw in the original, but of which, twelve years previously, some reflection had vitally affected his first great religious painting, the London altarpiece. There is also another significant difference from Raphael's picture. The Sistine Madonna is visibly walking forward. Parmigianino's Madonna advances her right leg, but it seems that the clouds beneath her are themselves drifting forward, bringing her with them, the light brightening as the vision nears the spectator.

It is the light that transforms Parmigianino's picture and enables him to achieve the difficult feat of capping one masterpiece with another. As in the *Madonna with Saint Margaret,* it creates an atmosphere of magic and mystery, heightened in this case by the dramatic storm clouds. Regarded simply as a design, the Dresden altarpiece is eccentric. In Raphael's picture the saints who flank the Madonna are kneeling. Parmigianino's Baptist and Saint Stephen (evidently modeled on two of the studio boys, who reappear in some of the genre drawings) are seated side by side. They sit close together in front of a balustrade on a shallow platform that drops vertically on the spectator's side. In this way they take up more of the picture space, both horizontally and vertically, than Raphael's saints. They are firmly delineated, the elongation kept within an acceptable limit, the draperies elegantly simplified. And the patron, who in one of the early sketches (P664r) had actually been relegated to a pit in the middle distance, with only the upper half of his body visible between the seated saints—an extraordinary idea—now kneels, reverently and inconspicuously, on the left. All this is surprising enough in what is outwardly an orthodox design for an altarpiece of the Madonna and saints. What remains is the element of genius; the focal point—the vision itself—is actually out of focus. This is achieved by a method different from the shorthand touch of the figures to the sides of the altarpiece of the *Madonna with Saint Margaret.* The Madonna and Child of the Dresden altar are not defined with flashing brushstrokes, as was the Saint Jerome in the Bologna picture, but are painted with a general faintness and lack of detail, such as Raphael had used for the angelic choir in his *Saint Cecilia* (fig. 7). As a result the vision really is a vision. Even the Sistine *Madonna,* perfect as she is both as form and on a human level, looks earthbound in comparison with Parmigianino's evocation of colored light.

124. PARMIGIANINO
Madonna and Child with Saint Stephen, the Baptist, and a Donor, c. 1540
Oil on panel, 99⅝ × 63⅜ in.
(253 × 161 cm)
Gemäldegalerie, Dresden, Germany
(cat. A8)

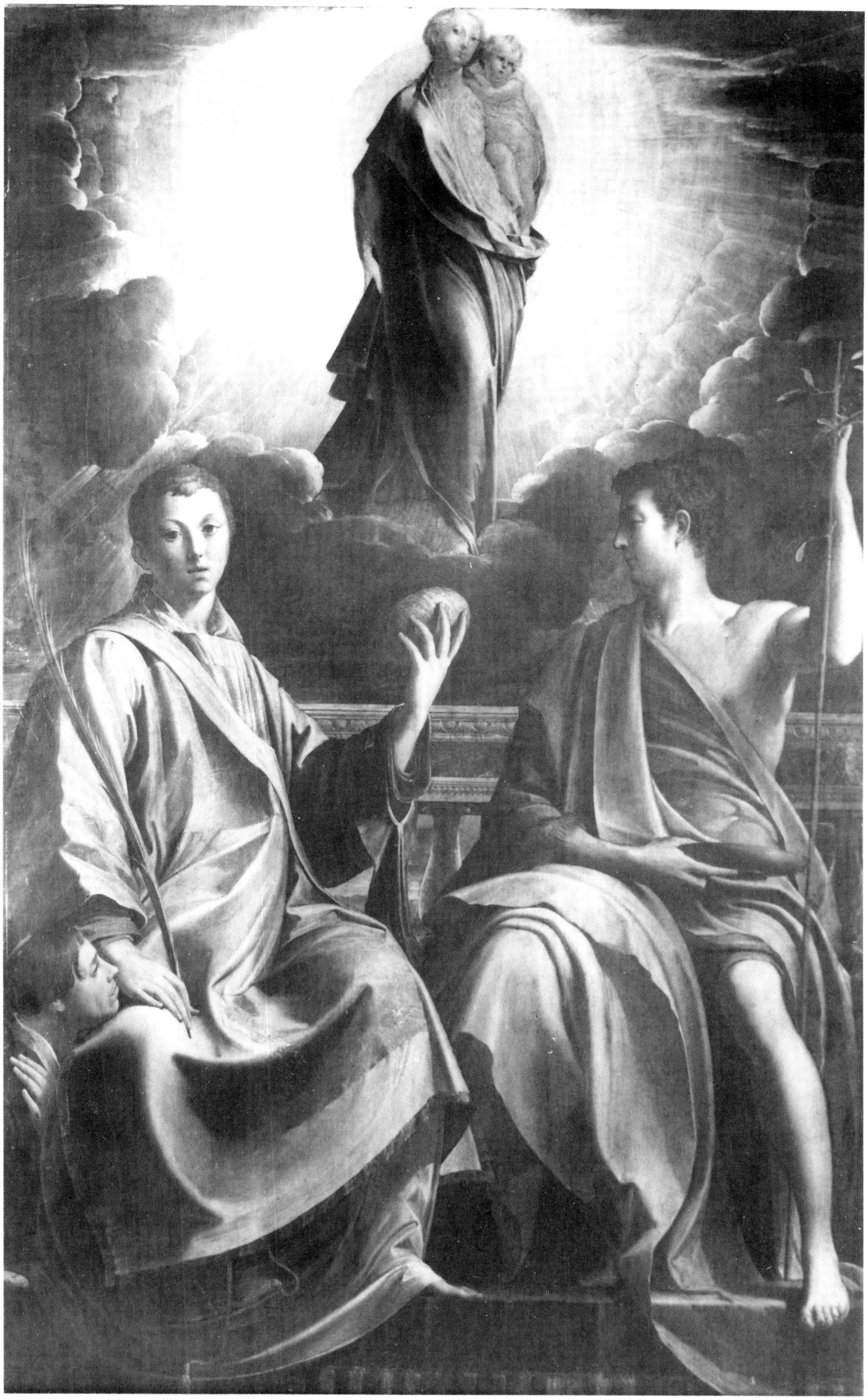

This was his last major work that survives. A *Lucretia,* named by Vasari as the last of all, is unidentified. Parmigianino's sketches for this subject, such as P25, P488, P523, P525, and P670, show a standing figure of the type that he had used, more or less indiscriminately, for *Judith, Circe,* and Augustus's *Sibyl.* Raphael's *Lucretia,* as engraved by Marcantonio, is also standing, though not resembling Parmigianino's sketches in other ways. But a *Lucretia* engraved by Enea Vico as after Parmigianino shows a seated figure, and the print corresponds in essentials with an elaborate drawing in Washington.[16] This was attributed by A. E. Popham to Bedoli—an attribution with which the present writer is inclined to agree, though the standard is higher than Bedoli's average in a drawing—but the figure is similar in type to the *Eve* of the Steccata.[17] It may be that the autograph sketches were for an earlier version of the subject and that Vico's print and the Washington drawing record the one mentioned by Vasari. In view of the rarity of Parmigianino's paintings of classical subjects, the loss of this one is the more deplorable. But it is difficult to imagine that it would have captured the mood of the epic heroine in the grand manner to the extent that Raphael did. Some idea of its technique may perhaps be obtained from the little painting of Pallas Athene at Hampton Court, which is certainly a very late work (fig. 125). It is vouched for by a sketch (P316) in the Morgan Library and by studies (P799) for the elaborate jewel that the goddess wears. This is similar to some of the details on the Steccata vault, though even more finely wrought in his final style, which has been well described by a modern critic as having "electrified delicacy as if the artist's nerves were on edge."[18] As with the saints in the Dresden altarpiece, and the portrait of the count of San Secondo, Pallas Athene's fingers are of spidery thinness.

Parmigianino died on August 24, 1540, and was buried in the Servite church called "La Fontana" at Motta San Fermo, outside the town of Casalmaggiore. He was thirty-seven. Vasari tells us that by his wish he was buried naked, with a cross of cypress on his chest. There is no reliable documentation on the cause of his premature death. At a guess one might suspect that it was perhaps a pulmonary ailment contracted from the fumes associated with alchemical experiments.

Of his art in general, the elegance that is associated with his name does indeed permeate his output. His traumatic relationship to Correggio has something in common with that of Anthony Van Dyck to Peter Paul Rubens. In both cases the younger artist lacked the mighty innovatory power of the older, but achieved in some ways even greater refinement.

Compared with the vast amount of work of many different kinds that Raphael, who died at the same early age, left behind him, the output of Parmigianino is small. Two major frescoes, about half a dozen altarpieces, about a dozen smaller religious pictures, and about the same number of portraits, together with a single mythology and a handful of etchings—other artists have achieved a comparable quantity in less than thirty-seven years. Certainly the superlative quality of the craftsmanship of most of Parmigianino's paintings, and of his preparatory drawings, compensates for the rarity, and certainly, too, there has been an element of bad luck: many of his smaller pictures, to judge by what Vasari says, have been lost. When poring over the reproductions of more than eight hundred drawings assembled in Popham's magisterial folios the student pauses over many that could have been, but probably never were, carried to the stage of a painting. Not only the inevitable Madonnas and Children. More teasing are the designs for less hackneyed subjects, or for a new approach to an old one—three mysterious figures, truncated by a parapet, witness the Visitation in the lunar beauty of the Parma drawing (P550; fig. 59), already discussed; fabulously graceful horses, fauns, satyrs, and other creatures of antiquity; exquisite landscape studies (P118; fig. 126); occasional pornography;[19] and a few scenes from the artist's daily life—one of the studio boys on

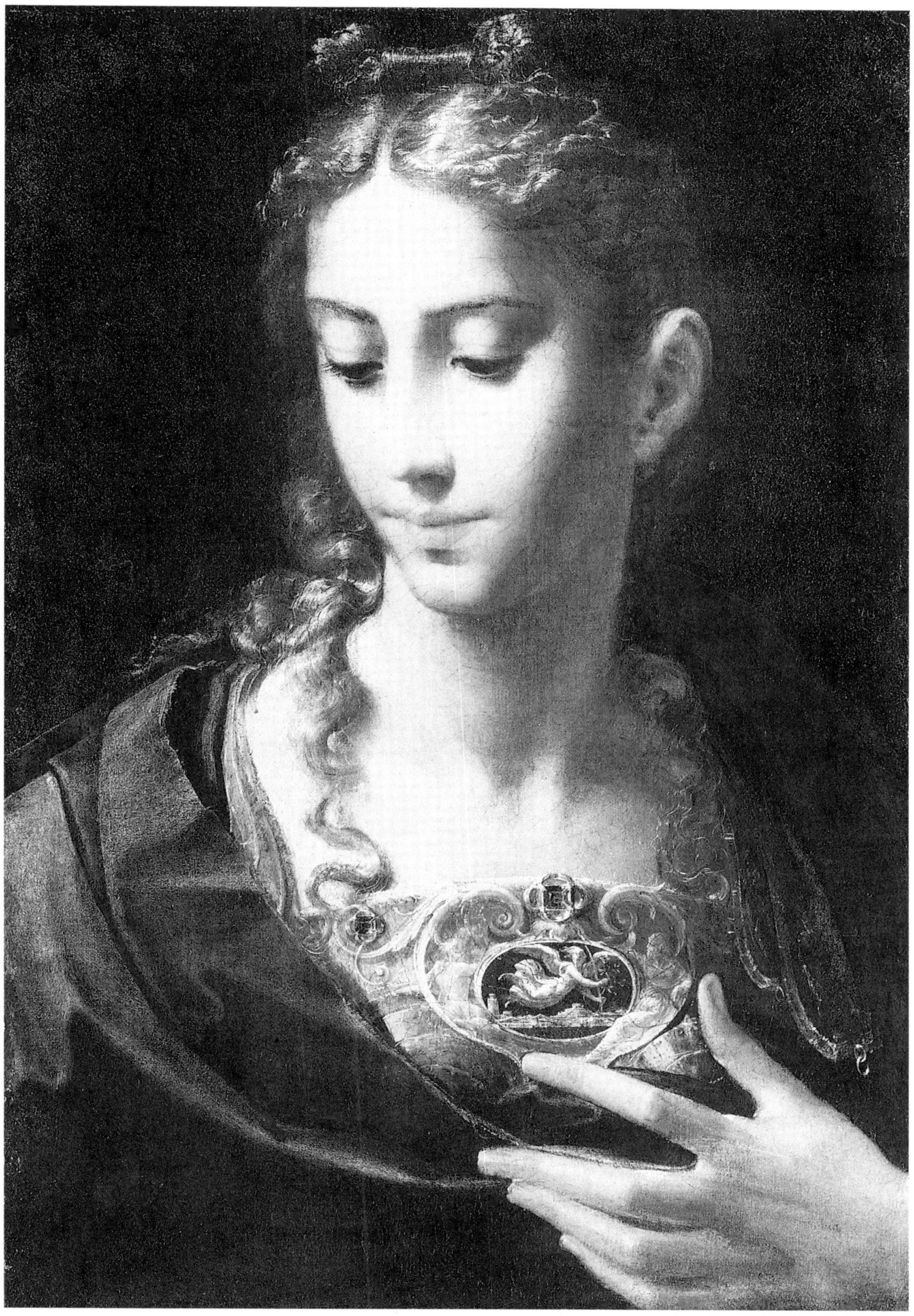

125. PARMIGIANINO
Head and Bust of Athene, n.d.
Oil on canvas, 25⅛ × 17¾ in.
(63.8 × 45.1 cm)
Hampton Court Palace, Hampton Court, England (cat. A15)

his hands and knees (P272), the studio boys in a ferry (P224), or Parmigianino himself with a bitch (P256; fig. 127). The last-named drawing is the only visual indication known to me of Parmigianino's physical stature—to judge by his nickname, conspicuously small. For the animal is evidently the same as the one who is shown clasping the leg of one of the studio boys in another drawing (P460; fig. 128). Here the dog appears of no more than medium size. But in the sketch with Parmigianino himself (P256) it would be colossal if the man were of normal size.[20]

In this twilit world of the drawings certain features surface from the artist's subconscious with the regularity of obsessions—alchemical vases or, even more puzzling, an extraordinary fondness for Phrygian caps. The most diverse characters are made to wear them in different contexts. Sometimes, perhaps subconsciously, Parmigianino persuades

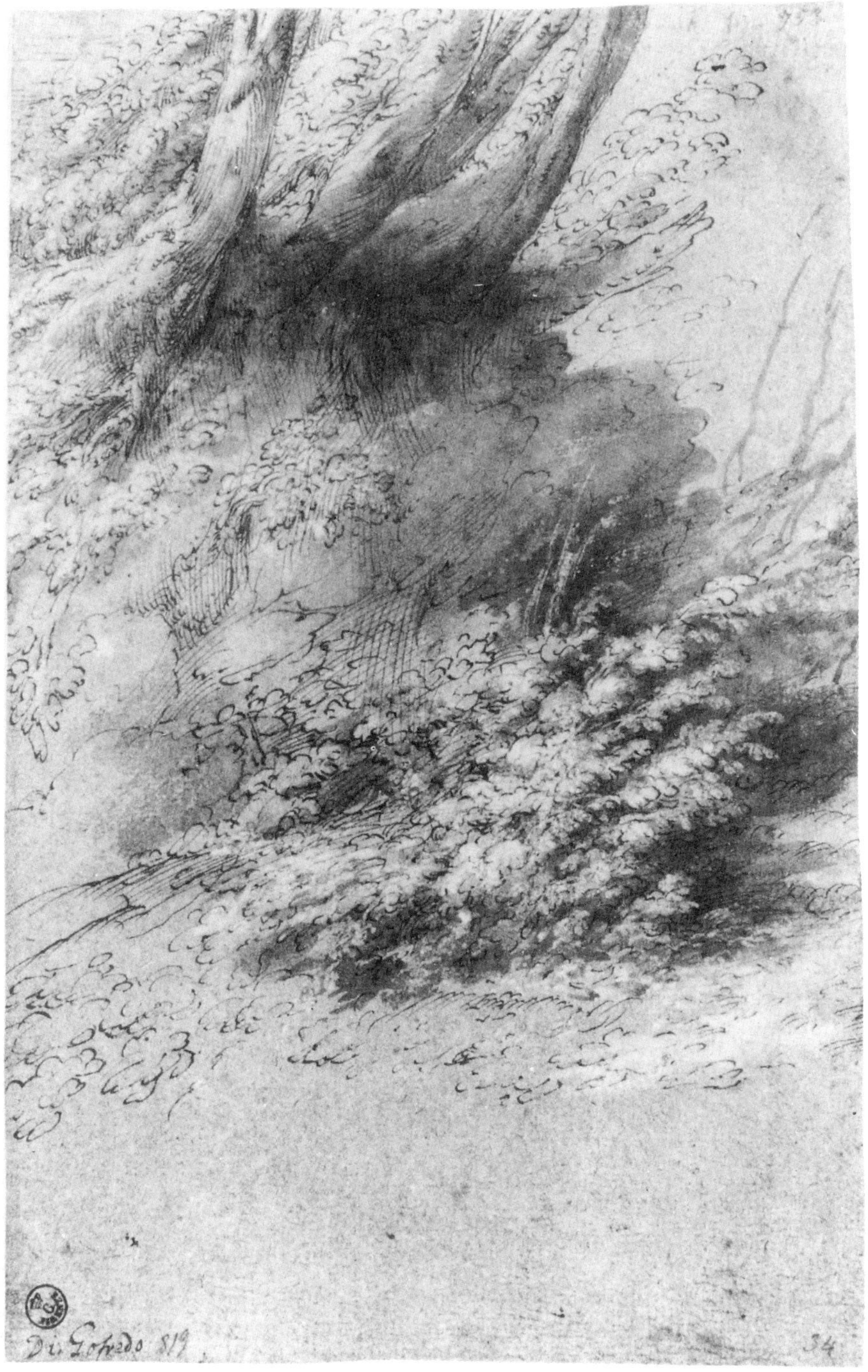

126. PARMIGIANINO
Study of trees, c. 1531–35 P118
Pen, brown ink, and watercolor on gray paper, 11 × 6⅞ in. (27.8 × 17.6 cm)
Galleria degli Uffizi, Florence

ordinary draperies to simulate their shape, and sometimes he combines them with another obsessive image—two bearded men deep in conversation in the middle distance. Another source of perpetual fascination was antique armor, with its curlicues and the glitter of its gold. If he had lived a little later he might, with this interest and his delight in sylvan subjects, have been the ideal interpreter of the story of Rinaldo and Armida, and of other episodes from Tasso.

At this point in the discussion of Parmigianino as draftsman a claim to supremacy may be made. For all this wonderful talent few of his paintings could be classed among the greatest Renaissance masterpieces—perhaps only the Dresden altarpiece and the *"Antea"* portrait. But the eagerness with which his drawings have been collected at all times since his death, and even during his lifetime, is a reliable gauge of their quality. If they lack

Below, left:
127. PARMIGIANINO
Man Holding a Bitch, n.d. P256
Pen and brown ink on paper, 12 x 8 in. (30.5 x 20.4 cm)
British Museum, London

Below, right:
128. PARMIGIANINO
Youth with a Bitch, n.d. P460
Pen and light brown ink on paper, 7⅜ × 4½ in. (18.7 × 11.3 cm)
Musée du Louvre, Paris

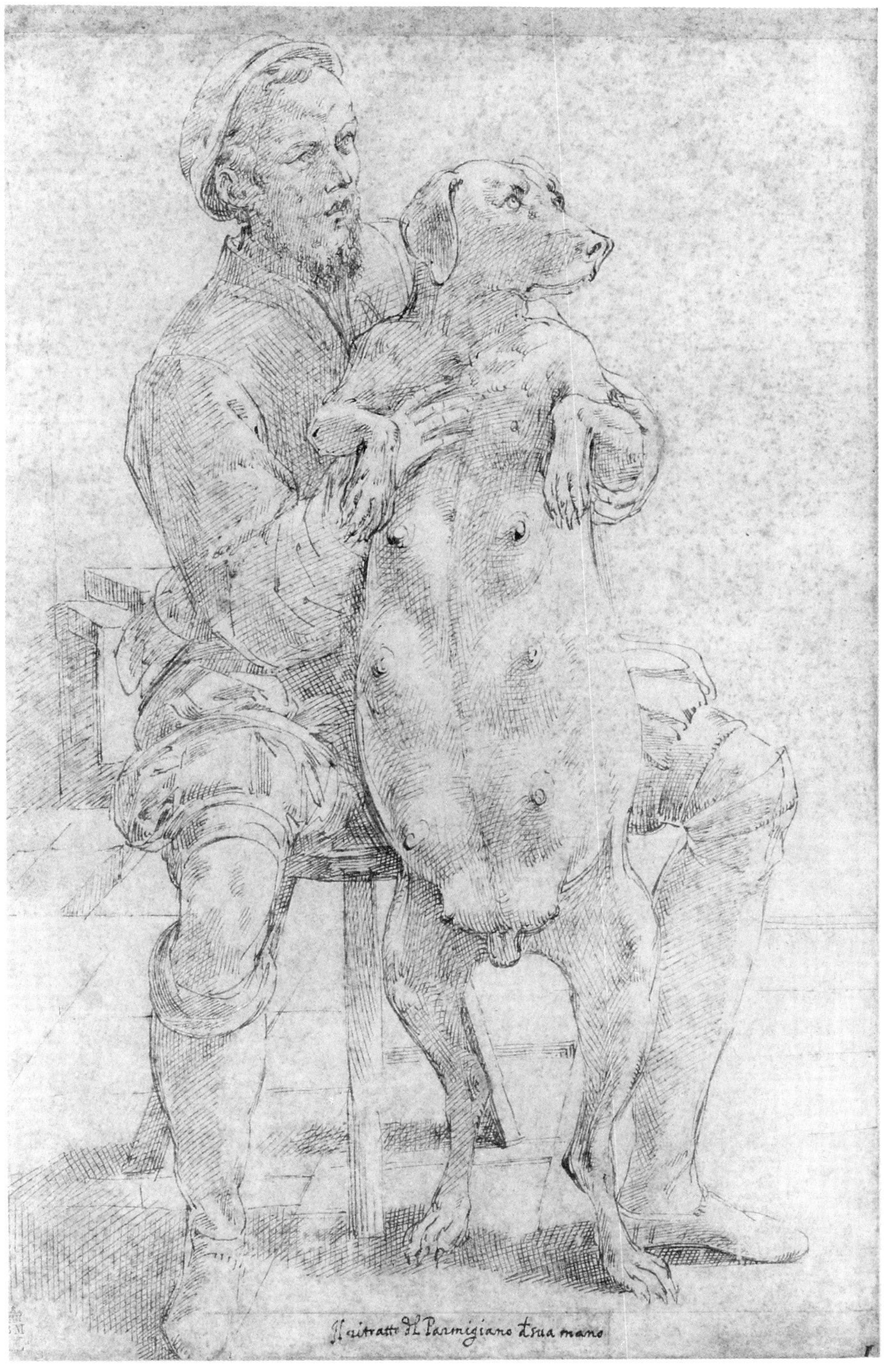

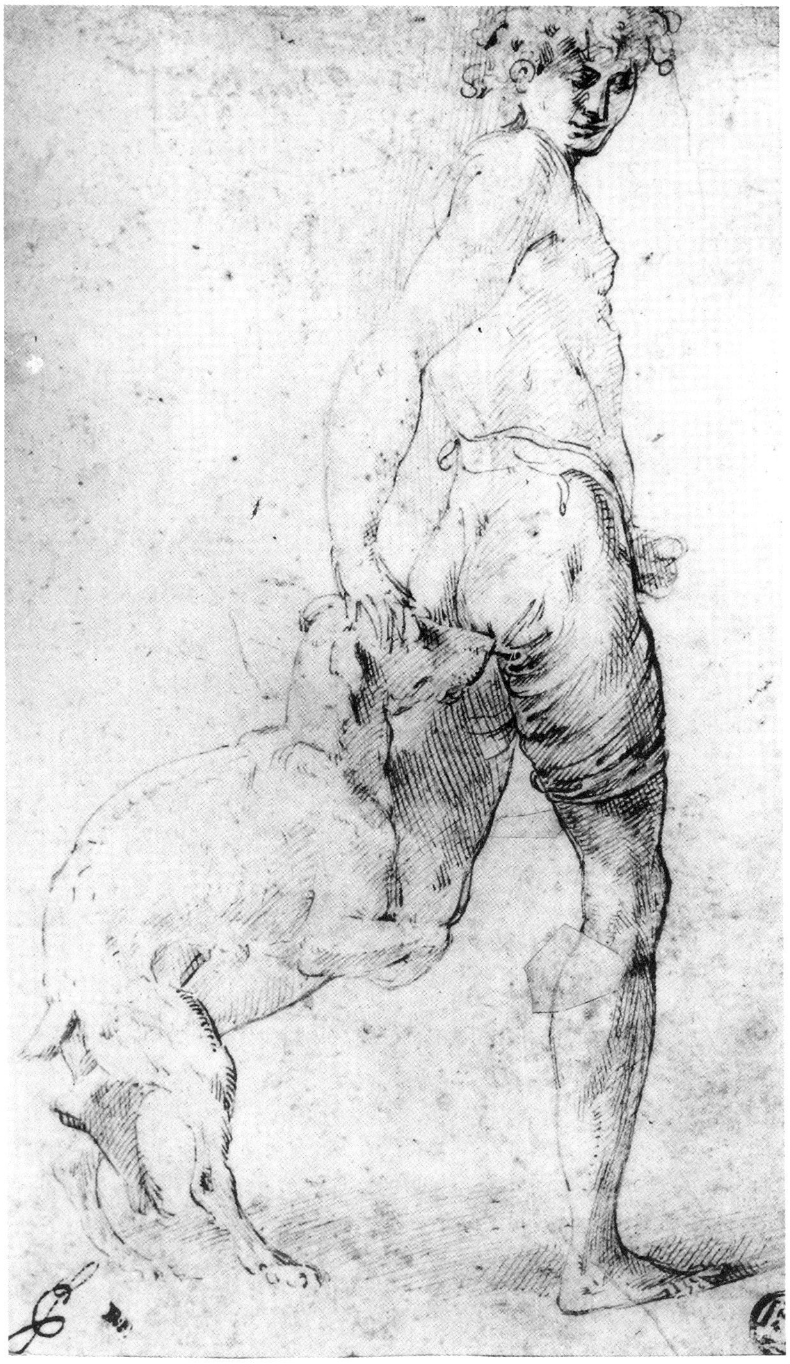

the profundity of Michelangelo's greatest drawings, they score in other ways. For refinement of idea and perception, and variety and beauty of technique, together with a quality of suggestion by which the spectator tends to imagine more than he is shown, I know of no draftsman who has surpassed Parmigianino. The superb quality of the drawings had one very practical consequence—the survival of so many of them. In this way we have knowledge of some of the fleeting and extraordinarily bizarre ideas that he toyed with and then discarded—an insight that, in the case of less avidly collected draftsmen, would have gone the way of the snows of yesterday. Thus in wrestling with the *Madonna dal Collo Lungo* we can see that he contemplated locating one of the saints—Saint Jerome—prone on the ground at the Madonna's feet, that the Christ Child in the *Madonna della Rosa* was briefly envisaged doing a high kick (P739, P740), and that at one stage in the evolution of the Dresden altarpiece the patron was sited in a cavity at the center of the base, with his head looking out toward the spectator.

As far as we know, Parmigianino never married. Judging from the totality of his art, I suspect that his instincts were bisexual. Vasari tells us he was a skilled lutanist. As regards the general level of his education, some notes on a drawing at Stockholm (P591) show that as late as the 1530s he was teaching himself Latin grammar.

In the twenty-odd years of his career he had undergone multiple influences, and he continued to absorb and develop them until the end. The juvenile impressions of Francia and Cima had been superseded by the more powerful forces of Pordenone and his colleagues at Cremona. Then came Anselmi from Siena and Correggio from the city of that name; and at some point he undoubtedly became aware of Mantegna's work at Mantua, of Dosso Dossi, and of some echo of Leonardo. One or more portraits by Lotto are also likely to have come his way, and even before the Rome journey he had some knowledge of Raphael and Michelangelo. In Rome itself these impressions and those of the antique were strengthened. There was also personal contact with Rosso, Sebastiano, and Perino del Vaga, and experience of the Roman work of Giulio Romano. Between Rome and Bologna the magic light of Beccafumi, together with Pontormo's revolution in spatial design, left an emphatic impression. On arrival at Bologna he set up as a printmaker and then developed his own version of the shorthand technique in painting. Neither this nor the Roman impressions lasted long, being soon overtaken by the renewed impact of Correggio, in a sense his evil genius. From now till the end of his life, when the influence of Raphael reasserted itself, the touch becomes harder and more precise, bringing with it stronger contrasts of color.

After his death, Parmigianino's influence persisted at Parma, thereby cutting out for the time being that of Correggio, except, after a decent interval, in cupola painting. The reasons for this, although complex, were nevertheless partly personal. The most prosperous and active painter at Parma throughout the middle years of the sixteenth century was Girolamo Mazzola Bedoli, and he happened to be Parmigianino's cousin by marriage. In his best religious paintings, such as the polyptych from the Cistercian abbey of San

Martino de' Bocci, now in the Parma gallery, Bedoli balances delicate figure painting effectively against a leafy background, but his portraits are much inferior to Parmigianino's. Bedoli, in his turn, was evidently followed by another gifted painter with personal connections with Parmigianino, namely Jacopo Zanguidi, called Bertoja.[21] He is of special interest in this connection since he worked in Rome and at Caprarola as well as at Parma,[22] and in this way he carried a little of the Parmigianinesque tradition to the Eternal City. But his early death in 1574 contributed to the waning of Parmigianino's influence in his hometown, a process that culminated when the Correggio revival started toward the end of the sixteenth century.

Mention has already been made of the influence of Parmigianino's Bolognese paintings on the young Florentine Francesco Salviati; perhaps also on the young Vasari. In addition, Parmigianino's influence was evident in Lombardy, in the work of the Procaccino family of painters, who transferred from Bologna to Milan in the 1580s. But the two painters who responded most sensitively and understandingly to Parmigianino's painting were both migrants, and we do not know to what extent, if at all, either of them may have come in personal contact with him. One of them, Andrea Schiavone, was a native of Dalmatia who settled in Venice. In the meantime he had copied Parmigianino's prints, which left an indelible mark on his paintings and drawings, as well as on his own prints (fig. 129). And in Schiavone's adopted home at Venice one of the devices that Parmigianino had used in his later work was to be of service to Veronese throughout his life. This was the sinking of the middle distance to a lower level than the foreground, thereby showing only the upper and more decorative portions of the subsidiary figures. The influence of Parmigianino's etchings has also been seen in Tintoretto, Jacopo Bassano, and the young El Greco.

129. ANDREA SCHIAVONE
Bellona, n.d.
Etching

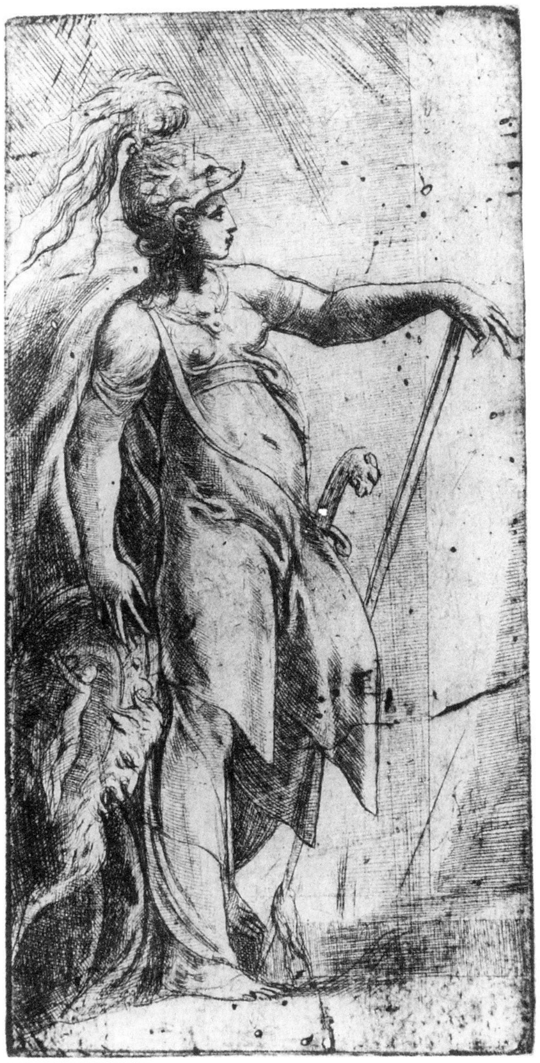

The other painter who profited most essentially from Parmigianino's example was Niccolò dell'Abate, who was from Modena. He emigrated in middle life to Fontainebleau, where, in paintings such as the *Aristaeus* (London; fig. 130), he adapted Parmigianino's style both of figure painting and panoramic landscape, but reversed the ratio of one to the other.[23] The elegant Parmigianinesque figures now complement landscapes such as those in Parmigianino's *Conversion of Saul* or the Uffizi *Madonna with Saint Zachariah* (fig. 107), whereas with Parmigianino himself the accent was the opposite, with the landscape setting off the figures. In other respects these beautiful pictures are precisely the kind of composition—naked figures in a sylvan setting—that Parmigianino executed exquisitely in some of his prints and that he could have painted, but unfortunately never seems to have done, with even greater skill. In addition, the dissemination at Fontainebleau of Parmigianino's own etchings greatly influenced the graphic work that was produced there, and at least one of his etchings—the *Entombment*—inspired, as I have suggested, a major work of French sculpture, Jean Goujon's marble relief *The Entombment* (Louvre).[24]

One of the later manifestations of Parmigianino's influence can be traced at the ducal court of Lorraine at Nancy in the opening years of the seventeenth century, where

130. NICCOLÒ DELL'ABATE
The Story of Aristaeus, n.d.
Oil on canvas, 74½ × 93½ in.
(189.2 × 237.5 cm)
National Gallery, London

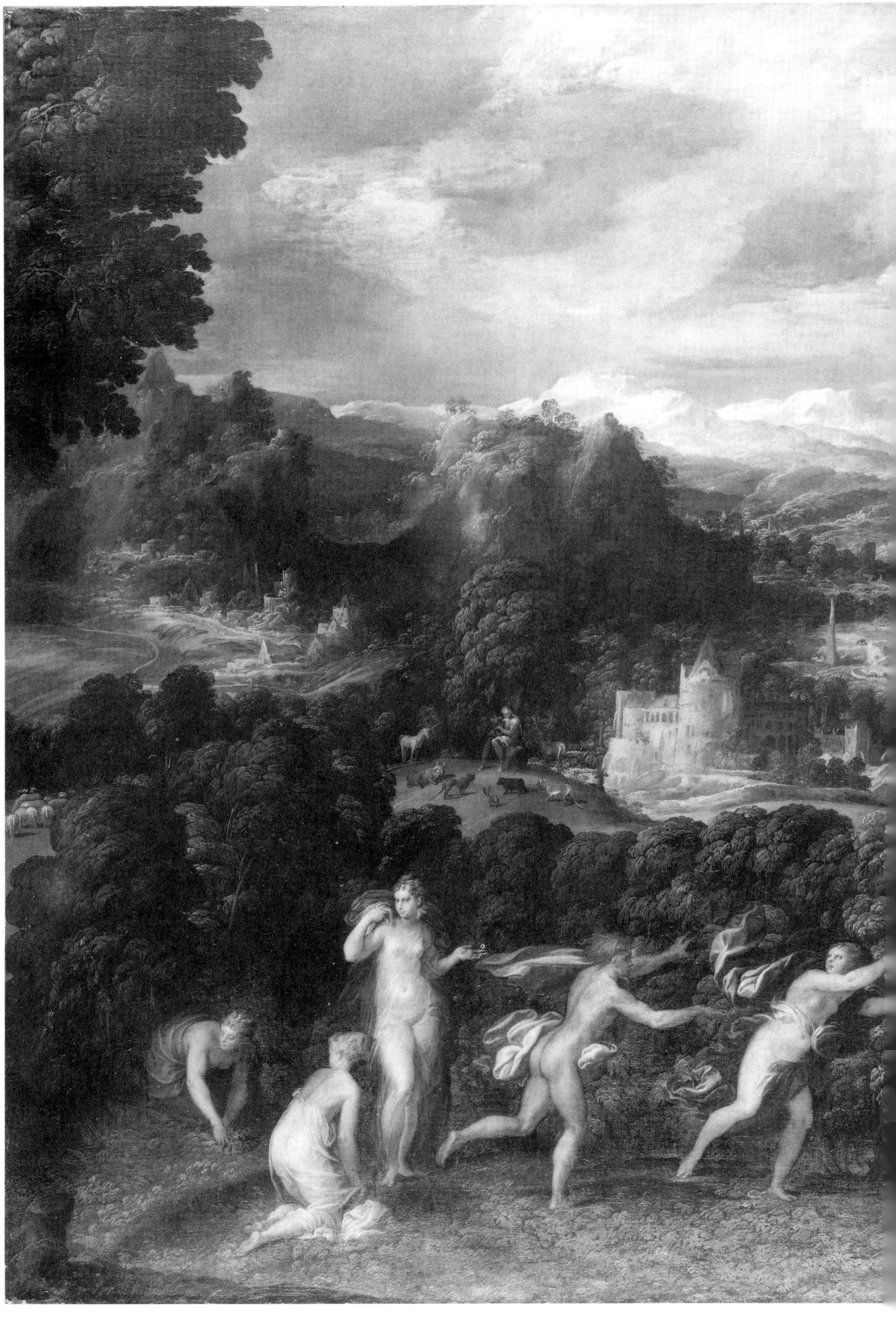

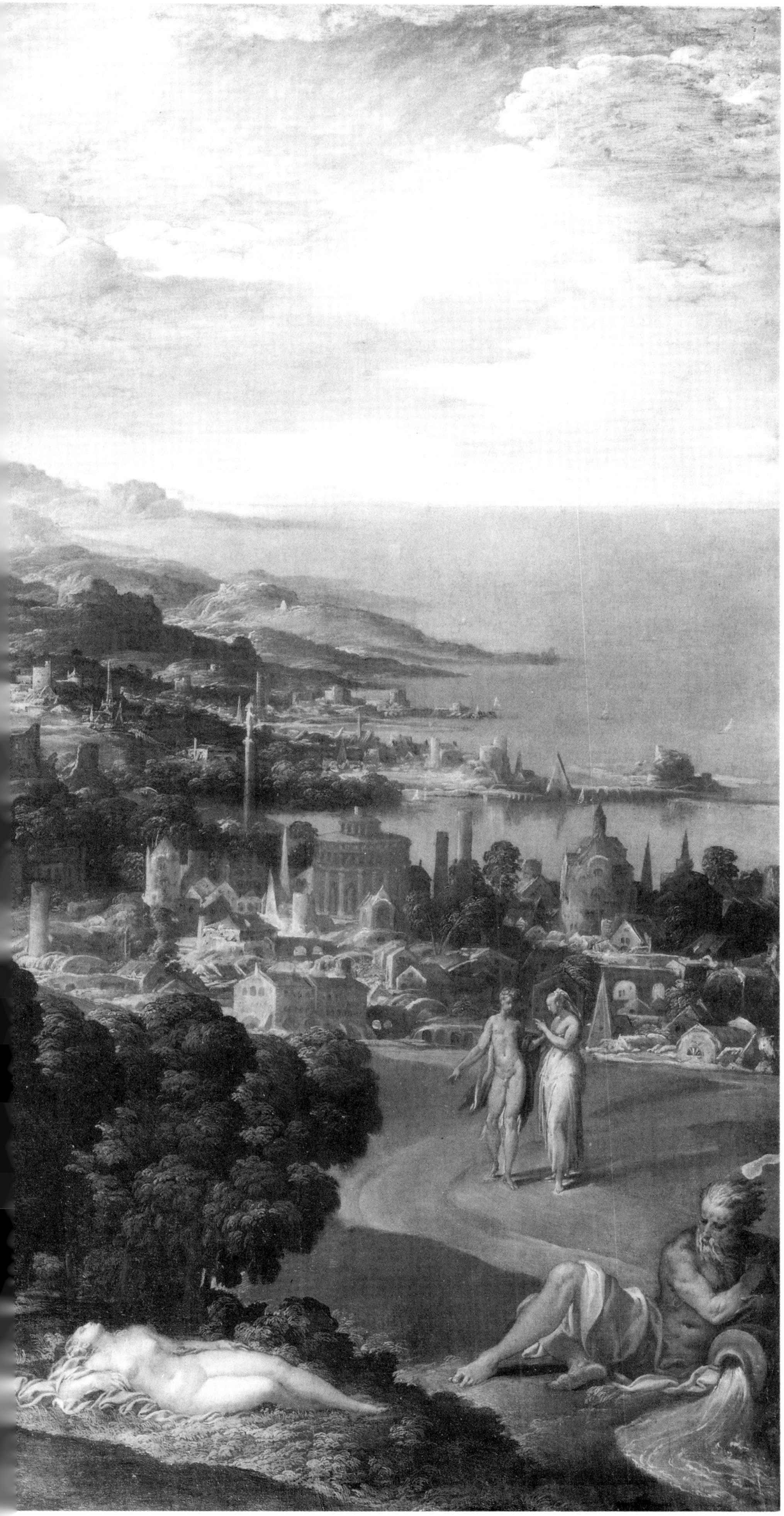

Jacques Bellange developed in some of his etchings the elongated and spiral anatomy of the *Madonna dal Collo Lungo* to an extreme degree (fig. 131). Another line of descent is fascinating in its prolonged and unpredictable transmigrations. The strange and still underestimated genius Bartholomäus Spranger was born in Antwerp in 1546.[25] He spent some time at Parma in the 1560s and then went on to Rome. There, in the Farnese circle, he would have renewed contact with, among others, Bertoja, whom he would have known at Parma. Like him, he worked briefly for the Farnese at Caprarola. He also made the acquaintance of his countryman, the painter and historian Karel van Mander, and at one stage was in contact at Florence with another of his countrymen, the great Giambologna. Giambologna recommended Spranger to the Emperor Maximilian II. Eventually Spranger settled at the court of the Emperor Rudolf II at Prague, where his art found an ideally sympathetic

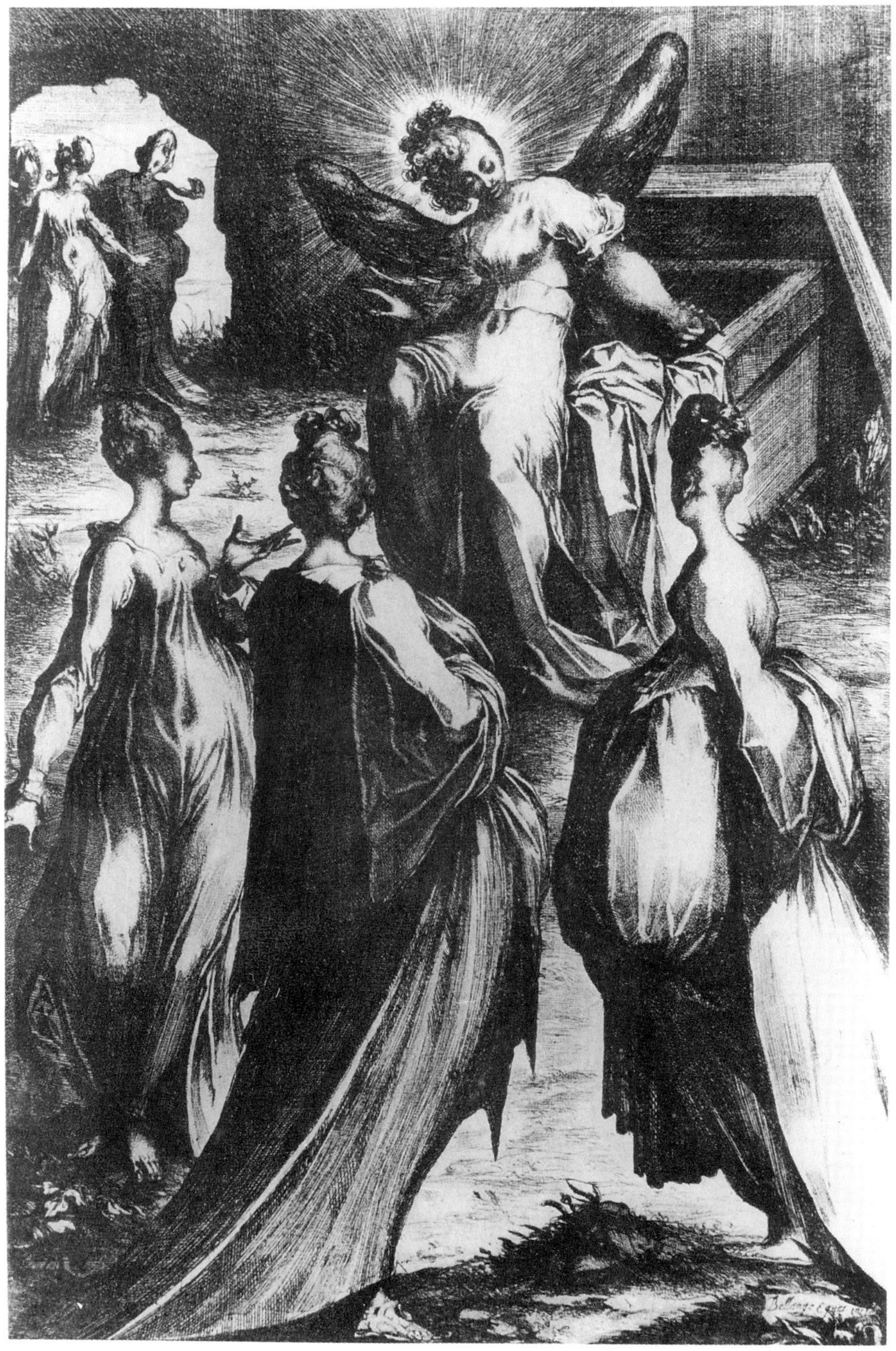

131. JACQUES BELLANGE
The Three Marys at the Sepulchre, n.d.
Etching touched with burin,
17¼ × 11⅜ in. (44.1 × 28.8 cm)
Museum of Fine Arts, Boston.
Otis Norcross Fund

outlet in paintings of erotic and allegorical subjects (fig. 132). These were in an individually eclectic style based on that of Parmigianino (particularly the *Madonna dal Collo Lungo*), with the addition of nudes in attitudes derived from Giambologna's bronzes. There is also perceptible influence from Baroccio, particularly in the coloring. Finally, as far afield as England, the designs of Inigo Jones for masques at the court of King James I owe not a little to his study of prints by and after Parmigianino. Jones's admiration of Parmigianino is mentioned by his friend, the third earl of Pembroke.

Up to this point the posthumous influence of Parmigianino had followed a fairly consistent pattern. One aspect of his art—the mannered elegance of his figures and the world of fantasy evoked by his prints—had chimed with the mood of life at royal and ducal courts as far apart as Parma, Fontainebleau, Nancy, Prague, and even London. But something of the same strain, by now much diluted, also took root in an unexpected place. This was bourgeois Holland. Some of Spranger's elegantly mannered designs had been introduced by Van Mander to the newly founded academy at Haarlem, where they vitally influenced painters such as Hendrick Goltzius and Cornelis van Haarlem, who developed them almost to the point of caricature. Finally this Haarlem style was transplanted by Abraham Bloemaert and Joachim Wtewael to Utrecht, where it flourished for a time before giving way to a more recent, and rather less surprising fashion, this time coming from Italy direct—the monumental realism of Caravaggio.[26]

The end of the sixteenth century saw the start of the seesaw process between the reputations of Correggio and Parmigianino—a phenomenon that has continued virtually to the present day. That they appeared on the same scene at the same time made it difficult for posterity to think of them separately, while the essential dissimilarity of their art ensured that as one rose in esteem the other tended to fall. The case of Annibale Carracci, the protagonist of the Correggio revival, illustrates this. Brought up in the partly Parmigianinesque tradition of mid-sixteenth-century Bologna, he reacted against his upbringing, specifically exalting Correggio at the expense of Parmigianino.[27]

Throughout most of the seventeenth century, with the spread of Baroque art from Rome to the court of Europe, Correggio was by far the more influential. He was correspondingly also more highly esteemed, though the preference expressed by Guido Reni, according to Scaramuccia (1674), for Parmigianino's *Saint Margaret* altarpiece as against Raphael's *Saint Cecilia* should be mentioned—particularly since it was probably the bold technique of this picture of Parmigianino's more than any other that influenced that of Reni's late, "unfinished" work.[28] In the eighteenth century the views of the two most knowledgeable and discerning critics, Anton Raphael Mengs and Sir Joshua Reynolds, were diverse. Mengs worshipped Correggio and had little to say about Parmigianino, while Reynolds concedes that Parmigianino is "perhaps equal" to Correggio. He adds that both "have fallen into the most hateful of all hateful qualities, affectation,"[29] and this charge is what, in the nineteenth century, was leveled by Jacob Burckhardt at Parmigianino (in connection—inevitably—with the *Madonna dal Collo Lungo*) but not at Correggio. In

Following pages:
Detail of fig. 132
BARTHOLOMÄUS SPRANGER
Triumph of Wisdom
(Angels)

Detail of fig. 110
PARMIGIANINO
Madonna dal Collo Lungo
(Angels)

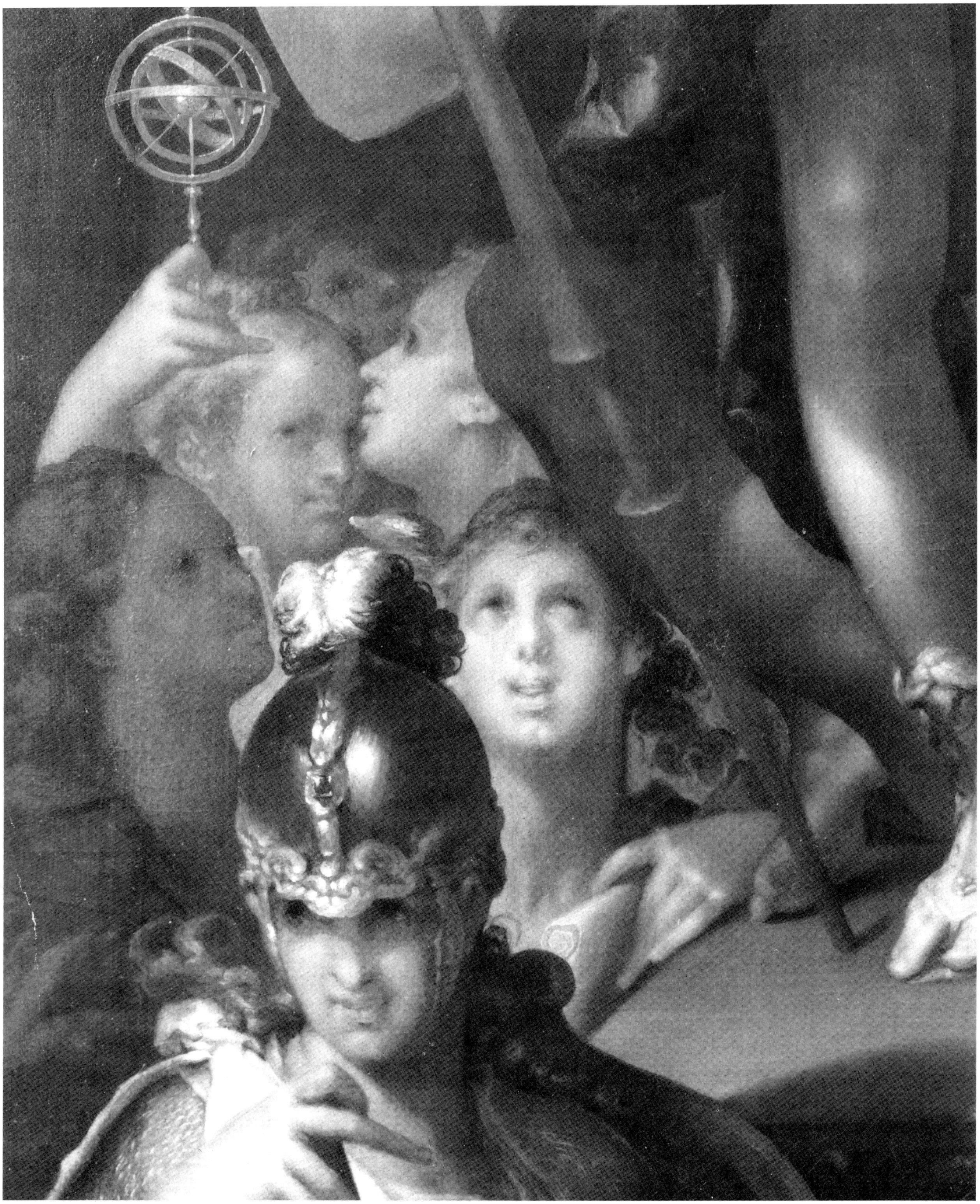

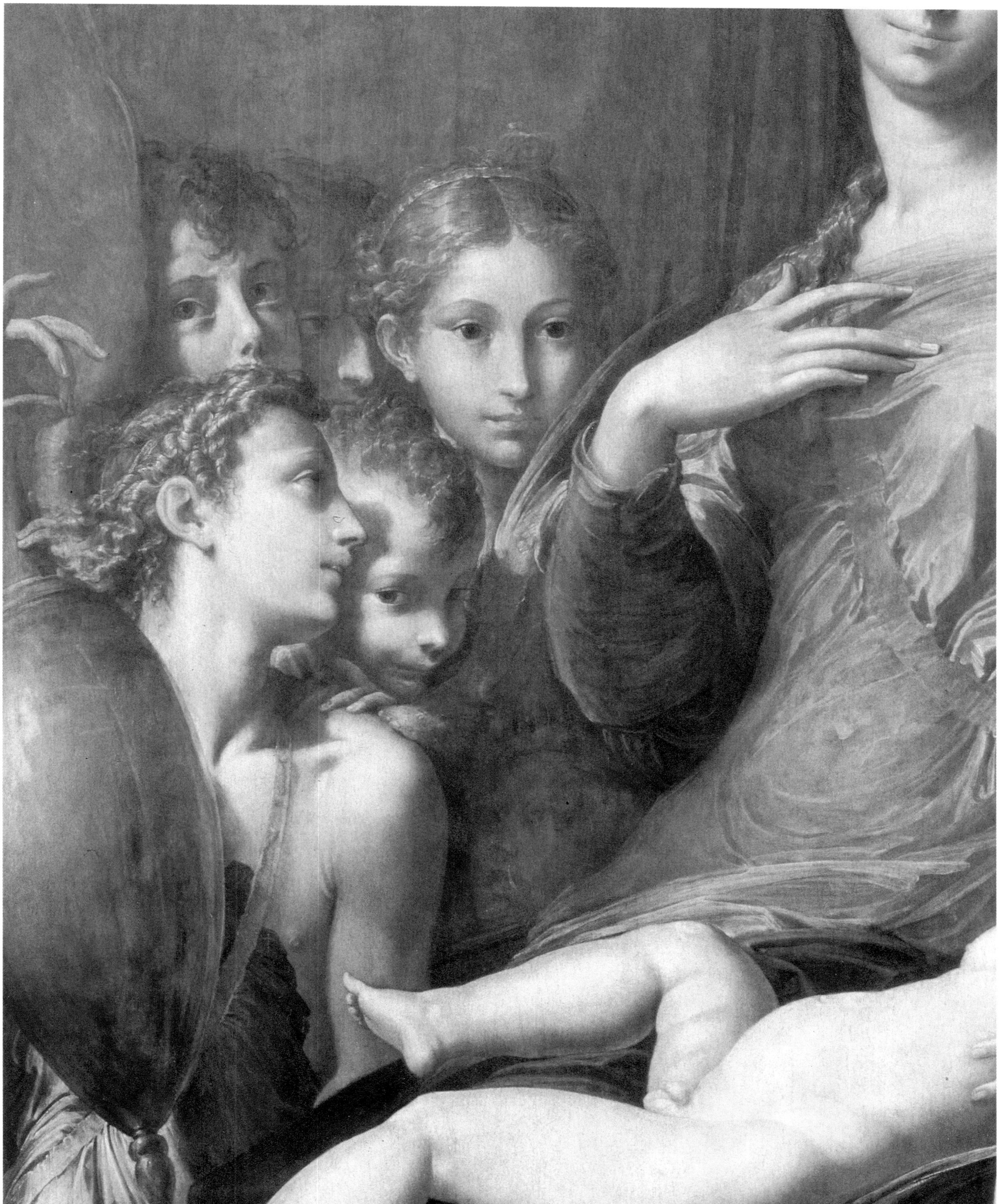

132. BARTHOLOMÄUS SPRANGER
Triumph of Wisdom, n.d.
Oil on canvas, 64⅛ × 46⅛ in.
(163 × 117 cm)
Kunsthistorisches Museum, Vienna

our own century the kaleidoscope has shifted again. Some of the most influential critics have been fascinated by Parmigianino while showing less interest in Correggio.

But no fluctuations in taste or in art-historical emphasis can ignore the summits of Parmigianino's art and craftsmanship: the finest portraits and the Dresden altarpiece, along with some ravishing details from larger works—the flowers, fish, and animals on the Steccata vault, the golden curls of the women and children in general, or the Madonna group in the London altarpiece—and hundreds of marvelous drawings. Though the more mannered elements of his style exercised, as we have seen, a vital influence on European court art in the generations following his death, it was not he but Annibale Carracci and his successors in the seventeenth century who found the true answer to Parmigianino's problem and that of his contemporaries of the post-peak generation—how to build on the legacy of Raphael and Michelangelo and the antique, of Correggio and Titian, without being overwhelmed by it. For this reason Parmigianino's lasting place in history is not so much that of a catalyst as that of exquisite virtuoso. But to humanity's loss he was loved by the gods.

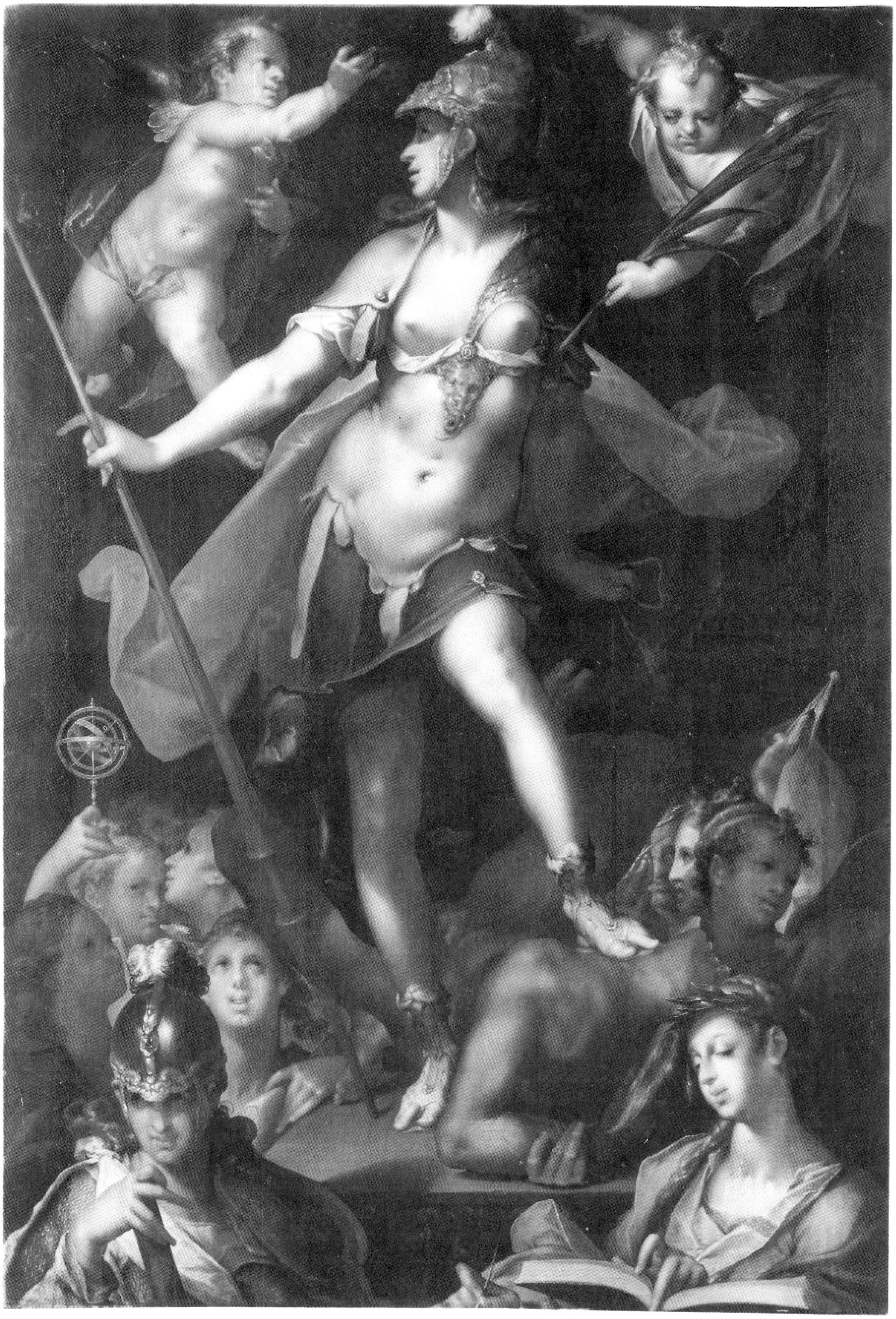

Appendixes

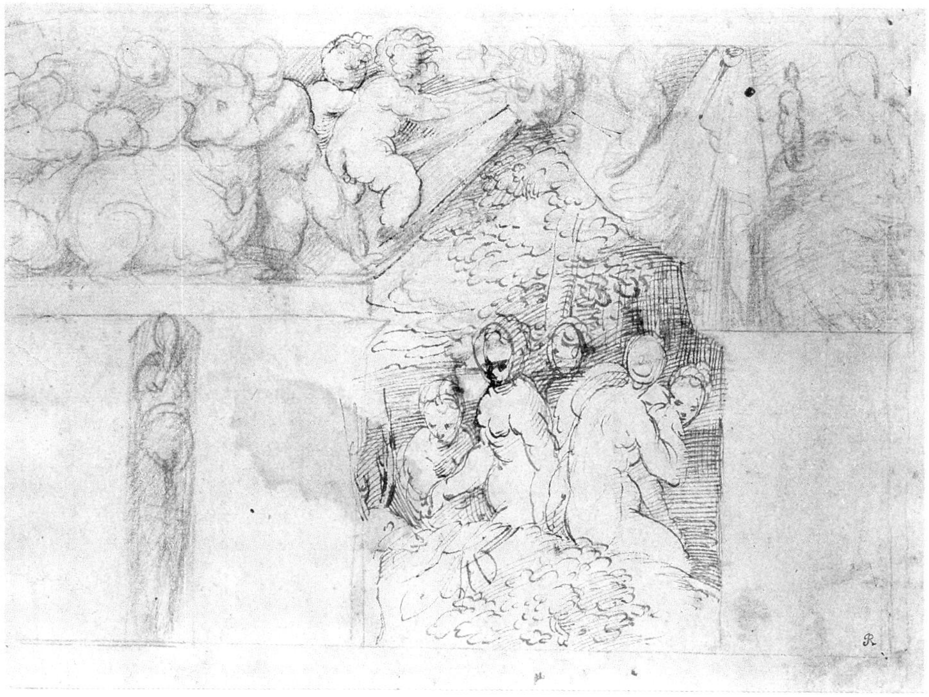

Notes

Works Cited

Appendixes

APPENDIX 1

A Note on Parmigianino's Patrons

It emerges, mainly from Vasari, that Parmigianino's patrons during the twenty years of his career included some of the local nobility of the Parma region such as the Sanvitale of Fontanellato or the Rossi of San Secondo, together with the authorities of Parma cathedral, of the monastery of San Giovanni Evangelista and of the church of the Steccata, and finally various bourgeois families such as the Baiardi at Parma and several at Bologna. And an important addition to our knowledge of his career comes from the recent deduction (Fornari-Schianchi 1990) that before going to Rome Parmigianino was briefly working as assistant to Correggio at San Giovanni Evangelista. But much remains obscure and would repay further research. For instance, attention has only recently been drawn to Parmigianino's habit, throughout his career, of painting small pictures without commission.

At the end of Parmigianino's sojourn at Bologna opportunities of patronage opened of a more ambitious kind than before or later. The coronation in February 1530 of Charles v by Pope Clement vii drew a concourse of notabilities to the city. Perhaps at the suggestion of Pietro Aretino, Parmigianino started a portrait of the emperor, apparently without being asked. Among those accompanying the Pope on this occasion were his young cousin, Ippolito de' Medici, and Paolo Giovio. It is not clear if Ippolito actually commissioned work from Parmigianino at this time, but we have Vasari's word that he bought small pictures that Parmigianino had painted in Rome and also the abandoned portrait of the Emperor. And I have suggested that it was at this time that Giovio commissioned the portrait of the *condottiere* Malatesta Baglione that is now in Vienna, for his museum in Como.

Among the unexplained aspects of the subject are two apparent failures by Parmigianino to secure princely patronage. Alessandro Farnese, later Pope Paul iii, had been appointed bishop of Parma as early as 1509. He actually visited the city in 1516 and again in 1519, but there is, apparently, no record of his presence there during Parmigianino's maturity, nor any sign of interest on his part in the local artists. More surprising at first was the apparent failure of Isabella d'Este and Federigo Gonzaga to employ Parmigianino. In Isabella's case the most likely explanation would be that Correggio's two allegories (now in the Louvre with the other paintings from her Studiolo) had filled the last two spaces in the small room. As to her son, Federigo, one is tempted to think that Giulio Romano, who was currently the Pooh Bah of the artists at Mantua, did not welcome another rival.

APPENDIX 2

A Note on Vasari's Sources

Vasari's meeting with Girolamo Mazzola Bedoli at Parma in 1566, which he mentions in his biographies of Garofalo and Girolamo da Carpi, evidently supplied him with information about Parmigianino's activity at Parma, namely his earliest work and also his latest. Such information was incorporated in Vasari's second edition (1568). Early works, such as the Berlin *Baptism* (cat. A2), the Bardi *Marriage of Saint Catherine* (A1), the two lost altarpieces—*Saint Francis* (B1) and *Bernardino da Feltre* (B2)—and the frescoes at San Giovanni Evangelista (A32 and 33), are discussed in the second edition but not in the first (1550). Similarly, the second edition gives more information than the first about late works such as the *Madonna dal Collo Lungo* (A9), the Dresden altarpiece (A8), and the lost *Lucretia* (B6). But for the Rome and Bologna periods the second edition adds little to what was already contained in the first. For the Roman works Vasari's main source was probably his fellow Arentine, Giovann'Antonio Lappoli, who had known Parmigianino in Rome. For the Bologna years the question is open. Vasari may have met Parmigianino himself when they were both there in 1529–30, though Vasari was very young at the time and does not claim to have met the artist. Otherwise he would have had to rely on what he could collect when he was again at Bologna in 1539–40. The account of Parmigianino's work that he gives in his second edition was followed closely by Borghini in his *Il Riposo* (1584).

APPENDIX 3

A Note on the Iconography of the Immaculate Conception

For centuries the attitude of Rome to the cult of the Immaculate Conception had been ambivalent. Sixtus iv, a Franciscan, approved the Feast in 1476, but it was more than 140 years later (1616) that the current pope, Paul v, issued a bull forbidding anyone to teach or preach a contrary view. Finally, in 1854, Pius ix issued the bull *Ineffabilis Deus*, which included the following definition: "La beatissima Vergine, nel primo istante della sua concezione, per singolare grazia e privilegio concessole da Dio onnipotente, in previsione dei meriti di Gesù Cristo Salvatore del genere umano, fu preservata immune da ogni macchia di peccato originale" (The most blessed Virgin, in the first moment of her conception, as a result of exceptional grace and privilege conceded to her by Almighty God, as foreseeing the merits of Jesus Christ, the savior of the human race, was preserved immune from all stain of Original Sin).

Given this situation, and the difficulty of illustrating such a doctrine intelligibly, it is not surprising that attempts to do so were long rare, and the iconography not standardized. In early-sixteenth-century examples, such as Piero di Cosimo's (Fiesole, San Francesco), Sogliani's (Uffizi), or Zaganelli's (Forlì), there is a two-tiered arrangement with celestial figures overhead and saints below. The two most elaborate versions that date from the second quarter of the sixteenth century—Bedoli's (Galleria Nazionale, Parma, from the Oratorio della Concezione) and Vasari's (Florence, SS. Apostoli) include many figures to illustrate the descent of Original Sin, but the characters are not the same in the two pictures. Nevertheless, as early as 1492 a simpler scheme had been illustrated by Carlo Crivelli (National Gallery), which already foreshadows the mode of presentation that became normal and common after the promulgation of the bull of Paul v in the seventeenth century. Crivelli showed the Virgin Mary standing, without the Christ Child and with her hands together in front of her chest. She is surrounded by symbols of her immaculate state.

Despite claims that have been made that paintings by Parmigianino such as the London altarpiece and the *Madonna dal Collo Lungo* represent the Immaculate Conception, neither of these nor any other of his paintings adhere to any of these pictorial schemes. Nor does Vasari specify the Immaculate Conception as the subject of any painting by Parmigianino. And while the contract for the London altarpiece shows that it was intended as an element in the context of the doctrine of the Immaculate Conception, it also specifies that the illustration of this (which does not survive) was to be separate from the main panel.

Notes

Chapter I

1. Vasari/Milanesi v, pp. 161–62. Kenneth Clark, *A Failure of Nerve* (1967), p. 3.
2. Dolce/Roskill 1968, pp. 182–83.
3. For Correggio's commissions see Gould 1976, pp. 25–26.
4. Fornari-Schianchi 1990.
5. Crowe & Cavalcaselle 1912, vol. 2, p. 296. It seems that the wife of the painter Tacconi, a native of Cremona who had worked for a time in Venice, adopted Parmigianino's father as her heir.
6. For the Berlin picture see particularly Freedberg 1950, pp. 151–53. Further bibliography in Rossi 1980, p. 85. Affò gives Parmigianino's age at the time as fourteen.
7. Fagiolo dell'Arco 1970, passim.
8. Bologna 1983, pp. 153 and 155ff.
9. Reynolds/Wark 1975, p. 271.
10. For the document see A. O. Quintavalle 1948, p. 48, n. 9.
11. The Scurano altarpiece reproduced by A. G. Quintavalle/L. Fornari 1971–72, pl. 19.
12. Rossi 1980, p. 86. For Bedoli's altarpiece see Milstein 1978, p. 157, and for his frescoes, pp. 74ff.
13. For the Del Bono chapel see Gould 1976, pp. 257–58 and 265–67.
14. Fagiolo dell'Arco 1970, passim. Also his pl. 4.
15. Surprisingly, I know no engraving of the *Horse Tamers* (Dioscuri) earlier than c. 1540.
16. For the contract see Martini 1865, pp. 170–80.
17. Fornari-Schianchi 1990 assumes that Parmigianino's share is one of his earliest works. But this dating depends on the traditional assumption, which rests on no sound evidence, that Correggio's cupola preceded the half-dome. For the evidence that the contrary was the correct sequence see the present writer's monograph on Correggio (1976) and more particularly his article in the *Gazette des Beaux-Arts,* May–June 1991.
18. For the documentation see A. G. Quintavalle/L. Fornari 1971–72, pp. 47–49.
19. Gould 1980. As with Correggio and Lotto, the influence between Parmigianino and Lotto was probably neutral. Lotto's portrait of *Odonti* (Hampton Court) is dated 1527 and may well show influence from Parmigianino's portrait of a collector (A19).
20. Fagiolo dell'Arco 1970 passim and pl. 76. Also Asmus 1983. The apparent incongruity between the foppish image and the military adjuncts may be misleading. In the nineteenth century the earl of Cardigan affected a similar appearance to Galeazzo Sanvitale (even to the whiskers). But his reckless courage at Balaclava was undeniable.
21. Raphael 1983, pp. 139–41.

Chapter II

1. Chastel 1980, passim.
2. Popham 1971, p. 11.
3. In addition, Parmigianino may have seen (in Rome) Rosso's studies for the painting. See Freedberg 1950, passim.
4. Some account of Ippolito's life is given in G. F. Young, *The Medici,* vol. 1, 1930 ed., pp. 494ff. But his birthdate (1511) is there given as 1509.
5. For Ghirlandaio, the Louvre portrait of an old man and a child and the New York portrait of Francesco Sassetti and son. For the Giorgionesque, the Uffizi portrait, long attributed to Cavazzola, of a knight and page.
6. Anselmi's frescoes reproduced by A. G. Quintavalle n.d., figs. 39 and 41.
7. Popham 1971, no. 190.
8. Blunt 1982. For the contract see Sandro Corradini in *Burlington Magazine,* January 1993, and article by Mary Vaccaro in the same issue, pp. 22ff.
9. Gould 1976, p. 203.
10. Wilde 1953, no. 16.
11. Pope-Hennessy 1963, catalog volume p. 36, suggests the Medici *Madonna* was carved "about 1521–3."
12. For example, his woodcuts called "La Ricerca e lo Sfruttamento dei Metalli." See Sanminiatelli 1967, pp. 130ff.
13. It has also been suggested that Parmigianino's design owes something to Leonardo's *Saint Jerome* (Vatican). The provenance of this is unknown, but it may well have been somewhere in Florence when Parmigianino was there. A further *Saint Jerome* (by Sodoma, National Gallery) also bears some relation to these works, particularly Pontormo's.

Chapter III

1. Gould 1976, pp. 121, 122.
2. Joannides 1983, nos. 304–311.
3. For Sansovino, one of the panels in the Saint Mark's sacristy door (reproduced Pope-Hennessy 1963, fig. 113). For Giambologna, gilt-bronze relief, Victoria and Albert Museum, reproduced C. Avory, *Giambologna,* 1987, pl. 197. For Goujon, marble relief, Louvre, reproduced exhibition catalog, Paris, 1972, pl. 520. It has been noted (M. Hirst, *Burlington Magazine,* CVIII, 1966, p. 401) that the pose of Christ in Parmigianino's *Entombment* etching is repeated in Perino del Vaga's frieze (the Adam figure) in San Marcello, Rome.
4. The series is Popham 1971, pls. 175–77. See also Reed/Wallace 1989 passim.
5. Scaramuccia 1674, p. 60.
6. Anselmi's picture reproduced A. G. Quintavalle n.d., figs. 65 and 66. A payment made to Parmigianino in 1529 in respect of the Steccata shutters argues another visit to Parma.
7. Goethe, *Italian Journey.* Entry for 18 October, 1786: "One would be content to die so long as this picture [Raphael's] could endure for ever."
8. Armani 1986, p. 313 (as Perino del Vaga).
9. Affò 1784, p. 67.
10. Gould 1975 II.
11. In the catalog of the *Exhibition of the King's Pictures* (R. A. London, 1946, no. 227) it is suggested that the sitter is the same as for the Saint Stephen in Parmigianino's Dresden altarpiece, and the present portrait dated very late accordingly. But the likeness is superficial. The sitter of Saint Stephen is more probably one of Parmigianino's studio boys, who appears in several of the late drawings (e.g., P224 and P58). Shearman 1983, pp. 182–83, employs an oversubtle analysis of certain details in the painting to cast doubt on the authenticity.
12. Wethey 1971, p. 84.
13. Affò 1784.
14. Gould 1976, p. 196.
15. Popham 1971, pls. 226–32.
16. For the inventory see Popham 1971, p. 264.
17. Negri 1680. There is, as far as I know, no specific documentation of Pietro Aretino's presence in Bologna at the time of the coronation, but it is implicit to Parmigianino's intended gift to him at this time. It is impossible to imagine someone of his interests staying away from such a gathering, but owing to the Vatican's hostility he would have had reason to lie low.

Chapter IV

1. Panofsky 1961, passim.
2. Popham 1971, 559, 665r, 770, 594.
3. Correggio's half-dome was destroyed in 1586 and copied on a larger scale.
4. Reproduced Fagiolo dell'Arco 1970, fig. 138.
5. For payments cf. Testi 1922, pp. 265ff., and A. O. Quintavalle 1948, pp. 162ff.
6. E.g., Popham 1971, pl. 323.
7. Freedberg 1950. Vasari is misleading in speaking of six figures, of which two are in color and the others chiaroscuro. He is followed by Borghini

(*Il Riposo*, 1584), whose biography of Parmigianino is a précis of Vasari's.

8. For the Domus Aurea see Dacos 1969. The attempt of Fagiolo dell'Arco 1970, figs. 134–37, to equate the creatures on the frames at the Steccata with the four elements is questionable, since he is forced to find one of them—fire—in an extraneous feature, namely the lamps held by the Wise Virgins.
9. Painting now in the Louvre. Parmigianino would be unlikely to have had access to the original, which was currently in the Studiolo of Isabella d'Este. But the group of the Muses had been engraved by Zoan Andrea. Correggio, who had contributed to the decoration of Isabella's Studiolo, could also have been an intermediary.
10. Reproduced Hartt 1958, pl. 429.
11. Popham 1971, p. 24. It is noteworthy that the identity of the figures in the north and south vaults (by Bedoli) is also uncertain (Milstein 1978 passim).
12. Reynolds/Wark 1975, p. 271.
13. Gould 1976, p. 219.
14. Facsimile of the letter in A. G. Quintavalle 1970, fig. 120.
15. Testi 1922, passim. Text of Giulio Romano's letter, p. 271. For Bedoli's contracts Milstein 1978, pp. 189–90 and 314. Parmigianino's claim, in his letter to Giulio Romano, that he could get the Steccata half-dome painted to his design without coming to Parma himself shows that he had reliable studio assistants at that stage of his life. In general, though, his paintings, like Correggio's, seem to show the minimum of studio assistance.
16. Degrazia 1984, p. 178. A painted version by Bedoli of this subject is in Naples (C7).
17. Popham/Di Giampaolo 1971, no. 71.
18. Shearman 1983, p. 184.
19. E.g., P496.
20. Conspicuous shortness of stature seems often to go with great creative talent. Among other instances are Van Dyck, Rembrandt, Mozart, Beethoven, Schubert, Leopardi, and Wagner.
21. A. G. Quintavalle, *Il Bertoja* (1963), p. 9, notes that Bertoja's father was a beneficiary of Parmigianino's will.
22. Vasari's remark (VII, p. 422) that a painter called Mirola had worked in the Palazzo del Giardino in Parma has led to uncertainty about the division of labor between him and Bertoja. The existence of similar landscapes that are documented as the work of the northern painter, Jan or Hans Soens, who was working in Parma from 1580, completes the confusion. See Degrazia 1991.
23. The Louvre picture reproduced Paris 1972, p. 9.
24. Reproduced Paris 1972, p. 388. For Parmigianino's impact on the Fontainebleau etchers see Zerner 1969.
25. Dacosta Kaufman 1985, passim.
26. Lowenthal 1986, passim.
27. Malvasia 1678, I, pp. 365–67.
28. Scaramuccia 1674, p. 60.
29. Reynolds/Wark 1975, p. 72.

Works Cited

Affò 1784. Ireneo Affò. *Vita del graziosissimo pittore Francesco Mazzola, detto il Parmigianino.* Reprint. Bologna, Italy: Forni.

Affò 1791. ———. *Memorie degli scrittori e letterati Parmigiani.* Reprint. Bologna, Italy: Forni.

Affò 1794. ———. *Il Parmigiano servitor di Piazza. . . .* Reprint. Bologna, Italy: Forni.

Armani 1986. Elena Parma Armani. *Perin del Vaga, l'anello mancante.* Genoa, Italy: SAGEP.

Asmus 1983. U. Davitt Asmus. "Fontanellato I: Sabatizzare il mondo: Parmigianinos Bildnis des conte Galeazzo Sanvitale." In *Mitteilungen des Kunsthistorischen Institutes in Florenz,* vol. 27.

Asmus 1987. ———. "Fontanellato II: La trasformazione dell'amante nell'amato: Parmigianinos Fresken in der Rocca Sanvitale." In *Mitteilungen des Kunsthistorischen Institutes in Florenz,* vol. 31.

Barri 1671. Giacomo Barri. *Viaggio pittoresco. . . .* N.p.

Béguin 1956. Sylvie Béguin. *Jan Soens paysagiste oublié: Oud Holland* (Mededelingen van het Rijksbureau voor Kunsthistorische Documentatie).

Béguin 1981. ———. "Un Nouveau Corrège au Louvre." In *Hommage à Hubert Landais.* N.p.

Bertini 1987. Giuseppe Bertini. *La Galleria del Duca di Parma: Storia di una collezione.* Bologna, Italy: Nuova Alfa.

Biondo 1549. M. Biondo. *Della nobilissima pittura.* N.p.

Blunt 1982. Anthony Blunt. *Guide to Baroque Rome.* New York: Harper & Row.

Bober/Rubinstein 1986. Phyllis Pray Bober and Ruth Rubinstein. *Renaissance Artists and Antique Sculpture: A Handbook of Sources.* London and Oxford: Oxford University Press, 1986.

Bologna 1956. Ferdinando Bologna. "Il Carlo V del Parmigianino." *Paragone* (Arte) 7:16.

Bologna 1983. *L'Estasi di Santa Cecilia di Raffaello da Urbino nella Pinacoteca Nazionale di Bologna.* N.p.

Bologna 1986. *The Age of Correggio and of Carracci: Emilian Painting in the Sixteenth and Seventeenth Centuries.* Bologna and Washington, D.C.: National Gallery of Art.

Campori 1866. Giuseppe Campori. *Lettere artistiche inedite.* Reprint. Sala Bolognese, Italy: Forni, n.d.

Chastel 1980. André Chastel. *The Sack of Rome, 1527.* The A. W. Mellon Lectures. Reprint. Princeton, N.J.: Princeton University Press, 1983.

Copertini 1932. Giovanni Copertini. *Il Parmigianino.* 2 vols. Parma: n.p.

Crowe/Cavalcaselle 1912. Joseph A. Crowe and Giovanni B. Cavalcaselle. *A History of Painting in North Italy.* Ed. T. Borenius. Reprint. New York: AMS Press, n.d.

Dacos 1969. N. Dacos. *La Découverte de la Domus Aurea et la formation des grotesques à la Renaissance.* London: Warburg Institute, University of London.

Dacosta Kaufmann 1985. Thomas Dacosta Kaufmann. *The School of Prague.* Reprint. Chicago: University of Chicago Press, 1988.

Dall'Acqua 1984. Marzio Dall'Acqua. *Correggio e il suo tempo.* Parma: Ministero per i beni culturali e ambientali.

Dall'Acqua 1988. ———. *Fontanellato.* N.p.

Degrazia 1984. Diane Degrazia. *Correggio and His Legacy: Sixteenth-Century Emilian Drawings.* Washington, D.C.: National Gallery of Art.

Degrazia 1991. ———. *Bertoia, Mirola and the Farnese Court.* Bologna, Italy: Nuova Alfa.

Dolce/Roskill 1968. *[Lodovico] Dolce's "Aretino" and Venetian Art Theory of the Cinquecento.* Ed. M. Roskill. New York: New York University Press.

Ekserdjian 1983. D. Ekserdjian. "Parmigianino's *Madonna of St. Margaret.*" *Burlington Magazine,* pp. 542ff.

Ekserdjian 1984. ———. "Parmigianino's First Idea for the Madonna of the Long Neck." *Burlington Magazine,* pp. 424ff.

Fagiolo dell'Arco 1970. Maurizio Fagiolo dell'Arco. *Il Parmigianino: Un saggio sull'ermetismo nel Cinquecento.* Rome: Mario Bulzoni.

Fontana 1689. G. G. Fontana. *Pallado Segretaria. . . .* N.p.

Fornari-Schianchi 1990. Lucia Fornari-Schianchi. *Un miracolo d'arte senza esempio.* Parma: n.p.

Freedberg 1950. Sydney J. Freedberg. *Parmigianino: His Works in Painting.* Reprint. Westport, Conn.: Greenwood Press, 1971.

Frölich-Bum 1921. Lili Fröhlich-Bum. *Parmigianino und der Manierismus.* Vienna: n.p.

Giordani 1842. G. Giordani. *Della venuta . . . in Bologna del . . . Pontefice Clemente VII.* N.p.

Gould 1975 I. Cecil Gould. *The Sixteenth-Century Italian Schools.* National Gallery Catalogues Series. Reprint. Seattle: University of Washington Press, 1987.

Gould 1975 II. ———. "Notes on Parmigianino's 'Mystic Marriage of St. Catherine.'" *Burlington Magazine,* pp. 230ff.

Gould 1976. ———. *The Paintings of Correggio.* Ithaca, N.Y.: Cornell University Press.

Gould 1980. ———. *Lotto and Correggio.* Atti del convegno internazionale di studi per il V centenario della nascita. N.p.

Gould 1982. ———. "Raphael versus Giulio Romano: The Swing Back." *Burlington Magazine,* pp. 473ff.

Gould 1992. ———. "A Parmigianino Madonna and Child and His Uncommissioned Paintings." *Apollo,* March.

Hartt 1958. Frederick Hartt. *Giulio Romano.* New Haven, Conn.: Yale University Press.

Joannides 1983. Paul Joannides. *The Drawings of Raphael, with a Complete Catalog.* Berkeley, Calif.: University of California Press.

Lamo 1560. Pietro Lamo. *Graticola di Bologna: Gli edifici e le opere d'arte della città nel 1560.*

London 1960. *Italian Art and Britain.* London: Royal Academy.

Lowenthal 1986. Anne W. Lowenthal. *Joachim Wtewael and Dutch Mannerism.* Doornspijk, the Netherlands: Davaco.

Malvasia 1678. Carlo Cesare Malvasia. *Felsina Pittrice: Vite de' pittori bolognesi.* 2 vols. Reprint. Bologna, Italy: Forni.

Martini 1865. Pietro Martini. *Studi attorno al Correggio.* N.p.

Mezzetti 1977. A. Mezzetti. *Girolamo da Carpi.* Milan: Silvana.

Milstein 1978. Ann Rebecca Milstein. *The Paintings of Girolamo Mazzola Bedoli.* New York and London: Garland.

Mortara 1846. Anton Enrico Mortara. *Della vita e dei lavori di Francesco Mazzola detto il Parmigianino.* N.p.

Negri 1680. G. F. Negri. *Basilica Petroniana.* N.p.

Olsen 1961. Harald Olsen. *Italian Paintings and Sculpture in Denmark.* Copenhagen: Munksgaard.

Oberhuber 1963 I. Konrad Oberhuber. *Parmigianino und sein Kreis.* Vienna: Albertina.

Oberhuber 1963 II. ———. *Parmigianino als Radierer.* Alte und Moderne Kunst.

Panofsky 1961. Erwin Panofsky. *The Iconography of Correggio's Camera di S. Paolo.* London: Warburg Institute, University of London.

Paris 1972. *L'Ecole de Fontainebleau.* Paris: Réunion des Musées Nationaux.

Pope-Hennessy 1963. John Pope-Hennessy. *Italian High Renaissance and Baroque Sculpture.* London: Phaidon.

Popham 1971. Arthur Ewart Popham. *Catalogue of the Drawings of Parmigianino.* 3 vols. New Haven, Conn.: Yale University Press.

Popham/Di Giampaolo 1971. A. E. Popham and Mario di Giampaolo. *Disegni di Girolamo Bedoli.* Viadana, Italy: Sodalizio Amici dell'Arte.

A. G. Quintavalle 1970. Augusta Ghidiglia Quintavalle. *Gli ultimi affreschi del Parmigianino.* Milan: Silvana.

A. G. Quintavalle/L. Fornari 1971–2. Augusta Ghidiglia Quintavalle and Lucia Fornari. *Arte in Emilia 4: Capolavori ritrovati e artisti inediti dal '300 al '700.* Parma, Italy: Tipografica La Nazionale.

A. G. Quintavalle n.d. [1960]. Augusta Ghidiglia Quintavalle. *Michelangelo Anselmi.* Reprint. Parma, Italy: n.p.

A. O. Quintavalle 1948. Armando Ottaviano Quintavalle. *Il Parmigianino.* Milan: Istituto Editoriale Italiano.

Raphael 1983. *Raphael dans les collections françaises.* Paris: n.p.

Reed/Wallace 1989. Sue Welsh Reed and Richard Wallace. *Italian Etchers of the Renaissance and Baroque.* Boston: Museum of Fine Arts.

Reynolds/Wark 1975. Sir Joshua Reynolds. *Discourses on Art.* Ed. R. Wark. New Haven, Conn.: Yale University Press.

Ricci 1894–5. C. Ricci. *Di alcuni quadri di scuola parmigiana conservati nel R. Museo Nazionale di Napoli.* Naples(?): Napoli Nobilissima.

Ricci 1895. ———. *Di alcuni quadri del Parmigianino già esistenti in Parma.* Archivio storico per le provincie parmensi, vol. 4, 1895 (published 1903).

Ricci 1896. ———. *La Reale Galleria di Parma.* N.p.

Rossi 1980. Paola Rossi. *L'Opera completa del Parmigianino.* N.p.

Sanminiatelli 1967. Donato Sanminiatelli. *Domenico Beccafumi.* Milan: Bramante.

Sanvitale 1857. L. Sanvitale. *Memorie intorno alla rocca di Fontanellato ed alle pitture che vi fece Francesco Mazzola detto il Parmigianino.* N.p.

Scannelli 1657. Francesco Scannelli. *Il Microcosmo della Pittura.* Reprint. Bologna, Italy: Nuova Alfa, 1989.

Scaramuccia 1674. Luigi Pellegrino Scaramuccia. *Le Finezze de' pennelli italiani. . . .* Reprint. Milan: n.p., 1965.

Shearman 1983. John Shearman. *The Early Italian Pictures in the Collection of Her Majesty The Queen.* Cambridge: Cambridge University Press.

Stockholm 1966. *Christina, Queen of Sweden.* Stockholm: n.p.

Testi 1922. Laudedeo Testi. *Santa Maria della Steccata in Parma.* Florence: n.p.

Vasari 1568. Giorgio Vasari. *Le Vite de' più eccellenti pittori scultori ed architettori scritte da Giorgio Vasari pittore aretino con nuove annotazioni e commenti di Gaetano Milanesi.* Florence: n.p. 1878–1885.

Voss 1933. Hermann Voss. *Ein wiedergefundenes Gemälde von Parmigianino.* Prussian Yearbook, Bd. 54, p. 33. Berlin.

Wethey 1971. Harold Edwin Wethey. *The Paintings of Titian, II: The Portraits.* London: Phaidon.

Wilde 1953. Johannes Wilde. *Italian Drawings in the Department of Prints and Drawings in the British Museum: Michelangelo and his Studio.* London: Trustees of the British Museum.

Zerner 1969. Henri Zerner. *The School of Fontainebleau: Etchings and Engravings.* London: Thames and Hudson.

Catalog

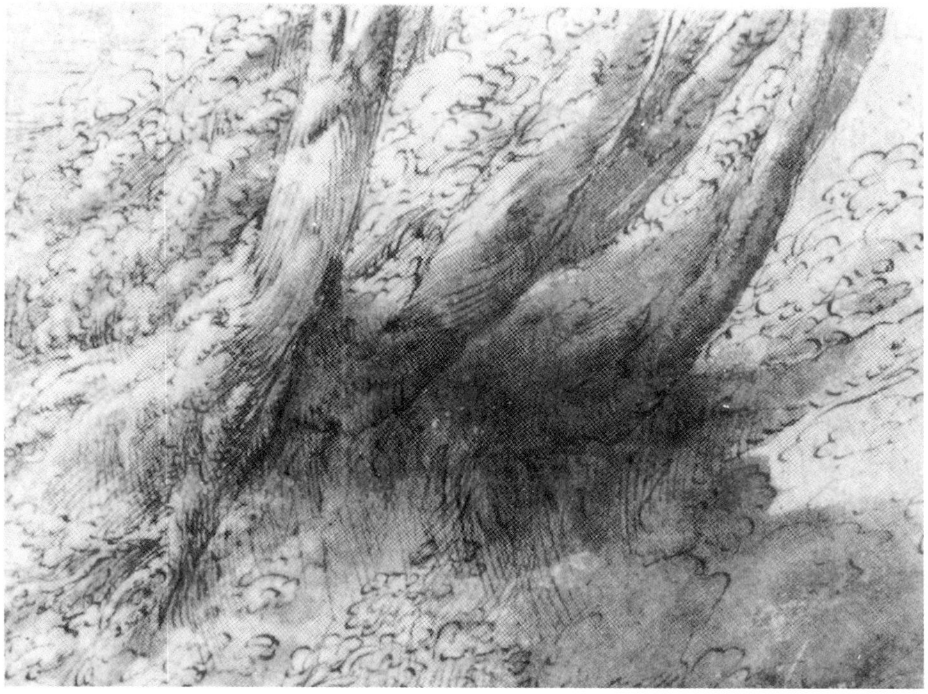

As explained in the preface to this book, the catalog has been planned for reference purposes. It aims to present essential facts and the minimum of padding. Discussion of debatable theories is relegated to the text. Pictures listed in the first section are those whose attribution to Parmigianino is supported by contemporary documents or by authentic drawings; or, lacking both, are those about whose authenticity I have little or no doubt. Some of the many others that have at times been attributed to Parmigianino are listed in a later section. The brief notes on condition relate to instances of damage and restoration that are visible to the naked eye in ordinary viewing conditions. Consequently they are far from comprehensive, and in many cases no notes of this kind have been attempted. I have not tried to list all of the very many copies that may still exist, but I have noted a few of the more accessible ones. Of the paintings cataloged in section A I have inspected all in the original, with the exception of the Copenhagen portrait.

ABBREVIATIONS

P = Popham 1971
P.O.C. = Popham as old copy
P.O.R. = Popham as old reproduction

SECTIONS

Part One. Paintings
A. Acceptable Paintings
B. Lost Paintings
C. Notes on Some Attributed Paintings

Part Two. Prints
D. Authentic Etchings
E. "F. P." Etchings
F. Chiaroscuro Prints after Parmigianino Mentioned by Vasari or Signed
G. Early Metal Engravings after Parmigianino Mentioned by Vasari or Signed

Part One. Paintings

A. Acceptable Paintings

BARDI (PARMA), ITALY

Santa Maria

A1 *The Mystic Marriage of Saint Catherine*
Tempera on panel, 80 × 51⅛ in. (203 × 130 cm)
(text p. 19, fig. 5)

Saint John the Evangelist holds a cup with a serpent in it in his right hand. His eagle is lower down on the left. Saint Catherine's wheel and martyr's palm are in the foreground. A wreath of leaves lies at the top of the plinth of the Madonna's throne. Saint John the Baptist stands on the right.

An area of damage extends upward from the base, under the Baptist's right heel as far as his left hand.

ESSENTIAL DOCUMENTATION

Vasari 1568. Painted at Viadana and therefore in 1521/22.

1630. Document printed by Campori 1866. Picture sold to Parma.

1860. Picture reported at the parish church of Santa Maria at Bardi (A. O. Quintavalle 1948).

1932. Not included in the edition of Berenson's *Lists.*

1935. Published as Parmigianino by Copertini (in *Aurea Parma*) and exhibited in the same year as Parmigianino in the *Mostra del Correggio,* Parma, no. 53.

1950. Included in addenda to Freedberg's catalog.

1968. Included in latest edition of Berenson's *Lists.*

RELATED DRAWINGS

P381 (Louvre), P76r (Uffizi), P598 (Venice), P709 (Chatsworth), P51 (Cambridge, Mass.), and P779 (formerly London, Sir J. Witt).

BERLIN

Staatliche Museen, formerly Bode Museum

A2 *The Baptism of Christ*
Tempera on panel, 76 × 50 in. (193 × 127 cm)
(text p. 18, fig. 4)

In the background (?) the *Temptation of Christ.*

The small angels above the dove may reflect the influence of those in Correggio's altarpiece *Madonna with Saint Francis,* painted in 1514–15 and therefore a novelty at the time when Parmigianino's picture was painted. Correggio's was for the church of San Francesco at Correggio, but has been at Dresden since the eighteenth century.

ESSENTIAL DOCUMENTATION

Vasari 1568. Painted when Parmigianino was sixteen years old and placed in the church of the Annunziata at Parma.

Affò 1784. Picture had been moved in the sixteenth century to the Torelli chapel of the new church at Capo di Ponte, Parma, where a tablet gave the artist's age at the time as fourteen. Sanvitale 1857 says sold to his family, 1706.

Waagen 1830. In his catalog of the Bode (later the Staatliche) Museum, says bought in 1821 from the English collector Solly.

Ricci 1896. Further details.

Voss 1933. History of the picture to which he had drawn attention in 1922. From 1884 to 1932 on loan to a church at Rederitz.

Though the pedigree has a break between Sanvitale and Affò's long description (1784) of the picture, then chez Sanvitale, it is sufficiently detailed to leave no reasonable doubt of its identity with the present picture. In recent times it was accepted by Freedberg 1950 but does not figure in any edition of Berenson's *Lists.*

BOLOGNA, ITALY

Pinacoteca Nazionale

A3 *Madonna and Child with Saints Margaret and Jerome, a Mitered Saint, and an Angel* (588)
Oil on panel, 80¼ × 58⅝ in. (204 × 149 cm)
(text p. 90, fig. 67)

The head of Saint Margaret's dragon emerges on the right, below Saint Jerome.

The paint in Saint Margaret's left hand is worn, also the flesh of the Christ Child.

The evidence for the identity of the mitered saint, left, is conflicting. Vasari calls him San Petronio. The Bologna Pinacoteca catalog of 1935 has Saint Augustine. An early document (Ekserdjian 1983) and Affò 1784 have Saint Benedict. Vasari (both editions) calls the angel Saint Michael. Saint Margaret (of Antioch) was patroness of childbirth.

ESSENTIAL DOCUMENTATION

Vasari 1550 and 1568. As in the church of the nuns of Santa Margherita, Bologna.

Lamo 1560. As in Vasari.

Affò 1784. As already in the convent church of Santa Margherita by August 1529 (see also Ekserdjian 1983). Soon afterward transferred to the Giusti chapel of that church and later to Palazzo Giusti.

1796/7. In France.

From 1815 in the Pinacoteca, Bologna.

RELATED DRAWING

P79 (Uffizi). Full-length composition. The head of the bearded saint appears on the left between that of the mitered saint and the Madonna. The angel is missing. Freedberg 1950 as copy.

ENGRAVING

Giulio Bonasone (Bartsch XV.126.61). Cat. G8.

San Petronio

A4 *Saint Roch and Donor*
Oil on panel, 106¼ × 77½ in. (270 × 197 cm)
(text p. 88, fig. 66)

The dog under Saint Roch's left thigh, and the wound on the latter, are normally associated with him.

The paint of the saint's yellow tunic has worn thin, revealing pentimenti.

The historical Saint Roch lived in the fourteenth century and was of French birth. His cult is associated with relief from the plague.

ESSENTIAL DOCUMENTATION

Biondo 1549. Said, evidently in error, to be in the church of "San Gioanni."

Vasari 1550. At San Petronio.

Lamo 1560. Says the donor was Baldassare da Milano.

Vasari 1568. Specifies the chapel in San Petronio as that of the Monsignori and the donor as Fabrizio da Milano.

Affò 1784. Mentions a full-size copy in pastel by Lodovico Carracci in Palazzo Tanari, Bologna.

F. Antal, *Pinacotheca*, 1928, pp. 48ff., redirects attention to the picture.

RELATED DRAWINGS

P21r and v (Besançon), P377r and v (Louvre), and P772v (Chatsworth): these three sheets are sketches for the saint in various attitudes. P351 (Christ Church, Oxford) is a fragment of a cartoon for the saint's head. A double sheet at New York (P298) has, on the right, apparently the head of a corpse in profile and an inscription with the name of Giorgio Anselmi with the date, September 21, 1530. On the left is a profile that may be of the same person as the donor in the San Petronio picture. According to Affò 1791 the poet Giorgio Anselmi died of the plague in 1528, and this date would accord better with the presumed date of the picture than the date 1530. The closeness of these dates to that of the painting, and the appropriateness (in a way) of the subject—Saint Roch, the healer—to commemorate a patron who died of the plague, would suggest a connection. But the discord between the two dates and between the three names involved—Giorgio Anselmi, Baldassare da Milano, and Fabrizio da Milano—leaves uncertainty whether either or both leaves of the New York sheet have any connection with the San Petronio painting.

ENGRAVING

Giulio Bonasone (Bartsch XV.130.70). Cat. G7.

EXHIBITED

Parma, 1935, Correggio exhibition no. 55.
Bologna, 1986, no. 61.

COPENHAGEN

Statens Museum fur Kunst

A5 *Lorenzo Cybo and His Page* (25)
Oil on panel, 49¾ × 41⅛ in. (126.5 × 104.5 cm)
(text p. 60, fig. 38)

Inscribed, bottom right, LAVRENTIVS CYBO MARCHIO MASSAE ATQUE COMES FERENTILLI ANNO MDXXIII. For the status of this inscription see text.

The sitter was a member of the papal guard. His hat is of the same type as that worn in Parmigianino's portrait of Galeazzo Sanvitale (A29). Marks on the present sitter's hat have been interpreted as the letters LL.

ESSENTIAL DOCUMENTATION

Vasari 1568 (in the context of pictures painted in Rome).

1763. Already at Copenhagen. Said to be ex-Cardinal Valente.

Another version is in the Columbia Museum of Art.

DETROIT, MICHIGAN

Detroit Institute of Arts

A6 *The Circumcision* (30.295)
Oil on panel, 16½ × 12¼ in. (42 × 31 cm)
(text p. 42, fig. 28)

The sacrificial doves are associated more with the Purification of the Virgin than with the Circumcision.

Until recently wrongly considered a copy.

ESSENTIAL DOCUMENTATION

Vasari 1550 and 1568 (as given by the artist to Pope Clement VII).

Leuchtenberg catalog (Munich) 1855 (p. 32, no. 42) as on copper.

1930. Given to Detroit Institute.

1932. Accepted by Berenson as Parmigianino.

1950. Rejected by Freedberg, who afterward relented (Bologna 1986).

RELATED DRAWING

P369 (Louvre). Sketch for whole composition.

EXHIBITED

Bologna 1986, no. 57.

DRESDEN, GERMANY

Gemäldegalerie

A7 *Madonna and Child (Madonna della Rosa)* (161)
Oil on panel, 42⅞ × 34⅞ in. (109 × 88.5 cm)
(text p. 113, fig. 88)

The visible portion of the globe under the Christ Child's left hand is intended to represent Europe (top left), North Africa (bottom left), and Asia (right).

ESSENTIAL DOCUMENTATION

Vasari 1550 (in context of the Bologna period). With Dionigi de' Gianni.

Vasari 1568. Painted for Pietro Aretino but switched to Pope Clement VII when he came to Bologna (1529–30). Then Dionigi de' Gianni. Currently (1568) in possession of his son, Bartolomei. Estimates fifty copies already made.

Scannelli 1657. "Il più stupendo Quadro . . . nella Casa de' Conti Zani."

1752. Sold by the Zani family to Augustus III for Dresden.

The numerous old copies include one at Hampton Court, probably ex-Charles I.

RELATED DRAWINGS

The following are for the whole group: P739, P702r and P740 (all three at Chatsworth), P494 and P493 (both Louvre), P88 (Uffizi). Perhaps also P675v (Amsterdam, private collection) and P223 (London, British Museum). Also P.O.R. 14, 15, 16.

ENGRAVING

By Domenico Tibaldi.

Gemäldegalerie

A8 *Madonna and Child with Saint Stephen, the Baptist, and a Donor* (160)
Oil on panel, 99⅝ × 63⅜ in. (253 × 161 cm)
(text p. 157, fig. 124)

The colors are currently (1988) distorted by discolored varnish. The Baptist's reed cross has sprouted leaves.

ESSENTIAL DOCUMENTATION

Vasari 1550. No details but in the context of the last works (therefore 1539–40).

Vasari 1568. Painted for church of Santo Stefano, Casalmaggiore.

1646. Appropriated by Francesco d'Este of Modena.

Scannelli 1657. In the ducal gallery at Modena. Parmigianino's last picture, unfinished at his death (this is probably untrue, but since Scannelli omits to say that the *Madonna dal Collo Lungo*, which really is unfinished, is in that state he may be confusing the two).

1746. Sold to Dresden.

Mortara 1846. Says donor's name was Matteo Cavalli.

RELATED DRAWINGS

The following are for the whole composition: P276 and P277 (both Biblioteca Nacional, Madrid), P664 (Windsor), and P.O.C. 33. For the Virgin and Child, P113 (Uffizi). For Saint Stephen, P673 (Windsor). Perhaps also the following: P109 (Uffizi), P711r (Chatsworth), P339 (Ashmolean), and P258-60 (British Museum).

FLORENCE

Galleria degli Uffizi

A9 *Madonna and Child with Angels (Madonna dal Collo Lungo)* (P1139)
Oil on panel, 84¼ × 52⅜ in. (214 × 133 cm)
(text p. 140, fig. 110)

Middle distance, right, Saint Jerome.

Inscribed: FATO PRAEVENTUS F. MAZZOLI. PARME / NSIS ABSOLVERE NEQUIVIT

The title—*Collo Lungo*—has been applied since the eighteenth century. This feature of Parmigianino's picture is referred to by Lanzi (1796), and in a footnote to the English edition (1828) Thomas Roscoe says "a long neck in virgins is inculcated by Malvasia, as a precept of the art . . . and the Cav. Lazzarini drew his Madonnas according to this rule." (Abate Luigi Lanzi, *The History of Painting in Italy*, ed. Thomas Roscoe [1828], vol. 4, p. 125.)

Much restoration in the past along the lines of the joins in the wood. The pediment and entablature of the building in the background is unfinished; also the farther columns.

ESSENTIAL DOCUMENTATION

December 23, 1534. Commissioned by Elena Baiardi. To be finished by Pentecost, 1535 (A. O. Quintavalle 1948).

1540. Death of Parmigianino.

1542. Picture set up in the Servite church, Parma.

Vasari 1550. Brief mention.

Vasari 1568. Mentions crystal urn with cross inside; also the artist's abandoning the work through dissatisfaction.

1698. Sold to Ferdinando de' Medici.

In France 1799/1800–1815.

There are a number of copies and partial copies.

RELATED DRAWINGS

The full series of drawings reproduced by Popham 1971, pls. 345–60. Another was sold at Sotheby's, London, July 4, 1988(8).

The main stages in the evolution of the design, as indicated by the drawings, can be summarized as follows:

1. B.M.1978-3-4-6 (Ekserdjian 1984), P.O.C. 33, and P363 (Louvre) locate the Madonna centrally, flanked by Saints Francis and Jerome (and, in P363, also by the heads of three other saints). The B.M. drawing and P.O.C. 33 have an arched top and a semicircular colonnade in the background.

2. P359 (Louvre) and P.O.C. 25 and P327 (Ottawa) show the Madonna displaced to the left. In P359 and P.O.C. 25 the youthful Baptist kneels, extreme left, and Saint Jerome stands on the right. In P327 the Baptist is replaced by an angel, but the saint on the right is probably still Saint Jerome.

3. P454 and P509 (both Louvre). The saints are now omitted from the foreground. The Madonna begins to regain the center and to assume her final pose. The posture of the Christ Child not yet established.

4. P661 (Windsor). Study for Saint Jerome. On the verso a sketch that may be an idea for the setting of the painting.

Galleria degli Uffizi

A10 *Madonna and Child with Saints Zachariah, Mary Magdalene, and the Infant Baptist* (P1138)
Oil on panel, 28¾ × 24⅜ in. (73 × 62 cm)
(text p. 139, fig. 107)

A copy is in the Corsini Gallery, Rome. Others are listed by Lanzi, *History of Painting in Italy* (English ed., 1828), pp. 126–27.

ESSENTIAL DOCUMENTATION

October 27, 1533. Bonifazio Gozzadini from Bologna agrees, in Parma, to complete payment by August of the following year in respect of a painting by Francesco Mazzola described as representing the Madonna and Child with the Baptist and Saints Zachariah and Mary Magdalene, the picture having been delivered to Gozzadini in the current year. Further documents of 1535 and 1538 show payment still outstanding (A. O. Quintavalle 1948).

Vasari 1550 and 1568. Unspecified picture for Conte Giorgio Manzuoli.

Lamo 1560. A picture of the Madonna and Child with the Infant Baptist, Mary Magdalene, and Saint Zachariah described as in the possession of Giorgio Manzuoli at Bologna. This is evidently the same as the one mentioned in both editions of Vasari. It was identified by Affò 1784 with the Corsini picture, though conceivably the Gozzadini picture might have passed to Manzuoli.

1605. Already in Medici possession.

RELATED DRAWING

P279 (Academia di San Fernando, Madrid). Full-length study, connected by Popham with the London *Marriage of Saint Catherine* (A18) but more probably for the present picture (Gould 1975 II).

ENGRAVING

Giulio Bonasone 1543.

Galleria degli Uffizi

A11 *Portrait of a Man ("Self-Portrait")* (A667)

Oil on panel, 39⅜ × 28 in. (100 × 71 cm). Now (1993) almost illegible through darkened varnish.

(text p. 107, fig. 82)

In the truncated painted relief on the wall a kneeling woman on the right holds out an amphora to a tall bearded man whose right arm swings across his body from his right shoulder.

A copy in the gallery in Parma has the remains of an inscription on the back, read by Ricci 1896 as "Franciscus Mazola pinxit seipsum anno MDXXX."

ESSENTIAL DOCUMENTATION

1773. Engraved as a self-portrait and as in the Uffizi.

FONTANELLATO (PARMA), ITALY

Rocca Sanvitale

A12 *Diana and Actaeon*

Frescoed room, 171⅜ × 137¾ in.; height 153½ in. (435 × 350 cm; height 390 cm)

(text, pp. 30–38, figs. 17–21)

A mirror in the center of the ceiling is inscribed RESPICE FINEM (contemplate the end). This was revealed during a modern restoration. It is assumed to be original, but had been covered up.

• *Window wall (short wall):*

Left lunette: hound.

Central lunette: nymph (? Ceres) with amphora and ears of corn.

Right lunette: hound.

The window is under the central lunette. The portion of the frieze on the left of the window is inscribed DEAS (the concluding word of the whole inscription). The inscription begins on the right of the window with the words AD DIANAM.

• *Long wall to the right of the window wall:*

Left lunette: two hounds.

Second lunette from left: two huntsmen.

Second lunette from right: nymph pursued by huntsmen.

Right lunette: single hound.

The portion of the inscription under these lunettes reads DIC DEA SI MISERVM SORS HVC ACTEONA DVXIT.A. TE CVR CANIBVS.

The nymph in the second lunette from the right is dressed in the same clothes as Actaeon with the head of a stag in the next lunette.

• *Short wall opposite window wall:*

Left lunette: Actaeon with the head of a stag.

Central lunette: Diana scooping up the water.

Right lunette: Two naked nymphs (the lower part of the body of the one on the left is damaged).

The portion of the inscription under these lunettes reads TRADITVR ESCA SVIS. NON NISI MORTALES ALIQVO.

• *Long wall to the left of the window wall:*

Left lunette: hounds.

Second lunette from left: shepherd blowing a horn.

Second lunette from right: stag (Actaeon) attacked by hounds.

Right lunette: hound, two human heads behind.

The portion of the inscription under these lunettes reads PRO CRIMINE PENAS FERRE LICET : TALIS NEC DECET IRA.

Complete inscription reads AD DIANAM. DIC, DEA, SI MISERVM SORS HVC ACTEONA DUXIT, A TE CVR CANIBVS TRADITVR ESCA SVIS. NON NISI MORTALES ALIQVO PRO CRIMINE PENAS FERRE LICET : TALIS NEC DECET IRA DEAS. (Tell, O goddess, if it was Fate that led unhappy Actaeon hither, why was he delivered by you to his hounds as food? It is not right for mortals to suffer punishment except in respect of a crime. Such anger is not seemly for goddesses.)

Of the various theories concerning the symbolic meaning of the fresco Fagiolo dell'Arco 1970 proposes an alchemical illustration of the conjunction of the masculine and feminine principles. Germano Mulazzini (in *Corti del Rinascimento nella provincia di Parma,* 1981) sees the cycle as the contrast between Paola Gonzaga (hypothetically identified in the Ceres figure) as Pomona and Diana as symbolizing the contrast between fertility and chastity. A further theory (U. Davitt Asmus in *Mitteilungen des kunsthistorischen Institutes in Florenz,* XXX, 1987) divides the fresco into three episodes—the pursuit of love, the fountain, and the death.

ESSENTIAL DOCUMENTATION

Fontana 1689.

Affò 1784.

Sanvitale 1857.

Dall'Acqua 1988.

RELATED DRAWINGS

P313 (Pierpont Morgan Library, New York), P418 (Louvre), P100 (Uffizi), and P715r and v (Chatsworth): all these are for putti. P313 has a rough sketch of Diana splashing Actaeon (still with human head, unlike fresco). Perhaps also P12r and v (Berlin) and P748 (formerly Donnington Priory).

FRANKFURT

Städelsches Kunstinstitut

A13 *Saint Catherine of Alexandria* (1496)
Oil on panel, 10¼ × 7½ in. (26 × 19 cm)
(text p. 39, fig. 26)

Two small angels, right. Panel probably cut down at the sides. No attribute for the saint is visible in the picture's present state, which is much retouched. But old copies show the saint's right hand on part of a wheel. X-ray photographs taken in 1932 revealed Parmigianino's work beneath repaint, and led to the demotion of the Vienna version (see below), long considered to be Parmigianino's original.

ESSENTIAL DOCUMENTATION

1913. Presented to the Städel Institute.

RELATED DRAWING

Probably P424 (Louvre): Study of woman's head.

COPY

Kunsthistorisches Museum, Vienna. Ex-Charles I of England. Still accepted as the original in Berenson's 1968 *Lists.* Other old copies include one in the Parma gallery.

HAMPTON COURT (ENGLAND)

Hampton Court Palace

A14 *A Young Man* (185)
Oil on panel, 38¾ × 32½ in. (98.5 × 82.5 cm)
(text p. 105, fig. 81)

A number of retouchings are visible.

The doorway in the background is similar to that in the *Marriage of Saint Catherine* (National Gallery, London, cat. A18).

The doubts expressed by A. O. Quintavalle 1948 and Shearman 1983 concerning the picture's authenticity are not justified, in the present writer's opinion.

Old copies at Holyrood and Knole.

ESSENTIAL DOCUMENTATION

c. 1666–7. Charles II of England inventory (as Parmigianino).

Hampton Court Palace

A15 *Head and Bust of Athene* (186)
Oil on canvas, 25⅛ × 17¾ in. (63.8 × 45.1 cm)
(text p. 160, fig. 125)
The brooch shows a flying figure and is inscribed ATHENE.

Very good condition.

ESSENTIAL DOCUMENTATION

Before 1660. Reynst collection, Amsterdam.

1660. Presented to Charles II of England.

Probably owned before 1561 by Francesco Baiardi. The dimensions in the relevant entry in the inventory at his death in that year (Popham 1971, p. 264) tally well enough. Another version was in the Muselli collection at Verona in the seventeenth century. See Shearman 1983, in which the difference in dimensions between the present ones and those given in the Baiardi inventory is exaggerated: 0.16 × 0.1 *oncie* equals 0.72 × 0.45 meters.

RELATED DRAWINGS

P316 (Pierpont Morgan, New York). Study for the whole picture.

P799r and v (homeless). Studies for the brooch.

KEDLESTON HALL (DERBYSHIRE, ENGLAND)

Kedleston Hall

A16 *Madonna and Child*
Oil on panel. Original painted surface c. 19⅛ × 14 in. (48.5 × 35.5 cm) (subsequently enlarged).
(text p. 96, fig. 71)

The green curtain behind the figures revealed by a recent restoration.

ESSENTIAL DOCUMENTATION

1758. Bought by William Kent (dealer) for the Curzon family from Arnaldi in Florence.

1992. C. Gould, *Apollo,* March 1992.

RELATED DRAWING

P227 (British Museum). The central group bears some relation to the design, but is not strictly a preparatory study.

LONDON

National Gallery

A17 *Madonna and Child with the Baptist and Saint Jerome* (33)
Oil on panel (arched top), 135 × 58⅝ in. (343 × 149 cm)
(text p. 67, fig. 49)

Extensive local damage due to flaking in the past.

Saint Jerome's right hand presses a palm branch to the stem of his crucifix. His cardinal's hat nestles among the dismembered jaws of a skull. See appendix 3.

ESSENTIAL DOCUMENTATION

January 3, 1526. Piero and Francesco Mazzola of Parma promise Maria Bufalina Caccialupi to deliver an altarpiece representing the Virgin and Child with Saint Jerome and Saint John the Baptist, also a representation of the Conception of the Virgin on one side and of Saints Joachim and Anna on the other "in cornicibus cappellae." This for a fee of 65 *scudi* and to be done within the next six months. Piero Mazzola's name was presumably only included for legal reasons. (Sandro Corradini, *Burlington Magazine,* January 1993; also article by Mary Vaccaro in the same issue, pp. 22ff.)

Vasari 1550. Picture commissioned by Lorenzo Cybo for a chapel at San Salvatore in Lauro, Rome. Nearly finished at the time of the sack (1527).

Vasari 1568. Commissioned by Maria Bufalina of Città di Castello for San Salvatore in Lauro. Stored for many years after the sack at Santa Maria della Pace, Rome, before being taken to the Bufalini church (Sant'Agostino) at Città di Castello.

Scaramuccia 1674 (p. 86). At Sant'Agostino at Città di Castello.

Affò 1784. Picture already withdrawn to Palazzo Bufalini, Città di Castello. Replaced in church by a copy.

c. 1789. Sold by the Bufalini family to James Durno, and by him to the marquess of Abercorn. Sold by the latter, before 1809. Then briefly Harris and Hart Davis until 1823, when bought by Holwell Carr for the British Institution, by whom presented to the National Gallery, 1826.

VERSION

A full-size copy was reported in Palazzo Mancini, Città di Castello.

RELATED DRAWINGS
An extensive list in Gould 1975 I and Popham 1971 (at P181). The only developed sketch for the whole composition is P181r and v (British Museum, here fig. 51). A slight sketch at Parma (P544v) includes all four figures. The other drawings are for individual figures. No drawings have been identified for the flanking representation of the Immaculate Conception and Saints Joachim and Anna.

ENGRAVING
Bonasone (Bartsch XV.127.62). Cat. G5.

National Gallery

A18 *The Mystic Marriage of Saint Catherine* (6427)
Oil on panel, 29¼ × 22½ in. (74.2 × 57.2 cm)
(text p. 98, fig. 74)

Bottom left, the numerals 379 (Borghese numeration).

Very good condition. The Christ Child's body may once have been draped.

Unidentified male saint, left.

Bologna period. Wrongly dated in the past to the Roman period.

Copies in the Wellington Museum (London), the Pinacoteca (Bologna), and the Museo Davio Bargellini (Bologna).

ESSENTIAL DOCUMENTATION
Vasari 1550. "Et un'altro ne fece ad un Sellaio suo amico bellissimo fuor di modo; dove era una Madonna dipinta, volta per fianco con bella attitudine, e parecchie altre figure" (and he did another for a friend, a saddler, extraordinarily beautiful, with a Madonna turned toward the side in a beautiful attitude and several other figures).

Vasari 1568. The same.

1693. Palazzo Borghese, Rome, no. 379 in the inventory, corresponding with the numeral painted on the surface. See Gould 1975 II. Probably acquired by Scipione Borghese (d. 1633).

1799–1800. In England, where bought by Ottley. Subsequently Young and Morland collections. From 1832 in the family of the earls of Normanton, from whom bought by the National Gallery, 1974.

RELATED DRAWINGS
Popham lists his nos. 48, 279, 367, 399, and 793 tentatively, but none of them is certainly preparatory.

ENGRAVING
Giulio Bonasone (Bartsch XV.121.47). Cat. G6.

National Gallery

A19 *A Priest or Collector* (6441)
Oil on panel, 35 × 25¼ in. (89 × 64 cm)
(text p. 46, fig. 31)

Bronze statuette and coins on the table in the foreground; marble relief behind perhaps representing Mars, Venus, and Cupid.

Early inventories (see below) consistently describe the sitter as a priest.

Copies in the Uffizi, Minneapolis, and formerly New York art market.

ESSENTIAL DOCUMENTATION
1587. Probably no. 14 ("ritratto di un prete di mano del Parmigianino," portrait of a priest by the hand of Parmigianino) in the *Guardaroba* of Ranuccio Farnese, Parma (Bertini 1987, p. 205).

c. 1680. Probably painting no. 224 ("Rittrato [sic] di un prete con beretta in capo, officio alle mani, et anello alla destra, del Parmeggianino [sic]," portrait of a priest with a biretta on his head and a breviary in his hands and a ring on his right hand, by Parmigianino). (Bertini 1987, p. 246.)

1708. No. 304 in Parma inventory ("Ritratto con beretta da prete") (Bertini 1987, p. 189).

1801. In England in Ottley collection.

1826. In Strafford collection, Wrotham, England.

1940. C. Gamba (*Emporium* XCII) as Parmigianino.

1977. Bought from the Strafford collection for the National Gallery.

Courtauld Institute, Seilern Collection

A20 *Holy Family with an Angel ("Nativity")* (49)
Oil on panel, 17 × 18⅝ in. (43.1 × 47.3 cm)
(text p. 39, fig. 24)

Another version illustrated in Rossi 1980, pl. X.

ESSENTIAL DOCUMENTATION
1830. Sir T. Lawrence sale (92). Previously Tries and Speck von Sternberg collections. Subsequently Rogers and Cook collections. Bought from the latter by Anton Seilern, 1966, and bequeathed by him to the Courtauld Institute, 1978. For this and the following picture see H. Braham, *The Princes Gate Collection* (London: 1981).

RELATED DRAWING
Perhaps P823v. Other sketches associated by Popham are questionably related.

Courtauld Institute, Seilern Collection

A21 *Madonna and Child* (50)
Oil on panel, 25 × 20 in. (63.5 × 50.7 cm)
(text p. 96, fig. 72)

The appearance of the Madonna's drapery caused the picture to be described as unfinished. But some of this effect may be due to the top pigment's having become transparent in the course of time.

Bologna period. Wrongly dated to the Roman period in the past. Perhaps the "Madonna abbozzata" bought by Vasari at Bologna.

ESSENTIAL DOCUMENTATION
1965. Bought from Lord Kinnaird by Anton Seilern, by whom bequeathed to the Courtauld Institute, 1978.

1981. H. Braham, *The Princes Gate Collection* (London), p. 34.

RELATED DRAWINGS
P616 (Albertina, Vienna). Study for the whole composition with the addition of an angel.

P550 (study for the *Visitation*) has similar buildings in the background.

MADRID

Museo del Prado

A22 *Saint Barbara* (282)
Oil on panel, 18⅞ × 15⅜ in. (48 × 39 cm)
(text p. 21, fig. 8)

The object in her hands is her emblem, a model tower.

Engraved (in reverse) by J. du Bois (seventeenth century) as after Raphael. Evidently one of Parmigianino's earliest panels. Not in the Prado catalog of 1952.

ESSENTIAL DOCUMENTATION

1866. Campori, *Lettere artistiche inedite*, p. 191. Possible identification with picture in the Muselli collection, Verona, 1662, and, more hypothetically, with a reference in the Este inventory of 1624.

1921. Overlooked by Fröhlich-Bum (1921) but accepted by other twentieth-century critics.

Copy in the Mauritshuis, The Hague (no. 354, as "Italian School," in the 1977 catalog). Other versions listed by Rossi 1980, p. 86, no. 3.

RELATED DRAWING

Perhaps P6v (Bayonne).

Museo del Prado

A23 *Holy Family with Angels* (283)
Oil on panel, 43¼ × 35 in. (110 × 89 cm)
(text p. 42, fig. 27)

The extra hands on the right are evidently those of a sacred angel.

ESSENTIAL DOCUMENTATION

Vasari 1550 and 1568, as brought by Parmigianino to Rome (in 1524) and presented to him by Pope Clement VII and by the latter to Ippolito de' Medici. Thereafter no trace until the nineteenth century.

Prado catalogs from 1858.

RELATED DRAWINGS

P396r (Louvre); perhaps P46 (Fitzwilliam Museum, Cambridge).

Museo del Prado

A24 *Pier Maria Rossi, Count of San Secondo* (279)
Oil on panel, 53⅛ × 15 in. (135 × 38 cm)
(text p. 149, fig. 119)

The attribution to Parmigianino as a late work has been generally accepted by twentieth-century critics except for the Quintavalle family and Fagiolo dell'Arco.

ESSENTIAL DOCUMENTATION

Vincenzo Carrari, *Istoria dei Rossi Parmensi* (1583), vol. 5, p. 216. As in the Rocca di San Secondo and as by Parmigianino.

A. Pezzana, *Storia della Città di Parma* (1837), vol. 4, pp. 51ff., quoting Federico Rossi (son of the sitter): *Elogia Virorum Rosciorum* as by Parmigianino.

Campori 1866, pp. 453–5. Undated inventory, said to be late seventeenth century, cites this portrait as by Parmigianino and the female portrait as by Correggio.

A probably relevant reference, not included by Freedberg 1950, is Scannelli's (1657, p. 311) to two portraits by Parmigianino with Marchese Serra at Milan, in which one of the sitters is specified as accompanied by three children.

The present picture was in Spain by 1686 (inventory of the Alcazar at Madrid of that date) and in 1772 is specified as at the Retiro, Madrid (current Prado catalog).

Museo del Prado

A25 *Camilla Gonzaga, Countess of San Secondo, with Three Children* (280)
Oil on panel, 50⅜ × 38⅝ in. (128 × 98 cm)
(text p. 149, fig. 120)

Attribution and comment as for the preceding picture.

ESSENTIAL DOCUMENTATION

Carrari, Campori, and Scannelli as for preceding male portrait.

1772 and 1794. In Madrid palace.

Freedberg 1950, fig. 162, and Milstein 1978, p. 379, publish a portrait at Philadelphia perhaps of the same sitter (C15) but disputed authorship.

RELATED DRAWING

P704 (Chatsworth).

MILAN

Castello Sforzesco

A26 *A Man in Black*
Oil on canvas, removed from panel, 23⅝ × 16⅞ in. (60 × 43 cm)
(text p. 46, fig. 30)

ESSENTIAL DOCUMENTATION

R. Longhi, "Correggio Giovane," *Paragone* 181 (1958), as Correggio.

Gould 1976, p. 288, tentatively as Parmigianino.

Bologna 1986, p. 159, as Parmigianino.

NAPLES

Galleria Nazionale di Capodimonte

A27 *A Young Woman ("Antea")* (108)
Oil on canvas, 53⅛ × 34⅝ in. (135 × 88 cm)
(text p. 149, fig. 116)

Datable to the mid-1530s by association with the *Madonna dal Collo Lungo.*

The historical Antea was a known courtesan who is mentioned in Cellini's autobiography; but the identification of the sitter with her is too late (1671) to be reliable, and since she appears to have been resident in Rome it is also highly implausible.

ESSENTIAL DOCUMENTATION

1671. Barri, *Viaggio Pittoresco*, as "Antea, mistress of Parmigianino" and as in Palazzo del Giardino, Parma.

c. 1680. Inventory of Palazzo del Giardino, Parma, no. 69 (Bertini 1987, p. 237).

1708. No. 129 in a Parma inventory (Bertini 1987, p. 126).

1734. Transferred from Parma to Naples.

Bologna 1986, no. 58.

Galleria Nazionale di Capodimonte

A28 *A Man ("G. B. Castaldo")* (109)
Oil on panel, 38⅝ × 32⅝ in. (98 × 83 cm)
(text p. 113, fig. 86)

The paint in the dress has sunk somewhat. The writing on the book is not now legible. His left hand, holding the book, rests on the pommel of his rapier.

Speculatively, but implausibly, attributed to Girolamo da Carpi (Longhi, *Ampliamenti nell'Officina ferrarese* [1940], p. 37, n. 2). The identification of the sitter with Castaldo is also speculative (Ricci 1894–5). There is a portrait listed as of Castaldo by Parmigianino, no. 10 in the 1587 Parma inventory (Bertini 1987, p. 205). Alternatively perhaps identical with a portrait of a Bolognese count mentioned by Vasari.

ESSENTIAL DOCUMENTATION

c. 1680. No. 246, inventory of Palazzo del Giardino, Parma, as Parmigianino (Bertini 1987, p. 247).

1708. No. 17, Parma inventory (Bertini 1987, p. 90). Still as Parmigianino.

1734. Transferred from Parma to Naples.

1940. Longhi (as above) as Girolamo da Carpi.

1950. Freedberg. Back to Parmigianino.

1964. As "School of Parma" in the Capodimonte catalog and still (1993) labeled as such.

1968. Berenson as Parmigianino, as in previous editions.

1977. A. Mezzetti, *Girolamo da Carpi*, as Parmigianino.

Galleria Nazionale di Capodimonte

A29 *Galeazzo Sanvitale, Count of Fontanellato* (111)
Oil on panel, 42⅞ × 31⅞ in. (109 × 81 cm)
(text p. 47, fig. 34)

Artist's name and date—1524—on the back.

Galeazzo Sanvitale lived from 1496 to 1550. (Cf. Dall'Acqua 1988 with biographical details that confirm the cabalistic interests of the sitter that are adumbrated in the present portrait.)

The sitter holds a medal inscribed with the figures 72. The badge on his hat has been interpreted as representing the Pillars of Hercules (Fagiolo dell'Arco 1970, fig. 77). The hat itself is of the same type as that worn by Lorenzo Cybo (see Copenhagen).

ESSENTIAL DOCUMENTATION

1587. Painting no. 11, "Un ritratto del C.te Galeazzo Sanvitale di mano del Parmegianino [sic]" (Bertini 1987, p. 205). This inventory is that of pictures in the *Guardaroba* of Ranuccio Farnese.

1708. Parma inventory, painting no. 285 (Bertini 1987, p. 185).

1734. Transferred from Parma to Naples.

1799–1900. Looted by the French.

Sanvitale 1857.

Asmus 1983.

RELATED DRAWINGS

P458r and v (Louvre), P748v (fig. 35), and P.O.R. III (what was apparently the original sold at Sotheby's, July 4, 1988, no. 6).

Galleria Nazionale di Capodimonte

A30 *Holy Family with the Infant Baptist* (110)
Tempera on canvas, 62⅝ × 52 in. (159 × 132 cm).
(text p. 103, fig. 79)

Rather worn in places.

Probably one of two paintings for Luca dai Leuti of Bologna (Vasari V, 227; see also private collection, Parma). Therefore datable to 1527–30. Freedberg's dating (1950) to 1535–39 has found no support. The truncation of the Baptist's head, which appears on the left, above that of the Christ Child and larger than it, suggests that the canvas may have been cut on this side, but the dimensions as given in the Farnese inventories from c. 1680 onward approximate to the present ones.

ESSENTIAL DOCUMENTATION

1653. Inventory of pictures in Palazzo Farnese, Rome (Bertini 1987, p. 210, no. 222).

1662. Inventory of pictures sent from Rome to Parma (Bertini 1987, p. 223, no. 1).

c. 1680. Inventory of Palazzo del Giardino, Parma (Bertini 1987, p. 237, no. 87).

1708. Parma inventory (Bertini 1987, p. 98, no. 38).

1734. Transferred from Parma to Naples.

Bologna 1986, no. 59.

RELATED DRAWINGS

P208, P209 (both British Museum)

P517r and v (Louvre)

P534 (Parma)

NEW YORK

Rosenberg & Steibel

A31 *Allegorical Portrait of Emperor Charles V*
Oil on canvas, 67¾ × 47 in. (172 × 119.4 cm)
(text p. 118, fig. 91)

The winged figure with laurel and palm sprigs is identified by Vasari as Fame. He identifies the child as the boy Hercules, but in one of the preliminary studies (P318r) this figure appears with wings and there are other putti on the far side of the globe. In its present state this important work gives the impression that Parmigianino brought it to the penultimate stage but abandoned it before adding the finishing touches.

A copy in the Residenz at Salzburg is ascribed to Rubens.

ESSENTIAL DOCUMENTATION

Vasari 1550 and 1568 as painted in Bologna (in 1529–30) and as acquired by Ippolito de' Medici and then by the cardinal and subsequently the duke of Mantua.

Not identifiable in the collection of King Charles I of England.

1857. Lent to Manchester (210) by William Angerstein.

February 23, 1883. W. Angerstein sale. Bought by Lesser and soon afterward in the Cook collection, Richmond.

Bologna 1986, no. 62 (with discussion of speculative attributions).

RELATED DRAWING

New York (Pierpont Morgan Library) P318r and v (see above). Perhaps P.O.R. 118.

☞ PARIS

Musée du Louvre

A32 *Marriage of Saint Catherine, and a Male Saint*
Oil on panel, 7⅞ × 10⅝ in. (20 × 27 cm)
(text p. 103, fig. 78)

Damaged in places and perhaps unfinished. Pentimento in the Christ Child's head. His face was earlier in profile. The male figure on the right holds a book.

Conceivably identical with no. 10 in the Baiardi inventory (see note under Lost Paintings).

ESSENTIAL DOCUMENTATION

A brand mark—DGH—on the back.

A label on the back signed by Frédéric Reiset identifies the picture with no. 556 ("A Madonna with Saint Catherine and Saint Joseph, unfinished") in Bathoe's edition (1758) of the catalog of James II's pictures. Reiset notes that he bought the picture in February 1839, at the Sommariva sale.

Acquired by the Louvre, 1992–93.

Copy in the Hermitage, Saint Petersburg, and a variant at Palazzo Campori, Modena (V. Lazareff, *L'Arte,* XXVII, 1924, pp. 169ff.).

RELATED DRAWING

P263. Head of Saint Catherine.

☞ PARMA, ITALY

San Giovanni Evangelista

A33 First chapel, nave aisle, left:
Frescoes: *Saint Agatha and Executioner*
Saint Lucy and Saint Apollonia
God the Father and Angels
(text p. 24, fig. 11)

ESSENTIAL DOCUMENTATION

Vasari 1568. Attributes as many as seven of the chapels to Parmigianino and as preceding the flight to Viadana in 1521.

Affò 1784. Corrects the number of chapels to two.

D. Ekserdjian, "Parmigianino in S. Giovanni Evangelista," in *Florence and Italy, Renaissance Studies in Honour of Nicolai Rubinstein* (1988), gives details regarding the patronage of the chapels.

RELATED DRAWINGS

P15r (Berlin): Saint Lucy and Saint Apollonia.
P396v (Louvre). Putti. P405 (Louvre). Putti.

San Giovanni Evangelista

A34 Second chapel, nave aisle, left:
Frescoes: *Two Deacons.* Marks that may be traces of an inscription—if so, now illegible—are on the arch that frames the figures.
Saint Vitalis. His name, now almost illegible, was inscribed on the arch above the horse's head.
The Four Temperaments
(text p. 21, figs. 9 and 10)

All these frescoes much damaged and discolored.

ESSENTIAL DOCUMENTATION

As for first chapel (A33).

RELATED DRAWINGS

P283 (Modena). *Saint Vitalis* (Popham as *Saint Secundus*).

P161 (British Museum). *Two Deacons.* The one on the right has a gridiron and is therefore Saint Laurence, who is often accompanied by Saint Stephen, but in the painting's present state neither figure has an attribute. The halo of the one on the left is almost obliterated.

For Parmigianino's putative share in the execution of one or more of Correggio's pendentive paintings see text p. 29 and fig. 14.

Santa Maria della Steccata

A35 Decoration of the choir vault.
Tempera on fresco.
(text pp. 126–39, figs. 96–100, 104, 106)

• *North side:*
Moses (grisaille). West end.
Three Foolish Virgins. Center.
Adam (grisaille). East end.

• *South side:*
Aaron (grisaille). West end.
Three Wise Virgins. Center.
Eve (grisaille). East end.

Friezes on both sides. Still life of books and lamps.

For the decoration of the coffers see text, p. 126.

ESSENTIAL DOCUMENTATION

(for texts see Testi 1922, pp. 265–72, and A. O. Quintavalle 1948, pp. 162ff.)

c. 1531. Parmigianino to paint the Coronation of the Virgin in the half-dome according to a drawing submitted, and to paint the choir vault. Fee to be 400 gold *scudi.* Work to be done in eighteen months.

May 10, 1531. Contract.

October 5, 1531. 100 *scudi* paid.

November 6, 1531. 100 *scudi* paid.

September 27, 1535. Church authorities claim refund of advance but relent in face of pressure from painter's friends. Fresh agreement allows two more years on pain of return of advance. Further 50 *scudi* allowed in three installments, two of which paid October 6 and November 20, 1535.

June 3, 1536. Further attempt by authorities to regain advance.

May 30, 1537. Angelo Mattei and Cipriano Bonelli commissioned to make bronze rosettes.

February 26, 1538. Another attempt to regain advance, but extension granted until August 26, 1539.

August 2, 1538. Rosettes to be gilded.

September 27, 1538. 25 remaining *scudi* paid.

September 19, 1544. Retrospective account of Parmigianino's imprisonment and of his attempt to damage the work.

Vasari 1550 and 1568.

RELATED DRAWINGS
Popham 1971 catalogs about 100 drawings (his plates 309–44), comprising studies for the vault as a whole, for the *Coronation of the Virgin* and for individual sections and figures and details. Three others were sold at Sotheby's, London, July 4, 1988 (7, 9, 10).

Santa Maria della Steccata

A36 *Saint Cecilia.* She holds a large viol in her left hand. The boy on the left holds a pipe in his left hand and two others over his right shoulder.
A37 *David.* He holds up a viol.
Organ shutters. Oil on canvas, present dimensions of each: 21⅞ × 109⅜ in. (538 × 278 cm)
(text p. 29, figs. 15 and 16)

Enlarged, 1580, by Jan Sons (Soens), who added the inner faces of the *Flight into Egypt.*

ESSENTIAL DOCUMENTATION
January 9, 1579. "Lo sportello dell'Organo . . . di quel famoso nostro Parmigianino . . ." Testi 1922, p. 178. Also Béguin 1956 and A. G. Quintavalle/L. Fornari 1971–2.

RELATED DRAWINGS
P435 (Louvre). *Saint Cecilia.* P37r and v (Budapest), recto for *Saint Cecilia,* verso for *David.*
P501r (Louvre). *Saint Cecilia* (?).

Galleria Nazionale

A38 *A Young Woman ("Turkish Slave")*
Oil on panel, 26⅜ × 20⅞ in. (67 × 53 cm)
(text p. 107, fig. 85)

ESSENTIAL DOCUMENTATION
1675. Leopoldo de' Medici (Uffizi inventory).
1704. Medici inventory. The fanciful title "Turkish Slave" used, presumably on the strength of the chain on the sitter's sleeve and of her headdress. But the latter is not an oriental turban but an Italian fashion of c. 1530 that is also seen in Parmigianino's portrait (*"Contessa Gozzadini"*) at Vienna (cat. A50).
1928. Passed from Florence to Parma as part of an exchange.

RELATED DRAWING
P489 (Louvre).

Galleria Nazionale

A39 *Self-Portrait*
Oil on paper, mounted on canvas, 8¼ × 6⅛ in. (21 × 15.5 cm)
(text p. 107, fig. 84)

On reverse, a pen drawing.

ESSENTIAL DOCUMENTATION
A. G. Quintavalle, *Tesori Nascosti* (1968). Identifies with entry no. 46 in the Baiardi inventory of c. 1561.
Rossi 1980 (p. 106, no. 61).

RELATED DRAWING
P490 (Louvre). The head on the right bears some resemblance to this.

Private collection; formerly on loan to the Galleria Nazionale

A40 *Saint Roch in the Desert*
Tempera on canvas, 11 × 8½ in. (27.8 × 21.5 cm)
(text p. 104, fig. 80)

Probably for Luca dai Leuti of Bologna (Vasari v, 227). (See also cat. A30)

Perhaps the "quadretto co'uno san Rocco bozzato di colore alto 0.7 largo 0.5 di mano del Parmesanino" that is no. 34 in the inventory of the Cavaliere Baiardi (Popham 1971, pp. 264ff.). In that case the fragment must have been cut from the parent picture at an early date.

ESSENTIAL DOCUMENTATION
L. Fornari-Schianchi, R. Tassi, and M. Lucco (Looklet), *Un Parmigianino ritrovato* (n.d.).

Palazzetto Eucherio Sanvitale

A41 *Madonna and Child*
Fresco fragment, grisaille.

Irregular shape. Most of the Christ Child survives, but very little of the Virgin. The Palazzetto Eucherio Sanvitale belonged in 1527 to Galeazzo Sanvitale, who had bought it from Scipione della Rosa (Lucia Fornari-Schianchi, "Palazzetto Eucherio Sanvitale: Qualche considerazione sulle decorazioni," in *La Reggia de là da l'Acqua,* 1991). Two copies, one formerly in the Armano and Pirri collections, the other at Capodimonte, and a print by Rosaspina after the former reproduce the composition before mutilation.

RELATED DRAWINGS
P813 (homeless)
P170 (British Museum)
Perhaps P424 and P425 (both Louvre).

☞ ROME

Galleria Borghese

A42 *A Prelate* (100)
Oil on panel, 20½ × 16½ in. (52 × 42 cm)
(text p. 113, fig. 87)

ESSENTIAL DOCUMENTATION
1693. Borghese inventory as Parmigianino and as "Portrait of Pianerlotto" (P. Della Pergola, *Galleria Borghese; I Dipinti,* vol. I [1955], p. 59).

The attribution to Parmigianino has been general except for A. O. Quintavalle 1948 (to Annibale Carracci).

Galleria Doria

A43 *Madonna and Child* (290)
and
A44 *Holy Family (Adoration of the Shepherds)* (292)
Oil on panel; each panel, arched top, 23¼ × 13⅜ in. (59 × 34 cm). Both currently (1993) discolored by varnish.
(text pp. 62–63, figs. 42 and 43)

ESSENTIAL DOCUMENTATION

S. Tonci, *Descrizione ragionata della Galleria Doria* (1794), as Parmigianino.

E. Sestieri, *Catalogo della Galleria ex-Fidecommissaria Doria-Pamphilj* (1942).

RELATED DRAWING

(for *Holy Family*), P778.

Galleria Spada

A45 *Three Heads*
Fresco, 28 × 23⅝ in. (71 × 60 cm)

Evidently a fragment, perhaps representing the Three Ages. The attribution to Parmigianino questioned, e.g., by Freedberg 1950, and ignored by Berenson. Since the restoration of 1969 clearly by Parmigianino.

ESSENTIAL DOCUMENTATION

F. Zeri, *La Galleria Spada in Roma* (1951).

A. G. Quintavalle, *Gli ultimi affreschi del Parmigianino* (1970), p. 14.

TAGGIA (IMPERIA), ITALY

San Domenico

A46 *Adoration of the Magi*
Oil on panel, 47¼ × 37 in. (120 × 94 cm)
(text p. 96, fig. 73)

ESSENTIAL DOCUMENTATION

1622–24. Already at Taggia (Armani 1986).

1631. Attributed to Perino del Vaga.

1957. Fiocco as Girolamo da Treviso ("Luca Cambiaso, Girolamo da Treviso e Pordenone" in *Matteo Marangoni Festschrift*).

1958. R. Longhi, *Paragone* 99. As Parmigianino and from the Bologna period.

1986. Armani (back to Perino).

1988. P. Amato, ed., *Imago Mariae* (Rome: Palazzo Venezia). Entry by Franco Boggero (as Parmigianino).

RELATED DRAWINGS

P586 (Stockholm). Study of negro's head, perhaps for the young king on the right.

P723 (Chatsworth)—a similar bearded head to that of the foremost king, but not necessarily connected.

P.O.R. 22 bears some slight resemblance.

VIENNA

Kunsthistorisches Museum

A47 *A Young Man with a Book* (610)
Oil on panel, 26⅝ × 20⅞ in. (67.5 × 53 cm)
(text p. 96, fig. 70)

ESSENTIAL DOCUMENTATION

1718. Prague inventory as "School of Correggio."

1723. At Vienna.

1950. Freedberg rejects attribution to Parmigianino.

1968. Berenson as Parmigianino (with query).

Kunsthistorisches Museum

A48 *Self-Portrait in a Convex Mirror* (609)
Oil on panel (convex), circular, 9⅝ in. (24.4 cm) diameter.
(text p. 53, fig. 36)

ESSENTIAL DOCUMENTATION

Vasari 1550 and 1568, as painted before the Rome journey (therefore not later than 1524) and successively in the possession of Pope Clement VII, Pietro Aretino, and Valerio and Elio Belli. Then, via Andrea Palladio, to Alessandro Vittoria.

1608. Rudolf II as by Correggio.

1777. At Vienna.

Kunsthistorisches Museum

A49 *Malatesta Baglione* (612)
Oil on panel, 46 × 38⅝ in. (117 × 98 cm)
(text p. 149, fig. 117)

ESSENTIAL DOCUMENTATION

Vienna 1783 catalog by Christian von Mechel as Parmigianino and as representing the *condottiere* Malatesta Baglione. The woodcut of Baglione in the 1575 (Basel, Switzerland) edition of Giovio's *Elogia virorum bellica virtute illustrium* evidently derives from the present picture and confirms the identification of the sitter.

1950. Freedberg rejects the Parmigianino attribution.

1968. Berenson as Parmigianino.

Kunsthistorisches Museum

A50 *A Woman ("Contessa Gozzadini")* (unfinished) (611)
Oil on panel, 19⅝ × 18¼ in. (50 × 46.4 cm)
(text p. 139, fig. 108)

The fashionable headdress is of the same type as that of the so-called *Turkish Slave* (cat. A38) and indicates a similar date of origin.

ESSENTIAL DOCUMENTATION

Perhaps Vasari 1550 and 1568 (he says Parmigianino never finished his portrait of Gozzadini's wife).

1659. Collection of Archduke Leopold William. At that time the format was larger, as shown in David Teniers II's view of the Archduke's pictures (Vienna no. 1161). Reduced to its present size by 1730.

Kunsthistorisches Museum

A51 *Conversion of Saul* (422)
Oil on canvas, 69⅞ × 50⅝ in. (177.5 × 128.5 cm)

ESSENTIAL DOCUMENTATION

Vasari 1550 and 1568, in the context of works executed at Bologna, as for Albio, a doctor from Parma. A footnote by Milanesi identifies "Albio" with Giovantonio Bianchi. Vasari's mention of "many figures" in Albio's picture is some argument against identifying it with the present work, though this is now generally admitted (there are only very few humans, and assorted animals, all on a very small scale, in the background).

1560. Lamo.

1912. In the depot of the Kunsthistorisches Museum.

1938. Included in the Vienna catalog with an attribution by Johannes Wilde to Niccolò dell'Abate.

1950. Freedberg rejects Niccolò dell'Abate attribution and substitutes Parmigianino.

1960. Still as Niccolò dell'Abate in the Vienna catalog.

1968. Not included by Berenson as Parmigianino.

1986. Bologna, no. 60 as Parmigianino.

RELATED DRAWINGS

P769 (Courtauld Institute, London, Seilern collection).

One other drawing—P768r and v (also Courtauld Institute, Seilern collection)—shows two designs, both in oblong format and differing not only from each other but also from the design of the greatest painting. These may represent earlier, discarded ideas for it.

Kunsthistorisches Museum

A52 *Cupid Cutting His Bow* (613)
Oil on panel, 53⅛ × 25¾ in. (135 × 65.3 cm)
(text p. 120, fig. 93)

A narrow strip along the top appears to be an addition.

ESSENTIAL DOCUMENTATION

Vasari 1550 and 1568 as for Baiardi, Parma, and then Marcantonio Cavalca.

c. 1561. No. 1 in Baiardi inventory (Popham 1971, p. 264).

1585. Antonio Perez, Madrid.

1603. Emperor Rudolf II, Prague.

From 1631 at Vienna.

1660. Boschini, *Carta del Navegar pitoresco.*

1702. Tolner, *Kurz lesenswürdige Erinnerung der Seltenheiten in und um Wien,* as Correggio.

1950. Freedberg as the Triumph of Love.

1970. Fagiolo dell'Arco as the "fuoco che favorisce la coniunctio" (the fire that encourages copulation).

The many extant old copies include those by Joseph Heintz at Vienna and Munich and a free copy by Rubens at Schleissheim (dated 1614), at which time the original was at Prague and Rubens was resident at Antwerp. Others at Hampton Court and the Prado.

RELATED DRAWINGS

P500 (Louvre), P543 (Parma), and P624v (Albertina) (?).

YORK, ENGLAND

City Art Gallery

A53 *A Man with a Book* (739)
Oil on canvas, lined, 27½ × 20½ in. (70 × 52 cm)
(text p. 46, fig. 32)

Impasto somewhat flattened.

Traces of letters on the book held by the sitter have been read (by Copertini in *Parma per l'Arte,* 1962) as I / AET / VLTRA, but are not legible now. Attributed to Correggio when recorded in 1810 (see below). Tentatively, and incorrectly, attributed to Bedoli by the present writer (1976, p. 288). Attributed to Parmigianino in the York catalog (1961) and by Heinemann (1965), as well as in the 1968 edition of Berenson. Also Bologna 1986 (56) and tentatively at Manchester (*Between Renaissance and Baroque,* 1965, 179).

Perhaps identical with a portrait in Charles I's collection (Van der Doort's inventory, ed. O. Millar, Walpole Society 37, p. 42) though that was specified as on panel.

Speculatively identified as a portrait of Correggio (Giuseppe M. Toscano, *Nuovi Studi sul Correggio* [1974], p. 158). There is no contemporary documented likeness of Correggio, and the image in the present portrait does not seem to be that of a painter.

ESSENTIAL DOCUMENTATION

Enamel copy by H. Bone sold at Christie's, London, June 16, 1970 (79), inscribed "London, August, 1810 . . . after the original by Correggio in the possession of Angelo Bonelli of Todi." Anonymous sale, Christie's, London, May 29, 1931 (76) as Correggio, bought by Wilson.

Presented to York by F. D. Lycett Green, through the NACF, 1955.

LOCATION UNKNOWN

(with Harari & Johns Ltd., London, 1990–91). In 1993 on loan to the Kunsthaus, Zurich

A54 *Adoration of the Shepherds ("Nativity")*
Oil on panel, 16½ × 16⅝ in. (41.9 × 42.3 cm)
(text p. 40, fig. 25)

ESSENTIAL DOCUMENTATION

C. Gould, "A Parmigianino Madonna and Child and His Uncommissioned Paintings," *Apollo*, March 1992.

RELATED DRAWINGS

Degrazia 1984, no. 40, is directly related. The following are related in part: P61, P137, P264, and P631.

LOCATION UNKNOWN

(with Harari & Johns Ltd., London, 1990–91)

A55 *Portrait of a Young Man (Self-Portrait)*
Oil on panel, 11¼ × 8⅞ in. (28.5 × 22.5 cm)
(text p. 120, fig. 92)

ESSENTIAL DOCUMENTATION

C. Gould, "A Parmigianino Madonna and Child and His Uncommissioned Paintings," *Apollo*, March 1992.

B. Lost Paintings

The following are mentioned by Vasari as Parmigianino's, but the originals have not been traced. Freedberg 1950 prints an extensive list from early catalogs, but it is no longer possible to check their authenticity.

B1 *Saint Francis Receiving the Stigmata and Saint Clare*
Early work. Placed in the church of the Frati de' Zoccoli (Franciscans) at Viadana.

B2 *Madonna and Child with Saint Jerome and the Blessed Bernardino da Feltre*
According to Vasari, the patron was portrayed as one of the figures. Copy in the Parma gallery and print by Giulio Bonasone. Related drawings: P275 (Biblioteca Nacional, Madrid) and P561 (Philadelphia Museum of Art).

B3 *Portrait of Bonifazio Gozzadini*

B4 Tondo of the *Virgin Annuntiate*
For Agnolo Cesi.

B5 *Holy Family with Angels*
For Luigi Gaddi.

B6 *Madonna*
Later sold in Bologna to Vasari. Said to be only "started" ("abbozzato"), so perhaps identical with the Courtauld Institute *Madonna* (A21).

B7 *Lucretia*
See under attributed paintings, C6.

B8 *Nymphs*
In Vasari's time with Niccolò Bufalini at Città di Castello.

B9 *Cradle of Children*
For Angiola de' Rossi of Parma, wife of Alessandro Vitelli of Città di Castello.

B10 The oblong *Mystic Marriage of Saint Catherine* (Parma) is not documented or supported by drawings, but is generally accepted as an old copy. (text p. 27, fig. 13)

The Baiardi inventory, which, in view of its early date (1561) and of Baiardi's intimacy with Parmigianino, must be considered reliable, lists some eighteen items as "colorito," that is, painted as opposed to drawn, by Parmigianino, of which the Vienna *Cupid*, the Hampton Court *Head and Bust of Athene*, the *Saint Roch in the Desert* fragment, and the small late self-portrait at Parma (A52, A15, A40, A39) survive and have been acceptably linked with the respective entries. Most of the other entries are too unspecified to attempt identification with existing works. The following are the most specific:

Baiardi no. 10. *Madonna and Child with Saint Catherine and Saint John.* Perhaps identical with A32.

Baiardi no. 14. Full-length portrait of *Bishop Rangone.*

Baiardi no. 20. *Saturn and Philyra.* Studies are P245, P387, P510, P654r and v, P655, P718v, and P.O.C. 20. Engraved by B. Lepicié (fig. 40). (text p. 61, fig. 40)

Baiardi no. 39. *Head of a Youth.* Underneath, a man and woman making love.

C. Notes on Some Attributed Paintings

It would not be feasible to attempt to discuss all of the many pictures that have been attributed to Parmigianino in early inventories and catalogs. Most of them can no longer be traced with certainty. The short list that follows is of some paintings, mainly in fixed locations, whose attribution to Parmigianino seems to me questionable, but for which claims have been made within comparatively recent times.

DRESDEN, GERMANY

Gemäldegalerie (formerly)

C1 *Portrait of a Youth*

Canvas, 40⅛ × 26¾ in. (102 × 68 cm)

From the Unger collection, Berlin. Consistently as Parmigianino until World War II, when it was destroyed. As Parmigianino (with a query) in Berenson 1968. Impossible to decide on the authorship now.

GLOUCESTERSHIRE, ENGLAND

Sudeley Castle

C2 *Mystic Marriage of Saint Catherine*

Published as Parmigianino (C. Whitfield, *Burlington Magazine,* 1982) but more probably Bedoli (Degrazia 1984, p. 180). Other versions are known.

MILAN

Private collection

C3 *A Man in Armor and a Female*

E. Arslan (*Emporium* 105 [1947]: 65–66) drew attention to similarities of design to Parmigianino's *Charles V* (A31). The small photograph suggests an interesting picture, but all efforts to trace it have come to nothing.

MODENA, ITALY

Galleria Estense

C4 *Holy Family with Saints and a Donor*

Canvas, 34⅝ × 24⅜ in. (88 × 62 cm)

No. 224 in R. Pallucchini's catalog of the Estense. Attributed since the nineteenth century to Rondani. A. G. Quintavalle (in *Paragone* 10, 1959) postulated the nucleus as Parmigianino, subsequently worked on by Rondani, and that Bedoli added the Saint Francis and Anselmi the Saint Joseph and the donor. So remarkable a cooperative undertaking would suggest highly unusual conditions of work, but it is true that the picture seems far from homogeneous. The Madonna has something in common with the one in the copy of Parmigianino's lost *Madonna and Child with Saint Jerome and the Blessed Bernardino da Feltre* (B2). But the picture as a whole is closer to one of equally questionable attribution in a private collection at Cremona (reproduced Milstein 1978, fig. 160).

NAPLES

Galleria Nazionale di Capodimonte

C5 *Portrait of Girolamo de' Vicenti*

Canvas, 43¼ × 35⅜ in. (110 × 90 cm)

Inscribed, top left: HERONIMVS DE VINCENTI / AETATIS SVAE AN XXVIII / MDXXXV

As Parmigianino in the Parma inventory of 1662–80 and as such in successive Naples inventories and catalogs. Taken by the French, 1799, and recovered in Rome. Still as Parmigianino in Freedberg 1950 (with query) and Berenson (1968). Attributed to Girolamo da Carpi by Longhi (*Ampliamenti nell'Officina Ferrarese,* 1940) and Mezzetti (*Girolamo da Carpi,* 1977), which attribution is probably correct. As Girolamo, Bologna 1986 (20).

Galleria Nazionale di Capodimonte

C6 *Lucretia*

Panel, 26⅜ × 20⅛ in. (67 × 51 cm)

Attributed to Parmigianino in the 1587 inventory of the *Guardaroba* of Ranuccio Farnese (Bertini 1947, p. 163). This early authority and the high quality of the painting militate in favor of the Parmigianino attribution, which has also found considerable support in modern times. Nevertheless it is certainly by Bedoli, as this kind of profile is typical of him (e.g., in the *Parma Embracing Alessandro Farnese* and *Woman Playing the Clavichord,* both in the Parma gallery).

Galleria Nazionale di Capodimonte

C7 *Portrait of a Man ("G. Bernardi da Castelbolognesi")*

Panel, 24¾ × 19¼ in. (63 × 49 cm)

The badge in the sitter's cap represents Leda and the Swan. In early seventeenth-century inventories variously as of or by Baldassare Peruzzi. Attributed to Parmigianino in the 1928 museum catalog and by Berenson. Attributed to Anselmi (A. G. Quintavalle n.d.) and by F. Bologna to Gregorio Pagani (1558–1605). The latter is unacceptable if only because the costume is considerably earlier.

Galleria Nazionale di Capodimonte

C8 *Portrait of a Youth with Hand on Hip*

Panel, 47¼ × 33⅞ in. (120 × 86 cm)

As Titian in the 1653 inventory of Palazzo Farnese, Rome. As Parmigianino in the 1708 Parma inventory. Consistently as Parmigianino (including Berenson 1932 and 1936) until 1940, when reattributed to Rosso by Longhi. Comparison with the Liverpool portrait of a man, signed by Rosso, leaves no doubt of the correctness of this attribution.

Galleria Nazionale di Capodimonte

C9 *Portrait of a Man ("Gian Martino Sanvitale")*

Canvas, 36¼ × 31⅞ in. (92 × 81 cm)

Dated 1536. Attributed to Parmigianino in the Palazzo del Giardino (Parma) inventory of c. 1680 and in the 1708 inventory (Bertini 1987). Attributed to Lotto by Berenson (1957) ("so-called Portrait of Henry VIII"). In the 1964 Naples museum catalog (p. 37) as "Anonimo del 1536." Attributed by Freedberg to Girolamo da Carpi. The design has much in common with that of the male portrait in the Galleria Nazionale (Palazzo Barberini), Rome, which is convincingly attributed to Girolamo da Carpi.

NEW YORK

Metropolitan Museum of Art

C10 *The Annunciation*

Panel, 33⅜ × 23⅛ in. (84.8 × 58.7 cm)

From Althorp. Published with an attribution to Parmigianino by Keith Christiansen in the catalog of the exhibition *Nell'Età del Correggio e dei Carracci;* Bologna, 1986. Evidently the model for Bedoli's altarpiece of the Annunciation for Santa Maria Annunciata at Viadana (now at Capodimonte, Naples) and as such attributable to him.

NORTHERN IRELAND

Barons Court (Duke of Abercorn)

C11 Portrait of an ecclesiastic identified with Cardinal Lorenzo Pucci. Crowe and Cavalcaselle (*Raphael: His Life and Works,* vol. 2 [1885], p. 351n.) describe the picture (not seen by them) as in the possession of the duke of Abercorn and as probably the one noted by Passavant (*Raphael d'Urbin,* vol. 2 [1860], p. 358) among those attributed to Raphael. Passavant states that it had passed from Palazzo Casale at Bologna to "M. Rossi" and thence to Sir Robert Gordon and Lord Aberdeen. He notes that the inscription on the paper held by the sitter was then "illisible," and describes the heads as "très-remarquable." In recent times attributed to Sebastiano del Piombo, and, by M. Hirst (*Sebastiano del Piombo* [1981], p. 92, n. 11), to Parmigianino. I have not seen this obviously impressive portrait, but a good black-and-white contact print seems to exclude Raphael, Sebastiano, and Parmigianino alike. On the strength of an analogy with the portrait called *Onofrio Bartolini* (Pitti, Florence), attributed to Girolamo da Carpi, I would tentatively suggest that painter for the present picture. The connection of both painter and sitter with Bologna would be consistent with this. Also the picture's provenance.

PARIS

Musée du Louvre

C12 *Portrait of a Young Man with His Hand to His Head*

Panel, 16½ × 13 in. (42 × 33 cm)

From the collection of the duke of Richelieu, 1665. After a record number of conjectural attributions—to Raphael, Bachiacca, Franciabigio, Sogliani, Francia, and Rondani—this portrait seemed to settle down as the work of Parmigianino until reattributed convincingly by S. Béguin, 1987, to Correggio as of c. 1520. The sitter is probably the young Parmigianino.

PARMA, ITALY

Galleria Nazionale

C13 *Adoration of the Shepherds*

Panel, 16⅝ × 12⅝ in. (42.3 × 32.2 cm)

Attributed to Parmigianino by Rossi 1980, no. 97, quoting A. O. and A. G. Quintavalle.

San Giovanni Evangelista

C14

• *Fourth chapel from west on the north side of the nave:*

Frescoes of Saint Nicholas of Bari and Saint Hilary of Poitiers.

Attributed to Parmigianino by A. O. Quintavalle 1948 and others, including Berenson (1968).

Commissioned of Parmigianino's uncles, but evidently not their work. I have difficulty in seeing Parmigianino here. Conceivably by the young Bedoli.

• *Sixth chapel from west:*

Frescoes of the Four Doctors of the Church.

Sometimes attributed to Parmigianino. Probably by Anselmi.

• *Vault of chapel to the left of the high altar:*

Frescoes of Saints Catherine and Agnes.

Once attributed to Parmigianino. Currently to Anselmi.

• *Vault of chapel to the right of the high altar:*

Frescoes of Saints Margaret and Cecilia.

Attributed to Parmigianino in old guide books. Also at times to Anselmi. Probably Bedoli.

PHILADELPHIA

Pennsylvania Museum of Art (W 96-1-6)

C15 *Portrait of a Lady*

Panel, 39 × 33⅞ in. (99 × 86 cm)

Acquired as Bronzino. Subsequently cataloged as Giulio Campi. Attributed to Parmigianino by Siren. Identified by Copertini and Freedberg with a picture in seventeenth- and eighteenth-century Farnese inventories, but that was more probably one still at Naples, attributable to Bedoli. The Bedoli attribution for the present picture rejected by Freedberg and Milstein. To judge from Parmigianino's portrait of the countess of San Secondo (Prado, A25), the sitter of this one may be the same.

RICHMOND, SURREY, ENGLAND

Cook collection (formerly)

C16 *Portrait of a Youth*

Slate, 13 × 7½ in. (33 × 19 cm)

Attributed to Parmigianino by Tancred Borenius in the Cook catalog. This attribution rejected by Freedberg and ignored by subsequent critics. This picture is however probably the original of which a miniature copy is in the Parma gallery, identified as representing Orazio Farnese (reproduced by Bertini 1987, p. 211). This miniature is one of a group of which others are copies after portraits by Titian of Pope Paul III and Pier Luigi Farnese. Orazio was Pier Luigi's third son, born in 1527. He would therefore have been about thirteen at the time of Parmigianino's death. From a chronological point of view the attribution to Parmigianino as a very late work would therefore not be impossible, and in the photograph published by Borenius looks equally impossible stylistically. Exhibited Burlington Fine Arts Club, London, 1912–13 (21).

VENICE

Cini collection

C17 *Holy Family and Angels*

Panel, 17¾ × 12¼ in. (45 × 31 cm)

Published as Parmigianino by Bologna 1956. Attributed to Bedoli by Milstein 1978. Probably the same hand as the similar picture below (C19). Rossi 1980, no. 33.

YORKSHIRE, ENGLAND

Castle Howard

C18 *Four Young Men*

Canvas, 87 × 73⅝ in. (221 × 187 cm)

Painted on two separate canvases, divided down the center and now joined, presumably originally flanking a central feature. Recorded as Tintoretto in Queen Christina's collection and as such through the Orléans and Bridgewater collections. Attributed to Parmigianino, Royal Academy, London exhibition, 1960, and Stockholm, 1966. Since then more generally as Bedoli. The turkey rugs, prominent in the present picture, were a feature used in portraits by artists as dissimilar as Lotto, Rosso, and Girolamo da Carpi, but on the whole Bedoli remains the most likely attribution. The bust on the right shows a crescent moon on the head, therefore presumably Diana. Each of the two central figures kneels at a prie-dieu. The figure on the left is clearly a servant. The status of the young man standing on the right is questionable. Freedberg 1950 saw a resemblance between him and the main figure in the Milan portrait of *A Man in Armor and a Female* (cat. C3). For myself, the two kneeling figures recall the two eldest boys in Parmigianino's portrait of the countess of San Secondo (A25) at a rather later age.

LOCATION UNKNOWN

C19 *Holy Family and Angels*

From Wilton, sold Christie's, London 19.iv.1957, as Bertoja, which seems possible, but attributed to Parmigianino by Longhi and others. Probably the same hand as C17. Rossi 1980, no. 32.

Part Two. Prints

D. Authentic Etchings

The etchings listed below are those that connect with authentic drawings by Parmigianino and that are assumed to be from plates that he worked himself. For etchings attributed to him without such support see the introduction to Popham 1971; A. Bartsch, *Le Peintre-graveur* (1803–21; illustrated edition 1978–); K. Oberhuber, *Parmigianino und sein Kreis* (Vienna: Albertina, 1963); K. Oberhuber, *Parmigianino als Radierer: Alte und moderne Kunst* (1963); and Reed and Wallace, *Italian Etchers of the Renaissance* (Boston: Museum of Fine Arts, 1989). See also the note at the end of the following section.

("B" = Bartsch + reference number)

D1 *Adoration of the Shepherds* B XVI.7.3.
Presumably the "Nativita di Cristo" mentioned by Vasari (V, 423). Related drawings: P368 (Louvre), P728 (Chatsworth), P593 (Stuttgart), P644 (Windsor), P.O.C. 6, and P.O.R. 5.

D2 *Entombment of Christ*
First version, with Christ's legs on the left (B XVIII.300.46) was attributed by Bartsch to Guido Reni. Related drawings: P555 (Parma), P62 (Darmstadt), and P765 (Courtauld Institute, London). Second version, with Christ's legs on the right (fig. 63; B XVI.8.5). Related drawings: P132 (Horne Museum, Florence), P197, P200, P201, P202 (all British Museum), and P408 (Louvre). One of these was presumably the Dead Christ Mourned by the Marys (Vasari V, 423).

D3 *Judith*
B XVI.6.1. Related drawings: P204 (British Museum) and P.O.R. 4.

D4 *Lovers in a Wood*
(text p. 84, fig. 60)
B XVI.14.14. Related drawing: ? P612 (Albertina, Vienna; fig. 61).

D5 *Madonna and Child*
B XVI.7.4. Related drawing: P368 (Louvre).

D6 *Resurrection*
(text p. 86, fig. 62)
B XVI.9.6. Related drawings: P643V (Windsor) and P310 (Morgan Library, New York).

D7 *Saint Philip*
B XVI.11.9. Related drawing: P473 (Louvre).

D8 *"Saint Thais"*
B XVI.12.10. Related drawing: P764 (Courtauld Institute, London).

D9 *Sleeping Cupid* (after detail in Raphael's *Massacre of the Innocents,* engraved by Marcantonio)
B XVI.13.11. Related drawing: P210 (British Museum).

NOTE

Of the etchings that are attributed to Parmigianino without the support of drawings, the most acceptable are the *Virgin Annuntiate* (B XVI.6.2), which presupposes knowledge of Michelangelo's Doni tondo, and the *Healing of the Lame Man,* after Raphael (B XVI.9.7). The latter may be what Vasari was referring to in stating that Parmigianino did an etching after a tapestry designed by Raphael (Vasari V, 423), but Vasari did not specify which of the tapestries. A further etching—*Standing Shepherd* (B XVI.13.12)—may perhaps be a development from a drawing at Chatsworth (P689) of a similar figure, but recumbent.

E. "F. P." Etchings

Bartsch catalogs twenty-six prints of this kind (B XVI, pp. 1–27). Repetitions, in the form of chiaroscuro woodcuts, were attributed by him to Antonio da Trento (B XIII, pp. 69ff.). The following are etchings inscribed "F.P." for which drawings by Parmigianino survive:

E1 *Saint Andrew*
B XVI.20.3. Related drawings: P96 (Uffizi) and P468 (Louvre).

E2 *Saint John the Evangelist*
B XVI.20.5. Related drawing: P469 (Louvre).

E3 *Saint Philip (?)*
B XVI.21.6. Related drawing: P473 (Louvre).

E4 *Saint Matthias*
B XVI.21.8. Related drawing: P470 (Louvre).

E5 *Saint Judas Thaddaeus (?)*
B XVI.22.12. Related drawing: P474 (Louvre).

E6 *Saint Paul*
B XVI.23.13. Related drawing: P471 (Louvre).

E7 *Fortitude*
B XVI.23.14. Related drawing: P725r (Chatsworth).

E8 *Hercules and Cerberus*
B XVI.23.15. Related drawing: P726r (Chatsworth). Verso has *Mutius Scaevola* (fig. 65).

E9 *Woman with Armillary Sphere*
B XVI.23.20. Related drawing: P725v (Chatsworth).

E10 *Hounds Coursing a Stag*
B XVI.24.16. Related drawing: P515v (Louvre).

E11 *Seated Philosopher*
B XVI.24.19. Related drawing: P724 (Chatsworth).

F. Chiaroscuro Prints after Parmigianino Mentioned by Vasari or Signed

By Ugo da Carpi (c. 1480–c. 1532)

Active successively in Milan, Venice, Rome, and Bologna. He claimed to be the inventor of the chiaroscuro method of woodcut.

F1 *Diogenes*
(text p. 76, fig. 56)
BXII.100.10. Vasari (V, 422) attributes the execution of this to Parmigianino himself and says it was better than any of the chiaroscuro prints by Ugo da Carpi. But it is signed by Ugo. Related drawings: P107 (Uffizi) and P714 and P729 (both Chatsworth). The plucked chicken in the background is assumed to refer to Plato's definition of man as a featherless biped. See also G4 (Caraglio's engraving from the same design).

By Antonio da Trento (c. 1510–1550)

Active in Bologna from 1527. By 1537 at Fontainebleau, where he died.

Vasari specifies the four prints that follow as the work of Antonio:

F2 *Martyrdom of Saints Peter and Paul*
B XII.79.28. See also Caraglio's metal engraving of the same design, G2. Related drawing: P190 (British Museum).

F3 *Augustus and the Sibyl*
B XII.90.7. Related drawings: P398 (Louvre) and P595 and 595r (Turin). Also P802 (homeless) and P.O.R. 68.

F4 *Naked Man Seen from the Back*
B XII.148.13. The subject is probably Narcissus. Related drawing: P2 (Amsterdam).

F5 *Madonna in an Oval*
B XII.56.12. Related drawing: P148 (Teylers Stichtung, Haarlem, the Netherlands).

The following two prints are not mentioned by Vasari but bear Antonio's monogram:

F6 *Saint John the Baptist in the Wilderness*
B XII.73.17. Related drawings: P4V (Amsterdam), P8 (Bayonne), P110 (Uffizi), P205 and P206 (British Museum), P370 and P371 (Louvre), P415 (Louvre), and P688 (Courtauld Institute, London).

F7 *Lute-player*
B XII.143.3.

By Nicolò Vicentino

Active in the middle of the sixteenth century.

F8 *Christ Healing the Lepers*
B XII.39.15. Signed by Nicolò but not mentioned by Vasari. Related drawing: P690 (Chatsworth).

Another print signed by Nicolò, *Madonna and Child with Four Saints*, B XII.64.23, includes the initials "F. P." but is questionably after Parmigianino. An *Adoration of the Magi*, B XII.30.3, relates to P137 (Frankfurt) and is attributed to Nicolò.

G. Early Metal Engravings after Parmigianino Mentioned by Vasari or Signed

Giovanni Jacopo Caraglio (c. 1500–1570)

In 1526 Caraglio was in Rome, where he engraved designs by Rosso and Perino del Vaga as well as by Parmigianino. In 1539 he was in Poland, and in 1558 at Parma. His engraving of Parmigianino's *Martyrdom of Saints Peter and Paul* has the word "Parmensis" after his signature. The others have "Veronensis."

G1 *Marriage of the Virgin* (signed)
B XV.66.1. Related drawing: P692 (Chatsworth); adapted from Rosso's altarpiece in San Lorenzo, Florence.

G2 *Martyrdom of Saints Peter and Paul* (signed)
B XV.71.8. Related drawing: P190 (British Museum). See also F2.

G3 *Adoration of the Shepherds* (bears monogram and date 1526)
(text p. 67, fig. 46)
B XV.68.4. Related drawing: P631 (Weimar).

G4 *Diogenes* (bears monogram)
B XV.94.61. Related drawings as for F1.

Giulio Bonasone

No reliable biographical information available, but his print after Raphael's *Saint Cecilia* bears the date 1531 and indicates his presence at Bologna at that time. Numerous prints survive, normally inscribed with his name and that of the artist whose work he was reproducing. The following are after Parmigianino:

G5 *Madonna and Child with the Baptist and Saint Jerome* (after A17)
B XV.127.62.

G6 *Marriage of Saint Catherine* (after A18)
B XV.121.47.

G7 *Saint Roch and Donor* (after A4)
B XV.130.70.

G8 *Madonna and Child with Saint Margaret and Others* (after A3)
B XV.126.61.

G9 *Circe*
After Parmigianino's drawing, P85.

G10 *Augustus and the Sibyl*
After Parmigianino's design for which P398 (Louvre), P595r (Turin), and P802 (homeless) are related.

G11 *Madonna and Child with Saint Jerome and the Blessed Bernardino da Feltre*
(text p. 26, fig. 12)
After Parmigianino's lost painting, B2.

Index

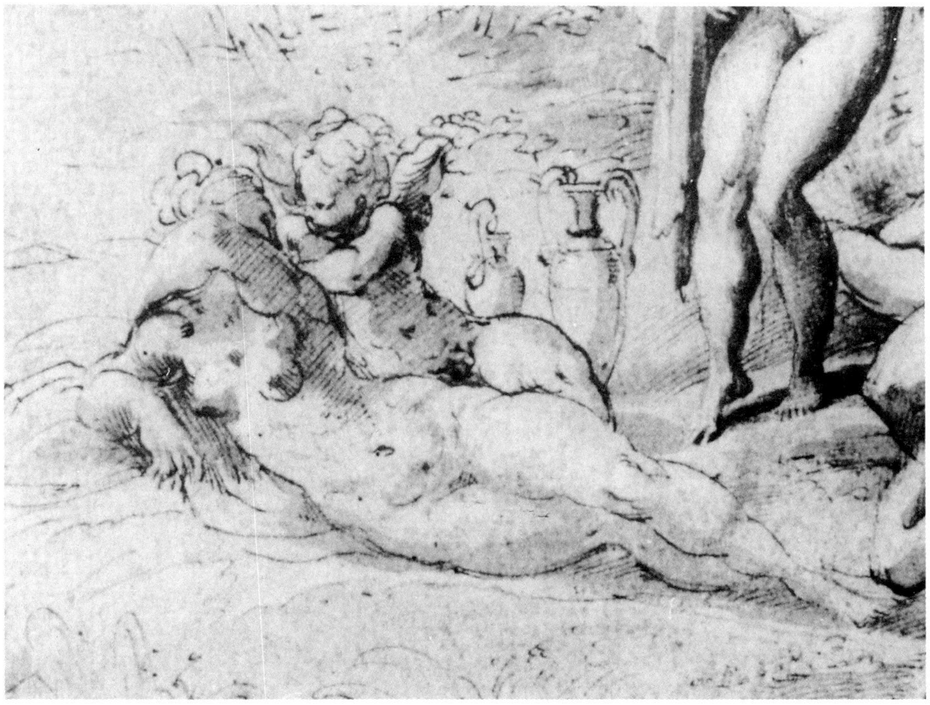

Note: *Italic* page numbers refer to illustrations. Parenthetical numbers are catalog numbers (with letters A–G) or Popham numbers (with letter P; see pp. 6 and 182 for key). Works are by Parmigianino unless otherwise noted; catalog numbers with C indicate doubtful attributions. When a work is mentioned in other catalog entries, the page of its main entry is marked with an asterisk. When details of an illustrated work are shown, the page showing the whole work is marked with an asterisk.

A

Aaron, Santa Maria della Steccata, 135, 190
Abate, Niccolò dell', 139, 165, 193; *The Story of Aristaeus,* 165, *166–67*
Abercorn collection, 186, 196
Aberdeen, Lord, 196
Academia di San Fernando, Madrid, 185; Study for *The Marriage of Saint Catherine,* 139, *142*
Adam, Santa Maria della Steccata, 135, 190
Adam (Michelangelo), Sistine ceiling, 58, 140
Adoration of the Magi (A46), 57, 96–98, *98,* 192
Adoration of the Magi (P137), 83; chiaroscuro after (attrib. Nicolò Vicentino), 83, 199
Adoration of the Shepherds (A44), *see Holy Family*
Adoration of the Shepherds (A54; "*Nativity*"), 39, *40,* 194
Adoration of the Shepherds (C13), 196
Adoration of the Shepherds (D1), 197
Adoration of the Shepherds (P631), 66, *66;* engraving after (G3; Caraglio), 65, 66, *67,* 199
Adrian VI, pope, 57
Affò, Ireneo, 98, 116, 177, 178, 182, 183, 185, 186, 190
Age of Correggio and Carracci catalog (Bologna, 1986), 183, 188, 189, 193, 195
Albertina, *see* Graphische Sammlung Albertina
Albio (Giovantonio Bianchi?), 139–40, 193
Alcazar, Madrid, 188
Allegorical Portrait of Emperor Charles V (A31), 59, 88, 118, *119,* 176, 189*, 195
Allegri, Antonio, *see* Correggio
Althorp, 195
Amato, P., 192
Ambrosiana, Milan: cartoon for *School of Athens* (Raphael), 58
Ampliamenti nell'Officina ferrarese (Longhi), 189, 195
Amsterdam, 184, 186, 198, 199
Ancona, 77
Andrea del Sarto, 12, 46
Angerstein, William, 189
Annunciation, The (C10; probably Bedoli), 195
Annunziata, church of the, Parma, 182
Anselmi, Giorgio, 90, 183
Anselmi, Michelangelo, 14, 76–77, 90, 157, 164, 195; Parma cathedral frescoes: altarpiece, 90, 177 n. III:6; unfulfilled contract, 28; San Giovanni Evangelista frescoes, 22, 196; *Saint Agnes* and *Saint Catherine,* 60–61, 177 n. II:6; Santa Maria della Steccata half-dome (after Giulio Romano), 157
Antal, Frederik, 183
Antea, 188; portrait of, *see Young Woman, A*
Antonella da Messina, 44
Antonio da Trento, 84, 85–86, 198; chiaroscuro woodcuts after Parmigianino: *Augustus and the Sibyl* (F3), 84, 198; *Lute-player* (F7), 199; *Madonna in an Oval* (F5), 84, 199; *Martyrdom of Saints Peter and Paul* (F2), 84, 198; *Naked Man Seen from the Back* (F4), 84, 198; *Saint John the Baptist in the Wilderness* (F6), 199
Antwerp, 168
Apollo (antique sculpture), sketch of (P518), 58
Apollo (periodical), 186, 194
Araldi, Alessandro, 18, 28
Arch of Titus, in *Madonna with Saint Zachariah,* 139, *139*
Aretino, Pietro, 55, 113, 116, 118, 176, 177 n. III:17, 184, 192
Aristaeus, see Story of Aristaeus, The
Armani, Elena Parma, 177, 192
Armano collection, 191
Arnaldi, 186
Arslan, Edoardo, 195
Arte, L' (periodical), 190
Ashmolean Museum, Oxford, 184; drawing (Raphael), 103–4; Studies after Correggio, 14, *15*
Asmus, U. Davitt, 177, 185, 189
Assumption (Torbido, after Giulio Romano), 133
Assunta (Titian), 67
Augustus III, king of Poland, collection of, 184
Augustus and the Sibyl, 160, 198, 199; chiaroscuro after (F3; Antonio da Trento), 84, 198; engraving after (G10; Bonasone), 199
Avory, C., 177

B

Bachiacca (Franceso d'Ubertino), 196
Baglione, Malatesta, 149; portrait of (A49), 107, 118, 149, *151,* 176, 192; woodcut print after, 149, *152,* 192
Baiardi, Cavaliere, 46, 88, 120, 121, 145, 191, 193, 194; portrait of (?), *see Priest or Collector, A;* posthumous inventory of holdings (1561), 121, 190, 191, 193, 194
Baiardi, Elena, 140, 184
Baiardi, Francesco, 186
Baiardi family, 176
Baldassare da Milano, 90, 183
Baptism of Christ, The (A2), 18, *18,* 21, 176, 177 n. I:6, 182
Barberini, *see* Galleria Nazionale Barberini
Bardi altarpiece, *see Mystic Marriage of Saint Catherine, The* (A1)
Baroccio, Federico, 169
Barons Court, Northern Ireland: portrait of an ecclesiastic (C11), 196
Baroque art, 169
Barri, Giacomo, 188
Bartolini, Onofrio, portrait of (attrib. Girolamo da Carpi), 196
Bartolommeo, Fra, 12
Bartsch, Adam von, 183, 187, 197, 198
Basel, 149, 153, 192
Bassano, Jacopo, 165
Bathoe, 190
Bayonne, 188, 199; study for *Saint Barbara,* 21
Beccafumi, Domenico, 12, 77, 164, 177 n. II:12
Bedoli, Girolamo Mazzola, 18, 23–24, 125, 155, 160, 164–65, 176; altarpieces: San Giovanni Evangelista, 24, 177; Santa Maria Annunciata, Viadana, 196; barrel vaults, Santa Maria della Steccata (after Parmigianino), 157, 178 n. IV:11; *Immaculate Conception,* 176; polyptych, Cistercian abbey of San Martino de' Bocci, 164–65; works attributed to, 193, 195,

196; *The Annunciation* (C10), 195; *Lucretia* (C6), 160, 178 n. IV:16, 195
Beethoven, Ludwig von, 178 n. IV:20
Béguin, Sylvie, 191, 196
Bellange, Jacques, 168; *The Three Marys at the Sepulchre*, 168, *168*
Belli, Valerio and Elio, 192
Bellini, Giovanni, 44
Bellona (Schiavone), 165, *165*
Berenson, Bernard, 182, 183, 186, 189, 192, 193, 195, 196
Berlin, 190, 195; Kupferstichkabinett, Studies for the Fontanellato fresco, 31–32, *39*, *175**, 185; Staatliche Museen (former Bode Museum), *The Baptism of Christ* (A2), 18, *18*, 21, 176, 177 n. I:6, 182
Bernardi da Castelbolognesi, G., portrait of (?) (C7), 195
Bernardino da Feltre, see Madonna and Child with Saint Jerome and the Blessed Bernardino da Feltre
Bertini, Giuseppe, 187, 188, 189, 195, 196
Bertoja (Jacopo Zanguidi), 165, 168, 178 n. IV:22, 197; father of, 178 n. IV:21
Bertoja, Il (A. G. Quintavalle), 178
Besançon, 183
Between Renaissance and Baroque, 193
Bianchi, Giovantonio (Albio?), 193
Biblioteca Nacional, Madrid, 184, 194
Biondo, M., 183
Bishop Rangone, 194
Bloemaert, Abraham, 169
Blunt, Anthony, 177
Boccaccio Boccaccino: frescoes, Cremona Cathedral, 15
Bode Museum, now Staatliche Museen, *see* Berlin
Boggero, Franco, 192
Bologna: artists, 11, 13, 15, 18, 83, 165, 169, 198; coronation (1530), 118, 176, 177 n. III:17; Parmigianino in, 7, 15, 18, 28, 55, 58–59, 77, 79, 83–122, 125, 139, 149, 164, 176, 187; works in, 117; Julius II statue (Michelangelo), 75; Museo Davio Bargellini, 187; Palazzo Casale, 196; Palazzo Giusti, 183; Palazzo Tanari, 183; San Giovanni al Monte, *Saint Cecilia* (Raphael), 20, 21; Santa Margherita, 183; *see also* Pinacoteca Nazionale; San Petronio
Bologna, Ferdinando, 195, 196
Bonasone, Giulio, 83, 185, 199; engravings after Parmigianino: *Augustus and the Sibyl* (G10), 199; *Circe* (G9), 199; *Madonna and Child with Saint Jerome and the Blessed Bernardino da Feltre* (G11), 26, *26*, 194, 199*; *Madonna and Child with Saint Margaret and Others* (G8), 183, 199*; *Madonna and Child with the Baptist and Saint Jerome* (G5), 187, 199*; *Marriage of Saint Catherine* (G6), 187, 199*; *Saint Roch and Donor* (G7), 183, 199*
Bone, H., 193
Bonelli, Angelo, 193
Bonelli, Cipriano, 190
Bordone, Paris, 46
Borenius, Tancred, 196
Borghese, Camillo, *see* Paul V
Borghese, Scipione, 187
Borghese gallery, *see* Galleria Borghese
Borghese palace, *see* Palazzo Borghese
Borghini, Raffaello, 176, 177–78 n. IV:7
Boschini, Marco, 193
Boston Museum of Fine Arts: *The Three Marys at the Sepulchre* (Bellange), 168, *168*
Botticelli, Sandro, 44
Brahan, H., 187
Brescia, 15, 46
Bridgewater collection, 197
Bridgewater Madonna (Raphael), 39
British Institution, 186
British Museum, London, 27, 107, 184, 186, 189, 190, 191, 197, 198, 199; *Diana and Nymphs*, 154, *154**, *201*; *Man Holding a Bitch*, 107, 162, *163*; portrait of Charles V and Paul III (Sebastiano del Piombo), 118; *Presentation in the Temple*, 58; *Standard-Bearer*, 154, *156*; Study for *Madonna and Child with the Baptist and Saint Jerome*, 70, 72, *72*, 187; Study for *Madonna dal Collo Lungo*, 142, *144*, 184; study for Sebastiano's Lazarus (Michelangelo), 75; Study for the vault of Santa Maria della Steccata, 126, 129, *130*, 135
Bronzino (Agnolo di Cosimo), 46, 196
Bruges: Nôtre Dame, *Madonna of Bruges* (Michelangelo), *73*, 73–75, 158
Budapest, 191; Szépmüvészeti Múzeum, *Madonna del Latte* (Correggio), 116, *117*
Bufalina [Caccialupi], Maria, 186
Bufalini church (Sant'Agostino), Città di Castello, 186
Bufalini family, 186
Bufalini, Niccolò, 194
Burckhardt, Jacob, 169
Burlington Fine Arts Club, London, 196
Burlington Magazine, 177, 186, 195

C

Cambiaso, Luca, 192
Cambridge, England: Fitzwilliam Museum, 188
Cambridge, Massachusetts: Fogg Museum, Study for the Bardi altarpiece, 18–19, *20*, 182
Camera di San Paolo, Parma (Correggio), 24, 31, 32, *38*, 125
Camilla Gonzaga, Countess of San Secondo, with Three Children (A25), 107, 149–53, *153*, 188*, 196, 197
Campi, Giulio, 196
Campori, Giuseppe, 182, 188
Capitoline Museum, *see* Museo Capitolino
Capodimonte, *see* Galleria Nazionale di Capodimonte
Capo di Ponte, church of, Parma, 182
Caprarola, 165, 168
Caraglio, Giovanni Jacopo, 199; engravings after Parmigianino: *Adoration of the Shepherds* (G3), 65, 66, 67, 199; *Diogenes* (G4), 65, 77, 83, 198, 199*; *Marriage of the Virgin* (G1), 57, 65, 66, 70, 199; *Martyrdom of Saints Peter and Paul* (G2), 65, 84, 199; after Rosso, *Saturn and Philyra*, 60, *61*

Caravaggio (Michelangelo Merisi), 122, 169
Cardigan, earl of, 177 n. I:20
Carmignano: Pieve di San Michele, *Visitation* (Pontormo), *78*, 79, *80**, 147
Caroto, Giovanni Francesco, 15
Carr, Holwell, 186
Carracci, Annibale, 169, 172, 191
Carracci, Lodovico, 183
Carrari, Vincenzo, 188
Carta del Navegar pitoresco (Boschini), 193
Casalmaggiore, 157; Servite church, 142, 160; *see also* Santo Stefano
Castaldo, Giovanni Battista, portraits of (A28), 107, 113, *114*, 189; (Titian), 113
Castello Sforzesco, Milan: altar (Mantegna), 122; *Man in Black* (A26), 46, *47*, 188
Castle Howard: *Four Young Men* (C18), 197
Catalogo della Galleria ex-Fidecommissaria Doria-Pamphilj (Sestieri), 192
Catalogue of the Drawings of Parmigianino (Popham), 6
Cavalca, Marcantonio, 193
Cavalcaselle, Giovanni Battista, 177, 196
Cavalli, Matteo, 184
Cavazolla (Paolo Miranda), 177 n. II:5
Cellini, Benvenuto, 188
Certosa di Galluzzo, Florence, frescoes (Pontormo), 77, 148
Cesi, Agnolo, 194
Charles I, king of England, collection of, 184, 186, 189, 193
Charles II, king of England, collection of, 186
Charles V, Holy Roman emperor, 118, 122, 152, 176; portraits of (A31), 59, 88, 118, *119*, 176, 189*, 195; (Titian), 118
Chastel, André, 177
Chatsworth, 107, 182, 183, 184, 185, 188, 192, 197, 198, 199; *Christ Healing the Lepers*, 65, 83; *Mutius Scaevola*, 86, *88*, 198; Study for *Madonna della Rosa*, 39, 118, *118*, 184; Study for *Marriage of the Virgin*, 66–67, *68*, 70, 199
chiaroscuro woodcuts, 83, 198
Christ before Caiaphas (Romanino), 16, *16*
Christ Church, Oxford, 183
Christ Healing the Lepers (P690), 65, 83; chiaroscuro after (F8; Nicolò Vicentino), 83, 199
Christ Healing the Sick, sketch for (P5), 65
Christian art, post-peak problem of, 12–13
Christiansen, Keith, 195
Christie's, London, 193, 197
Christina, queen of Sweden, collection of, 197
Christ on the Road to Calvary (Pordenone), 24–26
Cima da Conegliano, Giovanni Battista, 13–14, 164; altarpiece for Parma Cathedral, 21
Cini collection, Venice, *Holy Family and Angels* (C17), 196
Circe (P73), 154, *155*, 160
Circe (P85), 154, 160; engraving after (G9; Bonasone), 199
Circumcision, The (A6), 21, 42, *44*, 55, 183; Study for (P369), *45*, 183
Città di Castello, 194; Palazzo Bufalini, 186; Palazzo Mancini, 186; Sant'Agostino, 186
City Art Gallery, *see* York
Clark, Kenneth, 12, 177
Clement VII (Giulio de' Medici), pope, 42, 55, 58, 65, 113, 117, 118, 176, 183, 184, 188, 192
Columbia Museum of Art, 42, 183
Como, Museo di (Giovio's museum), 118, 176
Contessa di San Secondo, see Camilla Gonzaga
"Contessa Gozzadini", see Woman, A
Conversion of Saul (A51), 88, 139–40, 165, 193
Cook collection, Richmond, 187, 189; *Portrait of a Youth* (C16), 196
Copenhagen: Statens Museum fur Kunst, *Lorenzo Cybo and His Page* (A5), 42, *54*, *56**, 60, 107, 183*, 189
Copertini, Giovanni, 125, 182, 193, 196
Cornelis van Haarlem, 169
Coronation of the Virgin, Santa Maria della Steccata, 125–26, 191
Corradini, Sandro, 177, 186
Correggio (Antonio Allegri), 14–15, 17, 22, 26, 27, 29, 39, 46, 47, 72, 73, 76, 79, 85, 88, 104, 122, 125, 126, 135, 145, 164, 169, 176, 177 n. I:19, 178 nn. IV:9, 15, 193; departure from Parma, 15, 83; posthumous reputation, 164, 165, 169–72; works: Camera di San Paolo frescoes, 24, 31, 32, 33, *38*, 125; *Ganymede*, 122; *Holy Family*, 102, 103; *Holy Family with Saint Francis*, 26, 39; *Io*, 122; *Madonna and Child with Saint Jerome and Others*, 12, 13, *13*, 90, *94**, 96, 125, 144; *Madonna and Child with Saint Sebastian*, 72, *73*; *Madonna del Latte*, 116, *117*; *Madonna of Albinea*, 26; *Madonna of the Basket*, 145–47, *146*; *Madonna with Saint Francis*, 182; *Madonna with Saint George and Others*, 85, *87*; *Marriage of Saint Catherine*, 102, *102*; *Martyrdom of Four Saints*, 47; *Noli Me Tangere*, 83; Parma cathedral frescoes, 28, 125; *Pietà*, 85; *Portrait of Parmigianino(?)*, *52*, 53, 107; San Giovanni Evangelista frescoes, 14, 22, 24, 26, 28-29, 47, *49*, 125, 132, 135, *136*, 177 n. I:17, IV:3; Parmigianino's studies after, 14, *15*, 24; works sometimes attributed to, 62, 122, 188, 192, 193, 196
Correggio, Italy: San Francesco, *Madonna with Saint Francis* (Correggio), 182
"Correggio Giovane" (Longhi), 188
Corsini Gallery, Rome, 184, 185
Corti del Rinascimento nella provincia di Parma (Mulazzini), 185
Costa, Lorenzo il Vecchio, 15
Costantino, Sala di, *see* Sala di Costantino
Count of San Secondo, see Pier Maria Rossi
Courtauld Institute, London, 193, 197, 199; *Holy Family with Angel ("Nativity")* (A20), 39, *40*, 187; *Madonna and Child* (A21), 79, 96, 97, *97*, 118, 187*, 194
Cradle of Children (B9), 194
Cranach, Lucas, 46
Cremona, 195; cathedral frescoes, 15–16, 24–26, 39, 62, 164; *Christ before Caiaphas* (Romanino), 16, *16*; *Christ on the Road to Calvary* (Pordenone), 24–26; *The Flight into Egypt* (Melone), 39; style of, 18, 42
Crivelli, Carlo: *Immaculate Conception*, 176
Crowe, Joseph Archer, 177, 196
Cupid (antique sculpture), 121–22, *123*
Cupid Cutting His Bow (A52), *1*, 88, 120–22, *121**, 193*, 194; Study for (P543), 121, *122*
Curzon family, 186
Cybo, Lorenzo, 42, 186; portrait of (A5), 42, *54*, *56**, 60, 107, 183*, 189

D

Dacos, N. 178
Dacosta Kaufman, Thomas, 178
Dall'Acqua, Marzio, 17, 125, 185, 189
Darmstadt, 197
David (A37), *9*, 29, *31**, 191
David (Michelangelo), sketch of (P175), 58
Davis, Harris and Hart, 186
Dead Christ Mourned by the Marys, 197
Death of Meleager, The (antique relief), 85
Degrazia, Diane, 178, 194, 195
Del Bono chapel (Correggio), 24, 177
Dell'Abate, Niccolò, *see* Abate, Niccolò dell'
Della Pergola, P., 191
Deposition (Pontormo), 147, *148*
Deposition (Rosso), 148

Descrizione ragionata della Galleria Doria (Tonci), 192
Detroit Institute of Arts: *The Circumcision* (A6), 21, 42, *44*, 55, 183
Diana and Actaeon (A12), Fontanellato fresco, *10*, 30–38, *32*, *33*, *34*, *35**, *36–37*, 39, 185; sketch for (P313V), 33; Studies for (P12), 31–32, *39*, *175**, 185
Diana and Nymphs (P74), 154, *154**, 201
Dianti, Laura, portrait of (Titian), 60
Di Giampaolo, M., 178
Diogenes design, 77–79, 83; chiaroscuro after (F1; Ugo da Carpi), *76*, 77, 83, 177 n. II:13, 198; engraving after (G4; Caraglio), 65, 77, 83, 198, 199*
Diogenes (P551), 154
Dioscuri, see Horse Tamers
Dolce, Lodovico, 12, 13, 177
Domus Aurea, Rome, 132, 139, 178 n. IV:8
Doni tondo (Michelangelo), 197
Donna Velata (Raphael), 105
Donnington Priory, 185, 189; Study for the *Sanvitale* portrait, 47–51, *51*, 189
Doort, van der, inventory of, 193
Dosso Dossi, 15, 16, 46, 164; *Saint Sebastian with the Baptist and Saint Jerome*, 16, *17*
Dresden, *see* Gemäldegalerie
Du Bois, J., 188
Dürer, Albrecht, 46, 63, 65, 85; *Marienleben*, 42
Durno, James, 186
Dyck, Anthony van, 160, 178 n. IV:20

E

Ecole des Beaux-Arts, Paris: *Saint Christopher* (P528), 154
Edinburgh: *Bridgewater Madonna* (Raphael), 39
Ekserdjian, D., 183, 184, 190
Elogia virorum bellica virtute illustrium (Giovio), with woodcut of *Malatesta Baglione*, 149, *152*, 192
Elogia Virorum Rosciorum, 188
Emporium (periodical), 187, 195
England, Parmigianino's influence in, 169
engravings, 63–65, 197–98
Entombment (Fontana), 85
Entombment (Giambologna), 85, 177 n. III:3
Entombment (Goujon), 85, 165, 177 n. III:3
Entombment (Tintoretto), 85
Entombment of Christ (D2), 85, *86*, 165, 177 n. III:3, 197
Estasi di Santa Cecilia di Raffaello d'Urbino nella Pinacoteca Nazionale, L' (Bologna, 1983), 177
Este, Francesco d', of Modena, 184
Este, Isabella d', 176; Studiolo, 176, 178 n. IV:9
Este inventory (1624), 188
Eternal (Michelangelo), 26
Eve, Santa Maria della Steccata, 135, 160, 190
Exhibition of the King's Pictures, 177
Expulsion of Heliodorus (Raphael), 140
Eyck, Jan van, 43

F

Fabrizio da Milano, 90, 183
Fagiolo dell'Arco, Maurizio, 177, 178 n. IV:8, 185, 188, 189, 193
Failure of Nerve, A (Clark), 177
Fantuzzi, Antonio, 85–86
Farnese, Alessandro, 176; *see also* Paul III
Farnese, Orazio, portrait of, 196
Farnese, Pier Luigi, portrait of (Titian), 196
Farnese, Rannucio, 187, 189, 195
Farnese collection, 60, 189, 196
Farnese family and circle, 13, 168
Feast in the House of Simon (Marcantonio after Raphael), sketch after (P746), 58
Ferrara, 15, 16
Fiesole: San Francesco, *Immaculate Conception* (Piero di Cosimo), 176
Fiocco, Giuseppe, 192
Fire at the Borgo (Raphael), 132
Fitzwilliam Museum, Cambridge, England, 188
Flanders, 43
Flight into Egypt, Santa Maria Steccata, 191
Flight into Egypt, The (Melone), 39
Florence, 11, 12, 57, 77–79, 149, 165, 168; Parmigianino in (?), 57, 76, 77, 79, 177 n. II:13; portraiture, 46; works in: Certosa di Galluzzo, 77, 148; Horne Museum, 197; Santi Apostoli, *Immaculate Conception* (Vasari), 176; *see also* Carmignano; Palazzo Pitti; San Lorenzo; Santa Felicita; Uffizi
Florence and Italy, Renaissance Studies in Honour of Nicolai Rubinstein, 190
Fogg Museum, Cambridge, Massachusetts: Study for the Bardi altarpiece, 18–19, *20*, 182
Fontainebleau, 165, 169, 178, 198
Fontana, G. G., 185
Fontana, Prospero: *Entombment*, 85
Fontanellato, 14, 28, 176; Rocca Sanvitale frescoes, 21, 31; *Diana and Actaeon* (A12), *10*, 30–38, *32*, *33*, *34*, *35**, *36–37*, 39, 185; putti, 28, 29, 31, 32–33; Studies for, 33, 47, 185; (P12), 31–32, *39*, *175**, 185
Forlì: *Immaculate Conception* (Zaganelli), 176
Fornarina portrait (Raphael), 105
Fornari-Schianchi, Lucia, 14, 176, 177, 177 n. I:17, 191
Fortitude (E7), 198
Four Temperaments, The, San Giovanni Evangelista, 24, 190
Fourth Style, 135–39
Four Young Men (C18), 197
France, 11, 13, 18; paintings taken to, 189, 195
Francia (Francesco Raibolini), 13–14, 15, 18, 164, 196; *Madonna Enthroned with Saints*, 19
Franciabigio (Francesco di Cristofano), 46, 196
François I, king of France, 152
Frankfurt, 199; Städelsches Kunstinstitut, *Saint Catherine of Alexandria* (A13), 39, *41*, 186
Frari, church of, Venice: *Assunta* (Titian), 67
Frati de' Zoccoli, church of, Viadana: *Saint Francis Receiving the Stigmata and Saint Clare* (B1), 176, 194
Freedberg, Sydney J., 7, 18, 42, 177, 182, 183, 188, 189, 189, 192, 193, 194, 195, 196, 197
Fröhlich-Bum, Lili, 11, 188

G

Gaddi, Luigi, 194
Galeazzo Sanvitale, Count of Fontanellato (A29), 21, 38, 39, 42, 47–53, *50*, 60, 107, 183, 189*; Study for (P748V), 47–51, *51*, 189
Galleria Borghese, Rome: *A Prelate* (A42), 82, 113, *115**, 191
Galleria Borghese; I Dipinti (Pergola), 191
Galleria Doria, Rome: *Holy Family (Adoration of the Shepherds)* (A44), 60–61, 62, *62*, 102, 192; *Madonna and Child* (A43), 60–61, 62–63, *63*, 192
Galleria Estense (ducal gallery), Modena, 184; *Holy Family with Saints and a Donor* (C4), 195
Galleria Nazionale, Parma, 185, 186, 187, 189, 193, 194, 195, 196, 197; *Adoration of the Shepherds* (C13), 196; altarpiece (Rondani), 23; altarpiece for Parma Cathedral (Cima), 21; *Diogenes*,

Galleria Nazionale, Parma *(continued):* 154; *Immaculate Conception* (Bedoli), 176; *Madonna and Child with Saint Jerome and Others* (Correggio), 12, 13, *13*, 90, *94**, 96, 125, 144; *Madonna Enthroned with Saints* (Francia), 19; *Mystic Marriage of Saint Catherine* (after Parmigianino), 26, *27*, 42, 194; *Self-Portrait* (A39), 107, *111*, 157, 191*, 194; polyptych, abbey of San Martino de' Bocci (Bedoli), 164–65; Study for *Cupid Cutting His Bow*, *121*, *122*, 193; Study for *Madonna dal Collo Lungo* (P553), 144, *145;* Study for the *Visitation*, *78*, 79, *81**, 96, 154, 161, 187; *Venus, Mars, and Vulcan*, 154; *A Young Woman* (A38; *"Turkish Slave"*), 107, *112*, 191*, 193
Galleria Nazionale Barberini, Rome: Fornarina portrait (Raphael), 105; male portrait (Girolamo da Carpi), 195
Galleria Nazionale di Capodimonte, Naples, 189, 191, 195, 196; Annunciation altarpiece (Bedoli), 195; *Galeazzo Sanvitale, Count of Fontanellato* (A29), 21, 38, 39, 42, 47–51, *50*, 60, 107, 183, 189*; *Holy Family with the Infant Baptist* (A30), 103–5, *106*, 189*, 191; *Lucretia* (C6; probably Bedoli), 195; *Madonna del Gatto* (Giulio Romano), 102, *104; A Man* (*"G. B. Castaldo"*) (A28), 107, 113, *114*, 189; *Marriage of Saint Catherine* (Correggio), 102, *102; Parma Embracing Alessandro Farnese* (Bedoli), 195; *Portrait of a Man* (*"G. Bernardi da Castelbolognesi"*) (C7), 195; *Portrait of a Man* (*"Gian Martino Sanvitale"*) (C9), 195; *Portrait of a Youth with Hand on Hip* (C8; now attrib. Rosso Fiorentino), 195; *Portrait of Girolamo de' Vicenti* (C5; probably Girolamo da Carpi), 195; *Woman Playing the Clavichord* (Bedoli), 195; *Young Man* (Rosso Fiorentino), 59, *60*; *A Young Woman* (*"Antea"*) (A27), 107, 149, *150*, 163, 188
Galleria Spada, Rome: *Three Heads* (A45), 192
Galleria Spada in Roma, La (Zeri), 192
Gamba, C., 187
Ganymede (Correggio), 122
Garofalo (Benvenuto Tisi), 15, 155, 176
Gazette des Beaux-Arts (periodical), 177
"G. B. Castaldo," see Man, A
Gemäldegalerie, Dresden: *Madonna and Child (Madonna della Rosa)* (A7), 88, 96, 113–18, *116*, 122, 139, 164, 184; *Madonna and Child with Saint Sebastian* (Correggio), 72, *73; Madonna and Child with Saint Stephen, the Baptist, and a Donor* (A8), 12, 75, 152, 157–60, *159*, 160, 163, 164, 172, 176, 177 n. III:11, 184; *Madonna with Saint Francis* (Correggio), 182; *Madonna with Saint George and Others* (Correggio), 85, *87; Portrait of a Youth* (C1), 195
Ghirlandaio, Domenico, 44, 60, 177 n. II:5
Giambologna, 168, 169; *Entombment*, 85, 177 n. III:3
Giambologna (Avory), 177
Gianni, Bartolomei de', 184
Gianni, Dionigi de', 184
Giorgione (Giorgione da Castelfranco), 46; circle of, 60, 177 n. II:5
Giovanni da Udine: ceiling, Sala dei Pontefici (with Perino del Vaga), 55, 131–32, *134*
Giovio, Paolo, 118, 149, 176; *Elogia virorum bellica virtute illustrium* with Parmigianino's woodcut, *Malatesta Baglione*, 149, *152*, 192
Girolamo da Carpi, 113, 155, 176, 189, 195, 196, 197; *Onofrio Bartolini* (attrib.), 196; *Portrait of Girolamo de' Vicenti* (C5; attrib.), 195
Girolamo da Carpi (Mezzetti), 189, 195
Girolamo da Treviso, 192
Giulio Romano, 12, 15, 57, 65, 102, 157, 164, 176; *Assumption*, 133; half-dome, Santa Maria della Steccata, 157; *Madonna del Gatto*, 102, *104;* Parmigianino's letter to, 157, 178 n. IV:15
God the Father and Angels, San Giovanni Evangelista, 24, 26, 39, 190
Goethe, 177 n. III:7
Goltzius, Hendrick, 169
Gonzaga, Camilla, countess of San Secondo, portrait of (A25), 107, 149–53, *153*, 188*, 196, 197
Gonzaga, Federigo, 176
Gonzaga, Paola, 185
Gordon, Sir Robert, 196
Goujon, Jean: *Entombment*, 85, 165, 177 n. III:3
Gould, Cecil, 7, 177, 178, 185, 186, 187, 188, 194
Gozzadini, Bonifazio, 139, 184, 185; portrait of (B3), 194
Gozzadini, Contessa, portrait of (A50), 107, 139, *140*, 191, 193*
Graphische Sammlung, Weimar: Study for the *Adoration of the Shepherds* (P631), 66, *66*
Graphische Sammlung Albertina, Vienna, 187, 193; *Self-Portrait* (P600), 107, *111;* Study for *Lovers in a Wood*, *84*, 84–85, 197; Study for the vault of Santa Maria della Steccata, 134, *135*
Greco, El, 165
Guardaroba (R. Farnese), 187, 189, 195

H

Haarlem, 199; academy and style of, 169
Haarlem, Cornelis van, 169
Hague, The: Mauritshuis, 188
Hampton Court Palace, 184, 192; *Head and Bust of Athene* (A15), 160, *161*, 186*, 194; *Holy Family* (Correggio), 102, *103; Odonti* (Lotto), 177 n. I:19; *A Young Man (Portrait of a Youth)* (A14), 105–7, *110*, 177 n. III:11, 186
Hanover: Niedersächsisches, *Saint Jerome* (Pontormo), 77, *77–79*, 177 n. II:13
Harari & Johns Ltd., London, 194
Hartt, Frederick, 178
Head and Bust of Athene (A15), 160, *161*, 186*, 194
Head of a Youth, 194
Healing of the Lame Man (Raphael), etching after, 58, 85, 197
Heinemann, 193
Heintz, Joseph, 193
Henry VIII, king of England, portrait of (?), 195
Hercolani collection, 83
Hercules and Cerberus (E8), 198
Hermitage, Saint Petersburg, 190
Hirst, M., 177, 196
History of Painting in Italy, The (Lanzi), 184
Holbein, Hans, 46, 153
Holland, Parmigianino's influence in, 169
Holy Family (A44; *Adoration of the Shepherds*), 60–61, 62, *62*, 102, 192
Holy Family (Correggio), 102, *103*
Holy Family and Angels (C17), 196
Holy Family and Angels (C19), 197
Holy Family with an Angel (A20; *"Nativity"*), 39, *40*, 187
Holy Family with Angels (A23; Prado *Holy Family*), 21, 39, 42, *43*, 55, 58, 61, 188; study for (P396r), 42, 188
Holy Family with Angels (B5), 194
Holy Family with Saint Francis (Correggio), 26, 39
Holy Family with Saints and a Donor (C4), 195
Holy Family with the Infant Baptist (A30), 103–5, *106*, 189*, 191
Holyrood, 186
Horne Museum, Florence, 197
Horse Tamers (*Dioscuri;* ancient sculpture), 24–26, 177 n. I:15
Hounds Coursing a Stag (E10), 198
Huntsman (P282), 154

I

Ignudi (Michelangelo), drawings after, 26
Imago Mariae (Amato), 192
Immaculate Conception, iconography of, 70, 176
Imperia, *see* Taggia
Ineffabilis Deus (papal bull; Pius IX), 176
Io (Correggio), 122
Istoria dei Rossi Parmensi (Carrari), 188
Italian Etchers of the Renaissance (Reed and Wallace), 197
Italian Journey (Goethe), 177
Italy, portraiture in, 43, 44, 45

J

James I, king of England, 169
James II, king of England, collection of, 190
Joannides, Paul, 7, 177
Jones, Inigo, 169
Judith, 160
Judith (D3), etching, 197
Julius II, pope, statue of (Michelangelo), 75
Jupiter tonans (antique sculpture), 75

K

Kedleston Hall: *Madonna and Child* (A16), 96, 97, *97*, 186
Kent, William, 186
Kinnaird, Lord, 187
Kisters collection: portrait of Laura Dianti (Titian), 60
Knole, 186
Kunsthaus, Zurich, 194
Kunsthistoriches Museum, Vienna, 186; *Conversion of Saul* (A51), 88, 139–40, 193; *Cupid Cutting His Bow* (A52), *1*, 88, 120–22, *121**, 193*, 194; *Ganymede* (Correggio), 122; *Io* (Correggio), 122; *Malatesta Baglione* (A49), 107, 118, 149, *151*, 176, 192; *Self-Portrait in a Convex Mirror* (A48), 21, 42, 43, *51*, 53, 55, 107, 118, 192; *Triumph of Wisdom* (Spranger), 169, *170*, *173**; *A Woman ("Contessa Gozzadini")* (A50), 107, *140*, 191, 193*; *A Young Man with a Book* (A47), *95*, 96, 192
Kupferstichkabinett, Berlin: Studies for the Fontanellato fresco, 31–32, *39*, *175**, 185
Kurz lesenswürdige Erinnerung der Seltenheiten in und um Wien (Tolner), 193

L

La Fontana (Servite church), Motta San Fermo, near Casalmaggiore, 142, 160
Lamentation, etching, 85
Lamo, Pietro, 90, 183, 185, 193
Lanzi, Luigi, 184
Läocöon (antique sculpture), studies of, 58
Lappoli, Giovann'Antonio, 42, 57, 176
Last Judgment (Michelangelo), 75
Lawrence, Sir T., 187
Lazareff, V., 190
Lazzarini, Cavaliere, 184
Leonardo da Vinci, 12, 15, 46, 76, 83, 164; *Madonna with Saint Anne*, 61; *Saint Jerome*, 177 n. II:13
Leopardi, Giacomo, 178 n. IV:20
Leopold William, Archduke, 193
Lepicié, Bernard: *Saturn and Philyra* (after Parmigianino), 60, *61*, 194
Lesser, 189
Lettere artistiche inedite (Campori), 188
Leuchtenberg catalog, Munich, 183
Leuti, Luca dai, 104, 189, 191
Levey, Sir Michael, 7
Liverpool, 195
Lombardy, 62, 165
London, 169; Burlington Fine Arts Club, 196; cartoon for *Madonna with Saint Anne* (Leonardo da Vinci), 61; Harari & Johns Ltd., 194; Royal Academy, 177, 197; Wellington Museum, 187; *see also* British Museum; Courtauld Institute; Hampton Court; National Gallery; Victoria and Albert Museum
London altarpiece, *see Madonna and Child with the Baptist and Saint Jerome*
Longhi, Roberto, 113, 188, 189, 192, 195, 197
Lorenzini, 147
Lorenzo Cybo and His Page (A5), 42, *54*, *56**, 60, 107, 183*, 189
Lorraine, ducal court at Nancy, 165–68, 169
Lotto, Lorenzo, 46, 164, 177 n. I:19, 195, 197; *Odonti*, 177 n. I:19
Louvre, Musée du, Paris, 24, 27, 42, 107, 126, 177, 178, 182, 183, 184, 185, 188, 189, 190, 191, 193, 197, 198, 199; design for the Bardi altarpiece, 18; *Entombment* (Goujon), 85, 165, 177 n. III:3; *Madonna with Saint Anne* (Leonardo da Vinci), 61; *The Marriage of Saint Catherine, and a Male Saint* (A32), 103, *105*, *108–9**, 176, 190; *Parnassus* (Mantegna), 178 n. IV:9; portrait (Ghirlandaio), 177 n. II:5; *Portrait of a Young Man with His Hand to His Head* (C12), 196; *Portrait of Parmigianino(?)* (Correggio), *52*, 53, 107; sketch of Diogenes or Saint Jerome, 65, 79; Study for *The Circumcision*, 42–43, *45*, 183; *Youth with a Bitch*, 162, *163*
Lovers in a Wood (D4), *84*, 84–85, 197; Study for (P612), *84*, 84–85, 197
Lowenthal, Anne W., 178
Lucco (Looklet), M., 191
Lucretia (B6), 160, 176, 194
Lucretia (C6; probably Bedoli), 195
Lucretia (Raphael), 160
Lucretia (Vico, after Parmigianino), 160
Lute-player (F7; Antonio da Trento, after Parmigianino), 199
Lycett Green, F. D., 193

M

Mabuse (Jan Gossaert), 46
Madonna (B6; "Madonna abbozzata"?), 194
Madonna (Antonio da Trento), *see Madonna in an Oval*
"Madonna abbozzata," 118, 187, 194
Madonna and Child (A7; *Madonna della Rosa*), 88, 96, 113–18, *116*, 122, 139, 164, 184; Study for (P702r), 39, 118, *118*, 184
Madonna and Child (A16; at Kedleston Hall), 96, 97, *97*, 186
Madonna and Child (A21; at Courtauld Institute), 79, 96, 97, *97*, 118, 187*, 194
Madonna and Child (A41; at Palazzetto Eucherio Sanvitale), 38–39, 191
Madonna and Child (A43; at Galleria Doria), 60–61, 62–63, *63*, 192
Madonna and Child (D5), 197
Madonna and Child with Angels (A9; *Madonna dal Collo Lungo*), 13, 79, 90, 116, 140–48, *143**, 149, 157, 164, 168, 169, *171*, 176, 184*, 188; studies for, 142–44, 147, 164, 184; (B.M.), 142, *144*; (P553), 144, *145*; (P327), 144, *145*, 164

Madonna and Child with Four Saints (Nicolò Vicentino, after Parmigianino?), 199
Madonna and Child with Saint Catherine and Saint John, 194
Madonna and Child with Saint Jerome and Others (Correggio), 12, 13, *13*, 90, *94**, 96, 125, 144
Madonna and Child with Saint Jerome and the Blessed Bernardino da Feltre (B2), 26, 176, 194*; engraving after (G11; Bonasone), 26, *26*, 194, 199
Madonna and Child with Saint Margaret and Others (G8; Bonasone, after Parmigianino), 199
Madonna and Child with Saint Sebastian (Correggio), 72, *73*
Madonna and Child with Saints Margaret and Jerome, a Mitered Saint, and an Angel (A3; *Saint Margaret* altarpiece), 12, *12*, 13, 88, 90–97, *91**, *92*, *93*, 98, 147, 158, 169, 183; Study for (P79), 90, *94*, 98, 183; engraving after (G11; Bonasone), 199
Madonna and Child with Saint Stephen, the Baptist, and a Donor (A8; Dresden altarpiece), 12, 75, 152, 157–60, *159*, 160, 163, 164, 172, 176, 177 n. III:11, 184
Madonna and Child with Saints Zachariah, Mary Magdalene, and the Infant Baptist (A10), 88, 98, *124*, 139, *139*, 140, *141**, 165, 184–85
Madonna and Child with the Baptist and Saint Jerome (A17; London altarpiece), 13, 55, 65, 67–76, 69, 90, 142, 147, 148, 158, 172, 176, 186–87; studies for (P181r), 70, 72, 79, 187; (P107), 65, 79, 187; engraving after (G5; Bonasone), 199
Madonna and Saints altarpieces: for titles, *see* Madonna with Child and Saints altarpieces
Madonna with the Baptist and Saint Jerome, see Madonna and Child with the Baptist and Saint Jerome
Madonna dal Collo Lungo, see Madonna and Child with Angels
Madonna del Gatto (Giulio Romano), 102, *104*
Madonna della Rosa, see Madonna and Child
Madonna del Latte (Correggio), 116, *117*
Madonna Enthroned with Saints (Francia), 19
Madonna in an Oval (F5; Antonio da Trento, after Parmigianino), 84, 199
Madonna in Glory, composition, 70, 72–73, 158
Madonna in Glory (Titian), 77
Madonna of Albinea (Correggio), 26
Madonna of Bruges (Michelangelo), 73, *73*–*75*, 158
Madonna of Foligno (Raphael), 70
Madonna of the Basket (Correggio), 145–47, *146*
Madonna with Child and Saints (*Madonna and Saints*) altarpieces, 12–13; *see also Madonna and Child with Angels (Madonna dal Collo Lungo); Madonna and Child with Saints Margaret and Jerome, a Mitered Saint, and an Angel; Madonna and Child with Saint Stephen, the Baptist, and a Donor; Madonna and Child with the Baptist and Saint Jerome*
Madonna with Saint Anne (Leonardo da Vinci), 61
Madonna with Saint Francis (Correggio), 182
Madonna with Saint George and Others (Correggio), 85, 87
Madonna with Saint Jerome (Correggio), *see Madonna and Child with Saint Jerome and Others*
Madonna with Saint Jerome and the Baptist, see Madonna and Child with the Baptist and Saint Jerome
Madonna with Saint Margaret, see Madonna and Child with Saints Margaret and Jerome
Madonna with Saint Sebastian (Correggio), *see Madonna and Child with Saint Sebastian*
Madonna with Saint Zachariah, see Madonna and Child with Saints Zachariah, Mary Magdalene, and the Infant Baptist
Madonna with the Baptist, the Magdalene, and Saint Zachariah, see Madonna and Child with Saints Zachariah, Mary Magdalene, and the Infant Baptist
Madrid, 193; Alcazar, 188; Biblioteca Nacional, 184, 194; Retiro, 188; *see also* Academia di San Fernando; Prado
Malatesta Baglione (A49), 107, 118, 149, *151*, 176, 192; woodcut after, 149, *152*, 192
Malvasia, Carlo Cesare, 178, 184
Man, A (A28; *"G. B. Castaldo"*), 107, 113, *114*, 189
Manchester, 189, 193
Mander, Karel van, 168, 169
Man Holding a Bitch (P256), 162, *163*
Man in Armor and a Female, A (C3), 195*, 197
Man in Black (A26), 46, *47*, 188
mannerism, 11–12
Mantegna, Andrea, 65, 164; altarpiece, Castello Sforzesco, 122; funerary chapel of, *see* Mantua; *Parnassus*, 132, 178 n. IV:9
Mantua, 15, 65, 164, 176, 189; funerary chapel of Mantegna, Sant'Andrea, 32, 62–63; pendentive of (school of Mantegna), 62–63, *64*
Man with a Book, A (A53), 46–47, *49*, 51–53, 193
Manzuoli, Giorgio, conte, 185
Marcantonio, *see* Raimondi, Marcantonio
Margaret of Antioch, Saint, 183
Marienleben (Dürer), 42
Marriage of Saint Catherine, for the saddler, 96, 98
Marriage of Saint Catherine, Study for (P279), 139, *142*
Marriage of Saint Catherine (G6; Bonasone, after Parmigianino), 187, 199
Marriage of Saint Catherine (Correggio) 102, *102*
Marriage of Saint Catherine, see also at Mystic Marriage of Saint Catherine
Marriage of Saint Catherine, and a Male Saint, The (A32), 103, *105*, *108*–*9**, 176, 190*
Marriage of the Virgin, Study after Rosso (P692), 66–67, *68*, 70, 199; engraving after (G1; Caraglio), 57, 65, 66, 70, 57, 199
Marriage of the Virgin (Rosso Fiorentino), 57, 66–67, *68*, 177 n. II:3
Martini, Pietro, 177
Martyrdom of Four Saints (Correggio), 47
Martyrdom of Saint Cecilia (Marcantonio, after Raphael), 65
Martyrdom of Saints Peter and Paul (P190), 65; chiaroscuro after (F2; Antonio da Trento), 84, 198; engraving after (G2; Caraglio), 65, 84, 199
Massacre of the Innocents (Marcantonio, after Raphael): etching after a detail in, *Sleeping Cupid* (D9), 197; sketch after (P756), 58
Massys, Quentin, 46
Mattei, Angelo, 190
Matteo Marangoni Festschrift, 192
Maturino, 57
Mauritshuis, The Hague, 188
Maximilian II, Holy Roman emperor, 168
Mazzola, Filippo (father), 17, 177 n. I:5
Mazzola, Girolamo Francesco Maria, *see* Parmigianino
Mazzola, Michele (uncle), 17, 23, 27, 196
Mazzola, Pier Ilario (uncle), 17, 23, 24, 27, 125, 186, 196
Mazzola Bedoli, Girolamo (cousin by marriage), *see* Bedoli, Girolamo Mazzola
Mechel, Christian von, 192
Medici, Cosimo de', duke of Tuscany, 152
Medici, Ferdinando de', 184
Medici, Giulio de', *see* Clement VIII
Medici, Ippolito de', 55, 58–59, 118, 188, 189, 176, 177 n. II:4; portraits of (Sebastiano del Piombo), 118–20; (Titian), 55
Medici, Leopoldo de', 191
Medici, The (Young), 177 n. II:4
Medici collection, 107, 185, 191

Medici Madonna (Michelangelo), 75, *75*, 177 n. II:11
Melbourne: *Huntsman* (P282), 154
Melone, Altobello: Cremona Cathedral frescoes, 15; *The Flight into Egypt*, 39
Memling, Hans, 43
Mengs, Anton Raphael, 169
Metropolitan Museum of Art, New York: *The Annunciation* (C10; probably Bedoli), 195; Studies for *Moses*, 135, *137*
Mezzetti, A., 189, 195
Michelangelo Buonarroti, 11, 12, 14, 46, 57, 58, 73, 72, 75, 76, 102, 104, 147, 164; *David*, 58; Doni tondo, 197; drawings, 75, 164; *Last Judgment*, 75; *Madonna of Bruges*, *73*, 73–75, 158; *Medici Madonna*, 75, *75*, 177 n. II:11; *Pietà*, 58; *Prophet Isaiah*, 26; Sistine ceiling frescoes, 26; *Adam*, 58, 140; *Eternal*, 26; *Ignudi*, 26; Libyan and Persian sibyls, 102; statue of Julius II, 75; study for Sebastiano's Lazarus, 75; *Temptation*, 26
Milan, 15, 83, 165; works in, 188, 198; Ambrosiana, cartoon for *School of Athens* (Raphael), 58; Castello Sforzesco, *Man in Black* (A26), 46, *47*, 188; private collection, *A Man in Armor and a Female* (C3), 195*, 197
Milanesi, Gaetano, 177, 193
Millar, Oliver, 193
Milstein, Ann Rebecca, 177, 178, 188, 195, 196
Minneapolis, 187
Mirola, 178 n. IV:22
Mitteilungen des kunsthistorischen Institutes in Florenz (periodical), 185
Modena, 165; works in, 85, 190; Duomo, *Saint Sebastian with the Baptist and Saint Jerome* (Dosso Dossi), 16, *17*; Galleria Estense (ducal gallery), 184; *Holy Family with Saints and a Donor* (C4), 195; Palazzo Campori, 190
Montini, Bartolomeo, 125
Morgan Library, New York, 189, 197; study for *Diana and Actaeon*, 33, 185; study for *Head and Bust of Athene*, 160, 186
Morland collection, 187
Mortara, Anton Enrico, 184
Moses, Santa Maria della Steccata, 135, *136*, 190; Studies for (P301r), 135, *137*
Mostra del Correggio (Parma, 1935), 182, 183
Motta San Fermo, near Casalmaggiore: Servite church ("La Fontana"), 142, 160
Mozart, Wolfgang Amadeus, 178 n. IV:20
Mulazzini, Germano, 185
Munich, 193
Muselli collection, Verona, 186, 188
Museo Capitolino, Rome: *Cupid* (antique sculpture) 121–22, *123*
Museo Davio Bargellini, Bologna, 187
Museum of Fine Arts, Boston: *The Three Marys at the Sepulchre* (Bellange), 168, *168*
Mutius Scaevola (P726v), 86, *88*, 198
Mystic Marriage of Saint Catherine, The (A1; Bardi altarpiece), 18, *19*, 19–21, 26, 39, 176, 182; Study for (P51), 18–19, *20*, 182
Mystic Marriage of Saint Catherine, The (A18; in London), 86, 88, 90, 97, 98–103, 99*, *100–101*, *103*, 107, 139, 185, 186, 187*; engraving after (G6; Bonasone), 199
Mystic Marriage of Saint Catherine (B10), 26, 194; copy after, 26, *27*, 42, 194
Mystic Marriage of Saint Catherine (C2), 195
Mystic Marriage of Saint Catherine, see also at *Marriage of Saint Catherine*

N

Naked Man Seen from the Back (F4; Antonio da Trento, after Parmigianino), 84, 198
Nancy, ducal court, 165–68, 169
Naples, *see* Galleria Nazionale di Capodimonte
Narbonne, 75
National Gallery, London: *Immaculate Conception* (Crivelli), 176; *Madonna and Child with the Baptist and Saint Jerome* (A17), 13, 55, 65, 67–76, *69*, 90, 142, 147, 148, 158, 172, 176, 186–87; *Madonna of the Basket* (Correggio), 145–47, *146*; *The Mystic Marriage of Saint Catherine* (A18), 86, 88, 90, 97, 98–103, 99*, *100–101*, *103*, 107, 139, 185, 186, 187*; *A Priest or Collector* (A19), 21, 39, 46, *48*, 51–53, 107, 177 n. I:19, 187; *Raising of Lazarus* (Sebastiano del Piombo), *74*, 75; *Saint Jerome* (Sodoma), 177 n. II:13; *The Story of Aristaeus* (Abate), 165, *166–67*
National Gallery of Canada, Ottawa: Study for *Madonna dal Collo Lungo* (P327), 144, *145*, 184
Nativity, etching, 85
"Nativity," see Adoration of the Shepherds (A54); *Holy Family with Angel* (A20)
Negri, G. F., 177
Nell'Età del Correggio e dei Carracci exhibition catalog, 195; *see also Age of Correggio and Carracci*
Nero, Roman emperor, Domus Aurea of, 132, 139, 178 n. IV:8
New York, 183, 187; Ghirlandaio portrait, 177 n. II:5; *see also* Metropolitan Museum of Art; Morgan Library; Rosenberg & Stiebel
Nicolò Vicentino, 83, 199; chiaroscuro prints after Parmigianino: *Adoration of the Magi* (attrib.), 83, 199; *Christ Healing the Lepers* (F8), 83, 199; *Madonna and Child with Four Saints* (?), 199
Niedersächsisches, Hanover: *Saint Jerome* (Pontormo), 77, *77–79*, 177 n. II:13
Noli Me Tangere (Correggio), 83
Normanton, earls of, 187
Northern Europe, 11, 42; portraiture, 43, 45
Nôtre Dame, Bruges: *Madonna of Bruges* (Michelangelo, *73*, 73–75, 158
Nuovi Studi sul Correggio (Toscano), 193
Nymphs (B8), 194

O

Oberhuber, Konrad, 197
Odonti (Lotto), 177 n. I:19
Onofrio Bartolini (attrib. Girolamo da Carpi), 196
Oratorio della Concezione, Parma: *Immaculate Conception* (Bedoli), 176
Orléans collection, 197
Ottawa: National Gallery of Canada, Study for *Madonna dal Collo Lungo* (P327), 144, *145*, 184
Ottley collection, 187
Ovid, 33, 38
Oxford: Christ Church, 183; *see also* Ashmolean Museum

P

Pagani, Gregorio, 195
Palazzetto Eucherio Sanvitale, Parma, 38; *Madonna and Child* (A41), 38–39, 191
Palazzo Barberini, Rome, *see* Galleria Nazionale Barberini
Palazzo Borghese, Rome, inventory (1693), 187, 191
Palazzo Bufalini, Città di Castello, 186
Palazzo Campori, Modena, 190
Palazzo Casale, Bologna, 196
Palazzo del Giardino, Parma, 178 n. IV:22, 188, 189, 195
Palazzo Farnese, Rome, 189, 195

Palazzo Giusti, Bologna, 183
Palazzo Mancini, Città di Castello, 186
Palazzo Pitti, Florence, 196; *Donna Velata* (Raphael), 105; *Onofrio Bartolini* (attrib. Girolamo da Carpi), 196; portrait of Ippolito de' Medici (Titian), 55; *Vision of Ezekiel* (Raphael), 83
Palazzo Tanari, Bologna, 183
Palladio, Andrea, 192
Pallucchini, R., 195
Palma Vecchio, 46
Panofsky, Erwin, 177
Pantheon, Rome, 126
Paragone (periodical), 188, 192, 195
Paris, 178; Ecole des Beaux-Arts, *Saint Christopher* (P528), 154; *see also* Louvre
Parma: artists in, 13–14, 18, 164–65, 168, 199; Parmigianino in, 7, 13–53, 55, 72, 77, 83, 85, 88, 90, 120–21, 125–57, 176, 177 n. III:3; Parmigianino's influence in, 164–65, 169; patrons, 176; political turmoil, 13, 18; works in, 13, 189, 193, 197: altarpieces, 13–14; Correggio exhibition (1935), 182, 183; inventories (1587), 189; (1662–80), 195; (1708), 187, 188, 189, 195; *Pietà* (Correggio), 85; *Saint Roch in the Desert* (A40), 104–5, *107*, 191*, 194; by site: Annunziata, 182; Baptistery, 126; Camera di San Paolo (Correggio), 24, 31, 32, 33, *38*, 125; church of Capo di Ponte, 182; Oratorio della Concezione, *Immaculate Conception* (Bedoli), 176; Palazzetto Eucherio Sanvitale, *Madonna and Child* (A41), 38–39, 191; Palazzo del Giardino, 178 n. IV:22, 188, 189, 195; San Martino de' Bocci, abbey of, polyptych (Bedoli), 164–65; Servite church, 140, 184; *see also* Fontanellato; Galleria Nazionale; Parma cathedral; San Giovanni Evangelista; Santa Maria Bardi; Santa Maria della Steccata
Parma cathedral (Duomo), 26–28, 125, 176; altarpieces (Anselmi), 90; (Cima), 21; Cappella del Ferro (Rondani), 28; cupola, half-dome, and choir (Correggio), 28, 125; doors, 126; nave bays (Araldi), 28; north transept: wall, half-dome, and vault (contracted to Parmigianino), 14, 26–28; apses (Sammichini), 28; south transept (Anselmi), 28
Parma Embracing Alessandro Farnese (Bedoli), 195
Parma per l'Arte (Copertini), 193
Parmigianino (Girolamo Francesco Maria Mazzola; also called Francesco Mazzola, Francesco Parmigiano, Franciscus Mazola)
–arrest and imprisonment, 157, 190
–artistic formation, 13–21; apprenticeship, 17–18
–birth, 13
–characteristic features and motifs of his work: alchemical vases, urns, and amphorae, 18, 24, 98, 139, 147, 162; antique armor, 51, 163; Cremonese foliage, 46, 51, 60; crowding of heads and figures, 42, 147; hair, 13; magical lighting, 42–43, 90, 158; Phrygian caps, 162–63
–compared to: Correggio, 12–13, 32–33, 90, 135, 160, 169, 178 n. IV:15; Francia, 18; Michelangelo, 164; Raphael, 12–13, 17, 55, 160; Rosso, 66–67; Van Dyck, 160
–and Correggio, 14–15, 17, 27, 29, 125, 126, 160, 169; as his assistant, 14, 29, 176
–death, 160; Baiardi's acquisition of studio contents, 121; burial place, 142, 160; will, 178 n. IV:21
–as a draftsman, 160–64
–family of, 17; uncles, 17–18, 55, 76, 125; *see also* entries at Mazzola
–graphic reproduction of his work, 63–65, 83–86, 197–99; chiaroscuro prints, 83–84, 198–99; etchings, 63–65, 85, 165, 197–98; metal engravings, 199
–influence on other artists, 11, 85, 164–69; Abate, 165; Bassano, 165; Bellange, 168; Bloemaert, 169; Cornelis van Haarlem, 169; Correggio, 85; Giambologna, 85; Goltzius, 169; El Greco, 165; Goujon, 85, 165; Lotto, 177 n. I:19; in Parma, 164–65, 169; Perino del Vaga (?), 57; Reni, 169; Rosso, 60; Salviati, 165; Sansovino, 85; Schiavone, 165; Spranger, 168–69; Tintoretto, 165; Vasari, 165; Veronese, 165; Wtewael, 169
–influences on, 164; Anselmi, 14, 164; Beccafumi, 164; Cima, 13–14, 21, 164; Correggio, 14, 16, 22, 26, 27, 29, 32, 39, 72, 76, 79, 85, 88, 90, 96, 102, 104, 116, 122, 125, 135, 140, 145–47, 164, 182; Cremona frescoes, 15–16, 18, 42, 164; Dosso, 16, 164; Francia, 13–14, 18, 19, 164; Giovanni da Udine, 131–32; Giulio Romano, 102, 164; Leonardo da Vinci, 76, 164, 177 n. II:13; Lotto, 164; Mantegna, 32, 132, 164; Michelangelo, 26, 61, 73, 75, 76, 102, 104, 140, 147, 158, 164; Northern European artists, 42; Perino del Vaga, 131–32, 164; Polidoro da Caravaggio, 129; Pontormo, 77–79, 88, 147, 164, 177 n. II:13; Pordenone, 15, 24–26, 29, 164; Raphael, 21, 39, 65, 66, 65, 83, 85, 102, 103, 132, 139, 140, 158, 164; Rosso, 76, 164; Sebastiano, 75, 164
–interests: alchemy and magic, 12, 18, 24, 51, 58, 77, 129, 155, 160; graphics, 63; Latin studies, 164; lute, 164
–meetings and contacts with other artists: Anselmi, 14, 22; Araldi (?), 18; Correggio, 14, 22; Giulio Romano, 57; Michelangelo, 57, 75; Perino del Vaga, 164; Pontormo (?), 11, 79; Rondani (?), 18; Rosso (?), 11, 164; Sebastiano (?), 57, 75, 118, 164; Titian (?), 122; Vasari (?), 18, 176
–in Parma, 7, 11–53, 55, 72, 83, 125, 176; return, 15, 77, 85, 120–21, 125–57; visits from Bologna, 88, 90, 177 n. III:6
–patrons, 176; Baiardi, 46, 121, 140–42, 176; Gozzadini, 139; Ippolito de' Medici, 58–59, 118, 176; Sanvitale, 38, 176
–as a portraitist, 46–53, 105–113, 118, 149–53; *see also* entries at *Portrait*
–portraits of, 107; by Correggio, 52, 53, 107; *see also* entries at *Self-Portrait*
–posthumous reputation, 164–72
–shortness of stature, 162, 178 n. IV:20
–studio boys and assistants, 158, 161–62, 177 n. III:11, 178 n. IV:15
–travels and stays outside Parma: Ancona (?), 77; Bologna, 15, 18, 28, 55, 58–59, 77, 79, 83–122, 125, 139, 149, 164, 176; Casalmaggiore, 157–58; Florence (?), 57, 73, 76, 77, 79, 177 n. II:13; Fontanelleto, 14, 28; Rome, 14, 21, 28, 39, 42, 53, 55–79, 118, 120, 164, 176, 183; San Secondo, 149; Siena (?), 76–77; Venice, 122; Verona, 122, 139; Viadana, 21, 182, 190
–uncommissioned works, 39, 42, 59, 96, 120, 121
Parmigianino als Radierer (Oberhuber), 197
"Parmigianino in S. Giovanni Evangelista" (Ekserdjian), 190
"Parmigianino Madonna and Child and His Uncommissioned Paintings, A" (Gould), 194
Parmigianino ritrovato, Un (Fornari-Schianchi, Tassi, and Lucco [Looklet]), 191
Parmigianino und der Manierismus (Fröhlich-Bum), 11
Parmigianino und sein Kreis (Oberhuber), 197
Parnassus (Mantegna), 132, 178 n. IV:9
Passavant, Johann David, 196
Paul III (Alessandro Farnese), pope, 13, 176; portrait of (Titian), 196

Paul v (Camillo Borghese), pope, 176
Paul Preaching at Athens (Raphael): drawing after Marcantonio's print of the cartoon (P144), 58; etching after (?), 85
Peintre-graveur, Le (Bartsch), 197
Pembroke, 3rd earl of, 169
Pennsylvania Museum of Art, *see* Philadelphia
Perez, Antonio, 193
Perino del Vaga, 12, 57, 65, 97, 164, 192, 199; ceiling, Sala dei Pontefici (with Giovanni da Udine), 55, 131–32, *134*; frieze, San Marcello, Rome, 177 n. III:3
Perla, La (Raphael), 139
Peruzzi, Baldassare, 195
Petrucci, 147
Pezzana, Angelo, 188
Philadelphia: Pennsylvania Museum of Art, 194; *Portrait of a Lady* (C15), 188, 196*
Piacenza, 158
Pianerlotto, portrait of (?), 191
Pier Maria Rossi, Count of San Secondo (A24), 107, 149–53, *152*, 160, 188
Piero di Cosimo: *Immaculate Conception*, 176
Pierpont Morgan Library, *see* Morgan Library
Pietà (Correggio), 85
Pietà (Michelangelo), sketch of (P311), 58
Pinacotheca (Antal), 183
Pinacoteca Ambrosiana, *see* Ambrosiana
Pinacoteca Nazionale, Bologna, 183, 187; *Madonna and Child with Saints Margaret and Jerome, a Mitered Saint, and an Angel* (A3), 12, *12*, 13, 88, 90–97, *91**, 92, *93*, 98, 147, 158, 169, 183; *Saint Cecilia* (Raphael), *20*, *21*, 96, 83, 158, 169
Pirri collection, 191
Pitti Palace, *see* Palazzo Pitti
Pius IX, pope, 176
Plato, 198
Poetry (Raphael), sketch after (P168v), 26
Poland, 199
Polidoro da Caravaggio (Polidoro Caldara), 12, 57, 126; dado, Sala di Costantino 135–39; San Silvestro al Quirinale, 135–39
Pollaiuolo, Antonio, 65
Pontefici, Sala dei, *see* Sala dei Pontefici
Pontormo, Jacopo (Carrucci) da, 11, 12, 46, 77, 88, 147, 164; Certosa di Galluzzo frescoes, 77, 148; *Deposition*, 147, *148*; *Saint Jerome*, *77*, 77–79, 177 n. II:13; *Visitation*, *78*, 79, *80**, 147
Pope-Hennessy, John, 177, 177 n. II:11
Popham, Arthur Ewart, 6, 7, 24, 27, 70, 118, 134, 139, 160, 161, 177, 178, 184, 185, 186, 187, 190, 191, 193, 197
Pordenone (Giovanni Antonio de' Sacchis), 15, 29, 164, 192; Cremona Cathedral frescoes, 15–16, 24–26; *Christ on the Road to Calvary*, *24–26*
Portrait of a Collector, *see Priest or Collector, A*
Portrait of a Lady (C15), 188, 196
Portrait of a Man (A11; *"Self-Portrait"*), 107, *110*, 113, 185
Portrait of a Man (C7; *"G. Bernardi da Castelbolognesi"*), 195
Portrait of a Man (C9; *"Gian Martino Sanvitale"*), 195
Portrait of a Young Man (A55; *Self-Portrait*), 120, *120*, 194
Portrait of a Young Man with His Hand to His Head (C12), 196
Portrait of a Youth (A14), *see* Young Man, A
Portrait of a Youth (C1), 195
Portrait of a Youth (C16), 196
Portrait of a Youth with Hand on Hip (C8; now attrib. Rosso), 195
Portrait of Bonifazio Gozzadini (B3), 194
Portrait of Girolamo de' Vicenti (C5; probably Giromalo da Carpi), 195
Portrait of Parmigianino(?) (Correggio), *52*, *53*, 107
portraits. *References for additional portraits by or attributed to Parmigianino can be found under the following names:* Baglione; Castaldo; Charles V; Cybo; Gozzadini, Contessa; Pianerlotto; Pucci; Rossi, Pier Luigi; Rangone; Sanvitale, Galeazzo; *see also* entries at *Self-Portrait; Young Man; Young Woman*
portraiture, 43–53, 60; allegorical, 118
post-peak generation, 11, 12, 46, 79, 135, 172
Prado, Museo del, Madrid, 193; *Camilla Gonzaga, Countess of San Secondo* (A25), 107, 149–53, *153*, 188*, 196, 197; *Holy Family with Angels* (A23), 21, 39, 42, *43*, 55, 58, 61, 188; *Noli Me Tangere* (Correggio), 83; *La Perla* (Raphael), 139; *Pier Maria Rossi, Count of San Secondo* (A24), 107, 149–53, *152*, 160, 188; *Saint Barbara* (A22), 21, *21*, 24, 26, 188
Prague, 168–69, 192, 193
Prelate, A (A42), 82, 113, *115**, 191
Presentation of Christ in the Temple, 58; niche for (P273), 70, *71*
Priest or Collector, A (A19; London portrait), 21, 39, 46, *48*, 51–53, 107, 177 n. I:19, 187
Princes Gate Collection, The (Brahan), 187
Procaccino family, 165
Prophet Isaiah (Michelangelo), sketch after (P712v), 26
proto-mannerists, *see* post-peak generation
Pucci, Lorenzo, Cardinal, portrait of (?), 196

Q

Quercia, Jacopo della: statue, San Petronio, Bologna, 147
Quintavalle, Armando Ottaviano, 177, 182, 184, 185, 186, 190, 191, 196
Quintavalle, Augusta Ghidiglia, 177, 178, 191, 192, 195, 196
Quintavalle family, 188
Quirinal, Rome: *Horse Tamers* (Dioscuri) (ancient sculpture), 24–26

R

Raimondi, Marcantonio, 26, 63–65; prints after Raphael, 58; *Feast in the House of Simon*, 58; *Lucretia*, 160; *Martyrdom of Saint Cecilia*, 65; *Paul Preaching at Athens*, 58
Raising of Lazarus (Sebastiano del Piombo), *74*, *75*
Rangone, Bishop, portrait of, 194
Rape of Europa, study for (P12v), 32
Raphael, 11, 12, 14, 17, 46, 55, 57, 58, 65, 72, 85, 102, 105, 145, 160, 164, 188, 196; *Bridgewater Madonna*, 39; *Donna Velata*, 105; *Expulsion of Heliodorus*, 140; *Feast in the House of Simon*, 58; *Fire at the Borgo*, 132; Fornarina portrait, 105; *Healing of the Lame Man*, 58, 85, 197; late Madonnas, 139; *Lucretia*, 160; Madonna (Oxford drawing), 103–4; *Madonna of Foligno*, 70; *Martyrdom of Saint Cecilia*, 65; *Massacre of the Innocents*, 58, 197; *Paul Preaching at Athens*, 58, 85; *La Perla*, 139; *Poetry*, 26; Resurrection altarpiece, 85; *Saint Cecilia*, *20*, *21*, 83, 96, 158, 169, 177 n. III:7; print after (Bonasone), 191; *School of Athens*, 58, 65; Sistine *Madonna*, 12, 158; *Vision of Ezekiel*, 83
Raphael (Crowe and Cavalcaselle), 196
Raphael d'Urbin (Passavant), 196
Ravenna, battle of, 13
Rederitz, church at, 182
Reed, Sue Welsh, 177, 197
Reggia de là da l'Acqua, La, 191
Reiset, Frédéric, 190

Rembrandt van Rijn, 178 n. IV:20
Reni, Guido, 169, 197
Residenz, Salzburg, 189
Resurrection (D6), 85, *86*, 140, 197
Retiro, Madrid, 188
Reynolds, Sir Joshua, 21, 135, 169, 177, 178
Reynst collection, Amsterdam, 186
Ricci, C., 182, 185, 189
"Ricerca e lo Sfruttamento dei Metalli, La" (Beccafumi), 177 n. II:12
Richelieu, duke of, 196
Richmond: Cook collection, 187, 189; *Portrait of a Youth* (C16), 196
Riposo, Il (Borghini), 176, 178
Rocca di San Secondo, 188
Rocca Sanvitale, *see* Fontanellato
Roch, Saint, 183
Rogers collection, 187
Romanesque period, 13
Romanino (Girolamo Romani), 46; Cremona Cathedral frescoes, 15–16; *Christ before Caiaphas*, 16, *16*
Rome: artists in, 11–12, 14, 55–57, 83, 118, 165, 168, 198, 199; Parmigianino in, 7, 14, 21, 28, 39, 42, 53, 55–79, 118, 120, 164, 176, 183; portraiture, 46; sack (1527), 14, 57, 65, 76, 118; works in, 195; by site: Corsini Gallery, 184, 185; Galleria Nazionale Barberini, 105, 195; Domus Aurea, 132, 139, 178 n. IV:8; Galleria Borghese, *A Prelate* (A42), *82*, 113, *115**, 191; Galleria Spada, *Three Heads* (A45), 192; Museo Capitolino, *Cupid* (antique sculpture), 121–22, *123;* Palazzo Borghese, 187; Palazzo Farnese, 189, 195; Pantheon, 126; Quirinal, *Horse Tamers (Dioscuri)* (ancient sculpture), 24–26; San Marcello, 177 n. III:3; San Salvatore in Lauro, 67–70, 186; Santa Maria della Pace, 11, 186; Septizonium, 96; *see also* Galleria Doria; Vatican City
Rondani, Francesco Maria, 18, 195, 196; altarpiece with Saint Augustine, 23; Parma Duomo contract, 28
Rosa, Scipione della, 38, 125, 191
Rosaspina, Francesco, print by, 191
Roscoe, Thomas, 184
Rosenberg & Stiebel, New York: *Allegorical Portrait of Emperor Charles V* (A31), 59, 88, 118, *119*, 176, 189*, 195
Roskill, M., 177
Rossi, Angiola de', 194
Rossi, Federico, 188
Rossi, M., 196
Rossi, Paola, 177, 187, 188, 191, 196, 197
Rossi, Pier Maria, count of San Secondo, 152; portrait of (A24), 107, 149–53, *152*, 160, 188
Rossi family, 149, 176
Rosso Fiorentino (Giovanni Battista di Jacopo), 11–12, 21, 57–58, 60, 65, 76, 164, 197, 199; *Deposition*, 148; fresco, Santa Maria del Pace, 11; *Marriage of the Virgin*, San Lorenzo, 57, 66–67, *68*, 177 n. II:3, 199; *Portrait of a Youth with Hand on Hip* (C8; attrib.; formerly attrib. Parmigianino), 195; *Saturn and Philyra* (engraving by Caraglio), 60, *61; Young Man*, *59*, 60
Royal Academy, London, 197
Rubens, Peter Paul, 160, 189, 193
Rudolf II, Holy Roman emperor, 168; collection of, 192, 193

S

Saint, *see also* at San; Santa; Santi; Santo
Saint Agatha and Executioner (A33), 24, *25*, 26, 176, 190
Saint Agnes (Anselmi), 60–61
Saint Andrew (E1), 198
Saint Barbara (A22), 21, *21*, 24, 26, 188; study for (?) (P6), 21
Saint Catherine (Anselmi), 60–61
Saint Catherine of Alexandria (A13), 39, *41*, 186
Saint Cecilia (A36), 29, *30*, 39, 191
Saint Cecilia (Raphael), *20*, 21, 83, 96; engraving after (Bonasone), 199
Saint Christopher (P528), 154
Saint Francis Receiving the Stigmata and Saint Clare (B1), 176, 194
Saint Hilary of Poitiers, San Giovanni Evangelista (doubtful attrib.), 23, 196
Saint Jerome (Leonardo da Vinci), 177 n. II:13
Saint Jerome (Pontormo), *77*, 77–79, 177 n. II:13
Saint Jerome (Sodoma), 177 n. II:13
Saint John the Baptist in the Wilderness (F6; Antonio da Trento, after Parmigianino), 199
Saint John the Evangelist (E2), 198
Saint Judas Thaddeus (?) (E5), 198
Saint Lucy and Saint Apollonia, 24, 26, 190
Saint Margaret (Santa Margherita), convent church of, Bologna, 90, 183
Saint Margaret altarpiece, *see Madonna and Child with Saints Margaret and Jerome, a Mitered Saint, and an Angel*
Saint Mark, Venice: sacristy door (Sansovino), 177 n. III:3
Saint Matthias (E4), 198
Saint Nicholas of Bari, San Giovanni Evangelista (doubtful attrib.), 23, 196
Saint Paul (E6), 198
Saint Peter, Vatican: *Pietà* (Michelangelo), 58
Saint Petersburg: Hermitage, 190
Saint Philip (D7), 197
Saint Philip (?) (E3), 198
Saint Roch and Donor (A4), 88–90, *89*, 140, 183, engraving after (G7; Bonasone), 199
Saint Roch in the Desert (A40), 104–5, *107*, 191*, 194
Saint Sebastian with the Baptist and Saint Jerome (Dosso Dossi), 16, *17*
"Saint Thais" (D8), 197
Saint Vitalis (A34), *23*, 24–26, 190
Saint Vitalis (P283), 190
Sala dei Pontefici, Vatican: ceiling (Perino del Vaga and Giovanni da Udine), 55, 131–32, *134;* walls, 55, 65, 132
Sala di Costantino, Vatican, 57; dado (Polidoro da Caravaggio), 135–39
Salviati, Francesco, 11, 165
Salzburg, Residenz, 189
Sammichini, Orazio, 28
San, *see also* at Saint; Santo
San Domenico, Taggia (Imperia): *Adoration of the Magi* (A46), 57, 96–98, *98*, 192
San Francesco, Correggio: *Madonna with Saint Francis* (Correggio), 182
San Francesco, Fiesole: Immaculate Conception (Piero di Cosimo), 176
San Giovanni al Monte, Bologna: *Saint Cecilia* (Raphael), *20*, 21
San Giovanni Evangelista, Parma, 14, 176; frescoes, 14, 22–26, *27*, 28–29, 39, 125–26
–by Anselmi, 14; *Saint Agnes* and *Saint Catherine*, 60–61
–by Correggio, 14, 22, 24, *27*, 125; crossing arches, 132, 135, *136;* Del Bono chapel, 24, 177; cupolo, 14, 24, 28, 47, *49*, 177 n. I:17; putti for pendentives of (attrib. Parmigianino; *see below*); studies of (Parmigianino), 14, 24, *15;* half-dome, 26, 125, 126, 177 n. IV:3
–by Parmigianino, 14, 21, 24–26, 27, 29, 39, 176; first chapel (A33): *Saint Lucy and Saint Apollonia*, 24, 26, 190; *God the Father and Angels*, 24, 26, 39, 190; putti, 24, 42; *Saint Agatha and Executioner*, 21, 24, *25*, 26, 176, 190; second chapel (A34):

The Four Temperaments, 24, 190; *Saint Vitalis*, 21, *23*, 24–26, 190; *Two Deacons*, 21, *22*, 190; formerly attributed (C14): fourth chapel, with *Saint Nicholas of Bari* and *Saint Hilary of Poitiers*, 22–24, 196: sixth chapel and vaults of chapels to left and right of high altar, 196; recently attributed: putti for pendentives of Correggio's cupola, 14, 24, 28–29, *29*, 190
San Lorenzo, Florence, 199; Ginori chapel altarpiece, *Marriage of the Virgin* (Rosso Fiorentino), 57, 66–67, *68*, 199; *Medici Madonna* (Michelangelo), 75, *75*, 177 n. II:11
San Marcello, Rome: frieze (Perino del Vaga), 177 n. III:3
San Martino de' Bocci, Cistercian abbey of: polyptych (Bedoli), 164–65
San Michele, Pieve di, Carmignano: *Visitation* (Pontormo), 78, *79*, *80**, 147
Sanminiatelli, Donato, 177
San Paolo, Monastery of, Parma: Camera di San Paolo (Correggio), 24, 31, 32, *38*, 125
San Petronio, Bologna, 122; *Saint Roch and Donor* (A4), 88–90, *89*, 140, 183; statue over main door (Quercia), 147
San Salvatore in Lauro, Rome, 67–70, 186
San Secondo, 149, 176; Rocca di, 188
San Secondo, count of, *see* Rossi, Pier Luigi
San Secondo, countess of, *see* Gonzaga, Camilla
San Silvestro al Quirinale (Polidoro da Caravaggio), 135–39
Sansovino, Jacopo, 85; sacristy door, Saint Mark, Venice, 177 n. III:3
Santa, *see also at* Saint
Santa Felicita, Florence, 77; *Deposition* (Pontormo), 147, *148*
Sant'Agostino, Città di Castello, 186
Santa Margherita (Saint Margaret), convent church of, Bologna, 90, 183
Santa Maria Annunciata, Viadana: altarpiece (Bedoli), 195
Santa Maria Annunziata, Parma, 182
Santa Maria Bardi, Parma: *The Mystic Marriage of Saint Catherine* (A1), 18, *19*, 19–21, 26, 39, 176, 182; Study for (P51), 18–19, *20*, 182
Santa Maria della Pace, Rome, 186; fresco (Rosso), 11
Santa Maria della Steccata, Parma, 121, 125–26, 149, 154–57, 176
–altarpieces, commission for, 125
–choir vault (east barrel vault) (A35), 77, 125, 126–39, *127**, *128*, *131*, *132*, *133*, *136*, *138*, 147, 155, 160, 172, 177–78 n. IV:7, 178 nn. IV:8, 9, 11, 15; 190–91; coffers with rosettes, 126–29, 155, 190; friezes, 135, *138*, 190; grisaille figures, 135; *Aaron*, 135, 190; *Adam*, 135, 190; *Eve*, 135, 160, 190; *Moses*, 135, *135*, *137*, 190; maiden *(canephorae)* figures, 57, 132–35; Three Foolish Virgins, *2*, *128*, 129, *132**, 133–35, 147, 190; Three Wise Virgins, 129, *131*, 133–35, 147, 178 n. IV:8, 190; studies, 191; (P228), 126, 129, *130*, 135; (P310r; Moses), 135, *137*; (P618), 134, *135*
–half-dome: commission and designs, 27, 125–26, 129, 155–57; *Coronation of the Virgin*, 125–26, 191; completion of (Anselmi, after Giulio Romano), 157
–north and south barrel vaults (Bedoli; after Parmigianino), 157
–organ shutters, 27, 29, 177 n. III:6, 191; *David* (A37), *9*, *29*, *31**, 191; *Saint Cecilia* (A36), 29, *30*, 39, 191; enlargment and later additions to *Flight into Egypt* (Sons), 191
Santa Maria Gloriosa dei Frari, Venice: *Assunta* (Titian), 67
Sant'Andrea, Mantua, Mantegna's funerary chapel, 32, 62–63; pendentive of (school of Mantegna), 62–63, *64*
Santi Apostoli, Florence: *Immaculate Conception* (Vasari), 176
Santo Stefano, Casalmaggiore: altarpiece for, *see Madonna and Child with Saint Stephen, the Baptist, and a Donor*
Sanvitale, Galeazzo, Count of Fontanellato, 30, 38, 42, 177 n. I:20, 189, 191; portrait of (A29), 21, 38, 39, 42, 47–53, *50*, 60, 107, 183, 189*; Study for (P748v), 47–51, *51*, 189
Sanvitale, Gian Martino, portrait of (C9), 195
Sanvitale, L., 182, 185, 189
Sanvitale family, 149, 176, 182
Sassetti, Francesco, portrait of, 177 n. II:5
Saturn and Philyra, 60, 194; engraving after (Lepicié), 60, *61*, 194
Saturn and Philyra (Caraglio, after Rosso), 60, *61*
Scaevola, Mutius, depicted (P726v), 86, *88*, 198
Scannelli, Francesco, 184, 188
Scaramuccia, Luigi Pellegrino, 90, 169, 177, 178, 186
Schiavone, Andrea, 165; *Bellona*, 165, *165*
Schleissheim, 193
School of Athens (Raphael), 65; copy after cartoon for (P666r), 58
Schubert, Franz, 178 n. IV:20
Scurano altarpiece (Pier Ilario Mazzola and Michele Mazzola), 23, 177
Seated Philosopher (E11), 198
Sebastiano del Piombo, 46, 57, 118–20, 164, 196; *Raising of Lazarus*, *74*, *75*
Sebastiano del Piombo (Hirst), 196
Seilern, Anton, collection of, 187, 193
"Self-Portrait" (A11), *see Portrait of a Man*
Self-Portrait (A39), 107, *111*, 157, 191*, 194
Self-Portrait (A55), *see Portrait of a Young Man*
Self-Portrait (P600), 107, *111*
Self-Portrait in a Convex Mirror (A48), 21, 42, 43, *51*, 53, 55, 107, 118, 192
Septizonium, Rome, 96
Serra, Marchese, 188
Servite church ("La Fontana"), Casalmaggiore, 142, 160
Servite church, Parma, 140, 184
Servite Order, 140–42, 160
Sestieri, Ettore, 192
Sforza dynasty, 13
Shearman, John, 177 n. III:11, 178, 186
Sibyl, see Augustus and the Sibyl
Siena, 12, 14, 76–77
Siren, 196
Sistine ceiling (Michelangelo), 26; *Adam*, 58, 140
Sistine *Madonna* (Raphael), 12, 158
Sixtus IV, pope, 176
Sleeping Cupid (D9), 197
Sodoma: *Saint Jerome*, 177 n. II:13
Soens (Sons), Jan or Hans, 178 n. IV:22, 191
Sogliani, Giovanni Antonio, 176, 196
Solly, 182
Sommariva sale, 190
Sons, *see* Soens
Sotheby's, London, 184, 189, 191
Spada gallery, *see* Galleria Spada
Speck von Sternberg collection, 187
Spinario (antique sculpture), sketch of (P710), 58
Spranger, Bartholomäus, 168–69; *Triumph of Wisdom*, 169, *170*, *173**
Staatliche Museen, Berlin: *The Baptism of Christ* (A2), 18, *18*, 21, 176, 177 n. I:6, 182
Städelsches Kunstinstitut, Frankfurt: *Saint Catherine of Alexandria* (A13), 39, *41*, 186
Standard-Bearer (P255), 154, *156*
Standing Shepherd, 197
Stanze, Vatican (Raphael): *Expulsion of Heliodorus*, 140; *Fire at the Borgo*, 132; *Poetry*, 26; *School of Athens*, 65
Statens Museum fur Kunst, *see* Copenhagen

Steccata, *see* Santa Maria della Steccata
Stockholm, 164, 192, 197
Storia della Città di Parma (Pezzana), 188
Story of Aristaeus, The (Abate), 165, *166–67*
Strafford collection, 187
studies. *Studies by Parmigianino illustrated in the text are listed below; for other studies, see the main entry for the title or artist*
Studies after Correggio (P330), 14, *15*
Studies for the Fontanellato fresco (*Diana and Actaeon*) (P12), 31–32, *39*, *175**, 185
Study for *Adoration of the Shepherds* (P631), 66, *66*
Study for a niche (P273), 58, 70, *71*
Study for *The Circumcision* (P369), 42–43, *45*, 183
Study for *Cupid Cutting His Bow* (P543), 121, *122*, 193
Study for *Lovers in a Wood* (P612), *84*, 84–85
Study for *Madonna and Child with Saints Margaret and Jerome, a Mitered Saint, and an Angel* (P79), 90, *94*, 98, 183
Study for *Madonna and Child with the Baptist and Saint Jerome* (P181r), 70, 72, *72*, 187
Study for *Madonna dal Collo Lungo* (B.M.), 142, *144*
Study for *Madonna dal Collo Lungo* (P327), 144, *145*, 184
Study for *Madonna dal Collo Lungo* (P553), 144, *145*
Study for *Madonna della Rosa* (P702r), 39, 118, *118*, 184
Study for *The Marriage of Saint Catherine* (P279), 139, *142*
Study for *Marriage of the Virgin* (P692), 66–67, *68*, 70, 199
Study for the Bardi altarpiece (P51), 18, *20*, 182
Study for the *Sanvitale* portrait (P748v), 47–51, *51*, 189
Study for the *Visitation* (P550), *78*, 79, *81**, 96, 154, 161
Study of trees (P118), 161, *162**, *181*
Stuttgart, 197
Sudeley Castle: *Mystic Marriage of Saint Catherine* (C2), 195
Szépmüvészeti Múzeum, Budapest: *Madonna del Latte* (Correggio), 116, *117*

T

Tacconi, Francesco, 15, 177 n. I:5
Taggia (Imperia): San Domenico, *Adoration of the Magi* (A46), 57, 96–98, *98*, 192
Tassi, R., 191
Tasso, 163
Temptation (Michelangelo), 26
Teniers, David, 193
Tesori Nascosti (A. G. Quintavalle), 191
Testi, Laudedeo, 177, 178, 190, 191
Teylers Stichtung, Haarlem, 199
Three Foolish Virgins, Santa Maria della Steccata, *2*, *128*, 129, *132**, 132–35, 147, 190
Three Heads (A45), 192
Three Marys at the Sepulchre, The (Bellange), 168, *168*
Three Wise Virgins, Santa Maria della Steccata, 129, *131*, 132–35, 147, 178 n. IV:8, 190
Tibaldi, Domenico, 184
Tintoretto (Jacopo Robusti), 21, 165, 197; *Entombment*, 85
Titian (Tiziano Vecellio), 46, 51, 72, 122, 195; *Assunta*, 67; Madonna in Glory, Ancona, 77; portraits: Castaldo, 113; Charles V, 118; Laura Dianti, 60; Pier Luigi Farnese, 196; Ippolito de' Medici, 55; Paul III, 196; Venus and Adonis, 121
Tolner, 193
Tonci, S., 192
Torbido, Francesco, 15; *Assumption* (after Giulio Romano), 133
Toscano, Giuseppe M., 193
Tries collection, 187
Triumph of Wisdom (Spranger), 169, *170*, *173**
Turin, 198, 199
"Turkish Slave," see Young Woman, A
Two Deacons (A34), *22*, 190
Two Deacons (P161), 190

U

Uffizi, Galleria degli, Florence, 182, 183, 184, 185, 187, 191, 198, 199; *Circe* (P73), 154, *155*; *Circe* (P85), 154; *Holy Family with Saint Francis* (Correggio), 26, 39; *Immaculate Conception* (Sogliani), 176; *Madonna and Child with Angels (Madonna dal Collo Lungo)* (A9), 13, 79, 90, 116, 140–48, *143**, 149, 157, 164, 168, 169, *171*, 176, 184*, 188; *Madonna and Child with Saints Zachariah, Mary Magdalene, and the Infant Baptist* (A10), 88, 98, *124*, 139, *139*, 140, *141**, 165, 184–85; portrait (school of Giorgione), 177 n. II:5; *Portrait of a Man ("Self-Portrait")* (A11), 107, *110*, 113, 185; studies for Diogenes and Saint Jerome (P107), 65, 79; Study for *Madonna and Child with Saints Margaret and Jerome, a Mitered Saint, and an Angel* (P79), 90, *94*, 98, 183; study for *The Mystic Marriage of Saint Catherine* (P76r), 18; Study of trees (P118), 161, *162**, *181*
Ugo da Carpi, 83, 198; *Diogenes* (after Parmigianino) (F1), *76*, 77, 83, 177 n. II:13, 198
Ultimi affreschi del Parmigianino, Gli (A. G. Quintavalle), 192
Unger collection, Berlin, 195
Utrecht, 169

V

Vaccaro, Mary, 177, 186
Valente, Cardinal, 183
Vasari, Giorgio, 11–12, 17–18, 21, 22, 26, 29, 30, 39, 42, 43, 55, 57, 58, 59, 75, 76, 83, 84, 85, 86–88, 90–96, 98, 102, 104, 105, 107, 113, 117, 118, 121, 122, 126, 139, 147, 148, 149, 155, 157, 160, 161, 164, 165, 176, 177, 177–78 n. IV:7, 178 n. IV:22, 182, 183, 184, 185, 186, 187, 188, 189, 190, 191, 192, 193, 194, 194, 197, 198, 199; *Immaculate Conception*, 176
Vatican: Loggie, 57; *Saint Jerome* (Leonardo da Vinci), 177 n. II:13; Saint Peter, *Pietà* (Michelangelo), 58; Sistine ceiling (Michelangelo), 26; *Adam*, 58, 140; *see also* Sala dei Pontefici; Sala di Costantino; Stanze
Venice: artists in, 13, 165, 198; Parmigianino in, 122; portraiture, 46, 60; works in, 182; Cini collection, *Holy Family and Angels* (C17), 196; Saint Mark, sacristy door (Sansovino), 177 n. III:3; Santa Maria Gloriosa dei Frari, *Assunta* (Titian), 67

Venus and Adonis (Titian), 121
Venus, Mars, and Vulcan (P546), 154
Verona, 15; Parmigianino in, 122, 139; works in: cathedral, *Assumption* (Giulio Romano), 133; *La Perla* (Raphael), 139; Muselli collection, 186, 188
Veronese (Paolo Caliari), 122, 165
Viadana, 18, 21, 182; works in: church of the Frati de' Zoccoli, *Saint Francis Receiving the Stigmata and Saint Clare* (B1), 176, 194; Santa Maria Annunciata, altarpiece (Bedoli), 195
Viaggio Pittoresco (Barri), 188
Vicentino, Nicolò, *see* Nicolò Vicentino
Vico, Enea: *Lucretia* (after Parmigianino), 160
Victoria and Albert Museum, London, 177; *Presentation in the Temple* (P273), 58; Study for a niche (P273), 58, 70, *71*
Vienna, *see* Graphische Sammlung Albertina; Kunsthistoriches Museum
Virgin Annuntiate (B4; tondo), 194
Virgin Annuntiate (etching), 198
Visconti dynasty, 13
Vision of Ezekiel (Raphael), 83
Vision of Saint Jerome, The, see Madonna and Child with the Baptist and Saint Jerome
Visitation, Study for (P550), *78, 79, 81**, 96, 154, 161, 187
Visitation (Pontormo), *78, 79, 80**, 147
Vite de' più eccellenti pittori (Lives of the Artists) (Vasari), 11–12; *see also* Vasari
Vitelli, Alessandro, 194
Vittoria, Alessandro, 192
Volterra: *Deposition* (Rosso), 148
Voss, Hermann, 18, 182

W

Waagen, 182
Wagner, Richard, 178 n. IV:20
Wallace, Richard, 177, 197
Walpole Society, 193
Wark, R., 177, 178
Washington, D.C., 160
Weimar, 199; Graphische Sammlung, Study for *Adoration of the Shepherds* (P631), 66, *66*
Wellington Museum, London, 187
Wethey, Harold Edwin, 177
Weyden, Rogier van der, 43
Whitfield, C., 195
Wilde, Johannes, 177, 193
Wilson, 193, 197
Windsor Castle, 107, 184, 197
Witt, Sir J., 182
Woman, A ("Contessa Gozzadini") (A50), 107, 139, *140*, 191, 193*
Woman Playing the Clavichord (Bedoli), 195
Woman with Armillary Sphere (E9), 198
woodcuts, chiaroscuro, 83, 198
Wrotham, England, 187
Wtewael, Joachim, 169

Y

York, City Art Gallery: *A Man with a Book* (A53), 46–47, *49*, 51–53, 193
Young, George Frederic, 177
Young collection, 187
Young Man, A (A14; *Portrait of a Youth*), 105–7, *110*, 177 n. III:11, 186
Young Man (Rosso Fiorentino), *59*, 60
Young Man with a Book, A (A47), *95*, 96, 192
Young Woman, A (A27; *"Antea"*), 107, 149, *150*, 163, 188
Young Woman, A (A38; *"Turkish Slave"*), 107, *112*, *191**, 193
Youth with a Bitch (P460), 162, *163*

Z

Zaganelli: *Immaculate Conception*, 176
Zanguidi, Jacopo, *see* Bertoja
Zani family, 184
Zeri, Federico, 192
Zerner, Henri, 178
Zoan Andrea, 178 n. IV:9
Zurich, Kunsthaus, 194

Photography Credits

The photographers and the sources of photographic material other than those indicated in the captions are as follows:

Accademia di S. Fernando, Madrid, p. 142

Fratelli Alinari, p. 59

Archivio Fotografico Direzione dei Musei, Brescia, Italy, p. 16

Archivio Fotografico Musei Vaticani, Rome, p. 134

Archivio Fotografico Arnoldo Mondadori Editore, pp. 49 left, 73 left, 105, 107, 108–109, 119, 123, 148

Archivio M. R., Correggio (Reggio Emilia), Italy, pp. 2, 127, 128, 132

Ashmolean Museum, Oxford, England, p. 15

British Museum, London, pp. 72, 130, 144, 154, 156, 163 left, 201

Courtauld Institute of Art, Somerset House, London, pp. 40 top, 51 top, 68 right, 88, 97 right, 118

Ursula Edelmann, Frankfurt, p. 41

Fonds Albertina, pp. 84 right, 86 left, 111 left, 135

Fototeca Nazionale, Rome, pp. 62, 63

Founders Society, Detroit Institute of Arts, European Painting, p. 44

Gemäldegalerie Alte Maister/Var Veröffentlichung/Genehmigung der Galerie einholen, Dresden, Germany, pp. 87, 159

Antonio Guerra, Bologna, Italy, pp. 12, 20, 89, 91, 92–93, 143, 171

Harari & Johns Ltd., London, p. 120

Istituto Scala, Florence, pp. 9, 10, 25, 30, 31, 33, 34, 36–37, 43, 82, 112, 115

Kunsthistorisches Museum, Vienna, pp. 1, 51 bottom, 95, 97 left, 121, 140, 151, 169, 173

Kunstsammlungen zu Weimar, Weimar, Germany, p. 66

Kupferstichkabinett, Staatliche Museen zu Berlin, Preußischer Kulturbesitz, Gemäldegalerie. Photo: Jörg P. Anders, Berlin, pp. 18, 39, 175

Museo del Prado, Madrid, pp. 21, 152 right, 153

National Gallery of Canada/Musée des Beaux-Arts du Canada, Ottawa, p. 145 right

National Gallery Photograph/Royal Collection Photographic Services Department, London, pp. 48, 69, 74, 99, 100–101, 103 right, 110 left, 146, 161, 166–167

Niedersächsisches Landesmuseum, Landesgalerie, Hanover, Germany, p. 77

Nicolò Orsi Battaglini, Florence, p. 75

Luciano Pedicini, Naples, pp. 50, 102, 104, 106, 114, 150

Photo R.M.N., Paris, pp. 42, 52, 163 right

Photograph Services, The Metropolitan Museum of Art, New York, p. 137

Pineider, D., pp. 26, 61 left and right, 67, 84 left, 86 right, 89, 152 left, 155, 162, 165, 168, 181

President and Fellows, Harvard College, Harvard University Art Museums, Cambridge, Mass., p. 20

Prudence Cuming Associates Limited, London, p. 40 bottom

Marco Ravenna, Correggio (Reggio Emilia), Italy, p. 35

Rosenberg & Stiebel, New York. Scott Bowron Photography, New York, p. 119

Saporetti, p. 47

Soprintendenza Beni Artistici e Storici della Liguria, Genoa, Italy, p. 98

Soprintendenza Beni Artistici e Storici di Modena e Reggio Emilia, Italy, p. 17

Soprintendenza Beni Artistici e Storici di Parma, Italy, Gabinetto Fotografico, pp. 13, 19, 22, 23, 27, 29, 32, 38, 49 right, 78 top and bottom, 80, 81, 94 right, 111 right, 122, 131, 133, 136 left and right, 138, 145 left

Soprintendenza Beni Artistici e Storici per le provincie di Brescia, Cremona e Mantova, Mantova, Italy, p. 64

Szépmüvészeti Múzeum, Budapest, p. 117

Staatliche Kunstsammlungen, Dresden, Germany (Abteilung Foto), p. 116

Statens Museum fur Kunsts, Copenhagen, Hans Petersen, pp. 54, 56

Paolo Tosi, Florence, pp. 68 left, 73 right, 94 left, 110, 124, 139, 141

Victoria and Albert Museum, London, p. 71

Photographic research by Index, Florence.